The Political Theory of Aristophanes

The Political Theory of Aristophanes

Explorations in Poetic Wisdom

Edited by

Jeremy J. Mhire and Bryan-Paul Frost

Published by State University of New York Press, Albany

© 2014 State University of New York

All rights reserved

Printed in the United States of America

No part of this book may be used or reproduced in any manner whatsoever without written permission. No part of this book may be stored in a retrieval system or transmitted in any form or by any means including electronic, electrostatic, magnetic tape, mechanical, photocopying, recording, or otherwise without the prior permission in writing of the publisher.

For information, contact State University of New York Press, Albany, NY
www.sunypress.edu

Production by Eileen Nizer
Marketing by Anne Valentine

Library of Congress Cataloging-in-Publication Data

The political theory of Aristophanes : explorations in poetic wisdom / edited by Jeremy J. Mhire and Bryan-Paul Frost.
    pages cm
Includes bibliographical references and index.
ISBN 978-1-4384-5003-2 (hc : alk. paper) 978-1-4384-5004-9 (pb : alk. paper)
1. Aristophanes—Criticism and interpretation. I. Mhire, Jeremy J., 1977– II. Frost, Bryan-Paul, 1961–

PA3879.P58 2014
882'.01—dc23   2013012778

10 9 8 7 6 5 4 3 2 1

Contents

Introduction   1
   Bryan-Paul Frost

PART I

Chapter 1
Seeing Democracy in the *Clouds*   13
   John Lombardini

Chapter 2
The Meaning of Socrates' Asceticism in Aristophanes' *Clouds*   29
   Khalil M. Habib

Chapter 3
Rethinking the Quarrel Anew: Politics and Boasting in
Aristophanes' *Clouds*   47
   Jeremy J. Mhire

PART II

Chapter 4
Persuasion in Comedy and Comic Persuasion: Aristophanes
and the Mysteries of Rhetoric   69
   John Zumbrunnen

Chapter 5
Boundaries: The Comic Poet Confronts the "Who"
of Political Action   89
   Arlene W. Saxonhouse

Chapter 6
Aristophanes and the Polis 109
Stephanie Nelson

Chapter 7
On the Anabasis of Trygaeus: An Introduction to
Aristophanes' *Peace* 137
Wayne Ambler

Chapter 8
Aristophanes' Herodotean Inquiry: The Meaning of
Athenian Imperialism in the *Birds* 161
Kenneth DeLuca

Chapter 9
Learning the Lesson of Dionysus: Aristophanes'
Tragicomic Wisdom and Poetic Politics in the *Frogs* 183
Christopher Baldwin

Chapter 10
Wealth and the Theology of Charity 201
Paul W. Ludwig

PART III

Chapter 11
Anger in Thucydides and Aristophanes: The Case of Cleon 229
Timothy W. Burns

Chapter 12
The Comedy of the Just City: Aristophanes' *Assemblywomen*
and Plato's *Republic* 259
Peter Nichols

Chapter 13
Peisetairos of Aristophanes' *Birds* and the Erotic Tyrant of
Republic IX 275
Matthew Meyer

Chapter 14
Aristophanes' Feminine Comedies and Socratic Political Science   303
    Amy L. Bonnette

PART IV

Chapter 15
Leo Strauss's UnSocratic Aristophanes?   331
    Devin Stauffer

About the Authors   353

Index   357

Introduction

Bryan-Paul Frost

The purpose of this edited volume is to make available to students, the learned public, and academics alike a series of chapters that documents and describes the political wisdom of Aristophanes. For those individuals who are unfamiliar with Aristophanes—or who are uneasy with regarding this Athenian comic poet as a political thinker of the highest caliber—these chapters will hopefully make manifest his capacious range of vision, his trenchant insights, and his unique role as a civic educator; and for those who are more familiar with Aristophanes—or who are quite comfortable with regarding him as a towering thinker both in his own right and with respect to his appreciation and criticism of other such political thinkers and figures—then we hope that these chapters will reinforce and even deepen one's understanding of his philosophical thought, open up new avenues for scholarly investigation, and perhaps challenge in fruitful ways prevailing opinions and assumptions. All the chapters contained herein are original, and they were all written explicitly for this volume. The contributors include a wide assortment of individuals—from junior- to senior-level scholars, political scientists to classicists, and those from inside and outside the academy—and this diversity of background is often reflected in the various interpretive strategies and conclusions employed throughout. Although the editors themselves have assiduously avoided imposing any mandatory or uniform orthodoxy on the authors, all of the contributors are united in their belief that intertwined within Aristophanes' madcap comedies lies a genuinely philosophical engagement with issues of the utmost seriousness, complexity, and fundamental importance: indeed, it is hard to name a single political theme of foundational significance that is not in some way discussed in his eleven extant plays. An examination of the "About the Authors" section will reveal that all of the contributors are well versed in ancient political thought, in general, and/or Aristophanes, in particular, and that taken together, they have written dissertations, monographs, translations, and books on these subjects, as well as published peer-reviewed articles in some of the most prestigious academic journals in their fields. Those who enjoy this volume will have no difficulty in following up and furthering this enjoyment by consulting other works by the various contributors.

By his own admission (and this on several occasions in the plays), Aristophanes considered himself one of the—if not *the*—greatest comedians of all time, if not for all time. The historical record has only tended to confirm this (self-)assessment: Who does not fervently hope that someday, in the mustiest section on some neglected shelf of an unappreciated library, the remainder of Aristophanes' corpus will be discovered (something that one would certainly not wish on every author, past or present!). Obviously, many scholars are interested in Aristophanes for what we might call "antiquarian" or "historical" reasons, namely, that his comedies reveal valuable information about his life and times and about the character of ancient artistic festivals. But however important this information is, Aristophanes continues to remain popular and to scintillate his audience because his comedies are remarkably topical—even contemporary—regardless of the time period in which they are read or performed. It is difficult enough for an artist to get published in any age; it takes nothing short of a rare talent to be in print for some two thousand years. Although the reasons for his success could easily be the subject of one (or several) books, let us posit the following observation: the enjoyment of any particular piece of humor is exceptionally hard to sustain over the long term. Let's face it: there are many very funny individuals today (and in the past) whose humor and fame will (and did) last but a short time. If a comedian's material is based primarily upon specific events and individuals in the immediate present, then the appeal of that humor will be limited to the here and now. Of course, someone knowledgeable about the circumstances of this kind of humor can explain why these jokes were considered funny in the past—but we all know what happens to a joke when someone has to explain its humor to us. There is no doubt that Aristophanes' comedies revolved around his own particular historical situation, and we must admit that although we are knowledgeable about some of these unique circumstances, much of what was humorous to a contemporary Athenian audience is more than likely simply lost to us today. But Aristophanes' comedies do much more than poke fun at the here and now; they appeal to universal themes and topics that transcend, that is, are applicable to and comprehensible by, almost any particular political community. In other words, while his comedies may have plots and characters tied to contemporary Athens, the broad themes with which the plays deal are seemingly eternal in character and scope. For example, does a reader need to understand the Greek pantheon in order to recognize the poignant hilarity of Chremylus' Delphic discovery that the god Wealth has been blinded by the apparently more powerful god Zeus, or Poverty's arguments that Wealth's sight should not be restored lest the human economic condition be made even worse? Or, again, is it necessary to read the Platonic and Xenophonic corpus to recognize in Aristophanes' Socrates the typical and very modern "intellectual," someone who is ensconced in an ivory tower or think-tank pondering all sorts of inane and utterly irrelevant matters of interest only to him and his disciples? Or, finally, does one need to know the ins and outs of the Peloponnesian War to understand the sex strike perpetrated by Lysistrata and her cohorts? Substitute almost any destructive conflict in human history and one can easily make sense of trying to bring an end to a male-dominated conflict through the withholding of certain feminine favors (and the equally uproarious difficulty many of the women have in keeping the strike and not crossing the picket line). Examples could be drawn from each and every play, but the idea is clear: Aristophanes' comedies are not time bound because of their universality. Of course, our appreciation of Aristophanes only increases once we know more about the Greek pantheon, the Platonic and Xenophonic corpus, and the Peloponnesian War: indeed, the plays become even more amusing once we are immersed as fully as possible in the particular historical circumstances of ancient Athens and Greece. Nevertheless, because Aristophanes' comedies are of the highest order, lack of knowledge of the latter does not impede enjoyment of the former, and enjoyment of the former is only made richer by knowledge of the latter.

While the above observations might go a small way in helping to explain why Aristophanes has been perennially popular, it does not quite address why he can be considered philosophical, which is the claim of this book. To begin to answer this question, we can assert that Aristophanes' (or comedy's) deep kinship to philosophy is precisely the reason why Socrates banned comedy (and tragedy) from the education of the guardians in the city-in-speech in *Republic* III: in a phrase, Socrates saw that laughter is potentially liberating. To laugh at someone or something is not to take it seriously—to distance oneself from it and even to tower above it: it is to know or say that you would never fall for that old gag. This is why when a joke is good-naturedly played upon us, we are a bit thankful (if blushingly so) to the prankster for the enlightenment: we now see that we are the victim of that which we previously maintained we would never be so foolish as to do, or fall for, or believe in, or admit. In short, laughter calls into question whether we should take something as seriously as we might otherwise, or, more strongly, that once we laugh at something, it is never really possible to take it completely seriously again. It is true that comedy celebrates the low and not the high, and certainly the low is not the best judge of character; nevertheless, the only way you can know if something is fully and genuinely high is if you have seen its undercarriage, and this is something the high and mighty are often not willing to allow. Laughter then is potentially liberating because it calls into question, and thus subjects to critical scrutiny, all that shackles the mind to think or act in a predetermined manner, whether it be convention, shame, public opinion, custom, tradition, or religion. Laughter thus helps reveal to us that what we were once told was true may not be the whole truth. And what does Aristophanes mock and poke fun at if not every subject heretofore considered serious, if not reverential: the gods, the marriage bed, leading politicians, courage in war if not war itself, justice and moderation, the living and the dead, mastery and slavery, the young and the old, and so on. Of course, laughter is no sure sign that one is enlightened, but laughter may have more in common with philosophy than its counterpart. As has been observed before, while Jesus is reported to have wept in the Bible, Socrates is known to have laughed in the *Phaedo*.

This volume is divided into four sections, the first of which offers three chapters on *Clouds*, the undoubted favorite and/or most pertinent comedy for political scientists as a whole: here we have one of the very few direct testimonies as to the character of Socrates and (pre)Socratic philosophy. (The primacy of *Clouds* is starkly revealed by the table of contents of Leo Strauss's *Socrates and Aristophanes*: if one subtracts the "Introduction" and "Conclusion," then the book is rather elegantly divided into a longish chapter on "The *Clouds*" followed by a ten-part section that Strauss simply titles "The Other Plays.") John Lombardini begins this section by suggesting that at the core of Aristophanes' critique of Socrates in *Clouds* is a concern over the antidemocratic implications of the latter's purported scientific and philosophical activities. Lombardini focuses on Socrates' instruction of Strepsiades and the latter's successful attempt to fend off his creditors: just as Socrates mocks Strepsiades for his prescientific understanding of the cosmos, so Strepsiades mocks his creditors for their failure to grasp these same principles. Strepsiades thus uses this newfound knowledge to establish his superiority over his fellow democratic citizens by contending that he cannot and should not be held accountable by those who lack such knowledge, a belief with troubling implications in a society committed to core democratic values. Khalil M. Habib's chapter examines the character and meaning of Socrates' self-denying asceticism and whether that way of life stands up to critical scrutiny. Far from being a fully self-conscious and wholly self-sufficient being, Aristophanes reveals a deeply religious impulse behind this way of life—an impulse that is explicitly in conflict with Socrates' own self-understanding. Interestingly, Habib suggests that Socrates may have much more in common with Strepsiades than one might originally think: while Strepsiades is certainly more worldly and Socrates more theoretical, both seek an ordered stability and meaning in a world their own principles and actions seem to deny. And finally, Jeremy J. Mhire rounds out the section by maintaining that *Clouds* is intended by Aristophanes to be a defense of political life against the threat posed by Socrates' "pre-Socratic" philosophy. By averring that only the wise have a just claim to rule, Socrates necessarily collapsed the distinction between freedom and despotism and therefore denied the possibility of genuine political life being defined by the ability to rule and be ruled in turn. Aristophanes, by contrast, believes that true wisdom can only be attained in and through political life or, more poignantly, that it is only through a thorough appreciation and understanding of politics that one can adequately address the question as to the existence or character of the gods. At the end of this section, one cannot help but reflect upon a concern raised by all three chapters: Does Aristophanes' own way of life resolve the problems that he identifies with Socrates, Strepsiades, and the other characters of the comedy?

Section Two might be titled "Themes and Plays," with three chapters on the former and four on the latter. The effort here is to address topics that have a broad appeal and relevance and therefore would be applicable both inside and outside an academic environment or classroom. John Zumbrunnen starts off by asking a question central to Aristophanes' enterprise as a whole: How does one understand comic rhetoric or the rhetoric of comedy? While being wary of developmental arguments, this chapter draws on the earliest and latest of his comedies to consider continuity and change in the playwright's portrayal of persuasion in democratic politics. Produced in the 420s BCE, *Wasps*, *Acharnians*, and *Knights* consider the foibles of Athenian democratic politics in the context of the Peloponnesian War and the demagoguery of Cleon. *Assemblywomen* and *Wealth*, by contrast, appeared in the late 390s and early 380s as Athens slowly recovered from the long war and after the city had endured the temporary disruption of democracy.

In general, where the early plays focus on issues of war and peace and engage Cleon personally, the later plays explore the nature of persuasion in the context of radical social and economic change. Arlene W. Saxonhouse examines how Aristophanes' plays view the articulation of the different ways in which political membership can be constituted. In the *Acharnians*, a single individual attempts to act independently of any political body; in *Lysistrata*, it is the desire for sex and peace that brings the women together as political actors, not the physical or political boundaries that separate their cities; and in the *Ecclesiazusae*, old boundaries are broken down in order to open up political authority to new actors. In each play, the comic poet illustrates the challenges and tension-laden decisions underlying efforts to define the "who" of political action. Stephanie Nelson argues that Aristophanes is not primarily interested in contemporary political issues, but instead uses these issues as a way to examine Athens itself, or, in other words, the self-conscious understanding Athens has of itself as a city and the extent to which that understanding is consistent and wholly objective. Pursuing a range of plays, from *Knights* to *Frogs*, *Acharnians*, and *Birds*, Nelson suggests that Aristophanes in essence holds a mirror up to Athens and its citizens and asks whether their self-conceived image of themselves is more self-constructed than its purported natural and/or divine origins and character. Through his comedy, Aristophanes thus calls into question the very rationality of the polis. Thereafter follow fours chapters, each of which introduces a single play and what the authors see as its most significant implications. In *Peace*, Wayne Ambler analyzes Aristophanes' account of the political and philosophical events that eventually resulted in the Peace of Nicias during the Peloponnesian War. In Ambler's view, Aristophanes' play provides invaluable insight into how this Peace was (or any peace is) constituted, the obstacles to its achievement, whether the Greeks even ultimately wanted peace, and, finally, if not especially, to what extent the gods endorsed or aided in helping to bring about what turned out to be but a temporary reprieve to this murderous and destructive conflict. In *Birds*, Kenneth DeLuca explores how Athenian imperialism is reflected in Peisthetairos' own enterprise. This chapter (which in many ways is as much philological as it is philosophical) considers a wide array of themes—from the character of Tereus to the people of Thrace—many of them linked to or informed by (as his title suggests) Herodotus' *History*. Christopher Baldwin maintains that the *Frogs* presents us with some of Aristophanes' most mature reflections on the nature of poetry, the relationship between comedy and tragedy, and the role of the poet in political society. Situated at a time of political and cultural decline, with Athens about to lose the Peloponnesian War, Aristophanes displays what Baldwin calls his Dionysian wisdom to demonstrate how great artists (both tragic and comic) can instruct the city in such times and positively shape public opinion. And finally, Paul W. Ludwig points out that *Wealth* is the Aristophanic play that most closely engages with some of the founding principles of modern liberalism (e.g., that the accumulation of property yields happiness, that poverty causes crime, and that God is a loving and therefore charitable Being). But, as so often happens, the comedy also questions these very principles: Would the alleviation of poverty necessarily lead to an unmitigated increase in human happiness, and would such a situation cause us to lose the fear, reverence, and awe needed to maintain belief in the gods? After reading the totality of the chapters in this section, one can only marvel at Aristophanes' formidable philosophic acumen and the staggering breadth of his political instructiveness.

Section Three juxtaposes Aristophanes with several other of his Greek contemporaries in the hope that such in-depth comparisons will fruitfully illuminate all the thinkers involved. Timothy W. Burns opens the section with a figure central to Aristophanes, Thucydides, and the Peloponnesian War: the demagogue Cleon. Burns focuses on Cleon's angry (or waspish) desire for justice as well as on the role such anger plays in politics more generally. While both Thucydides and Aristophanes were inclined to peace throughout the war, and while both authors try to make their readers more gentle and less "Cleon-like" in and through their writings, it may be that Aristophanes sees some measure of anger as a necessary bulwark for the city's defense. Burns demonstrates that while Cleon was a central figure historically, an understanding of his soul philosophically is necessary to comprehend most fully political life and human nature more generally. The next two chapters by Peter Nichols and Matthew Meyer compare a work that is widely acknowledged to be influenced by, or even a refutation of, Aristophanes: Plato's *Republic*. Nichols looks at the resonances and dissonances between Socrates' three waves in Book V and Praxagora's revolutionary designs in *Assemblywomen*. Although both Plato and Aristophanes understand the ultimate impossibility of ever achieving perfect justice, what separate them most fundamentally are their differing understandings of the role and portrayal of philosophy in the best regime. Meyer contends that the difference between the erotic philosopher and the erotic tyrant in Book IX of the *Republic* might reveal a deeper quarrel between poetry and philosophy as to the highest way of life. Drawing upon the *Phaedrus* and *Symposium*, Meyer argues that while the eros of the philosopher is directed toward the contemplation of the Idea of the Good, the eros exhibited by Peisthetairos in *Birds* aims at a quest for power and the satisfaction of his sensual passions.

Amy L. Bonnette enlarges the comparison with the *Republic* to consider Socratic political science more broadly (i.e., to include both the Platonic and Xenophonic corpus) as it relates to Aristophanes' feminine comedies, or those with female choruses: *Lysistrata, Ecclesiazusae, Thesmophoriazusae,* and *Clouds*. Beginning with the Socratic thesis that politics and economics belong to the same art or science, Bonnette divides the plays into two groups: in the former two plays, the Socratic thesis tends to be confirmed, as Lysistrata and Praxagora are portrayed as rather competent rulers; in the latter two plays, there is a marked coolness and even hostility to Socrates and his like. Irrespective of what Aristophanes' final teaching is on the relationship between women and Socrates, any comprehensive understanding of his political science would do well to consider these four plays as a whole. And finally, Section Four contains but a single chapter on a book by one of the twentieth century's preeminent scholars, Leo Strauss's *Socrates and Aristophanes*. The centrality of this work for political scientists is readily indicated by the number of contributors who acknowledge their debt to Strauss in their notes and elsewhere. By Devin Stauffer's own admission, it is as impossible to do justice to Strauss's work in a single chapter as it is to do justice to Aristophanes in a single volume. Stauffer therefore aims to introduce us to some of the major puzzles and questions of the book, foremost among them being precisely what was Aristophanes' critique of Socrates, his way of life, and, perhaps most importantly, his understanding of the gods. Taken together, Sections Three and Four suggest a vast horizon of interpretive approaches and strategies both in respect to Aristophanes' influence on other thinkers and the vast scholarly literature surveying his thought. In sum, political theorists must sooner or later engage with Aristophanes.

As mentioned at the outset of this Introduction, the editors intend this volume for use by those who are already familiar, or wish to become so, with Aristophanes' overall philosophic thought; in this spirit, we hope that the volume finds its way into university classrooms in order to assist in inculcating a new generation of Aristophanes aficionados by those who have already been converted. It should be emphasized that no such book appears to be in print today. While there are certainly books on a specific theme(s) or play(s), and while there are volumes detailing his artistry, language, cultural influence, and so on, no edited edition exists that takes as its explicit focus his political philosophy as a whole. We therefore believe that this volume will fit in nicely with many traditional political philosophy courses (whether survey courses or those dedicated to a particular author or theme) as well as with the growing popularity of "Politics and Literature" both as a subfield in political science and as a focus of teaching on college campuses. Indeed, and ideally, we hope that this volume might persuade teachers to offer entire courses dedicated to an examination of Aristophanes' corpus: such courses could not only highlight Aristophanes' relationship to other key thinkers, from Thucydides to Plato, but also focus and discuss pivotal events in Western history, from the Peloponnesian War to the death of Socrates. While no single volume on Aristophanes can be complete, we have endeavored to survey in as comprehensive a fashion as possible what might be loosely termed his most political plays, themes, and influences, and all of his plays figure prominently in at least one chapter, while several plays make their appearance on multiple occasions. At the very least, the interpretations presented herein should allow students to receive a rich sense of all that Aristophanes has to offer, and especially how much work remains to be done.

Clearly, much more could said in introducing and therefore justifying a book dedicated to Aristophanes—but perhaps an overly longish Introduction would be a proof against reading the book in the first place. After all, could it not be argued that if you feel the need to justify a book about Aristophanes, then you obviously have no genuine appreciation for the artist himself? Who needs to justify laughter or a book that seeks to highlight laughter's wisdom? At any event, whether the book accomplishes this task will be decided by each and every reader. What the editors can confirm, however, is that each and every contributor involved in this project had an enjoyable time writing their chapter—and certainly learned and transmitted important insights about politics from that ever clever, bawdy, and utterly preposterous philosophic poet.

Part I

1

Seeing Democracy in the *Clouds*

John Lombardini

I.

At Plato's *Protagoras*, 319b3–d7, Socrates offers an analysis of the role technical knowledge plays in Athenian democratic deliberation. In technical matters, the *dēmos* willingly seeks advice from those possessing the corresponding *technē*, while dismissing those who claim authority based on their physical attractiveness, wealth, or noble birth. When it comes to political matters, however, the Athenians do not believe there is such a *technē*, and, hence, they allow anyone who wishes to offer political advice. Thus, though legally any Athenian citizen was entitled to speak regardless of the matter under discussion, Socrates' analysis points to a set of cultural norms that regulated how discursive authority was distributed in democratic Athens.

Those that violate these norms, Socrates notes, will meet with the laughter of their fellow citizens. Their laughter, in the scenario Socrates describes, serves to puncture the speaker's pretension to a type of knowledge he does not have, or to a type of authority that only the possession of such knowledge could grant. If we complete Socrates' hypothetical scenario, we can envision a second moment of laughter. Imagine the Athenians needed advice on a political matter, and an individual rose (let us call him Protagoras), addressed the assembly, and declared that he alone possessed the political *technē* necessary to give advice on such matters. Protagoras announces that anyone else who lacks this technical knowledge should relinquish his desire to speak because he lacks the competency to do so. We can imagine the Athenians laughing just as hard, if not harder, at Protagoras' claims: he would be attempting to exclude others from deliberation based on his claim to possess a type of knowledge they do not even believe exists.

In this chapter, I argue that we can use this (hypothetical) second moment of laughter as a lens to interpret Aristophanes' critique of Socrates in *Clouds*.[1] At the core of Aristophanes' critique of Socrates is a democratic anxiety concerning the antidemocratic authority of Socratic intellectualism. This anxiety comes to the fore if we focus on Socrates' education of Strepsiades, what the latter learns from Socrates, and how he deploys this knowledge against his creditors. Just as Socrates mocks Strepsiades for failing to understand his teachings, so Strepsiades exploits these same arguments in order to mock his creditors. Yet the latter scene carries with it an important twist: Strepsiades interprets the intellectual inferiority of his creditors as marking them as unfit to hold him accountable for his actions. Knowledge, in the form of technical knowledge of subjects like meteorology and grammar, is understood by Strepsiades as a necessary prerequisite for being entitled to challenge him.

To read *Clouds* in this way is to shift our interpretive focus from the threat Socrates poses to traditional authority—represented by the divine authority of Zeus and the parental authority of Strepsiades—to the danger his intellectualism poses to the specifically *democratic* operation of authority in ancient Athens. In the play, of course, Socrates worships the clouds rather than the gods of the traditional pantheon, and the style of argumentation Pheidippides learns from the Weaker Argument he then uses to undermine his father's authority. Given the later charges against Socrates—that he did not believe in the same gods the Athenians believed in, but introduced new gods, and that he corrupted the youth—this focus makes good sense. My argument here is not that this is an unimportant aspect of Aristophanes' depiction of Socrates; rather, it is that the emphasis on Socrates' challenge to traditional authority has obscured this other dimension of Aristophanes' critique.

This chapter begins by grounding this distinction between traditional and democratic authority through an analysis of the operations of authority in democratic Athens. In contrast to the traditional forms of authority wielded by the gods, the authority wielded by political actors in democratic Athens—like the *rhētor* and *ho boulomenos*—was far more contingent on the performance of certain socially constructed roles. The construction of such democratic authority, and the place of ordinary citizens within its operation, is the subject of the next section. Section three turns to the play itself, providing an overview of the education of Strepsiades at the *phrontistērion* and his use of this learning against his creditors. Section four addresses the role that mockery plays in both the interactions between Socrates and Strepsiades and those between Strepsiades and his creditors. Attending to such mockery illustrates how Socrates and Strepsiades deploy sophistical knowledge to discredit the authority of others. The conclusion considers the implications of this analysis for the vision of Socrates that emerges from reading *Clouds* in this way.

II.

The principle of *isēgoria* stood at the center of Athenian democratic ideology, so much so that Herodotus, writing in the second half of the fifth century, could use it as a stand-in for *dēmokratia* (5.78).[2] Commonly translated as the "equal right to speak," *isēgoria* symbolized each adult male citizen's ability to address the assembly. While under the sixth-century Solonian constitution all Athenian citizens were permitted to attend the assembly (and, hence, the vote of the *dēmos* was held to be sovereign), only elites were entitled to speak (most likely, those of the top two socioeconomic classes introduced by Solon's reforms). In the fifth-century democracy, in contrast, every adult male citizen in good standing was entitled to address his fellow citizens, a "right" enshrined in the question "Who wishes to speak?" (*tis agoreuein bouletai*), which initiated meetings of the assembly.[3]

Nonetheless, there were real distinctions in the authority wielded by Athenian citizens in democratic Athens. While every male citizen could speak in the assembly, it is unlikely that they all did. As M. H. Hansen explains, when thinking about democratic Athens, it is useful to distinguish between active and passive participation.[4] Only a small number of citizens regularly addressed meetings of the assembly, while a slightly larger group might have done so on a less frequent basis; most citizens, however, participated in politics through listening and voting. This ability to speak, hence, was most often exercised by a small number of wealthy elites—professional politicians known as *rhētores*—which in turn gave rise to certain norms governing who was held to possess the authority to speak.

Up through the beginning of the Peloponnesian War, the path to being an orator passed through the office of the generalship. The ten generals (one from each Cleisthenic tribe) were elected, rather than selected by lot—the only officials (until the mid-fourth century) so chosen under the democracy. During this period, Athenian generals all hailed from aristocratic families: Pericles, the best-known example, was a member of the prominent and powerful Alcmaeonid family from which Cleisthenes, whose late sixth-century reforms started Athens down the path toward democracy, was also descended. Cleon, his most (in)famous successor, did not share such a pedigree. Emblematic of the "new politicians" of the late fifth century, to borrow W. R. Connor's phrase, Cleon was a non-aristocrat, a tanner by trade, albeit a wealthy one.[5] In Aristophanes' *Knights*, his questionable ancestry serves as both a stand-in for questioning his authority and an explanation for his base activities. Thus, while every Athenian citizen was entitled to speak, social status was an important factor in assessing the authority that such speech held.[6]

The fact that most of the citizens who addressed and offered advice to the *dēmos* were elites of some stripe stood in tension with the egalitarian ethos that underpinned Athenian democratic practice. This anxiety was heightened by the fact that elite orators had been trained in the arts of persuasion that they could potentially deploy to deceive assemblymen and jurors and disrupt the ability of the *dēmos* to exercise sound political judgment.[7] Yet, as Josiah Ober has demonstrated, the ability of elite orators to offer advice to, and especially to criticize, the *dēmos* was effectively controlled via a mass ideology that channeled elite competition over the favor of the people into public benefits.[8] The various "dramatic fictions" that elite orators and ordinary citizens "conspired to maintain"—such as the rhetorically trained orator's portrayal of himself as an ordinary citizen—functioned as a check on the ambitions of elites while simultaneously authorizing their ability to oppose and critique the will of the people.[9] In this way, the Athenians managed to harness elite learning and harmonize it with a strong belief in the wisdom of the masses to best decide matters of public policy.

We can observe a similar dynamic at work in the judicial sphere. There was no public prosecutor in the Athenian judicial system; public cases could be prosecuted by any citizen who was willing—the *ho boulomenos*.[10] While legally any male Athenian citizen in good standing could try such cases, there were fairly clear social criteria for determining who counted as a legitimate prosecutor. In particular, as Danielle Allen has argued, the legitimate citizen prosecutor was one who was personally connected to, and hence justly angered by, the crime that had taken place.[11] These cultural norms served to distinguish between a legitimate prosecutor, on the one hand, and a sycophant, on the other hand. Though both had some personal interest in the case they were prosecuting, the latter's interest was perverted by the quest for pecuniary gain, a misuse of anger, or some combination of the two.[12] Thus, though each citizen had the equal ability to prosecute such cases, not all willing prosecutors were viewed as equally legitimate.

The type of authority exercised in democratic Athens, then, is certainly distinct from the type of traditional authority that has a prominent place in *Clouds*; it is also distinct from the authority possessed by the philosopher-kings of Plato's hypothetical Kallipolis. While all three are types of authority, they can be distinguished along two dimensions: 1) the norms that determine who is entitled to authority; and 2) the amount of deference such authority commands. The traditional authority of the gods, for example, is grounded in the obedience owed to time-honored rules and practices, and the deference it commands is unlimited.[13] The authority of the philosopher-kings, in contrast, was epistemic—it was grounded in the knowledge of the Forms that only philosophers could possess—and, as with traditional authority, the deference it commanded was total—no one else in the Kallipolis would have the knowledge necessary to challenge the authority of the philosopher-kings. Finally, the authority of the orator was governed by norms dictating that he must demonstrate his friendliness to the *dēmos* in order for his speech to carry weight. In contrast to both traditional forms of authority and the authority of the philosopher-kings, however, the deference such authority commanded was far more defeasible.[14]

Within a democratic context, like that of fifth-century Athens, each citizen is authorized to track the commitments and entitlements of his fellow citizens; it is precisely through this process of "keeping score" that authority is constructed. If Cleon, for example, convincingly demonstrates his affection for the *dēmos* and has given good advice in the Assembly in the past, I may be willing to defer to his authority in deciding what course of action the city should take. Yet if his policies start to produce deleterious consequences for the city or I happen to witness Cleon treating an ordinary citizen hubristically, I may no longer be willing to act in such a way that his advice counts as authoritative for me. That I have the authority to track Cleon's commitments in this way neither indicates, nor is predicated upon, the truth of my assessments (perhaps Cleon's policies will turn out to be beneficial in the long term, or what I witnessed was actually Cleon retaliating against a prior assault made against him); I possess such authority simply as a member of a democratic political community.[15] For the operation of authority to remain democratic, however, it requires that citizens exercise this authority to track each other's commitments and entitlements; this, in turn, demands that we recognize our fellow citizens as fit to hold each other accountable in these ways.

It is this last point in particular that can illuminate the dimension of Aristophanes' critique of Socrates that I wish to draw out in this chapter.

What Strepsiades learns from Socrates is that those without the knowledge he acquired at the *phrontistērion* are not fit to hold him accountable for his actions. To demonstrate this point, we must now turn to the play itself.

III.

As noted in the Introduction, most commentators on *Clouds* focus on Socrates' education of Pheidippides rather than on his relationship with Strepsiades. Given the historical fact that Socrates was prosecuted in 399 BCE on the charge of corrupting the youth, combined with Socrates' identification of Aristophanes as the individual perhaps most responsible for this public perception, this emphasis is unsurprising. It is Pheidippides, of course, who deploys the teachings of the Weaker Argument to question the authority of the gods, the city's laws, and his parents; the potential danger of sophistical teaching is thus forcefully displayed in the depiction of his corruption. Yet it is Strepsiades, and not Pheidippides, who successfully fends off his creditors at 1214–1302, despite the fact that the latter is sent to the *phrontistērion* for precisely this purpose.[16] Strepsiades' use of Socrates' teachings, moreover, presents its own challenge to authority—the equal authority of democratic citizens to hold each other accountable for their actions. It is Strepsiades' challenge to this aspect of democratic authority, and its connection to what he learns from Socrates at the *phrontistērion*, that is the focus of the following analysis.

When Strepsiades first attempts to persuade his son to become a student at the *phrontistērion*, he indicates that the students there engage in two types of intellectual activity. The first type is what we would call scientific: they "argue persuasively that the sky is a stove lid, and that it lies around us, and that we are the charcoals" (95–97); the second type is rhetorical: "these people teach, if someone gives them money, how to win any lawsuit, both right and wrong" (97–99).[17] It is clearly the latter that most interests Strepsiades, as is indicated by his frustration at the seemingly pointless intellectual exercises to which Socrates subjects him (655–56, 693, 738–39) and his desire to learn the weaker argument in order to escape repaying his debts (244–45). Still, these two types of intellectual activity are not as disconnected as they might appear; indeed, the argument that the sky is a barbecue lid is an example of how Socrates and his ilk are able to make the weaker argument appear the stronger.[18] It is as if Strepsiades were saying: "if these people can argue that the sky is a giant barbecue lid, surely they can help me come up with an argument to help me escape repaying my debts!"

What, then, is Strepsiades actually taught when he enrolls as a student at the *phrontistērion*? After observing the intellectual activities being undertaken at the school, the first thing Strepsiades is taught by Socrates is knowledge of divine matters (*ta theia pragmat'*, 250). He learns that the clouds are the only gods (365) and that Zeus, along with the other Olympian gods, does not exist (367). This prompts Strepsiades to ask who makes it rain, given that Zeus does not exist, which leads to the second subject he is taught: meteorology. Socrates explains that rain, thunder, and lightning are all caused by the physical motions of the clouds and that these motions themselves are caused not by Zeus, but by heavenly whirl (*aitherios dinos*, 379). Finally, Strepsiades is taught grammar; Socrates attempts to teach Strepsiades to identify the proper genders of nouns and proper names (658–93).

To claim, of course, that Strepsiades truly learns what Socrates attempts to teach him is something of an overstatement. On this point, Strepsiades' assessment of Socrates' atheism is illustrative. When Socrates explains that it is Whirl, rather than Zeus, that forces the clouds to crash against each other and produce thunder, Strepsiades immediately personifies Whirl, thinking that Whirl has replaced Zeus—Whirl now rules as king (*Dinos nuni basileuōn*)—much in the same way that Zeus replaced his father, Cronos (379–82). At the end of the play, Strepsiades reveals the full extent of his misunderstanding, having not simply personified the abstract concept of Whirl, but having taken Socrates to mean that an earthenware cup controlled the universe (1470–74).[19] Strepsiades' inability to think abstractly is further on display when Socrates attempts to instruct him in measurement and rhythm. With the former, Strepsiades can only think of grain measurements (639–40); with the latter, he mistakes the metrical finger (*daktulon*) for the fingers on one's hand (649–53). Thus, some of what Socrates attempts to teach Strepsiades fails to learn; other subjects he appears to have learned yet does not fully comprehend. In the end, this intellectual incompetence results in his expulsion from the *phrontistērion*.

Despite his ineptitude, Strepsiades successfully deploys the same arguments he is taught at the *phrontistērion* in fending off his creditors. When the first creditor arrives and demands payment, Strepsiades chastises the man for his belief in the traditional gods. While he begins by commenting on the creditor's laughable belief in the gods (*kai Zeus geloios omnumenos tois eidosin*, 1241), he continues by evincing the creditor's ignorance about the grammatical teachings Strepsiades learned at the Thinkery. When the first creditor asks whether Strepsiades will pay back the money, Strepsiades grabs a kneading trough and asks his creditor to name the object.

The creditor responds that the object is a kneading trough (*kardopos*), to which Strepsiades indignantly replies: "And you are demanding repayment, although being such a person? I would never pay back even an obol to anyone who would call a kneading *troughette* (*kardopēn*) a kneading *trough* (*kardopon*)" (1249–51). The test that Strepsiades lays out for the creditor cleverly recalls his own linguistic education at the Thinkery, and he castigates the creditor for "incorrectly" calling the kneading trough by a male name instead of a female one.

Strepsiades again displays his learning in his encounter with the second creditor. Again, when the creditor asks Strepsiades if he will repay the money he owes, Strepsiades asks "whether you think that Zeus, on each occasion, causes new water to rain or that the sun drags this same water back again from below" (1279–81). When the creditor replies that he neither knows nor cares which is the correct explanation, Strepsiades again comments on the gall of one who dares to ask for his money back, despite being ignorant of meteorological matters (*tōn meteōrōn pragmatōn*, 1284). When the creditor then asks that Strepsiades at least pay him back the interest on what he owes, Strepsiades pleads ignorance as to the nature of interest. When the creditor explains, quite simply, that it is the process by which money increases month by month and day by day, Strepsiades embarks on an extended scientific analogy, intent on proving that this creature (*thērion*) called interest does not exist. Noting that the sea is the same height that it was before despite the fact that rivers are flowing into it, Strepsiades highlights the absurdity behind the idea that money should increase in such a way when even the sea does not (1293–97). Strepsiades' interactions with his creditors, thus, demonstrate that he is at least competent at remembering and reconstructing the arguments he encountered at the *phrontistērion*.

Crucial, however, are the implications Strepsiades draws from these encounters. For Strepsiades, the ignorance of his creditors counts as a justification for refusing to repay his debts: their ignorance makes them unfit to hold him accountable for his actions. This is evident if we attend to the precise language used by Strepsiades. With the first creditor, as cited above, he declares: "And you are demanding repayment, *although being such a person* (*toioutos ōn*)? I would never pay back even an obol to anyone who would call a kneading *troughette* (*kardopēn*) a kneading *trough* (*kardopon*)" (1249–51, emphasis my own). His language is similar with the second creditor: "How could you be just in demanding repayment (*pōs oun apolabein targurion dikaios ei*) if you know nothing of meteorology?" (1283–84). What these scenes illustrate is not that those with expert knowledge should rule in place of ordinary citizens who lack such knowledge; rather, it is that Strepsiades deems his creditors unfit to hold him accountable based on their lack of such knowledge.

IV.

This refusal to recognize his creditors as equals is further illustrated by Strepsiades' use of the language of mockery against them: they are not just ignorant, but laughable on account of their ignorance. To understand Strepsiades' use of this language, however, we must return to his education at the *phrontistērion* and, more specifically, to Socrates' own use of this language against him. When Strepsiades declares that it is obvious that Zeus hurls down lightning bolts to incinerate perjurers, Socrates calls him a fool (*ō mōre*) for not recognizing that this idea flatly contradicts our observations concerning lightning strikes (there are many perjurers whom lightning has not struck, and it often strikes inanimate objects that cannot be perjurers) (398). Socrates later calls Strepsiades ignorant and barbaric (*amathēs houtosi kai barbaros*); accuses him of speaking nonsense (*lēreis*); tells him to stop blathering (*ou mē lalēseis*); refers to him as the most boorish, inept, stupid, and forgetful person (*ouk eidon houtōs andr' agroikon oudamou oud' aporon oude skaion oud' epilēsmona*) he has ever known; calls him a brainless lout (*agreios ei kai skaios*) and base (*ō ponere*, 688); and twice curses him (*eis korakas*, 646; *apolei kakist'*, 726). After he is completely fed up with Strepsiades' inability to learn, he commands him to leave the *phrontistērion*, calling him a most forgetful and idiotic old man (*epilēsmotaton kai skaiotaton*, 790). Socrates' abuse of Strepsiades, in short, is grounded in the latter's intellectual incompetence; Strepsiades appears laughable to Socrates precisely because he is his intellectual inferior, unable to comprehend his subtle teachings about the gods, grammar, and so forth.

From Socrates, then, Strepsiades learns not only the intellectual matters outlined in the previous section, but further to treat those ignorant in such matters with ridicule and contempt. The first evidence of this in the play is Strepsiades' behavior toward Pheidippides after the former leaves the *phrontistērion*. When his son swears by Zeus, Strepsiades calls him a fool (*tēs mōrias*) for still believing in Zeus at his age (817–18), and Pheidippides responds by asking his father why he is mocking him for this (*ti de tout' egelasas eteon*, 819). When Pheidippides then questions the worth of learning from people like Socrates, Strepsiades goes on to exclaim how ignorant and thick-witted (*hōs amathēs ei kai pakhus*) his son is (842). Finally, when Pheidippides refers to both a cock and a hen by the same name, Strepsiades calls him ridiculous (*katagelastos ei*, 849). Strepsiades later subjects his creditors to the same abusive language. He mocks the first creditor's rotundity with a joke about turning his gut into a wineskin (1237–39) and, as with Pheidippides, he tells him that swearing by the gods is laughable (*geloios*, 1241–42). He mocks the second creditor's woes (*mē skōpte m'*, 1265–66) and accuses him of speaking nonsense (*ti dēta lēreis*, 1273).

Strepsiades' encounter with the second creditor culminates in a threat to prosecute Strepsiades on a charge of hubris; though linked specifically to Strepsiades' physical assault of creditor, the idea of hubris well captures his general treatment of, and attitude toward, both the creditors. In democratic Athens, the charge of hubris (*graphē hubreōs*) pertained to cases of verbal and/or physical assault where the deliberate intent was the dishonoring or disrespecting of another.[20] To treat a democratic citizen hubristically was to deny that individual the equal respect and equal dignity he deserved qua democratic citizen;[21] it was akin to treating someone as an oligarchic ruler would treat a member of the disenfranchised lower class.[22] Strepsiades demonstrates, through both his mockery of and physical assault against his creditors, that he considers them to be his inferiors, neither fit to hold him accountable for his actions nor worthy of being treated with equal respect and dignity. This disdain for ordinary citizens is thus one of the key things Strepsiades learns from Socrates.[23]

Of course, Strepsiades' mockery of his creditors captures only one aspect of the humor contained in this scene. While Strepsiades construes his creditors as objects of ridicule for their lack of learning, Strepsiades himself is constructed as an object of laughter to the audience of the play. To a large extent, what makes Socrates and the intellectual activities at the *phrontistērion* laughable is their perceived uselessness—what practical benefit could one gain from knowledge of the orifice from which a gnat hums? Or from calling a kneading trough by its proper gender? Strepsiades' use of this knowledge to beat back his creditors is even more ridiculous, however, because it is predicated on the claim that knowledge of such useless matters is of the utmost importance to practical affairs. This is perhaps most apparent from Strepsiades' denial of the existence of interest, which he demonstrates using an analogy with the flowing of rivers into the sea (1285–96). When the second creditor, exasperated, pleads with Strepsiades to at least pay back the interest he owes, Strepsiades asks what sort of creature (*ti thērion*) this thing called interest is, to which the creditor responds that it is the process according to which an amount of money grows bigger each day as time flows (*huporreontos*). Strepsiades then asks whether the sea is bigger now than it had been previously, and the creditor answers that it is equal in size, because it would not be right (*dikaion*) for it to be larger. Strepsiades concludes that if it is not right for the sea to increase, even though rivers flow into it (*epirreontōn*), then the creditor has no right to demand that his money so increase. What makes Strepsiades' argument laughable is his attempt to deny the existence of interest—a social practice governed by Athenian laws and customs—on the basis of the movements of the seas. From the perspective of an ordinary Athenian citizen, such arguments would have appeared eminently ridiculous.

Ultimately, however, what makes Strepsiades laughable is his belief that those who lack the knowledge he gained at the *phrontistērion* are unfit to participate in the exchanging of reasons that is at the heart of the practice of democratic citizenship. Looking back to the reference with which this chapter begins, the audience's laughter at Strepsiades is like that of the hypothetical laughter the Athenians might direct at someone who claimed to possess a political *technē* that ordinary citizens did not possess and without which they would not be competent to participate in political deliberation. Compared with the antidemocratic laughter of Socrates and Strepsiades in the play, it is a democratic form of laughter, one that ridicules the challenge posed by Socratic intellectualism to the democratic operation of politics in Athens.

V.

Who is the Socrates who emerges from reading *Clouds* in this way? Martha Nussbaum argues that *Clouds* offers a critique of Socrates for neglecting the importance of the training and habituation of character in moral education and for lacking a positive teaching to replace the traditional values he has undermined. Nussbaum argues that the Platonic Socrates of the early dialogues is susceptible to the same critiques and that, in the *Republic*, Plato recognized the need for habituation in moral education and the need to supplement and correct Socratic practice. In short, Plato largely agreed with Aristophanes' critique of Socrates in *Clouds*, and his mature philosophy offers a means of balancing the negative Socratic *elenchus* with a concern for social stability.[24]

The reading of *Clouds* developed above highlights, in contrast, the specifically democratic dimension to Aristophanes' critique of Socrates, one that, I would argue, also left its mark on Plato's presentation of Socrates, and on

Xenophon's as well. Plato's Socrates, in the *Apology*, goes to great lengths to demonstrate the compatibility between his philosophic practice and the practice of Athenian democracy. While he implies, in the *Gorgias*, that he possesses a political *technē*, it is a *technē* that largely consists in elenctic questioning;[25] it is not, in other words, a type of knowledge that turns politics into a game for experts.[26] It is my hope that emphasizing this element of *Clouds* can illuminate some of the thematic connections across the Aristophanic, Platonic, and Xenophontic visions of Socrates that might be worth pursuing in the future.[27]

One such theme that emerges from Aristophanes' portrait, and is central to both Plato's and Xenophon's depictions of Socrates, is what we might call Socratic mockery. While Aristophanes depicts a Socrates who mocks and humiliates ordinary citizens for their ignorance, Plato and Xenophon depict this practice as a useful element in Socrates' attempt to improve his fellow citizens. If we take the *Philebus* as our guide, Plato's Socrates is engaged in exposing his interlocutors as laughable. He engages in mockery of his interlocutor's beliefs, either outrightly (as with Callicles) or ironically (as with Euthyphro). These semicomic elements are also central themes of Xenophon's presentation of Socrates; the *Symposium* details the semicomic elements of Socrates' character; the *Memorabilia* displays Socrates' mockery in his treatment of Euthydemus; and the *Oeconomicus* portrays Socrates using irony in an attempt to educate the young Critobolus. Rather than whitewash this aspect of Socrates' philosophical practice, both Plato and Xenophon attempt to explain its usefulness.

Notes

1. Since Dover's argument, in the introduction to his edition of the play, that the Socrates of *Clouds* is less a portrait of Socrates than of a generalized sophist, there has been no dearth of articles addressing the historical accuracy of Aristophanes' portrait, much of which challenges Dover's conclusion. For Dover's argument, see Kenneth Dover, "Introduction," in *Aristophanes: Clouds* (Oxford: Clarendon, 1968), xvii–cxxv. Adkins contends that the language of initiation surrounding the *phrontistērion* in *Clouds* likely reflected Socratic usage, and that Plato attempted to distance Socrates from such blasphemies (A. W. H. Adkins, "Clouds, Mysteries, Socrates and Plato," *Antichthon* 4 [1970]: 13–24); Havelock argues that the Socratic use of *psuchē* is ridiculed in the play (Eric Havelock, "The Socratic Self as It Is Parodied in Aristophanes' *Clouds*," *Yale Classical Studies* 22 [1972]: 1–18); Nussbaum reads the play as attacking Socrates for his neglect of the role of character and habituation in moral education, a criticism she argues is later taken up by Plato in the *Republic* (Martha Nussbaum, "Aristophanes and Socrates on Learning Practical Wisdom," *Yale Classical Studies* 26 [1980]: 43–97); Kleve

is perhaps the most staunch in his opposition, adopting Kierkegaard's claim that the Aristophanic Socrates is more faithful to the historical Socrates than either the Platonic or Xenophontic (Knut Kleve, "Anti-Dover or Socrates in the Clouds," *Symbolae Osloenses* 58 [1983]: 23–37); Edmunds argues that the clouds represent a hypostatized version of Socratic irony (Lowell Edmunds, "Aristophanes' Socrates," *Proceedings of the Boston Area Colloquium in Ancient Philosophy* 2 [1986]: 209–30); Nichols interprets the play as a defense of man's embodied existence against Socratic abstraction and the project of overcoming human limitation (Mary Nichols, *Socrates and the Political Community* [Albany, NY: SUNY Press, 1987]); Tomin points to the stark division between Socrates and the Worse Argument to argue that the Socrates of *Clouds* looks much more like the Socrates of Plato than Dover acknowledges (Julius Tomin, "Socratic Gymnasium in the Clouds," *Symbolae Osloenses* 62 [1987]: 25–32); Tomin also argues that lines 135–39 should be read as a joke about Socratic midwifery (Julius Tomin, "Socratic Midwifery," *The Classical Quarterly* 37 [no. 1, 1987]: 97–102, though see the criticisms of this view in Myles Burnyeat, "Socratic Midwifery, Platonic Inspiration," *Bulletin of the Institute of Classical Studies* 24 [1977]: 7–16, and Harold Tarrant, "Midwifery and the *Clouds*," *The Classical Quarterly* 38 [no. 1, 1988]: 116–22); Vander Waerdt argues that Socrates is portrayed as a follower of Diogenes of Apollonia and that this was true of Socrates at the time *Clouds* was performed (P. A. Vander Waerdt, "Socrates in the Clouds," in *The Socratic Movement*, ed. P. A. Vander Waerdt [Ithaca, NY: Cornell University Press, 1994], 48–86); Euben highlights the affinities between Aristophanes the comic poet and Socrates the philosopher (J. Peter Euben, "Where There Are Gray Skies: Aristophanes' *Clouds* and the Political Education of Democratic Citizens," in *Corrupting Youth* [Princeton, NJ: Princeton University Press, 1997], 109–38); Berg contends that Aristophanes illustrates the need for Socratic philosophy to be supplemented by poetry (Stephen Berg, "Rhetoric, Nature, and Philosophy in Aristophanes' *Clouds*," *Ancient Philosophy* 18 [1998]: 1–19); finally, Konstan maintains that while the Aristophanic Socrates is a combination of various characteristics of Protagoras, Hippias, Damon, Diogenes of Apollonia, and Anaxagoras, it was likely the fact that Socrates was not only an Athenian citizen, but a particularly bothersome one, that led to Aristophanes, and the other poets of Old Comedy, singling him out (David Konstan, "Socrates in Aristophanes' *Clouds*," in *The Cambridge Companion to Socrates*, ed. D. M. Morrison [Cambridge: Cambridge University Press, 2011], 75–90). For a more complete bibliography, see Konstan, "Socrates in Aristophanes' *Clouds*," 88–90.

2. The following section has been reprinted from John Lombardini, "Comic Authority in Aristophanes' *Knights*," *Polis* 29 (no. 1, 2012): 133–36. The author and editors gratefully acknowledge permission to reprint this material.

3. M. H. Hansen, *The Athenian Democracy in the Age of Demosthenes* (Norman: University of Oklahoma Press, 1991), 142.

4. Hansen, *The Athenian Democracy*, 306–7.

5. W. R. Connor, *The New Politicians of Fifth-Century Athens* (Princeton, NJ: Princeton University Press, 1971).

6. Paul Cartledge, "Comparatively Equal: A Spartan Approach," in *Spartan Reflections* (Berkeley: University of California Press, 2001), 69–73.

7. Josiah Ober, *Mass and Elite in Democratic Athens* (Princeton, NJ: Princeton University Press, 1989), 189.

8. Ober, *Mass and Elite*, 333.

9. Ober, *Mass and Elite*, 191, 318–24; Josiah Ober, "Power and Oratory in Democratic Athens: Demosthenes 21, *Against Meidias*," in *The Athenian Revolution* (Princeton, NJ: Princeton University Press, 1995), 105.

10. Private cases, in contrast, could only be prosecuted by the victim, or in the case of murder or a crime against a woman, by a male relative. See D. M. MacDowell, *The Law in Classical Athens* (Ithaca, NY: Cornell University Press, 1978), 57–58.

11. Danielle Allen, *The World of Prometheus: The Politics of Punishing in Democratic Athens* (Princeton, NJ: Princeton University Press, 2000), 50–59.

12. Allen, *The World of Prometheus*, 166.

13. Max Weber, *Economy and Society*, vol. 1, eds. Guenther Roth and Claus Wittich (Berkeley: University of California Press, 1978), 226–27.

14. As Jeffrey Stout argues, all discursive practices, even democratic ones, entail various degrees of authority and consent—what distinguishes democratic discursive practices, in this regard, from other types of discursive practices is that the former are relatively nondeferential (though not entirely nondeferential). See Jeffrey Stout, *Democracy and Tradition* (Princeton, NJ: Princeton University Press, 2004), 209–13, 278–83.

15. Stout, *Democracy and Tradition*, 279, offers the following example: "As in street soccer or sandlot baseball, all of the participants have the authority to 'keep score,' and each of them necessarily does so in light of his or her already-adopted commitments. That I have the authority to track commitments and entitlements, and thus to draw the fundamental normative distinction from my own point of view, does not make my commitments correct; nor does it make me entitled to them, in the sense that entails being epistemically justified in holding them. It simply puts me in the democratic game of giving and asking for reasons."

16. Tarrant speculates that in the version of *Clouds* performed in 423 BCE, Strepsiades successfully graduated from the *phrontistērion*. See Harold Tarrant, "*Clouds* I: Steps Towards Reconstruction," *Arctos* 25 (1991): 157–81.

17. All translations from *Clouds* are my own. The text used is that of Dover (see note 1 above).

18. This connection is emphasized by the language of Strepsiades' description: it is not simply that the men in the *phrontistērion* say or argue that the sky is a barbecue lid, but that they are persuasive in doing so (*hoi ton ouranon legontes anapeithousin hōs estin pnigeus*).

19. As Dover explains, the joke plays off of the similarity between the abstract word for 'whirling' or 'rotation' (*dinē*) and that denoting a type of cup (*dinos*). See Dover, "Commentary," 150.

20. N. R. E. Fisher, *Hybris: A Study of the Values of Honour and Shame in Ancient Greece* (Warminster, UK: Aris & Phillips, 1992), 148.

21. Josiah Ober, "Quasi-Rights: Participatory Citizenship and Negative Liberties," in *Athenian Legacies* (Princeton, NJ: Princeton University Press, 2005), 113–14.

22. Isocrates, *Against Lochites*, 4, in Isocrates, *Speeches*, vol. 1, trans. D. C. Mirhady and Y. L. Too (Austin: University of Texas Press, 2000). Cf. Ober, "Power and Oratory," 102.

23. *Clouds* 1068 is worth consulting on this point, where the Weaker Argument seems to construe being a *hubristēs* as an ideal for which one should strive. On this point, see Dover, "Commentary," 226.

24. Nussbaum, "Aristophanes and Socrates," 81–88.

25. Dana Villa, *Socratic Citizenship* (Princeton, NJ: Princeton University Press, 2001), 36.

26. As John Wallach has argued, though Socrates possesses a *technē logōn*, it is not a typical sort of *technē*. See John Wallach, "Socratic Citizenship," *History of Political Thought* 9 (no. 3, 1988): 409.

27. On the logic of such comparative exegesis, see Louis-André Dorion, "A l'origine de la question socratique et de la critique du témoignage de Xénophon: l'étude de Schleiermacher sur Socrate (1815)," *Dionysius* 19 (2001): 72–74.

2

The Meaning of Socrates' Asceticism in Aristophanes' *Clouds*

Khalil M. Habib

Of the eleven comedies by Aristophanes that have come down to us as genuine, only the *Clouds* features Socrates. Aristophanes' Socrates is depicted as an impoverished ascetic who teaches rhetoric in his "Thinkery" and spends his time suspended in a basket studying natural science. Aristophanes' Socrates openly denies the existence of Zeus (247, 366–81, 404–7, 1467–71), introduces new Cloud-divinities into the city (250–365), is indifferent to incest and father beating (1369–72), disrespects established law (365–425), and corrupts the young—"the very charges on which he was convicted twenty-four years after the *Clouds* was first performed" in 423 BC.[1] What is more, the *Clouds* is also the only play in which Aristophanes appears as a character and speaks his own name. Aristophanes plays the role of the leading member of the chorus of Clouds (515–85), and he can be seen on stage publicly admonishing Socrates for his arrogance, life of self-denial, imprudence, and lack of self-knowledge (360, 1460–1510). Not surprisingly, Aristophanes tells us that the *Clouds* is his "wisest" play (520).[2] Perhaps this is Aristophanes' way of presenting a contest of wisdom between Socrates and himself.

One could read the *Clouds* and conclude that Aristophanes is an esoteric Socratic; that is, Aristophanes is a wise poet who, while viewing nature as indifferent to human flourishing, has (unlike his Socrates) the good grace and prudence to keep quiet about it. Although I am sympathetic to this line of reasoning, I do not believe it is Aristophanes' deepest criticism of Socrates. Here is how the Clouds (Aristophanes' voice) first address Socrates on stage: "you [Socrates], *priest* of subtlest babble, tell us what you want. For we wouldn't listen to anyone else of those who are now sophist-of-the-things-aloft except for Prodicus: to him because of his *wisdom* and *judgment*, to *you* [Socrates] because of your *swagger* . . . and *barefoot you endure many evils and put on a solemn face for us*" (360–65, emphasis added). The Clouds mock Socrates as a boaster who swaggers around barefoot suffering hardships and putting on a solemn face to suffer for and impress the Clouds. Although Socrates, in the play, denies the existence of the gods, he seems to worship the Clouds, whom he later tells us are divinities that supply humans with "thought, dialectics, and intelligence" (316–18). The Clouds have no shape, and their formlessness reflects the "vortex," or essence, of nature that he claims to know through his science (348). Aristophanes' Socrates first appears, then, as a pretentious ascetic who renounces comforts and who subordinates himself to his science and lives a life of self-denial. Socrates' asceticism, however, is in conflict with his understanding of nature, as asceticism is a "form of self-sacrifice and, therefore, contains a religious instinct . . . [that] is in contradiction with science itself."[3] Hence, the Clouds refer to Socrates as a *priest* and describe him in religious rather than philosophic terms. Here is how Mark Kremer explains the problem:

> Natural science is above all a human activity, through which the natural scientist practices a form of self-forgetting. He finds security in his dedication to knowledge, but he has not examined the meaning of this dedication. In fact, his dedication makes no sense in light of his own understanding of nature because matter and motion are meaningless and unworthy of dedication. He practices a form of asceticism whereby he tries to avoid facing his own existence by subordinating himself to his science.[4]

In other words, Socrates cannot give living proof of the existence of the theoretical life he claims to live on the basis of his opinions about nature: "there is no order to which [Socrates] belongs and hence he can and must will where there is nothing."[5] Socrates does not comprehend how "his life and his science are in contradiction, and his unwillingness to face it is a mark of his ignorance."[6] This would explain why the Clouds view Socrates as a sophist who lacks wisdom and judgment. Perhaps this is Aristophanes' way of indicating that to grasp his critique of Socrates, we should begin to think about the necessity of reconciling the meaning of Socrates' asceticism with his lack of self-knowledge.[7] At the very least, the Clouds draw attention to it and, therefore, prod the reader to start thinking about Socrates' way of life. This chapter makes an attempt in that direction.[8]

I.

The opening scene of the *Clouds* begins in the bedroom of Strepsiades. It is dark, yet Strepsiades is awake:

> Strepsiades [*sitting up in bed*]: Oh! Oh!
> O Zeus the King, how long the *nights* are!
> *Boundless! Will day never come?*
> *I* heard the cock long ago,
> But the servants are still snoring. They wouldn't have before.
> Perish, then, *O War*, because among many other things,
> Now I can't even punish my servants!
> [Points to Pheidippedes.]
> Nor does this upright youth here
> Wake up at night; he farts away,
> Enwrapped in five blankets.
> But if it is so resolved, let's cover ourselves up and snore.
> But I can't sleep, wretched me, I'm being bitten—
> By expenses and stables and my debts
> because of this son of mine. He with his long hair
> rides horses and drives a chariot,
> and dreams of horses, while I am ruined
> as I see the moon bringing on the twenties:
> the interest mounts up. (1–20, emphasis added)

It is a striking feature of the *Clouds* that Aristophanes' only play devoted to an investigation of Socrates begins in a tone of despair and the haunting specter of death ("boundless night") and the longing for daylight (life). Strepsiades lies in bed bemoaning the war: Athens is in the midst of a terrible war it is destined to lose. The Peloponnesian War between Athens and Sparta (431–404 BC) provides an ominous backdrop of destruction and sets the play within the context of the decline of Greek civilization. What is more, Strepsiades' finances are in ruin. Although he was born to the lower class, Strepsiades has married into aristocracy. Yet his escape from poverty has run out, and so has his money; his son's extravagant preoccupation with chariot racing and the expense of keeping up an aristocratic lifestyle has bankrupted Strepsiades, sending him into serious debt. His own servants dare now to sleep in: they no longer take his authority seriously, for the present war between Athens and Sparta may well be welcomed by slaves who could easily defect and regain their freedom. His country, his life, and his finances are in shambles. Strepsiades is facing the imminent loss of everything he is attached to, and so he lies awake in the dark as though he were about to face his own oblivion. It is a journey into the end of the night for this old man, and so he longs for the consolation of daylight and relief from the "boundless night," which he fears might spell the end of his existence. He is a man who seeks freedom from the horror of losing everything, including his own life.[9]

With this opening scene, Aristophanes seems to be saying, "Here is a father who experiences the loss of his country, his wealth, and his grip over his servants and household as though he is about die. Let us see what happens when he turns to Socrates for a solution to his woes and to save himself and his family." After all, Strepsiades has heard that Socrates can teach anyone to win any argument, just or unjust, by teaching how to make clever arguments. The great natural scientist-philosopher has a reputation for making unjust actions appear just, and vice versa. What Strepsiades does not anticipate, however, is how the Socratic education erodes the bonds of the family and culminates in father and mother beating (1405–46), not to mention Socrates' cavalier attitude toward incest (1369–72). By the end of the play, Strepsiades will burn Socrates' schoolhouse down because he has discovered that everything Socrates stands for threatens society through dissolving family and, along with it, all meaningful attachments. It is fitting, then, that the play begins and ends with Strepsiades rebelling from oblivion and with his desperate attempt to affirm the meaning of his family and his existence within it. Just as his marriage failed to overcome poverty and necessity, so too will his Socratic education fail to satisfy his hope of saving himself and his family.

Strepsiades arrives at Socrates' Thinkery and bangs on the door with gusto. A disdainful, pale-faced devotee of Socrates answers the door and pretends that Strepsiades' graceless knock has just caused him to forget a certain novel discovery. When Strepsiades asks the pupil about the novel idea that miscarried, the student tells him that this can only be revealed to disciples. The Thinkery is shrouded in secrecy. Strepsiades informs the student that he has come from far, from the country in fact, to become a disciple, at which point the pupil eagerly discloses the secret. The pupil has not forgotten the novel idea after all.[10]

The student reveals how Socrates attempted to measure how many "flea-feet" a flea jumped by cleverly melting wax around the flea's foot, creating a wax "slipper," and then calculating the distance the flea jumped from Chaerophon to Socrates (148–52). The experiment to measure the infinitesimal, however, fails: "in taking this measurement, Socrates, of course, is trying to do the impossible, for the distance between himself and Chaerophon constantly changes."[11] Such is the indeterminacy of matter in motion. Socrates' experiment to measure the distance between himself and Chaerophon fails, as it "presupposes that they are both fixed points."[12] Through the absurdity of this endeavor, Aristophanes seems to raise doubts about the Socratic enterprise of understanding the world in terms of bodies or matter in motion. As we shall see later, Socrates' asceticism reveals a similar paradox: the denial of his body betrays a profound concern with avoiding his own oblivion, which makes no sense if everything passes away and if, as Socrates teaches, heaven is like an oven and men are like charcoals, burning and perishing away to nothing (95).

Before leaving this scene, I want to call attention to an episode that sheds light on the antiheroic character of the Socratic perspective. The student reveals to Strepsiades that someone asked Socrates whether gnats hum with their mouths or with their anuses. Socrates concludes that the gnat "sings" out of its narrow behind, for it is through this cavity that the sound of humming echoes as air is forced out (156–64). It is worth reflecting on the student's odd choice of the verb "to sing" (*adein*) to describe the sound of a gnat farting.[13] "To sing" would remind a Greek audience of the same verb used by both Hesiod and Homer when they invoke the Olympian Muses, the divine daughters of Zeus, to inspire them to "to sing" about the deeds of men of old and the gods. The *Iliad* and *Odyssey* stand alongside the *Theogony* and *Works and Days* at the beginning of Greek civilization and together give an account of the divine order. Singers on earth are gifts of the gods to mankind, and the Muses inspire these great poets "to sing" of the gods and to celebrate the race of gods and the actions of Greek heroes. In Aristophanes' play, however, the Socratics equate the divine singing of the poets and the subjects of their poetry with a sound a gnat makes when it passes gas.[14] This is consistent with Socrates' atheism and his teaching that heaven is like a stove and men are charcoal. Here Aristophanes points out that the Socratic perspective is both atheistic and antiheroic, and, worse yet, Socratic study of all the things under the earth (Hades) confirms their skepticism of the existence of the gods and reduces man's significance on earth to insignificant drivel—a perspective already implied by Socrates' view of Athens and Sparta as merely tiny dots on earth (210). In light of these remarks, it is easy to see how philosophy as practiced by Aristophanes' Socrates "prepared the break with the ancient city, its gods, and heroes, which made possible the authority of reason."[15] Mark Kremer further points out that "the age of reason belongs to a stage of human decay where the traditions and gods of the nobles no longer inspire and where there is need for new ends or limits"[16]—hence Strepsiades' attraction to a Socratic education at a time when Greek civilization is already in decline. This climate of decadence also allows Unjust Speech to triumph over Just Speech, as we demonstrate later.

This comic scene, however, is not yet over: while fixated on the revolutions of the moon, the student reports that a lizard dropped a turd on Socrates (171–73). This part of the story allows Strepsiades to laugh at what he sees as Socrates' odd fixation with such a trivial matter. Yet, from the perspective of Socrates, Strepsiades' concerns appear insignificant, and so the "natural scientist" has a chance to laugh at what concerns Strepsiades. From the perspective of an anxious father, Socrates loses his dignity; from the perspective of the whole, however, Strepsiades loses his, as human life is reduced to insignificance.

In any case, Strepsiades is now eager to enter the Thinkery and to meet Socrates. Once inside, he is shocked at the sight of his fellow students: "Hercules! Where do these beasts come from? . . . . [They look] like the Laconian captives from Pylos" (185). Strepsiades has never before seen such ill-appearing ascetics, and his visceral reference to Hercules only helps to underscore the pathetic, antiheroic appearance of these Socratics who spend most of their time indoors. The students of the Thinkery are bent over, busy studying the earth. The student explains to Strepsiades that, when bent over, the Socratics can investigate geology with their eyes and astronomy with their anuses.

Strepsiades instinctively relates their theoretical studies into nature to his earthly troubles and his stomach. When Strepsiades, for instance, sees the students of geology investigating the things beneath the earth (Hades), he assumes they must be searching for vegetables. Strepsiades thinks that geometers study and measure the earth in order to divide the land and distribute its resources, as opposed to their desire to seek the causes of the whole (203–5). Strepsiades notices how close Sparta and Athens are to one another on a map and becomes fearful (215–16), because if Athens' enemies are so close, he could be captured or killed. He asks his student host to move Athens' place on the map to a safer location. The student, by contrast, is unaware that Athens is at war or is simply indifferent; his view of the whole is detached from particulars and is cosmopolitan, and he looks at the world as a scientist rather than as a citizen.[17] The combination of Strepsiades' earthly concerns with his own self-preservation and his desperate turn to science for its utility constitute a feature of the Enlightenment and modern life. Aristophanes seems to suggest, anticipating the Baconian project, that science is exploited in the service of relieving man's physical discomfort, and so a theoretical understanding of nature is secondary, as theory is subordinated to applied science.[18] He appears to be asking whether this is the natural outcome of a marriage between the common mind and philosophy.

At this point, Socrates enters the stage suspended in a basket, floating high atop the clouds. He contemptuously addresses Strepsiades as "creature of the day" (223); that is, an insignificant being that takes him away from the study of nature. We learn that his disciples refer to Socrates as "Himself" rather than by his proper name (220)—for what is a conventional name to such men who seek after only the essence of things, as opposed to their accidental qualities, such as the name "Socrates"? Indeed, according to Socrates, the love of one's own distorts reality and gets in the way of discovering the "truth." He attributes his capacity to understand the nature of things to his "abstracting" himself from the earth and all things human.[19] Hence he literally suspends himself from all earthly attachments in order to gain the proper bird's-eye perspective required to see things as they "really" are (truth) and not as how one wishes or hopes for them to be. For this reason he is unconcerned with the current war between Athens and Sparta and views political communities as insignificant dots on a map. Justice, the law, and citizenship belong to convention and play no meaningful role in his massively important study of nature. The disproportion between the significance Strepsiades places on what matters to him and that inhabited by these natural scientists could not be greater: one is concerned with day-to-day matters, his body, and his food; the other floats suspended in the air studying natural science, detached from human beings and removed from the relations that form families and political communities.[20]

Strepsiades makes it clear at the outset in his discussion with Socrates that he wishes to confine his education to that aspect of philosophy that could alleviate his financial troubles. Each step in Socrates' educational program, however, through materialism and atheism, will erode everything to which Strepsiades is attached. The problem that Socrates' natural philosophy poses to Strepsiades will be deferred, but not indefinitely evaded, as we shall shortly see. For now, however, Strepsiades swears an oath to the gods to repay Socrates for his services, only to discover that his oath to the gods is futile because Socrates does not believe in Zeus. Still, Strepsiades is not so much bothered with Socrates' atheism (just yet) as much as he is amazed at how anyone could enforce an obligation without the fear of divine punishment. Socrates cannot be manipulated through either oaths or money, for he is neither fearful of divine retribution nor given to greed. "He" is an impoverished ascetic who lives from hand to mouth in order to survive, and he surrounds himself with ill-appearing, pale-faced young "cranks" who, significantly, never seem to make it outside the doors of their little schoolhouse. Although Socrates will accept payment for his teachings, or at least accept gifts (855–56), he is more concerned with gaining a new disciple. Socrates is invested in converting others to the "truth," that is, with spreading "His" knowledge. He is, therefore, more interested in discovering whether or not Strepsiades is eager to learn the nature of things from him.

II.

Socrates initiates Strepsiades into his Socratic teaching on justice by introducing him to the Clouds, the patron divinities of the Thinkery. The chorus of Clouds appears onstage with Aristophanes as the lead Cloud (518–62). Socrates says that the Clouds are goddesses who "supply us with thought, dialectics, intelligence, marvels, circumlocution, cheating, and comprehension" (316–18). They are formless and can take on any shape they wish. They reflect "a world that lacks distinct elements which limit a man's power," for the Clouds mirror the formless chaos of the material universe.[21] Their protean character enables them to make an unjust man appear just and vice versa, and they possess the power to teach one how to make clever arguments, making unjust actions appear just without fear of being caught (345). The Clouds, therefore, represent the formless world of nature and the art of rhetoric.

Strepsiades' pious fears, however, stand in the way of his scheme to defraud his creditors, for he believes that thunder is a sign of Zeus' anger and lightning a sign of Zeus' divine punishment (395). Socrates is less interested in Strepsiades' personal problems than he is with sharing his insight into the "reality" of things and gaining a new disciple for "Himself" and a devotee to the Clouds. For the moment, their conflicting motivations converge: Strepsiades needs to be convinced that the gods do not exist if he is to break his oaths without fear of divine retribution, while Socrates seeks a devotee. In order to teach Strepsiades the truth about the gods and divine punishment, Socrates tries to convince his acolyte that thunder and lightning occur naturally without any admixture of illusion connected to divine punishment. Because Strepsiades is not a natural scientist, Socrates cleverly explains the nature of thunder by appealing to Strepsiades' belly—a small part of nature Strepsiades knows all too well. Socrates tells Strepsiades that the sound of thunder is like the sound a stomach makes when digesting food or passing gas: it makes noise but means nothing. There are no divine rewards or punishments, and Zeus' divine justice is no different from Strepsiades' noisy stomach or a gnat passing gas.

By equating divine justice with Strepsiades' digestive process, Socrates reduces the universe to bodies in motion governed by necessity. Because the human body individuates humans from one another, there is no ground for justice in nature. The world of justice and injustice thus disappears. Only the art of rhetoric exists, persuading, through its powers over the imagination, of the existence of justice. Rhetoric becomes the sole means by which to establish justice or a common good in a world where only disparate bodies exist. And if there is no foundation for justice in nature, then justice becomes a matter of rhetorical formulations that can be twisted however one wishes. Socrates' teaching on justice is, therefore, informed by his understanding of nature. Socrates replaces the Athenian gods with Chaos and the Clouds. Although he no longer reveres the traditional deities, Socrates is zealously devoted to the "vortex" and wishes to draw potential admirers to it—even nitwits like Strepsiades. Once reverence for Zeus is destroyed and the authority of tradition and opinion is banished, Strepsiades may join Socrates on a quest to study nature free from prejudices.

Socrates forgets (or ignores) that Strepsiades is seeking his services in order to learn rhetoric so that he can twist justice as he wishes in order to restore his finances and preserve his own household. Socrates, however, has other plans. In order to reinforce his teaching about nature and to prepare Strepsiades for a life of asceticism and the study of natural science—the complete opposite of what Strepsiades seeks—Socrates has his newest student lie down in a flea-infested bed to test his ability to overcome his body and his attachment to his particularity. As Socrates surveys the whole from atop the clouds suspended in his basket, he instructs Strepsiades to "discover an abstract, universal thought" in order to teach him to see the whole free from the distorting effects of the love of one's own (695). Strepsiades is, of course, not cut out for asceticism; he simply cannot sacrifice himself for the truth. And he is equally not cut out for natural science and universal thought: he screams in anguish as the fleas bite him: "I am almost gone!" (720). For Strepsiades to think abstractly is an impossibility, because that would mean to think outside himself, to let go of his body and all of the attachments connected to it—his home, his family and servants, and his country. It is precisely the hope to preserve these things that sent him to Socrates' Thinkery in the first place. Where Socrates sees truth, Strepsiades sees death.

Socrates leaves Strepsiades alone for a moment to see whether or not he can arrive at an abstract thought. Upon his return, he discovers Strepsiades masturbating under a blanket (735). While he was supposed to overcome the particularity of his body in order to think high thoughts, which he a moment ago equated to death, Strepsiades cannot seem to let go of his penis. Whereas Odysseus holds onto a branch for dear life as the whirlpool sucks everything down beneath him, Strepsiades tries to save himself from oblivion by turning to himself, to the only part of nature that promises him continuity through procreation, an erotic and powerful longing to create a connection that cannot be taken away from him.[22] Yet Socrates seems to teach here that only by overcoming eros can Strepsiades become fully enlightened and Socratic, for eros does not lead to philosophy or anything eternal, as the Socrates of the *Clouds* understands it, but to the love of one's own and bodily satisfaction—after all, Strepsiades is alone in bed. Aristophanes' Socrates, unlike Plato's, is unerotic.

Nevertheless, Strepsiades manages to make a little progress, and for a brief moment he even impresses Socrates by relaying his plans to involve the moon and the sun in his schemes. First, Strepsiades plans to put the moon in a box to avoid paying interest on his loans, for there would be no way for his creditors to measure the passage of time without visible moon phases. Second, he says that he will use a magnifying glass to concentrate the sun's heat "and melt away the letters of [his] lawsuit" (770). Socrates praises him for both of these ridiculous schemes, as Strepsiades is finally starting to see how he can manipulate nature, in the forms of the moon and the sun, to triumph over convention and justice (755–75). Finally, however, Strepsiades concludes that he will commit suicide to get out of his debts, "since no one will bring a lawsuit against me if I'm dead" (780). This is the point when Socrates loses his patience with Strepsiades and throws him out of the Thinkery. Strepsiades' attachment to himself is so deeply ingrained that he actually believes he will survive his own death. Only now does Socrates realize that he cannot teach this man to think completely outside himself and to recognize the truth: there is no afterlife.

III.

Although he has been expelled from the Thinkery, Strepsiades refuses to give up, and so he sends his reluctant son, Pheidippedes, to learn in his place. Pheidippedes warns his father that he will regret his decision to force him to study with Socrates, a prediction that will prove correct. Unwillingly, Pheidippedes eventually accompanies his father to the Thinkery.

It is at this point in the play that Strepsiades and Pheidippedes come to witness the great debate between Just Speech and Unjust Speech, both of whom are personified on stage. Socrates leaves, being indifferent to the outcome of the contest, but the Clouds remain and watch. The debate between Just Speech and Unjust Speech immediately begins with unrestrained verbal abuse, resulting in the Clouds imposing order through rhetoric, because no common ground can be established.

Just Speech is a conservative from the Old Marathon Fighters of a past generation. He is an orator whose exhortations celebrate the venerable past when moderation ruled and when Marathon Fighters abstained from frivolous pleasures in the name of noble deeds. Just Speech tries to hold society up to a stern standard of justice and tells the audience that justice consists of obeying the gods and that man must do what the gods tell him to do, and not what the gods themselves do. He stands for those restraints on body and soul that are critical to the traditional running and preservation of society. He speaks of the earlier generation of youths who displayed reverence for the old by giving up their seats when their elders approached and who did not misbehave towards their parents and who never did anything shameful that would tarnish the statue of Awe (995). For him, the goal of education is to cultivate morally superior men with a sense of duty and self-sacrifice. Just Speech accuses the new progressive education, which laughs at and ridicules traditional education, for cultivating insolent, unheroic, and sensual citizens addicted to their private pleasures. His speech proves to be prescient for Strepsiades' family.

Unjust Speech, by contrast, is an excellent primer for reflection on the shameless use of dialectics and demagoguery to cast doubt on moral authority in the name of hedonistic self-indulgence. He is a nihilistic plebian who strips away shame and destroys reverence for tradition in order to encourage license. Whereas Just Speech uses oratory to hold society to a moral ideal, Unjust Speech flatters the audience's vices by pointing out the hypocrisy among the celebrated heroes of the past. Unjust Speech says that the gods say one thing and yet do quite another. Hercules, he claims, took warm, not cold, baths (1045), and he reminds the audience that Zeus banished his own father to Tartarus. The gods and heroes are really inclined toward self-interest and pleasure, too, he points out. What is good for the gods must be good for man.

Just Speech protests and predicts that if Unjust Speech's subversive teaching on injustice were to dominate society, then Athens would have a citizenry given to buggery. Unjust Speech responds by pointing out all the particular buggered men in the audience,[23] cleverly playing the "Hey, they are already doing it anyway" card. In other words, Unjust Speech knows that Just Speech needs the authority of the gods and public opinion on his side to triumph over vice; but if the authority of the gods is destroyed and the people are already corrupt, then stern speeches about justice will fall on deaf ears. When the impossibility of his own triumph over vice is brought before him, Just Speech flings his coat into the audience and abandons justice for injustice (1100; see 965).

Moral authority requires the assistance of convention and a poetry that speaks in its favor. Without the authority of the gods and the force of public opinion speaking on behalf of justice, the case for justice and the habits of self-restraint are destroyed and Unjust Speech is victorious. "The plebian instinct that emerges victorious and authoritative is characterized by the attempt to affirm oneself in the face of nobler types, which means that the dominant instinct is to eliminate fear and shame from life in order to form a perfect state of self-satisfaction."[24] In order to exercise his self-indulgent pleasures openly and without any moral restraint or censorship, Unjust Speech aggressively seeks to transform society by corrupting it. He uses his dialectical skills cynically to convert society into a mirror of himself: a democratic herd animal that longs for nothing beyond the satisfaction of self-interest and pleasure. Unjust Speech resembles our modern-day pornographers who justify their shameless tastes by pointing out the greater hypocrisy in society's moral authorities in order to whitewash the unjustifiable.

IV.

We witness the effects of the Socratic education on Strepsiades' household when he and Pheidippedes return home to celebrate their reconciliation and their newfound "wisdom." Their celebration quickly falls apart because Pheidippedes, requested "to sing" (that verb again!) a song by the traditional lyric poet, Simonides, contemptuously refers to him as old-fashioned. Pheidippedes insists on singing a song about incest by the more modern poet Euripides. When his father objects to his son's bad taste, Pheidippedes beats him.

Educated by Socrates, not only does Pheidippedes now take incest lightly (1369–72), but he also manages to justify beating his father "by appealing to nature, according to which it is just for the wise to punish the foolish for their own good."[25] Strepsiades is confused enough by his son's clever argument to concede his son's point, but Strepsiades draws the line when his son proposes to beat his mother as well. It is easy to see Aristophanes' point here: Socratic education undermines the sacred prohibitions protecting the family and the unqualified authority of experience: Strepsiades' age is his title to rule, "as it is in almost all regimes governed by ancestral custom. Age is a practical substitute for wisdom because, unlike wisdom, it is politically recognizable and easily defined. It is more feasible to teach force to respect age than to teach it to respect wisdom."[26] The reverence for age and tradition has obviously been undermined by Socrates' natural science and Unjust's victory over convention. Pheidippedes had been tamed by fear and shame, but, unbound from moral restraint and established law, he feels himself free to do any offensive thing that pops into his head!

The prohibition against incest and father beating is founded, Aristophanes implies, upon the authority of the gods, which in turn requires that the gods be harsh and punitive. This means that humans must do what the gods tell them to do, and not what the gods themselves do, as Just Speech had unsuccessfully tried to argue. It is for this reason that Leo Strauss points out that "the prohibition against incest, the obligation of exogamy, calls for the expansion of the family into the polis, an expansion that is necessary in the first place because the family is not able to defend itself. But the prohibition would lack the necessary force if there were no gods."[27] In other words, "the prohibition against incest is a quasi-natural bridge between the family and the city."[28] If the family is to flourish, it must become part of the city by welcoming divine authorities rather than philosophy into the household. The city, then, can be founded only when civic authorities have enough power to raise the virtue of piety above the authority of fathers. Aristophanes tells us that Socrates' teaching about nature and the gods presents a danger of undermining both the family and the city's religious authority. Aristophanes' deadly serious point here is that it is this teaching that places Socrates within the crosshairs of the city, ignites Strepsiades' ire, and, consequently, leads to Socrates' downfall. It is unfortunate that Socrates, whose head remains in the Clouds, is simply unaware of the political context and danger in which his Thinkery exists.

Strepsiades blames the Clouds for his son's deplorable conduct. They reply, "No, you yourself are responsible for these things by yourself, because you twisted yourself into villainous affairs" (1455). Strepsiades finally recognizes the truth of their words and takes responsibility for his own transgressions (1460). Only now, facing the consequences of his actions and the destruction of his household, does Strepsiades regret trying to defraud his creditors and getting around justice. He has, by the end of the comedy, gained the prudence to recognize and own up to his culpability in his misbehavior, his own neglect and lack of respect for traditional and ancient morals. It is more than Socrates manages to do.

V.

It may seem on the surface that Strepsiades has little in common with Socrates, an ascetic natural scientist who "abstracts" himself from his particular life and political community. Upon closer inspection, however, Aristophanes' comedy suggests that Strepsiades and Socrates share a similar hope, as both long for some meaningful connection to eternity. Strepsiades lives in a threatening world where fear and anxiety abound, where war and his financial troubles never cease, where the struggle to keep his family together is constant, where his longing for an anchor and refuge is ever present. He yearns for a stable order in which his existence and his family can find rest. Strepsiades is attached to his particularity and seeks immortality through his family. The thought of losing his material possessions, his family order, and his son's affection is too terrifying for him.

From the perspective of Socrates' natural science, Strepsiades' attachment to his family and his own existence is groundless. Socrates, by contrast, studies nature, which he defines as the "vortex," and concludes that there is no stability or meaning in the universe. Humans, like all civilizations, flourish, die, and disappear. Nothing lasts forever. Socrates scorns all earthly attachments and finds meaning in subordinating himself to his science and his devotion to the "vortex." In a crucial respect, however, Socrates' asceticism is presented as a way of not facing his own existence. His life of self-denial is a form of self-sacrifice and betrays a religious instinct that is in conflict with his alleged atheism, and his devotion to the "vortex" makes no sense in light of his understanding of the purposelessness of nature. His devotion to such an understanding of nature is, therefore, irrational and groundless. Aristophanes does not simply present Socrates as indifferent to worldly possessions; he attributes a religious characteristic to Socrates' way of life. Strepsiades remains on a worldly level as Socrates soars to a theoretical one.

Aristophanes' examination of Strepsiades and Socrates is a study of the human condition, of man's need for meaning in human existence and hope in the face of oblivion. Aristophanes seems to be suggesting that the possibility of the philosophic life depends decisively on whether or not such a life is rooted in nature. While Aristophanes tells us his own wisdom is a possession for all times for those few wise souls capable of comprehending it, he casts doubts over Socrates' claim to such wisdom throughout the play (535). The failure of Aristophanes' Socrates to justify his way of life any more than Strepsiades can opens a window into the meaning of political philosophy and Socrates' famous "second sailing" as presented by Plato.

Notes

1. Plato and Aristophanes, *Four Texts on Socrates*, 2nd ed., trans. Thomas G. West and Grace Starry West (Ithaca: Cornell University Press, 1998), 29. All citations to the *Clouds* are to this edition and appear in parenthesis in the text by line number.

2. For examples of interpretations that take the *Clouds* as a serious work of philosophy, see Paul A. Rahe, "The Aristophanic Question," in *Recovering Reason: Essays in Honor of Thomas L. Pangle*, ed. Timothy Burns (Lanham, MD: Lexington Books, 2010), 67–82; David Leibowitz, *The Ironic Defense of Socrates: Plato's Apology* (Cambridge: Cambridge University Press, 2010), 39–44; Martha Nussbaum, "Aristophanes and Socrates on Learning Practical Wisdom," in *Aristophanes: Essays in Interpretation* (Yale Classical Studies Series, vol. 26), ed. Jeffrey Henderson (Cambridge: Cambridge University Press, 1980), 43–61; Mary P. Nichols, *Socrates and the Political Community: An Ancient Debate* (Albany: State University of New York Press, 1987), 7–25; Charles Segal, "Aristophanes' Clouds-Chorus," *Arethusa* 2 (no. 2, 1969): 143–61; Leo Strauss, *Socrates and Aristophanes* (New York: Basic Books, 1966), 9–54; and Michael Zuckert, "Rationalism & Political Responsibility: Just Speech & Just Deed in the *Clouds* & the *Apology of Socrates*," *Polity* 17 (no. 2, 1984): 271–97.

3. Plato and Xenophon, *Apologies*, trans. and ed. Mark Kremer (Newburyport, MA: Focus Publishing, 2006), 42.

4. Plato and Xenophon, *Apologies*, 4.

5. Mark Kremer, "Introduction," in *Plato's Cleitophon: On Socrates and the Modern Mind*, trans. and ed. Mark Kremer (Lanham, MD: Lexington Books, 2004), 4.

6. Kremer, "Introduction," in *Plato's Cleitophon*, 4.

7. For an account of Aristophanes' self-understanding and its inadequacies, see Stanley Rosen's explication of Aristophanes' speech in Plato's *Symposium*, in Stanley Rosen, *Plato's Symposium*, 2nd ed. (New Haven: Yale University Press, 1988), 120–57.

8. My understanding of Aristophanes in general and of the *Clouds* in particular owes more than I can say to the classes and writings of Mark Kremer.

Without his understanding and guidance, this chapter might not have been possible. I am also deeply indebted to the writings of Mary Nichols and Leo Strauss. I am grateful to my friends and colleagues who read earlier drafts of this chapter. Their comments and criticism and discussions helped me to make needed improvements. I would especially like to thank Cressida Habib, Lou Bradizza, Clark Merrill, and Joseph L. Hebert.

9. Paul A. Rahe argues that the philosophical significance of the opening scene of the *Clouds* "foreshadows the question that Aristophanes poses persistently throughout the play: whether that which men call *logos* or rational speech is not, in fact, the fruit of flatulence." Rahe overlooks the obvious references to death in the opening scene and throughout the play and therefore fails to examine the self-forgetting lives of Socrates and Strepsiades. See Rahe, "The Aristophanic Question," 67.

10. See Strauss, *Socrates and Aristophanes*, 14.

11. Nichols, *Socrates and the Political Community*, 10.

12. Nichols, *Socrates and the Political Community*, 10.

13. Mary Nichols also observes the curious use of the verb "to sing" in reference to Homer. Her account of the use of the verb "to sing" in this scene parallels my own, but whereas she argues that "the Socratics fail to distinguish the singing of the Muses from the noises made by gnats" (*Socrates and the Political Community* 194n9), I suggest that the Socratics deliberately undermine the gods and heroes of Athens, which is more consistent with the atheism and antiheroic character of the Socratic school and the spirit of natural science. Notice also Socrates' adamant refusal to refer to the Clouds as heroines at 315.

14. This is, of course, reminiscent of the opening scene of the play when Pheidippedes passes gas as his father expresses great anxiety over his financial troubles.

15. Kremer, "Introduction," in *Plato's Cleitophon*, 39.

16. Kremer, "Introduction," in *Plato's Cleitophon*, 39.

17. Nichols, *Socrates and the Political Community*, 3.

18. See Francis Bacon, "Of the Advancement of Learning," in *The Works of Francis Bacon*, 15 vols., eds. James Spedding, Robert Leslie Ellis, and Douglas Denon Heath (London: Longman, 1857–74), 3:424–28.

19. As Stanley Rosen observes, "[the Socrates of the *Clouds*], we may assume, is still ignorant of, and defective in, the human Eros. He has not yet been softened, and so completed, by the feminine." Stanley Rosen, *Nihilism: A Philosophical Essay* (New Haven: Yale University Press, 1969), 145. For an account of the differences between the Platonic Socrates and the Aristophanic Socrates, see Stanley Rosen's explication of Aristophanes' and Socrates' speeches in his book *Plato's Symposium*, 120–58, 197–277.

20. Nichols, *Socrates and the Political Community*, 2.

21. Nichols, *Socrates and the Political Community*, 14.

22. For an extensive study of obscenity in Aristophanes, see Jeffrey Henderson, *The Maculate Muse: Obscene Language in Attic Comedy* (New Haven: Yale University Press, 1975). Henderson maintains that sexually obscene humor provides a pleasurable "release of hostile or sexual aggressiveness through laughter" (11).

23. West and West, *Four Texts on Socrates*, 159n180, point out that the city often punished adulterers caught in the act of "buggery" by shaving off their hair and thereby shaming them before the public. Unjust Speech, however, tells the audience that the most notorious adulterer in the audience has long hair (1100). Pheidippides also has long hair (15).

24. Kremer, "Introduction," in *Plato's Cleitophon*, 4.

25. Thomas G. West, "Introduction," in *Four Texts on Socrates*, 29.

26. Allan Bloom, "Interpretative Essay," in Plato, *The Republic of Plato*, trans. Allan Bloom (New York: Basic Books, Inc., 1968), 312.

27. Leo Strauss, "The Origins of Political Science and the Problem of Socrates," *Interpretation* 23 (no. 2, 1996): 331.

28. Leo Strauss, *The Rebirth of Classical Political Rationalism*, ed. Thomas L. Pangle (Chicago: University of Chicago Press, 1989), 123.

3

Rethinking the Quarrel Anew

Politics and Boasting in Aristophanes' *Clouds*

Jeremy J. Mhire

"Now let the two, trusting in their very shrewd speeches and thoughts and notion-coining ponderings, show which of them will be manifestly better as they speak. For now the whole hazard of wisdom is being risked here, and about it there is a very great contest among my friends."

Clouds 949–58[1]

Scholars of classical political thought have recently turned their attention to the comedies of Aristophanes, and with good reason: ancient equivalents to contemporary problems in political philosophy abound throughout Aristophanes' comedies, making the comic's corpus fertile ground for analyzing perennial political issues.[2] Indeed, what is perhaps most striking is just how well Aristophanes seems to have understood political life; that his plays still speak to us today, though they have as their basis caricatures of ancient figures and the vicissitudes of the ancient polis, says much about Aristophanes' political acumen. Moreover, because a comedy's drama must have a resolution so as to have a plot, scholars have also noted an additional resource: the comedies aim at ameliorating the dangers that beset political life by moderating the elements that give rise to those dangers. Aristophanes' comedies thus offer not only political analysis by way of literary device, but also lessons in political leadership, if not statesmanship, broadly conceived.

For these reasons, four of Aristophanes eleven extant plays have received careful attention, which leaves seven plays ripe for scholarly investigation.[3] Philosophers and political theorists alike would do well to attend to these remaining works, if not also to a more comprehensive account of the corpus as a whole that attempts to discern, to the extent possible, Aristophanes' understanding of political life as such.[4] Achieving such an account will require a new, more comprehensive method, however—one not yet at our disposal. Of the seven comedies remaining to be studied, one in particular—*Clouds*—is noteworthy in its absence. *Clouds* is the only play in which Aristophanes speaks to his readers in his own voice, asserting that of all his comedies, it is his wisest (522). This wisdom is presumably made manifest in the play's drama, which if nothing else aims to teach justice by way of example (1506–11). Yet claiming to teach justice in one way or another is an assertion not unique to *Clouds*.[5] Instead, Aristophanes gives *Clouds* pride of place because of *how* it teaches justice, namely, by showing that Socrates, the only character capable of challenging Aristophanes' claim to be wise, is in fact unjust. The poet's wisdom is his ability to teach the just things by showing unjust things pretending to be just, or what is the same, foolish things pretending to be wise (1458–64).

This suggestion presents a seemingly intractable problem for political philosophy, for if Aristophanes deemed Socrates to be both unjust and foolish because of his philosophizing, then political philosophy, which itself derives from that very philosophizing, is also indicted. Not only is political philosophy thought to be a species of the genus philosophy, but it was inaugurated when Socrates the philosopher of nature turned his attention toward political life. Regardless of whatever else it may mean, Aristophanes' quarrel with Socrates implies at least this: rather than a useful aid to philosophy—and thus also to political philosophy—for understanding political life, Aristophanes' *Clouds* indicts philosophy's very attempt to understand politics. Scholars looking to Aristophanes for insight into political life must first face this paradox: the poetry that would seemingly best aid philosophy is that which denies philosophy, or put another way, poetry's quarrel with philosophy is that philosophy misunderstands political life, and hence acts unjustly.

Aside from dismissing Aristophanes' criticism out of hand, one way to confront this paradox would be to draw a distinction between philosophy and political philosophy. Political philosophy is not a species of philosophy; either it differs fundamentally from philosophy or is in fact philosophy proper. The former possibility places political philosophy closer in practice to poetry than to philosophy; the latter implies that philosophy before political philosophy was misnamed—philosophy was originally more than the pursuit of wisdom. Both possibilities point toward the same conclusion: if we are to take Aristophanes seriously, then political philosophy must reassess its relationship to philosophy. At the very least, this means learning to see philosophy the way comic poetry once did, which, to adapt an adage by none other than Socrates himself, means reopening the ancient quarrel between poetry and philosophy.[6]

Such a proposal is neither as radical as it sounds nor as hostile to political philosophy in principle as one might imagine. To the extent that classical political philosophers such as Plato and Xenophon made use of the dialogue rather than the treatise as their written medium, both tacitly admit the significance of poetry to philosophy.[7] One can even go a step further: insofar as Socrates' turn to political phenomena represents a rejection of philosophy's original aim rather than a furthering of its scope, political philosophy and poetry are akin in rejecting philosophy as it was originally understood. Socrates' turn to political philosophy thus represents a rejection of his own philosophizing prior to the turn, or a rejection of the way he originally understood himself as a philosopher. At a minimum, the Socratic turn consisted in the discovery of self-knowledge; the theme of both poetry and political philosophy is the same as the Delphic injunction: know thyself.

But what does it mean to know oneself? More precisely, why does self-knowledge imply attentiveness to political life? I want to suggest that if we take *Clouds* seriously, it reveals an aspect of Socrates' "early" philosophizing that is normally overlooked: philosophy as originally practiced by Socrates asserted a quiet though unmistakable claim to rule. This does not mean Socrates regarded his claim as beneficial to political life; on the contrary, Socrates acts unjustly, according to Aristophanes, because of the harm his claim to rule does to politics. Aristophanes' teaching on justice implies that wisdom has a political function and hence that there are political obligations inherent in the quest for wisdom. By emphasizing wisdom's relationship to justice, Aristophanes also highlights ignorance's relationship to injustice; *Clouds* demonstrates Socrates' ignorance by connecting his lack of self-knowledge to his comical relationship with political life, specifically to Athens.

What follows makes a case for reading *Clouds* as a defense of political life. To do so, I venture two claims: first, that Aristophanes' caricature of Socrates presents the philosopher as a threat to political life. Socrates' "pre-Socratic" philosophizing threatened political life by attacking its nature; Socrates originally denied that there was any meaningful difference between politics and despotism. In doing so, Socrates asserted a distinctive claim to rule—the unmitigated rule of the wise—that necessarily disputed the possibility of ruling and being ruled in turn. Philosophy thereby denied the virtue of political life and therefore the possibility of genuine political freedom; necessity rather than freedom is characteristic of political life, according to Socrates.

Second, I claim that the plot of *Clouds*—particularly the dramatic consequences of Socrates' attack on politics—should be read as an attack on an attack, that is, as a defense of politics. Reading the play in this way has the effect of collapsing the distinction between the pursuit of wisdom and politics; Aristophanes asserts that wisdom is found in political life, rather than apart from it. To that end, I suggest that the dramatic action of *Clouds* asserts and thus defends the role wisdom must play in political life.

What's In a Boast? The Ubiquity of Laughter in *Clouds*

To understand fully *Clouds'* defense of political life, it is necessary to grapple immediately with the most obvious interpretive difficulty: *Clouds* is a work of art, which in this case means its argument comes in the form of a comic drama rather than a treatise. The aim of comedy in general is to make the audience laugh, though the aim of this comedy in particular is to teach justice wisely through the use of laughter. It does so in no small measure by making fun of those who would otherwise speak and think of justice as if it were the subject of a philosophical treatise. To approach *Clouds* on its own terms is to think of it not as philosophical poetry, but rather as a poetical presentation of philosophy. *Clouds'* argument should not be thought of as hidden in the drama; instead, *Clouds'* argument is the drama, which means that the reader of Aristophanes' plays must first enjoy them as plays, or better yet, must first enjoy them as comedies. And we enjoy them because they make us laugh; comedy, but especially Aristophanean comedy, is funny because it traffics in ridiculous and often unseemly things, things frequently thought but rarely said.[8] At a minimum, we should consider why such things are funny, or more precisely, why this particular comedy makes us laugh; why do we laugh at a philosopher in the act of philosophizing, and then also at his ultimate plight?

Yet not everything laughable in *Clouds* is philosophical in nature; the first character onstage, if not the main character of the play—Strepsiades—is ridiculous before any mention of Socrates or philosophy is made. To be sure, Strepsiades is ridiculous in his own way, yet his foolishness is similar to Socrates'; in fact, with the possible exception of the Clouds themselves, there is no character in *Clouds* that is good sense incarnate.[9] To lack good sense is to be without a proper measure of oneself; rather than saying they have bad sense, we would say they have no sense, which means no sense of themselves, especially with regard to what is good or bad for them. Every character lacks a sense of himself, which means every character lacks self-knowledge. The audience laughs at what transpires in *Clouds* because it makes public the most private of vices; every character behaves unjustly because of his ignorance, which is why every character is nearly brought to ruin. The audience is taught justice by learning to laugh at ignorance; the audience is also thereby taught to laugh at, and hence to look down upon, injustice as such (225–27).

Everything is laughable in *Clouds* because everything is foolish; only the play itself, or better yet, only the author himself, stands above foolishness as the author of foolishness. Recognizing this relationship between play and playwright is important, for otherwise the play's dramatic argument is likely to be confused with the philosophical propositions scattered throughout the play. In addition, if the play merits the claim of wisdom Aristophanes grants to it, then its foolishness must be in the service of something serious; if injustice is presented foolishly for the sake of teaching justice, then *Clouds* means to take seriously those who would practice justice—law-abiding citizens if not political life itself. To do so, Aristophanes' comedy must provide a means of defending politics otherwise unavailable to political life. The seriousness of political life is threatened by those who would make of it something trivial—those, in other words, who are themselves a natural subject of comedy. To defend politics in this way implies Aristophanes saw his comedy as constitutive of political life, which means that it too is an element of political life. It also implies that his characters, foolish though they may be, are themselves caricatures of elements within political life.

To state the obvious: reading *Clouds* as a defense of politics implies that politics is important and that comedy knows something about defending important things. Needless to say, *Clouds* itself must be something important, though not for that reason something serious; on the surface, important things may seem unimportant, if not ridiculous. If *Clouds* defends politics, then it does so by making serious or dangerous things seem unimportant or harmless; defending politics means making laughable that which threatens to make politics laughable. There are then threats to politics that must be taken seriously because they are not as important as they claim to be; the threat against which *Clouds* mounts a defense is a boast, one whose claim would be ridiculous were it not so serious.

But how would a boast threaten politics? Surely politics, or at least politicians, are prone to boasting; perhaps political life is itself something of a boast made on behalf of boasters, those otherwise called citizens. *Clouds* is about Athenians, performed for an audience of Athenians by a poet who was himself an Athenian; the play's plot never leaves the horizon of the city and therefore points to the city as its own horizon. The city is funny, though it may also be dangerous; the city's boasts can be the occasion of both laughter and tears. To boast is to make a serious claim or assertion. Yet it also misses the mark regarding that claim or assertion; a boaster claims more than what is true or asserts as wholly true what is in fact partly false. Boasts are *hybristic*, and *hybris* claims more than is justified; boasts are an admixture of wisdom and foolishness or of knowledge and ignorance. For that reason, a boaster is unjust with regard to the truth; in light of the truth, boasts appear immoderate, a vice to which political life is prone.

If *Clouds* is a defense of politics, then its effect should be a certain form of moderation. That is to say, the teaching of *Clouds* with regard to politics is the need politics has for moderation; citizens are prone to *hybris*, or making foolish boasts. This does not mean, of course, that every citizen boasts in the same way or to the same extent; though all citizens are prone to boasting, some may in fact be more brazen with respect to their claims. To defend politics, *Clouds* must caricature the many boasts that originate within politics—including the most outlandish—in order to moderate them. True to form, this is what the play does; *Clouds*' plot unfolds around Socrates' life in his think-tank, which can be funny only because it is a caricature of political life. Socrates' boasts caricature Athens' boasts, which is why the interaction of the two is a theme for comedy. Socrates is laughable because he takes seriously what to others is a laughing matter and disregards as trivial what to others is most important (165–68, 171–74, 180, 215–18). The dramatic inversion highlights Socrates' peculiar relationship to Athens and draws the reader's attention toward two aspects of the caricature that make its peculiarity possible.

First, the think-tank is portrayed as intentionally separated from everyday life. Physically, it is an enclosure, walled off and private, with both physical and contrived means of keeping others out (131–34, 140). Socrates' wish to remain apart from others is largely successful; he is relatively unknown outside the think-tank, though those who have heard of him know him to be a rogue or a charlatan (97–98, 102–4). *Clouds*' emphasis on the physical detachment of the think-tank is complemented by an equally droll depiction of private life within—the caricature's second key aspect. Strepsiades, the ill-fated though thoroughgoing rustic, voices his incredulity at the seemingly inhuman asceticism of the think-tank when he compares the students to the Spartan captives at Pylos (186). Later, once Strepsiades has decided to become Socrates' pupil in order to learn the art of clever speaking, he mentions being subjected to hunger, thirst, squalor, and the elements as the conditions of his tutelage (441–42, 834–39).

By exaggerating the think-tank's appearance from both without and within, Aristophanes does two things at once: he reveals the way Socrates originally understood Athens as well as the way Athens understood itself. Socrates and his students clearly wish to be separated from Athens; for whatever reason, Athens was originally anathema to philosophy. What goes on in the think-tank is the opposite of the happenings outside, and that because what is known outside is what is sought within. Socrates' think-tank is a mirrored reflection of Athens, though for that reason reversed. The Socrates of *Clouds* is a student of nature, investigating the things under the earth as well as the things aloft (143–95); the things above and below are obscured by the things in between—by those things not natural, but conventional.[10] He also teaches the art of clever speech, or better yet, the cleverness that ensues when speech investigates itself (658–66).[11] It is no accident that clever speech and an interest in nature coincide; the cleverness of the former is necessary in the pursuit of the latter. Nature is normally hidden, and for that reason it must be discovered by the use of novel means; Socrates' investigations are the means by which nature's mysteries are disclosed. This requires a number of tools either of Socrates' devising or adapted to his purposes.[12]

To be sure, Socrates did not discover the idea of nature; the Greek notion of *physis* is as old as Greek poetry itself.[13] Instead, Socrates is intent on learning the reach of the idea of nature; Socrates' investigations presuppose that the idea of nature is only the possibility of nature, which must be fully uncovered to be truly known. Nature remains a mystery until her secrets are forcibly extracted; the mystery rites of the think-tank are in full agreement with the think-tank's purpose (143). And lest Socrates' inquires be mistaken for nonsense rather than caricature, the idea of nature must also be uncommonly tantalizing; nature fully understood offers some promise otherwise unknown or unfulfilled. The correspondence of Socrates' speeches and deeds gives an important indication of what that promise is: to know nature would be to know the true reason(s) because of which things are what they are (368–70). Whatever that reason(s) may be, their ignorance of it is unimportant to most men; Socrates alone is both aware of and moved by his ignorance in this regard.[14] To know the reason of things is to know the cause of things, which here means to know how things come to be. The idea of nature bears within it the power to dispel falsehood, especially concerning the origins of things (247–48).

The comical relationship between Socrates and Athens helps to make sense of the enigmatic tension between nature and convention on display in *Clouds*; on the surface, nature is at odds with convention, a tension meant to be funny. Most men most of the time have no interest in nature; why things are the way they are is either of no interest to most Athenians, or they assume they know the reason(s) for this already (1282). Socrates denies what most Athenians assume; most are ignorant regarding the nature of things, according to Socrates. To that end, Socrates asserts boldly what Athens would deny emphatically, that "Zeus is not" (367). Socrates boasts that he knows what others do not; whereas most Athenians think Zeus causes things like rain, thunder, and lightning, Socrates sees instead physical interactions that bring forth effects the intelligibility of which needs no higher explanation (368). Zeus is powerless when confronted with necessity—*anagke*—a principle Socrates already acknowledges as the heart of things (367–71, 405).[15] All things are what they are not because of Zeus, but because they cannot be otherwise.[16] With no real power in the world, Zeus can have no real meaning in the world. For that reason, Zeus deserves no credit (247–48).

But Zeus is more than just the cause of the rain. He is also the author of the laws by which Athenians live (396–97); as the king of Gods and men alike, Zeus is both the father of Athens as well as its defender. For Athens, Zeus matters because he is the reason Athens matters; without Zeus, there would be no Athens. More specifically, Zeus is the source of Athens' law; it was Zeus who originally distinguished between "us" (we Athenians) and "them" (those who have different laws). Distinguishing Athens in this way also made her distinctive; "our" laws signify "our" way of life, which of course matters to "us." Who "we" are matters to "us" because it is important. Their distinctiveness was something in which Athenians took pride and hence something about which they could boast. It was not what they had in common with other cities that mattered most to Athenians but rather what set them apart; indeed, Athens' distinctiveness is crucial, as war is the occasion of *Clouds*' plot (1–7), while political boundaries and borders are a cause for concern even to the lowliest of citizens (215–17). Socrates' interest in nature makes no sense to most Athenians; all things are the way they are because Zeus wills it to be (1–3, 1292). Everything—Athens included—has its own way or manner, which is determined by the answer to a prior question: What is a God? To this question, Athens asserts an answer Socrates denies: Zeus is a God for us (366–67, 1240–41).

For Socrates, nature is philosophy's alternative to Zeus; nature is to philosophy what Zeus is to politics. This, of course, is no small boast.

Indeed, the think-tank is to Socrates what Athens is to a citizen; the philosopher is a natural subject of comedy because he is a comic imitation of a good citizen. An imitation, however, presupposes some more fundamental relationship with the thing imitated; the surface tension between nature and convention is possible only because of a deeper connection between the two. If Socrates' boasts are in fact an imitation of Athens' boasts, then the idea of nature should itself be an imitation—a comic equivalent—of Athenian convention.[17] By caricaturing philosophy, and thus encouraging his audience to think of philosophy comically, Aristophanes provides a glimpse into the way philosophy originally understood the idea of nature; nature, according to Socrates, has two aspects: it is both a standard that distinguishes things (681–82) and a distinctiveness among things (339, 1201–5, 1240–41). On the one hand, that there is an idea of nature at all presupposes some standard for distinguishing between what is natural and what is not natural; all natural things are alike in a way unique to them alone. Things that are not natural differ from natural things with respect to their origins; unlike nature (*physis*), which has necessity as its ultimate cause, things not natural—conventional things (*nomoi*)—have human origins, origins that differ with respect to time and place and are therefore the result of chance rather than necessity (1421–22).

On the other hand, the idea of nature is itself distinctive, and distinctive things differ from things without distinction because of their importance. Nature has both a power and an appeal because it reveals non-natural things as they truly are, a revelation that is at odds with the way those things were originally understood, and thus to the manner in which they first appear. Nature transcends convention and is therefore superior to convention on its own terms or with regard to the truth convention itself asserts (223). Nature's challenge to convention denies conventional authority, making it appear ridiculous and hence unimportant; the *hybris* of Socrates' boasts may be funny, but their implications are serious. Every convention asserts divine origins of one sort or another, yet in light of nature, those origins appear more alike than different; all conventions, in other words, have something in common, something they wish not to admit. In truth, no city is distinctive with respect to its origins; every convention hides the truth—each is like every other with regard to its human origins. Every city thinks of itself as being important and justifies that importance by linking its self-understanding to origins that are beyond politics—to divine origins. But that justification hides nature, and that because nature undermines the way the city wishes to understand itself. There is nothing special about Athens with regard to its origins, origins that are common to all other cities.

It is easy to overlook why something makes us laugh; Socrates was a boaster because his interests in nature necessarily set him at odds with Athens. According to Socrates, there was nothing that set Athens apart from any other city, which means there was nothing about which it could boast. Philosophizing about nature, however, is another story; to be able to recognize what is common is not itself a common virtue, which means it is a mark of distinction to distinguish correctly. Those who can understand nature are necessarily at odds with those who understand themselves according to convention. Socrates' rejection of Athens is then the flip side of his love of the truth; the love of the truth hates the falsehood that convention represents (361–71, 368, 828, 1471). To that end, Socrates' inquiries range from the low to the high because they aim to be as comprehensive as convention. Socrates wishes to dispel the falsehoods that hide nature, which means everything becomes a question. Socrates' philosophizing culminates in a cosmogony; not Zeus but cosmic whirl governs the whole (379–81). For that reason, not Athens but the think-tank is most distinctive.

When Boasts Become Dangerous: The Nature of Politics

Given that philosophy originally deemed politics unimportant, it is perhaps a bit strange that Aristophanes considered Socrates a threat worth taking seriously. At first glance, Socrates of *Clouds* posed a threat to Athens by attacking its foundation; Socrates was a threat to Zeus, who is the source of Athens' law. For that reason, it comes as no surprise later in the play when the family, another institution built upon the laws of Zeus, is also threatened by Socrates' philosophizing (1403–5, 1441–44). Yet the assertion of Zeus can hardly be countered, to say nothing of refuted, with the substitution of a question; Socrates boasted that he knew already what in fact he only questioned, or that what separated him from most Athenians was more crucial than what they had in common. If anything was threatened by philosophy, it was philosophy itself; Socrates' *hybris* was, after all, the basis of a caricature, which means its justification was somehow laughable. But what exactly does this mean?

Socrates is funny because his philosophizing is funny, or, better yet, philosophy is funny because nature is funny; if nature is the comic equivalent of convention, then nature is funny because it trivializes something important, which means that it is itself something unimportant or trivial. It thus appears one way while being another; nature presupposes an element of irony. Thinking of nature comically suggests that the truth Socrates sought to discover was itself a partial falsehood; if all conventions have in common how they understand their origins, specifically that they understand themselves to have a divine author, then convention too has a nature. All conventions understand themselves in the same way, which means no city is truly distinctive; either every city has the same origins, or there are as many Gods as there are cities. All questions reduce to the question of nature, which means all things, even conventional things, are in fact natural. But if all things are natural, then nothing is distinctively natural; distinguishing between nature and convention seems to require defending each from the other. However that may be, the vast disproportion between philosophy's original reach and its grasp make Socrates' boasts a worthy subject of caricature. It would not, however, justify Aristophanes' own boast: to be both wise and just.

Moreover, if Socrates were an actual threat to Zeus, then Aristophanes' defense of politics would in fact be a defense of the Gods; the poet must come to the aid of Olympus in its quarrel with philosophy. But that would be a terrible joke; of all the classical Greek poets, Aristophanes would be the last to be mistaken as most pious. In fact, *Clouds* seems to suggest that there is no defense possible for convention on its own terms (1052–53, 1086–87, 1102–4). This quarrel between poetry and philosophy cannot be understood as derivative of a more fundamental quarrel—that between philosophy and the Gods, or between reason and revelation. Instead, the threat Socrates posed to Zeus and to the family must derive from a more fundamental quarrel within politics; the original quarrel between the poets and the philosophers was a political quarrel. Put another way, the true threat to political life comes from within politics, from the contest over what is most important and thus over who makes the decisions regarding important matters. The quarrel between poetry and philosophy is thus a political contest, properly understood; *Clouds* too boasts when it claims to be both wise and just, which means it makes a claim about what is important and about what must be defended.

For *Clouds* to do what I am suggesting, the boasting to which politics is prone must indicate something important about the character of political life. All politics are conventional, but not all conventions are political. The difference between the two is essential and is the key to Aristophanes' defense of politics. There is a standard to every convention—what is common to all—as well as something distinctive to only a few; the two ways in which Athens understood itself were at odds with one another. True, Athens asserted that it was distinctive because its origins were divine; it either denied that other cities had similar origins or regarded those cities as unimportant regardless of their origins. But Athens also boasted of another uniqueness; Athens alone claimed to be free. Athenians distinguished themselves from others by having embraced political life, which means they asserted the importance of political freedom. Political life understands itself as the way of life of free men, which is free only in opposition to the slavish or necessitous ways of despotism.

This difference between politics and despotism is important to political life and hence was important to Athens; the distinction between a citizen and a slave is one that matters to citizens (491–94). Political life claims to give to itself its own laws freely and attempts to enforce and defend those laws justly and equitably (1266–78). The free man is a citizen because only a citizen can claim to rule himself; citizenship distinguishes some men from others on the basis of an important distinction. To be a free man therefore assumes excellence; the difference between freedom and despotism is a matter of virtue. This is not to say, of course, that political life is without difficulty; politics needs defending because it is precarious. Freedom can be misunderstood and hence confused with necessity, for instance. But political life does assert that it is important and thus worth defending; the distinctiveness of politics lies in the way(s) of the citizen, which represents the manner most excellent and distinctive of man.

What was distinctive about Athens was not its origins so much as its ends; the distinctiveness of political life presupposes some virtue without which it would be no different from mere convention. The distinction between politics and despotism stands or falls by the meaning of freedom; political life's distinctiveness—its excellence—assumes some knowledge of the meaning of freedom. Distinctive things are precarious precisely because they are not common, however; citizens can mistake politics for despotism, which means they can abuse their capacity to rule themselves. The possibility of confusing freedom with necessity is given to free men alone and is the reason Socrates posed a threat to Athens. The think-tank denied what Athens assumed—that Athens possessed a certain virtue that made it superior to other despotic conventions (915–18). If political life assumes that freedom is distinctive of its own nature, then Athens claimed to have self-knowledge by identifying freedom with self-rule. According to Athens, virtue equals knowledge. By separating from Athens, Socrates denied that Athenians truly participated in ruling and being ruled in turn.

Ruling and being ruled in turn implies moderation, that virtue most remote from the heat and strife that characterize political life.[18] If political life does presuppose virtue, then it would seemingly demand of its citizens that they too possess virtue; the citizens in any political community should be distinctive. But in Athens the opposite was true; in Athens, freedom meant that many rather than only one or a few could participate in political life. Athens assumed that many had virtue, or that what is most excellent was common. This Socrates denied; political life could not be common to many, and that because the virtue demanded by politics is possessed by very few. Socrates did not deny that virtue is knowledge but did deny that many could possess such knowledge. The proof of this is given in the way Athens understood itself; Athens claimed that its origins were divine, which means that the Gods were the source of its laws. If that were true, however, Athens could not claim to be free; not men but Zeus gives the laws to men. According to Athens' own self-understanding, there is no meaningful distinction between political life and despotism; with respect to the question of law, Zeus rules men either as children or beasts. Zeus the lawgiver is either Zeus the father or Zeus the shepherd.

To reiterate: according to Socrates, Athens was caught in a contradiction, one that arose because of the city's claim to be political. If Athens were truly free, then it would have no need of divine origins. Conversely, if the source of Athenian law were Zeus, then political life would be unnecessary. The idea of political life is incommensurable with the divine origins of law, or, put another way, the divine origins of convention are at odds with the ends of political life. The virtue of the free man is *hybristic*, and hybris is a vice to the pious man (915–18, 1002–5), while the way of life of piety is anathema to the idea of political life (1047–52, 1055–57). Piety is a virtue common to all men, but freedom is not; the possibility of free men makes the divine origins of the law superfluous, if not dangerous. For Athens to boast of both freedom and divine origins was, according to Socrates, to enlist the Gods in support of men. Better yet, it was to enlist the Gods in support of some men over other men; in every city some men rule others. Yet the competition that occurs within political life—disagreements over matters of importance to citizens—was of no concern to Socrates; most men most of the time are ignorant, according to Socrates. For that reason, most men should not rule; it is not justice but tyranny for the ignorant to govern the wise, regardless of the form it takes. Athenian political life was in fact a boast that hides the truth; all politics are conventional, and all conventions are despotic. Political life hides the true possibility of freedom from men; the philosopher experiences his life with non-philosophers as necessitous, if not slavish. To defend any such arrangement would make of Zeus a tyrant rather than a king, and Gods that do not defend justice are no Gods at all (398–402).

Socrates originally denied all conventional authority, which necessarily undermined Athens' legitimacy. Only the wise know the truth, and hence only the wise should be granted the privileges that pertain therein. Socrates admits as much when he argues that his idleness—his essentially parasitic relationship to Athens—is just (339). This can be just—Socrates could have a legitimate right to his idleness—only if philosophy itself claims the status of authority by displacing any and all contrary claims to rule. It is Socrates who, in denying political life, substitutes instead the justice of nature; the original idea of nature already presupposed the notion of natural right. For that reason, there is a notion of the best regime hidden in plain sight of the plot; Socrates as the head is already Socrates the king, which is only to say that the think-tank as regime is characterized by the rule of the philosopher-king.[19] Socrates' regime is the rule of the wise, which wishes neither to rule nor be ruled.

By revealing the nuances of Socrates' self-understanding, Aristophanes indicates a deeper link between philosophy and the world in which it emerges; despite its overt hostility toward political life, the original goal of philosophy was the same as the end of political life—to be free. Indeed, Socrates makes clear this link between his thinking and politics by conceiving of nature as necessity, for necessity is only necessitous in light of freedom, if not to a free man as such. Political life itself gives rise to the notion of freedom; rather than concealing it, political life seems to open up the possibility of freedom to man. To be sure, freedom may be obscured in the vicissitudes of politics; the competing factions within a city, to say nothing of the claims raised by other cities, testify to the problems that beset political life.[20] Nevertheless, these competing claims provide evidence of what is at stake; whereas there can be but one claim that arises from necessity, political life is the effect whose cause is the competition of differences. The condition of both political life and freedom is then chance, not necessity (1428–32).

It is worth mentioning again that every character in *Clouds* is ridiculous in his own way, yet each is foolish in the same way. If this is true, it suggests to us the following: every character is foolish because he forgets if not rejects outright his role in political life. Not only Socrates but Chaerophon, Strepsiades, and ultimately Pheidippides as well see themselves as apart from rather than a part of political life.[21] Each understands his freedom apart from Athens rather than in and through Athenian political practice. As disgruntled elements of political life, however, they also reveal why political life stands in need of a defense; political life is tenuous, which means it bears within itself this tendency to forget the necessary connection between living freely and life in the city. To take this a step further, Socrates' indifference to political life is not then apolitical, but rather antipolitical; the freedom Socrates seeks is despotic in nature rather than trans-political. Both he and his disciples reveal this aspect of philosophy's original self-understanding when they deny that the wise owe any debt or have any obligation to the ignorant (339, 1201–5, 1249–51, 1283–84). Philosophy originally denied what political life assumes: that there are important matters both for and among equals. Socrates' philosophizing represents how and why an element of political life, through its own ignorance, can destroy political life.

Clouds as a Defense of Political Life

To argue, as I have, that Aristophanes wrote *Clouds* as a defense of political life means that teaching justice and making an audience laugh are not incommensurable. This does not mean, however, that the two are perfectly compatible. Teaching justice assumes that justice is not known, or is imperfectly known. And if teaching justice is requisite to defending politics, then the threat to political life is its own ignorance with regard to the question of justice. In a way, this seems obvious; Socrates could be caricatured only because he was a boaster—he claimed to know what in fact he did not, or claimed not to know what he in fact did. The philosopher's *hybris* makes him a threat (362–63); Socrates denied that politics is important, an importance assumed by any defense of politics. But why is politics important? Was Socrates not right to reject Athens' claim to rule him, especially given its own ignorance with regard to the question of justice? And though he may have tried to remedy this, was Aristophanes' own relationship to political life really any different from Socrates'?

Undoubtedly the think-tank is meant to be quixotic, and I have argued that this ridiculousness is both possible and effective because it is a caricature of Athens, that is, an imitation of something serious. Athens is serious because Athens is politics, and politics is serious. Politics is serious because it is important; if there is a difference between important and unimportant things, then politics is certainly among the former rather than the latter. Politics is important to people who are important, or to people who think of themselves as important; it is for that reason unimportant to unimportant people, people who do not believe themselves to be important (43–48, 69–73). Politics is synonymous with importance; political things are to important things as despotic things are to unimportant things. Importance thereby distinguishes political life from despotism; to be important is distinctive of political life.

To defend politics is to defend importance, the sense one has of one's worth or how one is distinctive, and how that distinctiveness matters. To claim importance is to claim merit; it is to claim that what sets one apart merits admiration. Importance is admirable, and to be admirable is to be worthy of admiration. Men admire what is not easily attained, that which is excellent and which is therefore perhaps also noble (403, 1047–50). To do what others cannot is distinctive (961–62); to do what is excellent is noble (985–86). To be worthy of importance is to have some virtue; to be admirable because of one's virtue is to have honor. Politics is thus important because it involves honor; people who believe themselves to be important believe that honor matters, and that they have some measure of honor. To defend politics is to defend the importance of honor; a proper defense of honor requires a defense of virtue's importance.

Politics is about honor; honor presupposes that there are dishonorable things or ignoble actions, and the difference between the two matters to honorable men. Honorable men take pride in who they are; they are ashamed at the thought of acting dishonorably, to say nothing of doing so (1009–23). Yet their pride in themselves is not as simple as the love of one's own; they take pride in their virtue or excellence, which is the reason for their high esteem of themselves. To defend politics is then to defend the honor of politics; politics must be defended from those who would deny the importance of political life, those, in other words, who deny that politics matters. Treating politics trivially is not itself trivial; the threat to honor is that politics is at best a laughing matter, or that if not quite shameful, then certainly a matter of contempt (233). Politics is at risk of being laughed at, at being a laughing matter. It follows that a defense of serious things should come in the form of a nontrivial comedy.

Politics is a contest, one in which the participants matter because they are important (1238–39). For that reason, the contest itself matters and is important. Citizens are important when they assert their importance among other citizens of equal importance. Every citizen need not be important in the same way, but politics does assume the differences that occur between citizens are not such that only some have honor, while others are treated trivially. To be clear, I am not suggesting that Aristophanes' defense of politics is in fact a defense of democracy; *Clouds* is not defending the many's claim to rule, but rather that there are many claims to rule, each of which has to be protected from its own *hybris*. The differences between citizens are never so great that some citizens can treat others with contempt. *Hybris* is a threat to the city, and that because it is a threat to one's peers. Ironically, the contest of politics is possible only with a certain level of respect, which means that it falls to a comic poet to defend publicly the importance of respectability. This does not mean, of course, that *Clouds* must be perfectly respectable (1083–84, 1097–1100). Nor does it mean that comedians are averse to boasting.

Clouds ends with an element of strife; the think-tank is destroyed by a disgruntled father who was first a disgruntled citizen (6–7). In the end, Strepsiades gets angry with Socrates; his indignation is kindled by his son's indifference to important matters, indifference taught to him by Socrates (1377–78). Philosophy originally taught would-be philosophers and non-philosophers alike that politics did not matter; if politics does not matter, then neither the Gods nor the family matters. Defending politics does entail a certain defense of the Gods, who make an appearance *ad oculos* in *Clouds*. The Gods council indignation, the sense of injustice that arises when one's importance has been slighted (1507–9). Socrates was indifferent to politics and hence to indignation; an indignant man, at the advising of an indignant God, destroys the think-tank. *Clouds* is a comedy rather than a tragedy because Socrates escapes with his life; an honorable defense of politics—a proper use of indignation—is the most serious subject of comedy. Perhaps for that reason it is also a demonstration of wisdom, *ad oculos*.

It is fair nonetheless to ask if Aristophanes fully grasped the extent of his own claim, for even if such boasts are funny, who would believe that by laughing at others one was becoming wiser? More importantly, comedy's deed always seems to undercut its speech; laughter cannot but cast aspersions on all things, especially the most serious. The very mode by which comedy attempts to teach justice would seemingly undercut any and every nod to serious matters; to attempt to teach justice by imitating injustice dramatically is to try to teach virtue by imitating vice. To imitate vice, however, is to give a voice to vice, or better yet, to give a voice to the desires and opinions from which vice arises. To imitate vice is to inflame vice by drawing attention to, and hence engaging with, vice. Virtue would seemingly not be a natural subject of poetry; it is most certainly not a natural subject for comedy. Is the comic not then a teacher of injustice rather than justice? Is he not for that reason, like the philosopher, a teacher of tyrants rather than citizens?

To defend politics is then to defend justice, which inevitably means to teach justice. And to teach justice means to know justice, which also means to know virtue. *Clouds* defends politics by defending virtue; it thus possesses wisdom regarding virtue. It does so by recognizing that virtue is uninteresting, not to the passions and desires as such, but to the nonpolitical passions and desires as such. Vice is interesting insofar as it is connected with the non-political, despotic passions; virtue is interesting only insofar as it is connected with the political passions. These political passions—the claim that one is important and worthy of rule—are assertive rather than needy; they are connected with virtue only when their surety turns into a need. The theme of *Clouds* is not then virtue; rather, the theme is a question—what is virtue?—for which the play attempts to create a passion. Comedy is that element of political life that asks of itself a question it would not otherwise raise.[22] In doing so, it asks all citizens alike to be mindful of the gods: know thyself.

Conclusion

The distinction between poetry and philosophy turns out to be a very fine one indeed; philosophy originally differed from poetry with respect to the question of self-knowledge. Undoubtedly political philosophy—or better yet, the original political philosopher—took this claim very seriously; it is not unreasonable to suppose that Socrates turned toward questions of the good, the just, and the noble only when he came to understand their importance, an importance that stands or falls by the status of political life. In a sense, this means Socrates had to learn to laugh at his own boasts; at the very least, he had to learn to think comically about philosophy. Perhaps this lesson was the result of a withering though friendly caricature, one that emphasized the political nature of his quarrel with poetry.[23] Or perhaps he simply had to be beaten at his own game; there is nothing like a boastful bubble burst by a superior boaster to prompt a turn toward self-scrutiny. However that may be, scholars who fail to take seriously *Clouds*' relevance to political philosophy do so at their own risk, for they hazard falling victim to the same lack of self-understanding that promises to make of their work a caricature.

In particular, scholarship would do well to consider further the implications of Aristophanes' critique: How does political philosophy—particularly Socratic political philosophy—really differ from what is already implied in the comedian's plays, both *Clouds* and otherwise? Is Socratic political philosophy, at least as it was practiced by Plato and Xenophon, truly poetry rather than philosophy? If not, what further insight into nature, but especially into the nature of politics, is gleaned by political philosophy, but not understood by poetry? Is there a distinctively philosophical answer to the question of justice that is implied in the quest for the knowledge of justice? Whatever may be the answer to these questions, it behooves scholars to keep in mind that it was a poet rather than a philosopher who was the first to ask them.

Notes

1. All in-text citations will be to Thomas G. West and Grace Starry West, eds. and trans., *Four Texts on Socrates* (Ithaca, NY: Cornell University Press, 1984).

2. Leo Strauss, *Socrates and Aristophanes* (Chicago: University of Chicago Press, 1966), was the first scholar to argue seriously for Aristophanes' relevance to political philosophy. Following Strauss's lead, other political theorists have recently turned their attention to Aristophanes' corpus, including John Zumbrunnen, "Elite Domination and the Clever Citizen," *Political Theory* 32 (2004): 656–77, and "Fantasy, Irony and Economic Justice in Aristophanes's *Assemblywomen* and *Wealth*," *American Political Science Review* 100 (2006): 319–33; Kenneth De Luca, *Aristophanes's Male and Female Revolutions* (Lanham, MD: Lexington Books, 2005); and Paul Ludwig, "A Portrait of the Artist in Politics: Justice and Self-Interest in Aristophanes's Archarnians," *American Political Science Review* 101 (2007): 479–92.

3. This is not to say, of course, that these seven plays have been systematically ignored by scholars of classical political thought. On the contrary, most if not all of Aristophanes' corpus has received scholarly attention, often within the context of research concerning the Platonic dialogues. However, only the *Acharnians*, the *Knights*, the *Assemblywomen*, and *Wealth* have received their own scholarly treatments, and no study dedicated to the political theory of Aristophanes more generally has yet to emerge.

4. For the purposes of this chapter, I gloss over the professional distinction between political philosophers and political theorists, referring to both under the more comprehensive heading of political philosophy.

5. *Acharnians*, for instance, claims to do this explicitly (655).

6. Cf. *Republic* 607b3–c1.

7. *Republic* 393a2–96e2.

8. *Republic* 606c2–9.

9. Cf. Strauss, *Socrates and Aristophanes*, 312.

10. Cf. *Apology* 19b5–c6.

11. This differs from the Unjust speech, which Socrates is not said to teach, but which is housed inside the think-tank. Moreover, regardless of whatever else it may mean, Socrates' attempt to instruct Strepsiades in the correct use of language already presupposes the "ideas" to which language should correspond.

12. These include baskets, wax, compasses, and maps, among other things.

13. Cf. Homer, *Odyssey*, X.303–40.

14. Socrates' motivations are important here, as they imply that knowledge of ignorance is not the same as self-knowledge.

15. In addition to necessity, *anagke* can also mean force or constraint.

16. Stated differently, no thing can both be and not be at the same time and in the same respect, that is, the principle of contradiction.

17. Cf. Strauss, *Socrates and Aristophanes*, 140.

18. Socrates' extreme continence would then be the abstraction, or even caricature, of political life's virtue.

19. Cf. *Republic* 473c8–e4.

20. On this point, consider Ludwig, "A Portrait of the Artist," 487.

21. The Clouds alone see themselves—or wish to see themselves—as a part of the greater whole, which includes the city (577–79).

22. Cf. Leo Strauss, *What Is Political Philosophy?* (Chicago: University of Chicago Press, 1988), 94.

23. Cf. Leo Strauss, *The Rebirth of Classical Political Rationalism* (Chicago: University of Chicago Press, 1989), 105.

Part II

4

Persuasion in Comedy and Comic Persuasion

Aristophanes and the Mysteries of Rhetoric

John Zumbrunnen

I.

It comes as no particular surprise that Aristophanes, as a comic poet writing in democratic Athens, would treat rhetoric and its place in politics as a central source of material. Rhetoric played an important role in the major institutions of Athenian political life. If we believe Thucydides (and, in a way, even his Pericles), the Athenian Assembly was not the site of deliberative conversation among many equal voices but, instead, was dominated by a relative handful of prominent politicians who did most of the talking.[1] If we take seriously the image of the law courts we find in the *Apology* and elsewhere, then rhetoric was central there as well. Given the role of oratory in Athenian politics and its significance to elite observers and critics of Athenian democracy, it only makes sense that it would be of central concern to Aristophanes as well.

In Aristophanes' day as in our own, comedy can work fairly easily on the surface of political rhetoric. Though most political actors aren't particularly funny when they try to be, they often enough say unintentionally hilarious things. At a slightly deeper level—though still an easy target for someone like Aristophanes—we have the matter of political hypocrisy.

Politicians say one thing one day, another thing—sometimes the opposite thing—the next day; or they say one thing and do another; or they critique others for saying or doing things that they themselves have said or done. Comedy can engage with this kind of rhetorical hypocrisy simply by exposing it (Jon Stewart's often brilliant montages of elite rhetorical foolishness perhaps being the contemporary model of this). If effectively carried out, exposing hypocrisy will bring laughter and, just perhaps, some change in the opinions or actions of the audience. Comedy might hope, that is, to fashion a demos more attuned to hypocrisy and other foibles and failings of elite rhetoric. Indeed, Aristophanes at various points presents himself as a civic educator of sorts. He claims in the parabasis of *Acharnians*, for instance, that he "deserves rich rewards" for having saved the Athenians from their tendency to be "citizens vacant and vain" or "citizens of Simpletonia" and from being easy prey for the rhetorical ploys of elites (*Acharnians* 628–35).[2]

The extent to which Aristophanes actually does challenge the Athenians, much less save them from themselves, is a matter for debate. Backing up his claims that he educates rather than simply amuses, he often enough declares that he does not fall prey to the temptation simply to write what pleases his audience. In the parabasis of *Peace*, for example, he has the chorus leader offer this bit of praise of the poet himself: "By getting rid of such poor, lowbrow buffoonery, he's [i.e., Aristophanes has] made our art great and built it up to towering size with impressive verses, conceptions, and uncommon jokes" (*Peace* 745–49). Rather than appeal to the least common denominator, Aristophanes suggests, he has challenged his audience. Of course, as any reader of the plays knows, Aristophanes often appeals precisely to the least common denominator; he seems to delight in lowbrow buffoonery. Then, too, this passage itself aims to appeal to the flattering self-image of the demos, to the spectators' pride in appreciating great art and "uncommon jokes." Aristophanes, it would seem, does not shy away from the tricks of the trade that he critiques in other poets.

Thinking both of the character of Aristophanes' humor and of comedy's deep implication in the politics and culture of the city, Malcolm Heath has argued that Aristophanes' "plays are so nicely attuned to the prejudices and expectations of Aristophanes' audience" that we ought to "hesitate" in seeing them as expressing Aristophanes' considered political views. We need not accept this "domestication" thesis to recognize that the comic poet must figure out what will appeal to his audience and shape his comedy accordingly.[3] Aristophanes works in the context of an audience that arrives with ways of thinking about politics arrayed somewhere on a continuum from completely rigid to completely malleable. If the comic poet wants to get laughs, win first prize, *and* persuade or convince or educate his audience, then he must successfully appeal to what his audience already knows or at least to what it thinks it knows.

In this, Aristophanes finds himself in the same situation as the orators he so often mocks. Comedy and rhetoric, that is, both work in the context of the prejudices or preexisting opinions of the audience. Aristotle puts the point simply early on in the *Rhetoric*: "we must use, as our modes of persuasion and argument, notions possessed by everybody."[4] In the *Gorgias*, Plato turns the same basic insight about the nature of persuasion into a sharp criticism of the way in which received opinions shape the arguments and eventually the very soul of the orator. "Each demos," Socrates argues, "takes pleasure in hearing sentiments which are in harmony with its own nature and detests the reverse." The best teacher for an orator, then, is "whoever can fashion you to be most like [the demos]."[5]

I do not stress this basic similarity in the tasks of the orator and the comic poet simply as a way to apply the Platonic critique of the orators to Aristophanes, nor do I intend to add weight to the sort of arguments Heath makes about the domestication of comedy. I mean in part simply to offer a reminder of the democratic character of Aristophanic comedy: it is written first and foremost for a theater audience consisting of ordinary citizens of Athens, and it must appeal to that audience. But I also mean to throw into sharper relief the fact that, even as he aims at his own sort of comic persuasion, Aristophanes, like the philosophers, wonders about and worries over the nature of persuasion itself. His comedy, that is, engages not only with how rhetoric is used in Athens, but also with how rhetoric works, with how persuasion happens. Let me here highlight two passages, one from early in Aristophanes' artistic career, the other from much later. Both suggest the mysterious nature of persuasion, though they conceive of that mystery in different ways.

The first comes from *Wasps*. Produced in 422 BCE, the play revolves around the struggles of Bdelycleon to curb his father Philocleon's love not only of the Athenian demagogue Cleon but also of service as a juror in the Athenian law courts. In part, Bdelycleon proceeds by trying to convince his father that Cleon exercises a kind of mastery over his followers, turning men like Philocleon into his slaves. In the midst of this argument, Philocleon declares: "Heavens me, what are you saying? You're shaking me to my very depths, pulling me closer to your viewpoint, doing I don't know what to me!" (*Wasps* 696–97). The mystery of rhetoric here concerns just what effect it produces on listeners. What does rhetoric do to its audience? What sort of "shaking" does persuasion involve? How does rhetoric move listeners from one "viewpoint" to another?

The second passage comes from Aristophanes' latest surviving play, *Wealth*. Produced in 388 BCE, *Wealth*'s plot imagines the success of its hero, Chremylus, in bringing economic justice to the world. He does so by restoring the sight of the heretofore blind god Wealth. He must first, though, defeat the goddess Poverty in a rhetorical agon. As Poverty makes powerful arguments about how she spurs humans to hard work while Wealth makes them lazy, Chremylus defiantly declares: "Now get lost and stop your grumbling. Not another word! You won't persuade [*peiseis*] me even if you convince [*peisēs*] me" (*Wealth* 599–600). Henderson's translation of this sentence tends to downplay the paradoxical nature of the claim Chremylus makes. The double appearance of forms of *peitho* suggests that we read the line more literally as "you won't persuade me even if you persuade me."

The mystery here, then, concerns not how persuasion works but how one can be both persuaded and not persuaded. On the simplest level, this is a matter of resistance on the part of the listener. As I argue below, though, the passage—and the play—raise deeper questions about the relationship between rhetoric and reality. In *Wasps*, we might say, the mystery of rhetoric concerns how it moves listeners from one viewpoint to another. In *Wealth*, it is more accurate to say that the mystery of rhetoric concerns whether or to what extent it can move listeners from one reality to another—whether rhetoric itself can change reality and transport listeners from a world in which poverty rules to one in which justice prevails.

In this chapter, I consider this seeming change in Aristophanes' engagement with rhetoric and its mysteries. I begin by situating the mystery of rhetoric as it appears in *Wasps* in the context of rhetoric's similar treatment in two other early plays: *Acharnians* and *Knights*.[6] I then turn to the different understanding of rhetoric that emerges in *Assemblywomen* and *Wealth*.[7] This way of proceeding may seem to verge upon making an argument about the development of Aristophanes' comedy over the course of his long career. Such arguments are dangerous. We after all have complete versions of only eleven of more than forty Aristophanic comedies, too few to say anything definitive about what changes and when. Still, I do find such an argument tempting, though cast not so much as a matter of the poet's development as of the changing context for his poetry. *Wasps* appears early in the Peloponnesian War and in the midst of Aristophanes' seemingly bitter struggle with Cleon. *Wealth* appears more than a decade after the war's end. Insofar as comedy, like rhetoric, works with its audience's prejudices and preoccupations, context matters. Indeed, in the conclusion I turn to the Aristophanic comedy most favored by political theorists, thinking about the possibility that *Clouds* failed in part because its engagement with the mysteries of rhetoric was out of step with prevailing Athenian concerns.

II.

Aristophanes' first surviving plays revolve around the dislocations and political distortions seen during the early years of the Peloponnesian War. In *Knights* and *Wasps,* the playwright focuses his ire on Cleon's rise to prominence in Athens. *Acharnians*, by contrast, focuses more broadly on the ill effects of rhetoric in wartime Athens. The play opens with its hero, Diceapolis, complaining of the "umpteen million loads" of pains brought on by the war (*Acharnians* 1–2) and promising to go to the Assembly and "shout, interrupt, revile the speakers, if anyone speaks of anything except peace" (*Acharnians* 38–39). To Diceapolis' dismay, the Assembly will not hear talk of peace; in response, he concludes his own treaty with the Spartans and retreats to the Attic countryside.

The plot of *Acharnians* in this way frames a straightforward critique of rhetoric as practiced in Athens: it serves the interests of war, not peace. Later in the play we learn more about how this happens. Confronted by the angry chorus of Acharnians, Diceapolis pleads for the chance to speak in his own behalf yet says that he is "very apprehensive": "I know the way country people act, deeply delighted when some fraudulent personage eulogizes them and the city, whether truly or falsely; that's how they can be bought and sold all unawares. And I know the hearts of the oldsters, too, looking forward only to biting with their ballots" (*Acharnians* 370–76). The criticisms of "country people" and "the oldsters" Diceapolis offers here converge on a complaint about rhetoric familiar from Plato in particular: that it relies—or preys—upon the prejudices of its audience. In the case of the oldsters, Diceapolis' concern is straightforward: as his rhetorical opponents, the Acharnian chorus can depend upon the oldsters' desire to punish. In the case of the "country people," his concern is more nuanced: the chorus will be able to appeal to their self-love and so to win their support.

There are some unexplored complexities or tensions here. Is the audience for rhetoric malleable (like the country people) or recalcitrant (like the oldsters)? But the underlying apprehension is clear enough: facing an unwary audience, the skillful orator can manipulate their prejudices for his own gain. Diceapolis himself soon turns this source of apprehension into his own rhetorical resource. Before he actually speaks to the chorus, he borrows the "ragments of Telephus" from Euripides: "For the beggar I must seem to be today: to be who I am, yet seem not so. The audience must know me for who I am, but the chorus must stand there like simpletons, so that with my pointed phrases, I can give them the finger" (*Acharnians* 440–44).

Diceapolis here suggests that his rhetorical strategy rests on disguise and so on deception.[8] Deception works, though, in the context of the basic prejudices of the audience. Diceapolis gains rhetorical advantage by appearing as a beggar, knowing the chorus will sympathize. In taking advantage of the prejudices of the audience, rhetoric need not always deceive. In calling for the punishment of the Diceapolis, the Acharnians can, Diceapolis himself suggests, simply appeal to the punitive desires of the oldsters. But deception, it would seem, often attends the basic rhetorical reliance on preexisting opinions. Properly disguised, Diceapolis can seize upon the chorus's sympathy for beggars, though he is not himself one. Appealing to the self-love of country people, the chorus itself can "buy and sell" them though they remain "unaware."

This deception and manipulation of the country people points toward the basic plot of *Knights*, which appeared the year following *Acharnians*. *Knights* offers an allegory of Athenian politics, in which the Athenian demos appears as a single character, Demos of Pnyx. Demos is the head of a household and master of several slaves, who represent prominent Athenian political actors including Nicias and Demosthenes. The play's conflict revolves around the role of a new "paphlagonian" slave, who represents Cleon and who has, by endlessly flattering Demos, managed to gain control of the household. As the play unfolds, Demos is bested by a sausage seller in a series of rhetorical contests in which the competitors attempt to outdo one another in flattering and making promises to Demos.

This allegorical plot appears to raise the stakes from *Acharnians*. Now the question is not whether some elites deploy rhetoric to keep peace off the agenda of public discussion but, more fundamentally perhaps, whether some use rhetoric to turn the relationship between elites and ordinary speakers upside down, to turn the masters into slaves and vice versa. Still, the underlying concern with rhetoric is the same: it plays upon existing prejudices to deceive or manipulate. Along these lines, the slaves Nicias and Demosthenes describe the first actions of the Paphlagonian slave: "Last market day [Demos] bought a slave, Paphlagon, a tanner, an arch criminal, and a slanderer. He sized up the old man's character, this rawhide Paphlagon did, so he crouched before the master and started flattering and fawning and toadying and swindling him with odd tidbits of waste leather" (*Knights* 43–49). Later, when the sausage seller worries that "it's an amazing idea, me being fit to supervise the people," Nicias and Demosthenes advise him to "always keep the people on your side by sweetening them with gourmet bons mots" (*Knights* 215–16). In *Knights,* whether the Athenian people will remain enslaved by the likes of Cleon or place themselves under the wise "stewardship" of one like Agoracritus depends on which would-be elite best takes advantage of the underlying character, desires, and prejudices of the people themselves.

At the outset, I quoted a passage from *Wasps* in which Philocleon points toward the mysterious character of persuasion, saying that his son's arguments are "pulling me closer to your viewpoint, doing I don't know what to me." *Acharnians* and *Knights* suggest the basics of a by and large straightforward Aristophanic explanation of this mystery. Persuasion works to pull the listener to another viewpoint by appealing to the listener's prejudices, often doing so by means of deception. *Wasps* confirms this. In making thematic the relationship between Cleon and his followers, the play takes up the same issues of mastery and slavery as *Knights*. While in *Knights* these issues work at the level of characterization and plot, in *Wasps* they become subjects of the rhetoric of the characters. Bdeylcleon thus appeals directly to his father's desire for mastery or, put differently, to his deeply held conviction that in Athens he is and must be master. Bedylcleon's arguments work in a revelatory frame, showing the old man that Cleon's claims to act in accordance with the basic power of the ordinary Athenian are not to be believed. Answering his own rhetorical question about where the wealth that comes from empire ends up, Bedylcleon declares: "[It goes] to the 'I won't betray the Athenian rabble and I'll fight for the masses' bunch! You choose them to rule [*archēin*] you, father, because you've been buttered up by these slogans" (*Wasps* 666–67). Bedylcleon thus aims both to show the real motives that lie behind Cleon's flattering words and to reveal Cleon's success in turning citizens like Philocleon into his slaves.

Bdelycleon's argument points to a potential problem with the basic understanding of persuasion and its mysteries that I have been developing. Like *Acharnians* and *Knights¸ Wasps* by and large points to an understanding of persuasion as a matter of a speaker manipulating the prejudices of an audience, sometimes and perhaps often through deception. Persuasion on this understanding rests upon or enacts a particular relationship between speaker and audience. When Bdeylcleon makes that relationship itself the subject of his own revelatory rhetoric, he raises the possibility that rhetoric may work to shape the relationship upon which it rests—a possibility that Aristophanes takes up in earnest in his latest plays. *Wasps*, though, remains by and large within an understanding of persuasion as working in the context of preexisting prejudices. Just like Cleon, Bdeylcleon appeals to Philocleon's self-regard and specifically to his sense that he is the proper master in Athens. The chief difference is that Cleon deceives in order to use rhetoric for his selfish ends, while Bdelycleon does not. Once we see that rhetoric works by playing on existing opinion, our chief task, these early plays suggest, is to determine if it does so with or without deception.

We can also think about Aristophanes' posture as civic educator in this context. *Acharnians* and *Knights* point toward a certain kind of intelligence or cleverness as a possible antidote to the deceptive manipulation of the audience by orators. We have already seen Diceapolis suggesting that though his disguise may fool the chorus of Acharnians, the audience will "know me for who I am." Along similar lines, Aristophanes in the parabasis of *Knights* tells us that although no mask maker would paint a mask that actually resembled Cleon, spectators would know whom the Paphlagonian slave represents because "the audience [*theatron*] is smart [*dexion*]" (*Knights* 230–33). Comedy's spectators, that is, possess an intelligence or cleverness or dexterity that allows for seeing through the masks elite actors wear. Or, to the extent that Aristophanes' claim is prescriptive rather than descriptive, comedy aims to fashion spectators clever enough to see Cleon for who he is. The clever spectator or listener or citizen will, that is, recognize not only that all orators aim to appeal to their most basic beliefs in order to persuade but also that some do so by deception and for their own selfish purposes.

III.

I turn now from the earliest of Aristophanes' surviving plays to the latest: *Assemblywomen* and *Wealth*. The playwright's sustained interest in rhetoric and in the place of deception and disguise as rhetorical resources continues in both plays, particularly in *Assemblywomen*. *Assemblywomen* opens with the heroine Praxagora walking onstage, speaking to a lamp that she holds. She refers to the lamp's "supervisory eye," which can be made "privy to our plot," for the lamp is "an accomplice that never blabs to the neighbors" (*Assemblywomen* 5–15). Usually a witness to "Aphrodite's maneuvers," the lamp here aids Praxagora's plot. Praxagora's coconspirators—the women of Athens—gather by the light of the lamp but rely, too, on the lamp's discretion, on the fact that its light will not shine so brightly as to reveal the deception upon which they embark.

Praxagora's plot depends upon her convincing the men of Athens to hand the city's affairs over to the women. The success of the scheme will thus depend upon the rhetorical performance of the women once they arrive in the Assembly; their rhetorical strategy in turn relies upon deception. On one level, all of this works according to a logic familiar from the early plays. The "means of persuasion" (to borrow from Aristotle) that are available to Praxagora are shaped and delimited by the prejudices of the audience to whom they must appeal: the men of Athens who gather on the Pnyx. In *Acharnians*, Diceapolis borrows the rags of Telephus in order to appeal to the chorus' assumed sympathy for beggars. Praxagora's ultimate rhetorical success depends upon successfully navigating a deeper and fully institutionalized prejudice that only men are fully citizens, able to speak and vote in the Assembly. She and her coconspirators must, then, both look and sound like men if they are to carry the day. At Praxagora's direction, the women of Athens thus don false beards and their husbands' clothes; one says that she "threw my razor out of the house right away, so that I'd get hairy all over and not look female at all" (*Assemblywomen* 65–66). Speaking as men speak proves rather more difficult. Practicing their speeches, one woman mistakenly swears "by the Two Goddesses" (*Assemblywomen* 155); another, "by Aphrodite" (*Assemblywomen* 189), as no man would. Another, to Praxagora's dismay, greets the "assembled ladies" (*Assemblywomen* 165–66).[9]

If there is a simple similarity between Diceapolis dressing as a beggar to deceive the chorus and the women of Athens working to appear as men in order to deceive the Assembly, the disguises are significantly different, at least in degree and perhaps in kind. This difference is reflected, too, in the wonderful ironies of Praxagora's rhetorical effort. Not only Diceapolis' disguise and rhetoric, but also the action he wants his audience to take, fit with the prejudices of his audience; he wants his audience to see him as a beggar and, their sympathy for beggars activated, show him mercy. Praxagora wants her audience to see her as a man and, in line with their assumptions about gender roles, take her as a legitimate speaker; but she ultimately wants them to act in a way that calls into question those very assumptions. In arguing that women should replace men as the rulers of the city, she at once draws upon her disguise as a rhetorical resource yet aims to overturn the prejudices that give that disguise its meaning and power. Diceapolis depends on a stable rhetorical relationship that rests on unchallenged assumptions and prejudices. As soon as she wins the day, Praxagora has destabilized the rhetorical relationship upon which her victory has depended.

Praxagora's strategy for the Assembly thus points the way to a different sort of question about rhetoric. In thinking about Aristophanes' earliest plays, I have stressed the playwright's concern with the way in which rhetoric depends on the existing prejudices of the audience, often enough by employing deception. *Assemblywomen* from the start raises issues about the extent to which rhetoric can alter or overturn those prejudices. This goes beyond the matter of whether rhetoric can challenge the presumption in favor of men's political dominance. With her newly gained power, Praxagora initiates two radical reforms: both property and sex will hereafter be communally distributed. The remainder of the play makes clear that these policies are not self-executing dictates. They rely on the power of persuasion beyond the Assembly to change Athenian understandings of human action in the world.[10]

I focus here on Praxagora's egalitarian reform of property relations.[11] Once she has secured power for the women of Athens, Praxagora offers the following: "I propose that everyone should own everything in common [*koinōnein*], and draw an equal living. No more rich man [*ploutein*] here, poor man [*athlion*] there, or a man with a big farm and a man without land enough for his own grave, or a man with many slaves and a man without even an attendant. No, I will establish one and the same standard of life for everyone" (*Assemblywomen* 588–92). This equalizing of material well-being will, she claims, fundamentally alter human motivations and so human action. "No one will be doing *anything* as a result of poverty [*penia*] because everyone will have all the necessities" (*Assemblywomen* 605–6). This means that there will be "no more mugging, no more envying the next guy, no more wearing rags, no more poor people, no more wrangling, no more dunning and repossessing" (*Assemblywomen* 565–67).

Praxagora calls upon the Athenians to bring their private goods to the agora so that they might be redistributed equally. It soon becomes clear, though, that implementing her scheme will not be so simple. Aristophanes treats us to a conversation between Praxagora's neighbor and a "Dissident" who calls into question the very basis of Praxagora's plan.[12] The Dissident doubts that the Athenians will go along with the plan; it is "not in our national character," he says. More relevant to my purposes here is the Dissident's assertion that "on the strength of mere words I'm hardly about to throw away the fruits of my sweat and thrift in this sort of mindless way" (*Assemblywomen* 750); "I intend to be cautious, until I see what most people do," he concludes (*Assemblywomen* 770). The Dissident, that is, doubts whether "mere words" can change "what most people do."

Like her strategy for seizing power in the Assembly, Praxagora's attempt to enact her reforms—or, more precisely, the reaction to that attempt—points to questions about the power of rhetoric to alter settled patterns of human motivation and behavior. The play offers no clear-cut answer to these questions. Praxagora carries the day in the Assembly and works to enact her reforms, and the play ends in celebration. We are presented with the possibility, then, that rhetoric can alter human practices that we might otherwise think rooted in deep and abiding aspects of human existence. Still, the presence both of the Dissident and of those who would work to evade Praxagora's scheme of sexual redistribution suggests potential limits on this reconstructive power of rhetoric.[13] Along similar lines, *Wealth* raises and then leaves unanswered fundamental questions about the power of words to shape or reshape human reality; but the later play also points toward a particular stance we might take toward this mystery of rhetoric.

Like *Assemblywomen*, *Wealth* makes a scheme for economic redistribution a central plot element and, though it ends in joyous celebration of that scheme, calls into question the possibility of its ever happening in the world outside the theater. Indeed, *Wealth* in a sense makes this possibility seem more remote. Where *Assemblywomen* locates the barrier to redistribution in the recalcitrant self-interest of human beings, *Wealth* suggests that the advent of economic justice would require a reworking of the relationship between humans and the gods. The play's hero, Chremylus, has gone to Delphi to ask the Oracle whether his son should follow in his father's footsteps and so be just but poor or, instead, "become a criminal, unjust, completely unwholesome, considering that's the way to get ahead in life" (*Wealth* 37–38). The Oracle in its riddling way has told Chremylus that "the first person I encountered on leaving the shrine I was told to stick to and persuade to come home with me." That first person turns out to be the god Wealth, who is old and blind—and thus unable to distinguish between, and so appropriately reward and punish, the just and unjust.

These early lines already suggest the deep questions about the power of rhetoric that the play will raise. Because the first person he meets is in fact Wealth, Chremylus becomes entangled in a battle with the gods. Wealth at first resists Chremylus' plan to restore his vision. He has, he says, been blinded by Zeus, who "scares the pants off me" (*Wealth* 122). Chremylus must, then, first persuade Wealth to resist Zeus. He does so by arguing that not Zeus but Wealth himself is "the most puissant [*krastiste*] of all divinities [*daimonōn*]." The desire for Wealth, he argues, dominates human actions: "it's you and you alone who motivate everything, the good and the bad alike; you can be sure of that" (*Wealth* 180–81). As for the gods, Wealth undergirds Zeus' power, both because Zeus is himself rich and because humans pray and sacrifice to Zeus first and foremost to gain Wealth.

On one level, all of this works simply as a rhetorical strategy by which Chremylus aims to get Wealth to act as he wishes. The strategy succeeds.

Though still hesitant, Wealth agrees to Chremylus' plan, and his sight is restored through the offstage ministrations of Asclepius.

Chremylus thus argues on behalf of a world in which Wealth, his sight restored, can judge the just and the unjust and so in which all humans become just and the arbitrary power of Zeus is undercut. Beyond this, though, Chremlyus presents a view of an alternate world in which universal wealth produces universal justice. This alternate world becomes the subject of a rhetorical agon when the goddess Poverty appears.

Poverty arrives onstage as an old woman with a "crazed and tragic look" (*Wealth* 423)[14] and proceeds to call into question the account of the world and of human action in it that Chremylus has offered. Humans, she argues, act not out of desire for wealth, but out of fear of poverty. She claims herself to be "the sole source of all your blessings" (*Wealth* 470–71). She "sits by the artisan like a taskmaster, compelling him . . . to seek his livelihood" and so ensuring that he does not starve (*Wealth* 533–34). In a world ruled by Wealth, she says, "you'll find men with gout, potbellies, bloated legs and disgustingly fat"; the reign of Poverty, by contrast, means men who are "lean, wasp-waisted and hard on the enemy" (*Wealth* 557–59). Wealth encourages not only gluttony, but also corruption, while the poor are upright. Here, Poverty cites those politicians who "when they get rich on public funds immediately become wrongdoers, plotting against the masses and warring against the people" (*Wealth* 565–70). In place of Chremylus' vision of a world where wealth rewards justice, Poverty depicts a world where hunger, need, and the fear of deprivation not only motivate the productive behavior necessary for human life but also ensure some semblance of personal and civic virtue.

Most commentators think that Poverty gets the better of these arguments and that Chremlyus offers half-hearted and unconvincing responses.[15] Still, Chremylus in a sense wins the exchange. Wealth's sight is restored. In the play's later scenes, we see a newly enriched Just Man, a now wealthy older woman able to attract the attentions of a young man, and an informer who must find a new way to make money. In addition to being good fun, all of this perhaps suggests the possibility that the powerful arguments of Poverty might be overcome, or at least resisted. Indeed, here we can return to the passage I quoted in the Introduction, in which Chremylus declares his own intention—and ability—to resist what Poverty says: "Now get lost and stop your grumbling. Not another word! You won't persuade [*peiseis*] me even if you convince [*peisēs*] me" (*Wealth* 599–600). What can this mean? How can Chremlyus be convinced by Poverty yet not persuaded—or, as the Greek suggests, how can he be persuaded yet not be persuaded?

One possibility is that Chremlyus can detect the process of persuasion as it occurs and stop it before it is complete. This would perhaps involve something like the sort of cleverness discussed in the last section. Chremlyus would, then, see the way in which Poverty's rhetoric pulls him toward her point of view and, precisely because of this insight, be able to resist in time. The passage, though, suggests something different. It suggests that the process of persuasion can be complete, yet the auditor still cannot be persuaded. In the language I have been using, Chremylus suggests that Poverty's arguments might appeal successfully to his prejudices and persuade him of her worldview, yet he might still cling to a different worldview. He can, that is, be persuaded by her description of a world in which the fear of poverty motivates human action yet resist that description, holding to his view of an alternative rule where Wealth rules.

This is comedy, and so we should recognize the element of absurdity here and the way in which Chremylus' absurd line might play to laughter in the theater. We might also, though, see in this passage, and in *Assemblywomen* and *Wealth* more generally, an Aristophanic interest in rhetoric's ability to construct and reconstruct what we take as reality. Beyond playing to existing prejudices about what is and is not possible or desirable, rhetoric might, these plays suggest, aim to alter those prejudices in ways that in turn alter what is real. On this way of thinking, comedy might go beyond cultivating a cleverness that resists the deception and manipulation in which rhetoric so often traffics. It might instead work to cultivate a comic sensibility akin to that of Chremlyus. Aristophanes' spectators, that is, might learn to recognize and hold onto multiple worldviews, to inhabit different realities, and so to respect the stubbornness of facts while working toward changing the world as they had thought it to be. I have elsewhere described this sensibility as a kind of comic recognition, which appreciates both the rhetoric of change and the rhetoric of continuity as live possibilities.

IV.

I have here suggested that we find in Aristophanes' surviving works two relatively distinct ways of understanding and responding to the mysterious nature of rhetoric and persuasion. With the trepidation about developmental arguments expressed at the outset, I have also suggested that these different approaches to rhetoric seem to map on to different moments in Aristophanes' career. Written in the early years of the war and engaged directly with the role of demagoguery in bringing about and continuing that war, the earliest surviving plays concern themselves with the mysterious way in which rhetoric can change the minds of listeners. In a way familiar largely from both Plato's critique of rhetoric and Aristotle's more sympathetic treatment, *Acharnians*, *Wasps*, and *Knights* see the key to this mystery of rhetoric's effectiveness in the orator's often deceptive engagement with the prejudices of the audience. Aristophanes points toward a certain sort of cleverness, an ability to see through the deceptive masks elites construct for themselves, as an antidote. By contrast, the latest surviving plays appear in the wake of war, as Athens worked to rebuild itself. Here, the mystery of rhetoric centers on the possibility that it may be able to remake—to rebuild or reconstruct—the very reality in which speakers and listeners live. This is partly a matter of whether rhetoric can alter the prejudices upon which it seemingly depends, though *Wealth* in particular raises the question of whether rhetoric can move in a thoroughgoing way the worldviews of its audience. With more fundamental mysteries of rhetoric in mind, Aristophanes points in *Assemblywomen* and *Wealth* toward the need for an ability to recognize and inhabit multiple rhetorical realities, an openness to the possibility of change coupled with a recognition of our limited ability to reorder our world. I do not mean to suggest that these two ways of thinking about rhetoric are mutually exclusive, but they do point to distinct concerns: on the one hand, to the possibilities and consequences of rhetorically activating recalcitrant ways of thinking, and, on the other hand, to the possibilities and consequences of rhetorically altering those ways of thinking.

As I said at the outset, we ought to be wary of taking these arguments too far. We in particular ought to proceed carefully in making any claims about Aristophanes' artistic or political development. Again, our evidence for such claims in quite limited. That evidence is also not univocal. The concerns about the deceptive manipulation of prejudices that appear most strongly in the earliest plays run throughout the Aristophanic corpus. Likewise, Aristophanes' own recognition of the de- and reconstructive power of rhetoric is not limited to the later plays. The most obvious example here is *Clouds*, or at least the revised version of that play that has come down to us. *Clouds* has attracted more attention among political theorists than any other Aristophanic comedy, no doubt because of its (misleading) portrayal of Socrates. For my purposes here, though, the more significant character is Strepsiades, who tries but fails to learn sophistic rhetoric from Socrates and so insists that his son Phidippides study at the Thinkery. Phidippides emerges with the ability to use rhetoric not only to deceive and manipulate his father's creditors, but also and more fundamentally to upend the traditional *nomoi* of Athens. Most pointedly for Strepsiades, he uses rhetoric to defend father beating. Referring to *Clouds*' famous agon between Right and Wrong Speech, Kenneth Dover concludes that "Phidippides learns from Wrong a nonchalant, selfish nihilism."[16] He learns, too, the kind of rhetoric that enables and uses such nihilism.

In this way, *Clouds* would seem to fit better with *Assemblywomen* and *Wealth* than with other earlier plays. Again, I take this as another piece of evidence warning against an argument about the development of Aristophanes' concerns with rhetoric. We might well, though, take *Clouds* and in particular its failure to win first prize as indicative of the relationship between Aristophanes' comedy as civic education and the context of particular comedies. On the question of the mysterious nature and political and social import of rhetoric, *Clouds* appears less in tune with its time. Rather than taking warmongering demagogues as its subject matter, as do *Acharnians* and *Knights*, *Clouds* focuses on the obscure teachings of a Socrates who, as Michael Zuckert puts it, appears as "a rather isolated figure, unknown and of little interest to most of the city."[17] The more successful *Acharnians*, *Knights*, and *Wasps* suggest that the pressing questions of rhetoric in Athens in the 420s concerned how speech could deceive and manipulate, not how or whether it could reshape the basic contours of social and political reality. From this point of view, we might think that Aristophanes in *Clouds* raised an issue that was not or at least not yet an issue for his audience.

Beyond this contextual argument, it may also be that *Clouds* fails to address satisfactorily the mystery of rhetoric with which it engages. *Assemblywomen* and *Wealth* on my reading both engage with the same basic mystery; both consider the possibility that rhetoric might work to undermine or reshape the political and social prejudices or norms or *nomoi* of Athens. Challenging the political dominance of men, or imagining a world in which economic justice and widespread economic well-being prevail, is, in this sense, akin to overturning the prohibition on father beating. All three plays consider these sorts of possibilities. Importantly, the difference between *Clouds*, on the one hand, and *Assemblywomen* and *Wealth*, on the other hand, does not lie in accepting or rejecting the results of rhetorical transformations of reality. The significance of the Dissident in *Assemblywomen* and of Poverty in *Wealth* suggests abiding doubts about these transformations, just as does Strepsiades' suffering at his son's hand in *Clouds*.

The more telling difference lies, I think, between Strepsiades' burning of the Thinkery and Chremlyus' response to the arguments of Poverty. *Clouds* stands out among Aristophanes' surviving plays for the darkness of its ending, which replaces the dancing with which other plays conclude. Faced with his son's newfound rhetorical ability to alter the fundaments of Athenian common life, Strepsiades' only response is destruction. One is tempted here to say that in *Clouds*, comedy raises questions to which it has no answers, that Aristophanes has shown us an abyss—the malleability of reality by rhetoric—which he concludes ordinary people like Strepsiades cannot abide. Might a Strepsiades armed with Chremylus' sort of comic recognition, his ability not to be persuaded even when persuaded, to abide the lure of another rhetorically constructed reality while remaining in one's own world—might such a Strepsiades have reacted differently? And if so, might *Clouds* have ended not with destruction, but with a kind of comic confidence that could, if not welcome, at least abide or cope with both the sort of rhetoric that emerges from the Thinkery and the Socratic philosophy with which it is in the play falsely equated?

This way of thinking about *Clouds* and its theatrical failure brings us back to the domestication thesis—to the idea that Aristophanes' art is at least shaped and perhaps contained by its deep and complex ties to the institutions of Athenian life and Athenian culture. In its most extreme form, the domestication thesis is, I think, unsustainable. It requires ignoring or explaining away all those moments in which Aristophanes is in fact harshly critical of Athenian politics and culture, and it requires reading Aristophanes' flights of fancy, his frequent seeming celebration of fantastical change, as consistently and fully undermined by an irony or cynicism that suggests nothing can in fact change. We do better, I think, to consider Aristophanes as aiming at a kind of comic persuasion of his audience marked by the very mysteries of rhetoric in which the playwright shows such great and sustained interest. Comedy engages with and responds to the deeply ingrained thinking of its audience, sometimes playing to the lowest and worst prejudices for a laugh. It also, though, wonders about—and asks its audience to wonder about—the possibility that by laughing and talking and thinking we might change our world.

Notes

1. When Thucydides shows us Athenian politics, it consists of a speaker or speakers appearing before a silent demos. As for Pericles, though his Funeral Oration is often enough cited as the most friendly contemporaneous account of Athenian democracy, the great statesman himself suggests that in practice only some Athenians spoke, while most listened and decided: "we are able to judge proposals even if we cannot originate them." Thucydides, *The Peloponnesian War*, in *The Landmark Thucydides: A Comprehensive Guide to the Peloponnesian War*, ed. Robert B. Strassler, intro. Victor Davis Hanson (New York: The Free Press, 1996), II 40.

I have treated the silence of the mass of Athenians and the implications of this silence for our understanding of rhetoric and its place in Athenian democracy in my *Silence and Democracy: Athenian Politics in Thucydides' History* (University Park: Penn State University Press, 2008).

2. Aristophanes here deploys a word of his own making, "*chaunopolites.*" Rogers offers "citizens vacant and vain" in Aristophanes, *Aristophanes: The Acharnians, the Knights, the Clouds, the Wasps,* trans. Benjamin B. Rogers (Cambridge: Harvard University Press, 1924). Henderson has "citizens of Simpletonia" in Aristophanes, *Aristophanes: Acharnians, Knights,* trans. Jeffrey Henderson (Cambridge: Harvard University Press, 2000). Throughout this chapter, I rely on Henderson's translations of Aristophanes, as found in the Loeb Classical Library editions.

3. Malcolm Heath, *Political Comedy in Aristophanes* (Göttingen, Germany: Vandenhoeck and Ruprecht, 1987), 40–41. See also A. W. Gomme, "Aristophanes and Politics," *Classical Review* 52 (July 1938): 97–109; Stephen Halliwell, "Aristophanic Satire," *The Yearbook of English Studies* 14 (1984): 6–21; David Konstan, *Greek Comedy and Ideology* (New York: Oxford University Press, 1995); and Anthony Edwards, "Aristophanes' Comic Poetics: TpyΞ, Scatology, ΣkΩmma," *Transactions of the American Philological Association* 121 (1991): 157–79. The language of "domestication" comes from J. Peter Euben, *Corrupting Youth: Political Education, Democratic Culture, and Political Theory* (Princeton, NJ: Princeton University Press, 1997), 114, who rejects this view of Aristophanes' art as fully determined by his need to appeal to his audience.

4. Aristotle, *The Rhetoric and Poetics of Aristotle,* trans. W. Rhys Roberts (New York: The Modern Library, 1984 [1954]), 1355a25. Later, Aristotle summarizes the argument of Book 1 of the *Rhetoric* in similar terms, saying, "we have considered the received opinions on which we may best base our arguments so as to convince our hearers" (1377b15).

5. Plato, *Gorgias,* trans. Walter Hamilton and Chris Emlyn-Jones (New York: Penguin, 2004 [1960]), 513b–c. Socrates here argues in the context not only of the orator's quest for the love of the demos but also of Callicles' quest for the love of Demos, son of Pyrilampes.

6. I offer a fuller reading of *Acharnians* and *Knights* in John Zumbrunnen, "Elite Domination and the Clever Citizen: Aristophanes' *Acharnians* and *Knights,*" *Political Theory* 32 (no. 5, 2004): 656–77, and in John Zumbrunnen, *Aristophanic Comedy and the Challenge of Democratic Citizenship* (Rochester, NY: University of Rochester Press, 2012).

7. I offer a fuller reading of *Assemblywomen* and *Wealth* in John Zumbrunnen, "Fantasy, Irony, and Economic Justice in Aristophanes' *Assemblywomen* and *Wealth,*" *American Political Science Review* 100 (no. 3, 2006): 319–33, and in Zumbrunnen, *Aristophanic Comedy.*

8. On the role of disguise in *Acharnians,* see Jon Hesk, *Democracy and Deception in Classical Athens* (Cambridge: Cambridge University Press, 2000), 264–67; Niall Slater, "Space, Character and απατη': Transformation and Transvaluation in the *Acharnians,*" in *Tragedy, Comedy and the Polis,* ed. Alan Sommerstein (Bari,

Italy: Levante Editori, 1993), 397–415; and Thomas Hubbard, *The Mask of Comedy: Aristophanes and the Intertextual Parabasis* (Ithaca, NY: Cornell University Press, 1992), chap. 2.

    9. Of course, Praxagora and the other "women" were played by male actors, thus heightening the play on gender roles in *Assemblywomen*.

    10. In his reading of *Assemblywomen* in *Political Dissent in Democratic Athens: Intellectual Critics of Popular Rule* (Princeton, NJ: Princeton University Press, 2002), Josiah Ober argues that Aristophanes takes to the extreme and so puts to the test the Athenians' commitment to equality. My suggestion here is that *Assemblywomen* likewise exaggerates and so tests another central tenet of Athenian democracy having to do with the role of speech as a means not only of making collective decisions but also of reconstructing the world humans share.

    11. On the scheme of sexual equality, see in particular Arlene Saxonhouse's analysis in chapter 1 of her *Fear of Diversity: The Birth of Political Science in Ancient Greek Thought* (Chicago: University of Chicago Press, 1992).

    12. This character is in fact denoted simply as "man [*anēr*]." I follow Alan Sommerstein, "Aristophanes and the Demon Poverty," *The Classical Quarterly*, New Series 34 (no. 2, 1984): 314–33, 316, and Kenneth S. Rothwell, *Politics and Persuasion in Aristophanes' Ecclesiasuzae* (Leiden, Netherlands: E. J. Brill, 1990), 7, in using Dissident. Henderson uses "selfish man."

    13. Saxonhouse, *Fear of Diversity*, for example, argues that Praxagora's scheme of sexual communism works to suggest the dangers of replacing diversity with unity. On another note, though, the play ends with plans for a grand celebratory feast. Praxagora's husband suggests that the food for the feast will come not from communal property but from private stores, and so everyone must "hurry home" before the feast can happen (1144–47). See Sommerstein, "Aristophanes and the Demon Poverty," and Rothwell, *Politics and Persuasion*, 6–7, for discussions of how this undermines the idea that Praxagora can in fact through words change "what most people do."

    14. James F. McGlew, "After Irony: Aristophanes' *Wealth* and its Modern Interpreters," *American Journal of Philology* 118 (Spring 1997): 35–53, and Sommerstein, "Aristophanes and the Demon Poverty," both emphasize the frightful appearance of Poverty as designed in part to elicit the audience's sympathy with Chremylus and Blepsidemus. Aristophanes also plays here with gender stereotypes. Chremylus, in admonishing Blepsidemus to stay for the agon with Poverty, asks, "Do you want it said that two men fled in terror from one woman?" As in *Assemblywomen* and elsewhere, the joke can cut either way. On the one hand, it suggests a general sense of women as weaker than men, as nothing to be feared. On the other hand, it reminds the audience of the power of this particular goddess.

    15. A. M. Bowie, *Aristophanes: Myth, Ritual, Comedy* (Cambridge: Cambridge University Press, 1993), 290; Leo Strauss, *Socrates and Aristophanes* (Chicago: University of Chicago Press, 1996), 295–96; Douglas M. MacDowell, *Aristophanes and Athens: An Introduction to the Plays* (Oxford: Oxford University Press, 1995), 334–35.

16. Kenneth J. Dover, *Aristophanic Comedy* (Berkeley: University of California Press, 1972), 112.

17. Michael Zuckert, "Rationalism and Political Responsibility: Just Speech and Just Deed in the 'Clouds' of Aristophanes and the 'Apology' of Socrates," *Polity* 17 (1984): 271–97, 278. I offer my own reading of *Clouds* in chapter 2 of Zumbrunnen, *Aristophanic Comedy*.

5

Boundaries

The Comic Poet Confronts the "Who" of Political Action

Arlene W. Saxonhouse

Herodotus—after giving us detailed background information about the ambassador Alexander, who has been sent by the Persian king's close confidant Mardonius—records (so to speak) Alexander's speech to the Athenians. The speech largely repeats Mardonius' words of warning to the Greeks, advising them not to fight the Persian king, but to become his ally instead. Then Herodotus (8.141) reports:

> Now, the Lacedaemonians had heard that Alexander had come to Athens to bring the Athenians into agreement with the barbarian. They remembered also the prophecies that they themselves, with all the rest of the Dorians, must be expelled from the Peloponnese by a combination of Medes and Athenians, and they were mightily afraid that the Athenians would come to terms with the Persian. So they resolved to send messengers. For the Athenians had delayed and waited, knowing full well that the Lacedaemonians would learn that an envoy had come from the barbarian about the possibility of an agreement. . . . So the Athenians acted deliberately (*epitêdes ôn*), in order to make the declaration of their position to the Lacedaemonians most publically.[1]

This passage, taken almost at random from Herodotus' *Histories*, illustrates the ease with which Herodotus refers to "the Lacedaemonians" and "the Athenians" as political actors. They analyze; they worry; they strategize. When he writes of the "barbarian," it is singular, and we know that behind Alexander, behind Mardonius, stands Xerxes, the Great King. He—singular—is the one who makes decisions and acts. The Athenians, the Lacedaemonians, the Thebans—all plural—are the ones who act when we turn to the Hellenes.

In Thucydides' work, the troubles begin when the Epidamnians send ambassadors to the Corcyreans seeking help against the exiled nobles. The nobles may have been expelled from Epidamnus, but the remaining people (*ho demos*) act so as to protect the city. As Thucydides' story moves on, the Lacedaemonians decide this; the Athenians decide that. But who are these Lacedaemonians? Who are these Athenians? Generals like Archidamus and Pericles and Alcibiades and Athenagoras may persuade the Spartans or the Athenians or the Syracusans, but they are not the "actors" who decide for the collectivity.[2] How do we know who is the political actor when we speak of communities not ruled by a king or a tyrant?

Entailed in the articulation of who the political actor may be is the process of defining boundaries, assessing who is included and who is excluded from participating in the decisions that are made by a group. Who is in and who is out? While the Persian king may receive advice from his advisors (not always with happy outcomes for the advisors), he is the one who decides and acts. The Athenians may listen to the speeches of Pericles or Alcibiades, but in the end it is the Athenians sitting in their assembly, raising their hands as they vote, who act, deciding to go to war with Sparta or to send an expedition to Sicily. Philip Manville, in his book *The Origins of Citizenship in Ancient Athens*, argues that it was under the influence of Solon at the beginning of the sixth century BCE that Athenian "citizenship" was born with "the creation of boundaries—spatial, legal, and even psychological."[3] Solon "created" this Athenian citizenship in part by establishing individual rights to own property, instituting laws concerning inheritance, in effect ending slavery among those who had been or became landowners in Attica, and, in particular, instituting a "new civic spirit"[4] by affirming the power of the laws to offer justice to citizens. All of these efforts led, according to Manville, to a population who saw themselves as part of "*hêmetê polis*"—"our polis."[5] Over the rest of the sixth and fifth centuries, membership in and exclusion from "our polis" meant the development and refining of the criteria of what it meant to be an Athenian citizen—to be included in the "Athenians" who acted and who engaged in political decision making. As comfortable as the language of "the Athenians" may seem to us today, there is a long story about its creation that Manville's work chronicles. Aristophanes' comedies, by questioning the boundaries that came into play during the calcification of the meaning of citizenship for the Athenians, highlight the problematic nature of our facile linguistic constructions about who acts when we say the Athenians—or any political groups—"act." Such language always includes some and excludes others, and every polity must address the criteria that constitute membership in the political actor.

Aristophanes' works illustrate a range of alternative constructions for assessing the "who" of political action. In doing so, they illuminate one of the fundamental political challenges: given that boundaries—even those that often seem natural, such as those between the sexes—are not according to nature, how do they come into being, and, especially in terms of what follows below, what consequences flow from different constructions of those boundaries? Aristophanes' comedies illustrate the permeability of boundaries, questioning the naturalness they acquire over time, but they show as well the unsettling consequences of not constructing boundaries. In Aristophanes' first comedy, the *Acharnians*, a single individual, a man named Dikaeopolis (or "Just City"), decides on his own that he is fed up with the war between the Athenians and the Spartans and arranges for his private, individual peace with Sparta. Separating himself from Athens to become an independent political actor in the inter-poleis sphere, Dikaeopolis makes his own foreign policy and then benefits from the actions that take him outside the decision matrix of his fellow citizens. He constitutes a city that is inhabited by one citizen. Yet he engages in decisions concerning war and peace and carries on trade as an independent city by himself. At the opposite extreme, the *Lysistrata* expands the boundaries to create a political actor—the female race, as Lysistrata herself calls it—that transcends rather than narrows traditional boundaries in order to constitute a Panhellenic movement. The *Ecclesiazusae*, working within the structure of the city itself, breaks down the boundaries between the sexes that previously had been such a central feature in the description of the political actor. In contrast to a city with citizens, the Athens of the *Ecclesiazusae* becomes a family with family members. But unlike the story of Lysistrata, the effort is not to dissolve boundaries between cities, only within the city of Athens itself.

Aristotle, in the beginning of Book 2 of the *Politics*, points out that it is necessary that "citizens" share in some things and not others, and he proceeds to look at the range of different regimes according to what they share—wives and children as in Socrates' city from the *Republic* or common meals in Crete and Sparta, and so forth. Behind Aristotle's investigation lies the point that sharing is essential to the political community but that each regime must define the boundaries of sharing, of what is to be common (*koinos*) and what is to be private (*idios*). Different regimes will identify different shared qualities or objects, and Aristotle makes clear his preference for limitations on what is shared by the political community in contrast to the Socratic proposals for Kallipolis in the *Republic*. When Dikaeopolis decides that he will separate himself from his city, that decision is based on his awareness that being included as a member of the Athenian polity and sharing the goals and aspirations of the Athenians does not bring him the individual pleasures he seeks.[6] He does not wish to share in the war that the Athenians are fighting and instead seeks his private peace. Lysistrata creates her conspiratorial actor through a shared longing for sex. The females of the *Ecclesiazusae* come together from a shared concern for the welfare of the city, but that shared concern turns into a sharing of all things and the dissolution of the barriers between families, not to mention the barrier between public and private.

The *Acharnians*

Aristophanes' comedies tend to begin with complaints: a father complaining about his son's spending habits, two men on the road complaining about the failure of their guide bird to get them where they want to go, a woman complaining about the failure of other women to come to an important meeting. The *Acharnians* is no different: Dikaeopolis begins with a complaint. He has arrived at the Pnyx ready to attend the assembly with a view to persuading the city to seek peace. "O City, O City," he laments (27).[7] He calls out to the city as if it were one, and he as a member of that city imagines that he will make the city move as one. He wants the city to act as a unit of which he is a part, but he finds that there is no one there to listen to him. He is alone on the Pnyx in the early dawn, and that aloneness is what comes to characterize our Just City throughout the comedy (though as the play proceeds we may come to question how just he actually is or whether justice can be associated with alone-ness).[8]

Dikaeopolis has come into Athens from the countryside to persuade the other citizens to secure peace with her enemies, but he pines for the peace of the countryside where the merchants would not bombard him and he would escape the busy-ness of the city. He longs for the quiet he enjoys in his own deme and for the deme itself (*eirênês erôn . . . ton d'emon demon pothôn*, 31–32) where they do not know the language of "buy."

Membership in the city means war and the commerce of the agora, that is, social interaction, though later in the comedy we will find him building his private agora, admitting perhaps that the isolation of which he dreams at the beginning is not a viable fantasy. At this early point in the comedy, however, he wants to be away from the shared hustle and bustle of the city, from the interdependence of those buying and selling. The quiet that he imagines awaits him on his own farm when he returns with his own private peace treaty will isolate him from others and distance him from the political action of the city. As the action of the play begins, all he sees in the city is the corruption of the ambassadors sent to Persia and the inaction of the Assembly.

In reaction to the failure of the city to pursue peace seriously and because of his longing for peace, he decides to turn himself into a city of one and arranges for a peace for himself alone (*monôi*, 131), "along with the children and the wife" (132). And off goes Dikaeopolis' private ambassador, who returns from Sparta with treaties for five, ten, and thirty years. Dikaeopolis selects the thirty years version and declares himself free of war and hardships, heading home to enjoy the Dionysia celebrated in the country (201–2). He has made his private peace. He has acted politically without the polis of Athens. As awkward as the linguistic construction sounds, he is his own polis.

This comedy, then, is built on the absurd premise of one man making a peace on his own with another city. The absurdity lies in the fact that this individual Athenian acted as if he were or could be free of the city, as if he were a tyrant like the Persian king but without the masses subject to his choices and decisions, as if (contrary not only to Aristotle) the boundaries around an individual and his family could be sufficient to create a polis. Individuals who are not tyrants do not make their own treaties with other cities. Individuals are not the actors in relations between cities. Cities—"the Lacedaemonians," "the Athenians" (plural)—are. Exile, exclusion of the citizen from the circle of the political actor, from the life of the city, is meant to be a hardship, a punishment. Dikaeopolis nevertheless craves the life of an exile, to be freed from all the choices the city makes. He longs for what others consider a punishment, but this is, after all, a comedy.

The Chorus in this comedy, consisting of the Acharnians of the comedy's title, comprises the Athenian citizens whose farms have been ravaged by the Spartans and who unhappily find themselves living within the boundaries of a city that is at war with Sparta. They are not pleased to discover that someone is making a treaty, "bearing truces (*spondophoros*)" (216), with the Spartans, and they pursue Dikaeopolis in order to hold him accountable for his self-separation from the political body. They, as a Chorus, are angered about the destruction of "my lands" (228). They will protect their vines, except, as all of the members of the Chorus say, "I will defend my vines" (226). The unity of the Chorus such that (for the most part) its members can speak as one at this point in the comedy comes from their shared loss of resources, from their shared membership in a deme, from their shared hostility to the ravagers of their lands. Leo Strauss sees them as "embody[ing] the spirit of the city: They are old men, Marathon fighters, the most passionate haters in Athens of the Spartans."[9] As such, they oppose the man who has denied sharing in the "spirit" and history of Athens by choosing to separate himself from the city they are defending.

While the angered Acharnians give vent to their spleen, Dikaeopolis appears with his wife and daughter to celebrate the thirty years of peace that is his alone and sing a song to Phallus, the symbol of private pleasures that will follow from the treaty that he has made only for himself (*spondas poiêsamenos emautôi*, 268–69). His joy in his private treaty, though, is disrupted when the Acharnians begin to throw stones at him, saying that he alone among them makes peace with the enemy (*hostis hêmôn monos/ speisamenos*, 290–91) and that he is a traitor (*prodota*, 289) of the fatherland. The city has defined for them their common friends and enemies.[10] Dikaeopolis defines them without reference to choices or actions of the city. Dikaeopolis, though, is not a traitor. He has not betrayed the city to its enemies. Another translation of *prodotos* is "abandoner," which more accurately captures what Dikaeopolis has done. He has abandoned the city by leaving its established political boundaries. He acts politically on his own while letting the Athenians deal with their affairs. He has not transferred his allegiances from one active city to another. He emphatically affirms twice during the comedy that "I hate the Spartans" (496, 509–10), and he twice adds to that affirmation that he would be happy if Poseidon would send an earthquake to swallow up the Spartans. His abandoning of the city of Athens and becoming his own city emerges from his eagerness for peace rather than war, not from a desire to attach himself to or seek inclusion in another collective body.

As with all of Aristophanes' comedies, the play goes in many directions and has multiple goals. One of the directions in this comedy is the exploration of the consequence of an absurd action such as Dikaeopolis takes.[11] And the consequence of the absurdity of the premise is portrayed as—maybe—not quite so absurd. In both the interchange with the Chorus before he acquires the rags from Euripides that are intended to make him appear more sympathetic and in the speech that he gives adorned in those rags, Dikaeopolis speaks of the Spartans as perhaps not being responsible (*aitious*, 310) for the war from which he chooses to withdraw. Later he will ask why the Athenians blame the Spartans (*Lakônas aitiômetha*, 514), and he even goes so far as to say: "It was one of our men (*hêmôn gar andres*), not the city (*tên polin*) I say" (515) who acted. He repeats himself in the next line to emphasize his point: "Remember this, it was not the city, I say" (516). From his stance outside the city, as the individual political actor suing for his own individual peace, he sees behind the unity of the city that he had apostrophized in the early moments of the play. He sees the individuals who act rather than the city as the political actor. He can blame those scurrilous men who initiated the Megarian Decree and not view it as the action of the city as a whole (517–19). In the way that only the comic poet could arrange, Dikaeopolis finds that the real source of the war involving all of Greece—what Thucydides calls "the greatest movement"—lies in the actions of three prostitutes (528–29).

When Dikaeopolis first suggests that the Lacedaemonians are not to blame for the Athenians' problems, the Acharnians can only see this as heresy; they respond by saying that anyone who does not blame the Spartans for their troubles is entirely evil (*panourge*, 311). Dikaeopolis, in contrast, by separating himself from the perspective the city offers him, is even able to see that perhaps the Spartans might be the "injured ones" (*adikoumenous*, 314). Freed from the boundaries of sharing that unite the Athenians in their battle with Sparta, Dikaeopolis takes the outsider's stance (given that this is a comedy, I avoid using the language of objectivity), a stance that enables him to see what the individuals within the city's compass, because of their shared perspective, cannot perceive. The creation of boundaries and their crystallization precludes the openness of a vantage point that enables observers to see multiple sides of the controversies. The Just City is just in this respect. Isolation or aloneness enables him to be the just observer.

Dikaeopolis may perhaps appear less than just, though, when the personal benefits of his new status become apparent. Having stepped outside the confines of the city, he almost becomes a modern-day liberal individual practicing the principles of what we today would call free trade. Unlike Athens protecting its economy through the creation of barriers against imports from other cities, Dikaeopolis trades with everyone in order to acquire whatever goods he desires. It is the Athenian general Lamachus representing the city who announces to the assembled cast onstage and in the audience: "I with every Peloponnesian will be at war and everywhere I will annoy them, with ships, with foot soldiers according to all my power" (620–22). In contrast, Dikaeopolis, having made his own treaty, immediately announces to the Peloponnesians that they and the Megarians and the Boeotians are all welcome to come to his agora. Not bound by the language of a city at war, he enjoys the pleasures that those within the city, respecting the borders that exclude those outside the city, cannot.

Nevertheless, when Dikaeopolis appears onstage after the Chorus' long speech, he himself begins by setting up the boundaries that will demarcate his market. The word for boundary introduces the first line of his speech: *horoi men agoras eisin oide tês emês* ("These are the borders of my agora," 719). Even as he opens his market to all and erects the stele announcing his treaty with Sparta so that it will be clearly visible to all, he acknowledges the need for boundaries, the clarification of where his space begins and where it ends. A series of visitors to his agora engage in a series of trades (not always of the most elegant kind, but after all this is comedy), and his commercial transactions, such as they are, provide the sort of indulgences appropriate for the comic stage. The members of the Chorus, so hostile previously, but observing the pleasures he enjoys, now see a "blessed man" (*eudaimonei g' anthrôpos*) sitting in his marketplace (836). By the end of this scene, even the general Lamachus, who had proclaimed eternal enmity with Sparta, is sending his slave to make purchases in Dikaeopolis' market.

Instead of being called a traitor or "abandoner," Dikaeopolis now finds himself called a wise and super-smart man (*ton phronimon andra, ton hupersophon*, 971–72) for whom goods seem to come almost automatically (*automata*, 977). Watching Dikaeopolis lead this life of pleasure affects the Chorus. The anger they felt towards him dissolves, and they now say that they will never welcome Polemos (War) into their homes. A transformation has taken place. War, not the enemy Sparta, sets their vines on fire (986–87). Others now appear in Dikaeopolis' agora wanting a piece of his peace, as a tiller of the soil says, "even if it is only five years" (1021). But Dikaeopolis, who has chosen to isolate himself from the world of those who share, decides to keep the peace for himself. He has defined himself by his independent political action, and if he were to share his peace with Sparta—or even just make something common (*koinos*)—he would put himself back into the construction of a city.[12] He does, however, share the peace with a young bride, "since she is a woman and does not deserve (*azia*) war" (1062).

The comedy basically ends with the contrast between Dikaeopolis anticipating and then enjoying the feast that is his because he became his own political actor making his own treaty with Sparta, and Lamachus preparing for battle with ostrich plumes in his helmet but no bird meat—only stale salt fish—on his table. When Lamachus returns from battle injured and rattled, Dikaeopolis is exulting in his gustatory and sexual delights and is hailed the *kallinikos* (1028), the gloriously triumphant one. According to the inversions of comedy, the one finding peace apart from the city is the one who is granted the title normally assigned to military heroes. The comedy indeed turns the world upside down as the sharing of the city is joyously abandoned for the private pleasures that can only be experienced by rejecting the city's encompassing boundaries.

Dikaeopolis' solipsistic delight may, however, evoke some discomfort as the audience watches the portrayal of this pleasure-grubbing individual. Forgotten is the nobility that the city can offer to its members, the glories that are captured in Pericles' Funeral Oration where the soldiers make for themselves "shrines wherein their glory is laid up to be eternally remembered upon every occasion on which deed or story shall call for its commemoration" (2.43).[13] Such memorials await only the man who welcomes incorporation into the whole that the city has become, not the one who escapes from its psychological boundaries and indulges in his tables laden with roasted thrushes and pigeons. It is almost as if Aristophanes in this comedy is capturing well *avant la lettre* the tension between the self-centered liberal individual of the modern age and his or her republican counterpart, along with the pacifist and militaristic stances of each. In this comedy, it is the "liberal," pleasure-seeking individual focusing on peace and eschewing the language of friends and enemies who wins, though there remains the undercurrent of the virtues and nobility that are lost with the creation of the unique rather than the corporate actor.

The *Lysistrata*

At line 142 of the *Lysistrata*, Lysistrata, the protagonist of Aristophanes' comedy about a sex strike, says to Lampito, who hails from Sparta and has heeded Lysistrata's call to come to an early-morning meeting: *Zumpsêphisai moi* (Vote with me!). Using the verbal form of *psêphos* (vote), Lysistrata has alerted us to the political background of her actions. She is urging Lampito to participate in a group that will decide on a communal action intended to have both political and private consequences, namely, ending the war and bringing their husbands back to their beds. Even though the women come from distinct cities with distinct political regimes and boundaries—cities that are currently at war with one another—Lysistrata imagines (and will create) a Panhellenic conspiracy calling forth women from across Greece to come to her assembly as ambassadors (*presbeira*, 86). In addition to Lampito from Sparta, there are women from Thebes and from Corinth. Creating a little United Nations of women, they deliberate and take action, agreeing (albeit with some resistance) to the sex strike Lysistrata proposes, with the expectation that it will force their absent husbands to cease hostilities and return home, to create a world in which "no one of the men shall lift a sword against others" (49–50). Of course, this is comedy, and, of course, the women do not constitute a city, but the language that Aristophanes gives them enables them to capture the unity of purpose that characterizes the political agent. By acting together, they imagine that they can change the world, and—at least on the comic stage—they do.

When Lysistrata initially reveals her plan to her Athenian co-conspirator Calonike, she envisions that this newly formed political actor composed of women from a multitude of cities will be the salvation of the whole of Greece (*holês tês Helados . . . hê sôtêria*, 29–30). As she says, they will ensure that "the affairs of our city (*en hêmin tês poleôs pragmata*) do not cease to be," and not only "our city," but the affairs of the Peloponnesians and the Boeotians as well (33–35). Emphasizing the effect of a unified political actor composed of women, Lysistrata almost repeats herself shortly after: "If the women come together here, those from Boeotia and those from the Peloponnese, we together (*koinêi*) shall save Hellas" (39–41). The *koinê* Lysistrata uses emphasizes the shared or common endeavor of a political actor created by their common goals.

In Aristophanes' *Ecclesiazusae*, the women will take over the assembly within the framework of Athenian democracy; here, Lysistrata founds her own assembly where the women gather, deliberate, and vote. She creates—albeit briefly—a new political actor. Unlike Dikaeopolis, she cannot achieve her goal alone or even just within the boundaries of the city in which she lives. By founding this new political actor, Lysistrata violates a range of previously established boundaries. Her Panhellenism specifically ignores the boundaries that separate poleis at war, and she ignores the boundary between the male and female spheres of action that characterizes all the cities of ancient Greece, one that seems naturally to exclude the female from entering the public realm of deliberation even if—or especially if—it concerns the salvation of Greece.[14] The Panhellenic actor that Lysistrata creates is female. The political actor in ancient Greece is male. While Lysistrata breaks down the conventional boundaries, she creates new ones. No men belong in her deliberative body; they are the outsiders who are now subject to the decisions of the newly united women. Lysistrata ignores the rules defining who was entitled to be a citizen that had developed over the sixth and fifth centuries in Athens; new rules defining the community for shared political action are articulated to revise the boundaries that had been marked by gender, family, and territory.

When the action of the play begins, the women from Sparta arrive in Athens under the cover of early-morning darkness; next, a Theban and a Corinthian woman arrive. When she welcomes Lampito, Lysistrata calls her "My dearest (*philtatê*) Spartan woman" and remarks on her beauty. We need to remember that when Lysistrata says these words onstage, Sparta and Athens are at war with one another. Thucydides, to mark the transition from peace to war, writes at the very end of Book 1 of his *History* that the Spartans and Athenians mingled with one another (uneasily) without official messengers, but then, in the very first lines of Book 2, he explains that once the war began, there was no "mingling" without official messengers. The permeable boundaries between the cities become fixed barriers during war; movements across those boundaries are acts of war. For the women of the *Lysistrata*, ignoring those boundaries is an act of friendship and peace. The women blatantly ignore the force of the barriers established by the male citizens that each city hardened when the war began.

As the old barriers crumple, however, new barriers emerge; there must be something that unites the members of the new community to enable that community to come into being—the "What is shared?" question that Aristotle asks in Book 2 of the *Politics*. In the case of the *Lysistrata*, that shared something is, of course, sex, or more specifically the desire for sex. As Manville develops in his discussion of the emergence of Athenian citizenship, complex factors from land ownership to ancestry come into play to identify who is in and who is out and how membership in the citizen body is to be defined. In Aristophanes' comic world, it is the predominant desire for sex that constructs the criteria for membership for Lysistrata's new community. And because the desire for sex is universal, the sharing comes to include all rather than exclude. When the women from across Greece are assembled, Lysistrata asks them all: "Do you not long for the fathers of your children when they are away at war?" (99–100). With apparent delight, Lysistrata remarks: "Oh how utterly lewd is our whole race (*genos*)" (137). They all experience sexual loneliness when their husbands are away at war. It is just that shared lewdness that allows the "race of women" to become an effective political actor.[15] The women are not simply a gender in contrast to the men, at least in Lysistrata's opinion; they are a race, a stock, united by more than their opposition to the men. They are bound by common longings, which they show are shared by men as well. They define themselves not by opposition to others, but by identifying what unifies them. When the women swear allegiance to one another, they do so with objects different from those that men might use. The comedy of the women swearing by a wine sack emphasizes how much they differ from the men, but the premise of this play assumes that everyone—male and female—shares the desire for sex. This bond sanctions the Panhellenism that ends the play as Lysistrata says to both Spartan and Athenian men: "You purify yourselves with the same water at the altar like kinsmen (*zuggeineis*) at Olympia, at Pylae, at Pytho—how many others I could name if I had to speak at length" (1129).

In a well-known passage, Lysistrata compares the handling of the affairs of the city to weaving; the imagery emphasizes the blending together of all into a panel of common or shared goodwill (*koinên eunoian*). Significantly, her weaving metaphor includes the metics and any stranger (*xenos*) "who is your friend," and then she even adds, "by Zeus, the cities, which are colonies of this land." She proposes that they think of these lands, though they lie apart from one another, as the source from which wool is drawn and woven together into one big cloak for the people (*tôi dêmôi*, 579–83). The task, as the women see it, is to bring together what is distant rather than to separate what is near. The solution to their husband's warmongering is to ignore the boundaries rather than fortify them. In a comic reference to trade restrictions set up by the Athenians, the leader of the Women's Chorus complains that her nearby friend (the sexually suggestive Boeotian eel) cannot come because of decrees that have been passed by the men (700–4). Barriers—trade barriers, as in the *Acharnians*—preclude joy. Pleasures arrive only when the boundaries that separate cities from one another dissolve.

The boundaries that demarcate cities may allow for the virtues associated with battles and extolled in Pericles' Funeral Oration, but they work against the satisfaction of our carnal (and comic) desires. Initially, the men mistakenly—as Lysistrata sees it—place war and its potential for glory above the desire for sex as the uniting factor. The men do not understand themselves, and central to the action of the play is the effort to make them aware of desires that are more powerful than those that unite them in seeking glory for the city. The men see the unity of the political actor in terms of physical and psychological boundaries that let them share a land, a history, a *politeia* and ancestry that define the city. The women understand unity in terms of the common needs that come from their bodies. The men think that preserving the sanctity of those boundaries that separate cities allows for the glory that comes from a war that protects those boundaries. Pericles in Thucydides speaks of the "admiration of the present and succeeding ages" that "will be ours, since we have not left our power without witness, but shown it by mighty proofs; and far from needing a Homer for our panegyrist, or others of his craft whose verses might charm for the moment only . . . we have forced every sea and land to be the highway of our daring" (2.41). Lysistrata intends to show the men on Aristophanes' stage—and in the audience—that while a longing for admiration such as Thucydides' Pericles promises may appear to motivate and unite them, the real basis for unity is a private longing for the pleasures of sexual relations.

As Helene Foley points out, the denouement of the comedy "emphasize[s] the common, not the exclusive interests of the sexes."[16] The regular joke on Aristophanes' stage is that the men's bodies make evident the power of sexual desire, a desire that comes to trump any infatuation with an immaterial Periclean vision. The political understanding of the women concerning what unites them and leads them to political action is that what they share comes from their own bodies and not from the search for noble glory either for themselves or for the cities to which they belong. Once the men change perspectives away from exclusion based on the physical separation of cities that leads to war and its imagined glories, they can refocus on inclusion—the longing for sex that they all share with one another, male and female. These desires become visually apparent with the arrival of the Spartan emissary, whose cloak will not stay close to his body, a difficulty faced by his Athenian counterpart as well. Acknowledging their evident shared sexual needs, the men find that they need to join the Panhellenic peace and focus on what is common rather than on what separates them as citizens.

The underlying tension in this play, as in the *Acharnians* as well, is whether by abandoning the war and the securing of their boundaries, men forsake as well what it means to be human, turning themselves into physical bodies and satisfying only their physical longings. Abandoning war, they abandon as well Pericles' vision and transform themselves into peaceful creatures copulating with their wives. Having made this transition, though, are they still human? Aristophanes' comedy often achieves its humor by turning the human being into an animal, sometimes literally, as in the *Birds*, but more often by highlighting the carnal drives that control the human being, from eating to evacuation to sex. Though the needs and longings of the physical body point out to the Spartans and Athenians their commonality and lead to the end of the war so that all parties can satisfy those longings, we might ask whether the men then lose the capacity to rise above those shared physical longings. Are the boundaries that mark the city needed to define a political actor who is more than a simple physical being longing for sexual satisfaction?

We are back to Aristotle's question about sharing: If it is only our desiring animal nature that we share, does the Panhellenism that Lysistrata proposes appeal? As with Dikaeopolis becoming a single citizen in his own polis, not sharing anything, only exchanging through commerce so as to enjoy the sensual pleasures of piggies and wine, does this remove human beings from sharing the communal goals that raise them above their base desires? While the *Lysistrata* began as an effort by the women to bring their men home so that they could have sex again, Lysistrata's dream goes further. From the beginning, Lysistrata affirmed that the women are not simply the self-centered pursuers of sexual pleasures in their own homes. They are to be the saviors of Greece. The Chorus of old women attacks the Acropolis in order to gain access to the treasury with the hope that the women can then deliver Hellas and the citizens (*politas*) from war and madness (432–43). But the Proboulos, speaking for the old men, confronts them: How shall they preserve themselves if the money is taken away from the city? Lysistrata responds that the women, unlike the men, do not need war. And so they will not only save themselves, but they also will save the men (498), and as she later explains, they will save all of Hellas in common (*koinei*, 525)—all without engaging in war. Not only the city will be preserved; Hellas in common (*koinêi*, 525) will be saved.

In the bantering back and forth between the old men defending the Acropolis and the women attacking it about whether war is the purview of men or women, there is the undercurrent of how to define boundaries. The men at war and the Athenian men up on the Acropolis defending the treasury understand war as protecting the boundaries that separate Athens from other cities in Greece. The women claiming that they are the ones whom war concerns (535) want to erase the boundaries that allow for wars between the cities. The comedy, though, does not end by following the Panhellenic principles of the women who were ready to dissolve the lines separating them from one another. Instead, when *Diallagê* (Reconciliation, 1113), appears, the delegates divide her up for themselves as if she were a carcass, and when peace is secured with pledges of mutual trust, Lysistrata proclaims: "Each of you may reclaim his own wife and go home" (1185). From the unity of the women acting on the political stage breaking down old boundaries, the privacy of the individual homes surfaces as the Athenian delegates urge the Spartans to lead away their wives (1275). Lysistrata's Panhellenism fades with the accomplishment of her ends. The common satisfaction of physical desires is not sufficient to unite all or to overcome the boundaries that have been established between cities.

A curious choral intervention comes toward the end of the comedy. The Men's Chorus invites all to take whatever possessions the Chorus has but then qualifies the offer by noting that there is nothing in the house "unless someone has sharper eyes than mine" (1201–2). The Chorus offers grain as well—but there isn't much; the Chorus declares that the doors are open to all—but a dog guards the entrance (1205–15). The contradictions in the Chorus' speech capture the dialectic of the comedy. On the one hand, we have the openness of Lysistrata's Panhellenism, according to which the boundaries that separate cities and their citizens dissolve. Yet at the conclusion of the play, the Chorus reaffirms the status of boundaries that define what is ours and what belongs to another. Panhellenism comes across as a comic fantasy; the boundaries that lead to conflict and war do not. While the Athenian delegate urges that they never forget the peace that the great souled Aphrodite fashioned (1289–90), the Spartan delegate, amid the festivities of the final song and dance, honors the Spartan gods (1296–1321).

The *Ecclesiazusae*

The curious invitation that the Chorus makes at the end of the *Lysistrata* mocks the imagined unity Lysistrata's envisions. It is a reminder that the real effort of the women is not the shared political community of Panhellenism, but the retreat into the privacy of the family, where each wife attends to her own husband and each husband's longing is satisfied by his own wife.[17] Praxagora in the *Ecclesiazusae* creates a city in which all is shared: sex, wine, houses. Nothing is private. Boundaries disappear. Praxagora is the force behind the coup d'état that is to save the city from the worthless men who have been her leaders. The initial impetus is the preservation of Athens the city, and Praxagora's speech explains how the female can save Athens because women preserve the old way of doing things. The examples they offer—from dying wool to roasting barley to taking lovers (214–28)—do not tell us how such skills will save the city. Indeed, that knowledge of the old ways to which they initially appeal plays no role in the radically new regime Praxagora is about to institute.

To be in a position to implement Praxagora's plans to save Athens, the women must first take over the Assembly (*ecclesia*) and vote power to themselves. Whereas the women of the *Lysistrata* sexualized themselves with rouge and diaphanous gowns, the women of the *Ecclesiazusae* desexualize themselves, transforming themselves insofar as is possible into males—growing hair where Athenian women plucked, tanning their bodies, and speaking in deep voices. They need to elide the differences between the male and the female and ignore those boundaries that separate them. In order to make the argument (such as it is) for giving political power to the women, Praxagora points out how well the women handle the affairs of the household—from dying wool to cooking to baking to deceiving their husbands (214–40). She conceives of the city simply as a big household. The difference between the two is nothing more than size.[18] Violating the principles that Aristotle articulates at the beginning of the *Politics*, when he emphasizes the difference between the city and the family, Praxagora highlights the similarities between the two and enacts legislation that makes the analogy more than an analogy, that is, the city becomes the family sharing all. The walls that divide households are demolished. Privacy disappears, and no boundaries separate the family from the public realm of the city. The two meld into one.

Praxagora's proposal is radical in so many ways, but let me focus on the obliteration of the boundaries between public and private. Sally Humphreys writes in her book on the family: "The contrast between public and private life in classical Athens was sharp. . . . Monumental architecture clearly differentiated public buildings, religious and secular, from private houses."[19] Praxagora proposes (and gets passed) laws that remove those traditional distinctions. Monumental architecture no longer distinguishes public from private. The port becomes the wine cellar for the city; the monumental architecture of the courtrooms and the stoas becomes the architecture of the dining rooms. In Athenian democracy, the lottery was used to determine which jurors went to which courtrooms. In Praxagora's new regime, in which courtrooms will not be necessary, that machinery will be used to determine the dining rooms to which citizens will go for feasting and drinking. Jugs and mixing bowls for the wine will be stored in the speaker's dais.

One of the claims that Praxagora makes about why women should be given the chance to rule in Athens is that they are so good at sharing—be it their own possessions or secrets. They are not controlled by those distinctions that separate the private from what is common. When they acquire power, they decree that there is to be no private ownership of property, a provision that leads to the scene with one man lamenting the loss of his adored chamber pot. Similarly with sexual relations; they are no longer exclusive, because any man can sleep with any woman. So that all can share in sexual pleasures, and not only the young and beautiful, a man must sleep with an ugly old woman before he can enjoy a young woman. Likewise for the women, who must first sleep with old men before they can enjoy the lovemaking of a youth. This provision allows for the infamous scene of three old hags fighting over the opportunity to sleep with a young man, who is himself eager to sleep with his beautiful young girlfriend. Under the new regime that Praxagora establishes, theft and adultery lose their meaning as boundaries between property and marital partners dissolve. Further, all will share parents; older men become fathers to all and older women mothers. Thus, in addition to theft and adultery losing their meaning, so does incest. The beautiful young maiden, who must wait for her lover to sleep with the old hag, warns that the city will be populated with Oedipuses (1042).

When Praxagora's husband wonders how this plan to make all common will work, Praxagora explains: "I shall first of all make the land common (*koinên*) and the silver and whatever belongs to each one" (596–98; cf. 661, 671). She describes how the women will nourish the inhabitants of the city from the common treasury. A neighbor realizes that now "life will be from what is common (*ek koinou*)" (610). Praxagora explains to her husband that if his cloak is taken away, he will be able to go to the central store and bring back a better one "out of what is common (*ek tou koinou*)" (671). Reiterating her plan to her somewhat dense husband, who asks in some amazement, "What way of life will you make?" she repeats the theme she has articulated numerous times before: "A common one for all. I say that I will make the city one household ripping down everything into one so that it is possible to walk into each others' places" (673–75).[20]

The political regime and legal system entrusted with the enforcement of the boundaries between different families and with the punishments that attend the transgression of those boundaries become irrelevant. No judgments in law courts will take place because with no individual families or households, no crimes will be committed. As the family spreads to take over all, the city recedes into nothingness. Indeed, the consequence of this breaking down of all barriers and the elimination of the city is the obliteration of the political actor. There is no political actor without boundaries. Athens in a sense disappears, and all that is left is a family to satisfy the pleasures of the body with food, wine, and sex from a common source. Scarcity is not a problem because slaves will do all the work. The fantastical vision of the delightful city become family, though, ignores the threats that might come from beyond the borders of the city itself. The issue of war is not considered. While Praxagora has dissolved the boundaries within the city, she has not dissolved those boundaries that separate one city from another, as Lysistrata had tried to do with her Panhellenism. Praxagora has ignored the threat of war and thus eliminated the need for the political actor.[21] Once the city becomes a family and all is shared in common, the question of who acts fades into meaningless and the entire city follows the Chorus' call to feasting and celebration, one not qualified by any warning about scarcity of goods or about threatening watchdogs, as at the end of the *Lysistrata*.

From her initial practice speech to her co-conspirators on, Praxagora had ignored the differences between the polis and the household; the former was just a larger version of the latter. Both could be governed (and saved) by the same principles. When Aristotle introduces his *Politics* by affirming the difference between the polis and the household, he does so because he sees in the polis the venue for the human being to reach a fulfillment that goes beyond reproduction and preservation of the body. That fulfillment, though, depends on just the sort of distinctions that Praxagora wants to remove. By ignoring the boundaries that articulate the differences between city and family, between noble and ignoble, she eliminates politics from human experience. Unlike Lysistrata, who aimed at expanding the boundaries of the political actor to the whole of Hellas, and unlike Dikaeopolis who created the singular political actor, Praxagora makes the political actor disappear. Perhaps we should pay more attention to her name—one doing things in the marketplace—than to the title of the comedy—women attending the assembly. The political actor of the title gets overshadowed during the course of the play by the economic—in the full sense of that word—actor.

Conclusion

In Book 3 of the *Politics*, Aristotle clarifies for his readers what the city is not: it is not defined by the sharing of location, by agreements not to commit economic injustices, or by the practices of intermarriage. His understanding of the city entails sharing, but sharing of a particular kind: that of a regime or way of life focused on a shared concern with virtue. Aristophanes is a comic poet, and we cannot expect from him the consistency of argument that we might expect to find in Aristotle. While Aristophanes clearly intends to make his audiences laugh and smirk, he also captures the concerns that motivate Aristotle in his exploration of what in the world the city may be. The three comedies considered above point to the difficulty of defining what it is that we share in order to become political beings, beings that are more than pleasure-seeking animals. They clearly point to the instability of the traditional boundaries that define community and that originate in convention and history, but they also suggest how a desire to ignore those conventional and historical boundaries complicates the identification of the political actor. And they make clear what is lost when the "who" of political action becomes obscure. The comic characters freed from conventional boundaries enjoy themselves in a multitude of ways related to the body, but can they, without a clearly defined polis, go beyond those limited pleasures?

The challenge of Aristophanes' playful exploration of the status of boundaries and of the nature of what is shared leads to some darker questions that we usually do not associate with comedy. They force us to consider the degree to which we value boundaries that demand exclusion along with inclusion. They lead us to address with perhaps some discomfort the degree to which Carl Schmitt's emphasis on the identification of friend and enemy, an emphasis that requires boundaries without attention to whether they are natural or not, becomes a central part of our understanding of the polity and of the political actor. Schmitt wrote in *The Concept of the Political*: "Political thought and political instinct prove themselves theoretically and practically in the ability to distinguish friend and enemy. The high points of politics are simultaneously the moments in which the enemy is, in concrete clarity, recognized as the enemy."[22] The comedies discussed above all want to escape the identification of the enemy and focus on commonalities. At the same time, though, they point to the consequences of such an escape. Aristophanes enables us to look at these troubling concerns with the comic's eye, and in the absurdity of the theatrical presentations they capture some of the dark challenges such issues present.

Notes

1. I use the translation of Herodotus by David Grene, *Histories* (Chicago: University of Chicago Press, 1987).

2. Maurice Pope, "Thucydides and Democracy," *Historia: Zeitschrift für Alte Geschichte* 37 (no. 3, 1988), develops this argument.

3. Philip Brook Manville, *The Origins of Citizenship in Ancient Athens* (Princeton, NJ: Princeton University of Press, 1990); see also chapter 9 in Josiah Ober, *Athenian Legacies: Essays on the Politics of Going on Together* (Princeton, NJ: Princeton University Press, 2005).

4. Manville, *The Origins of Citizenship*, 150.

5. Manville, *The Origins of Citizenship*, 156.

6. Compare Alcibiades' speech to the Spartans in Thucydides 6.89–92.

7. All translations of Aristophanes are my own except as noted.

8. The relation of Dikaeopolis as the Just City to Socrates' Kallipolis in Plato's *Republic* with regard to this issue is worthy of further reflection, for which I do not have space here.

9. Leo Strauss, *Socrates and Aristophanes* (New York: Basic Books, 1966), 60.

10. I make reference to thought of Carl Schmitt in the conclusion to this chapter, but I alert the reader at this point to the shadow of Schmitt lurking over discussions of the necessity of boundaries.

11. Paul W. Ludwig, "A Portrait of the Artist: Justice and Self-Interest in Aristophanes' *Acharnians*," *American Political Science Review* 101 (no. 3, 2007): 479–92, appropriately calls these sorts of absurdities "thought experiments" (479).

12. Ludwig, "A Portrait of the Artist," 479, sees the contradictions here between Dikaeopolis' name and his lack of willingness to show a concern with others.

13. For Thucydides, I use the translation by Richard Crawley, *The Peloponnesian War*, intro. T. E. Wick (New York: Random House, 1982).

14. See further Helene Foley, "The 'Female Intruder' Reconsidered: Women in Aristophanes' *Lysistrata* and *Ecclesiazusae*," *Classical Philology* 77 (no. 1, 1982): 1–21.

15. We might note the different goal of the women here from that in the *Ecclesiazusae*. The latter are eager to save the city; the women of the *Lysistrata* want to abandon the city as the defining unit and focus on the pleasures of the individual.

16. Foley, "The 'Female Intruder' Reconsidered," 5.

17. It has often been remarked on that the *Lysistrata* ignores the obvious presence of prostitutes in the ancient Greek cities. Apart from considering how acknowledgement of the availability of prostitutes would have destroyed the plot, the comedy also relies on the affirmation of sex as practiced within the context of the family, thus capturing the conflicting needs of the family and the city. See further Arlene W. Saxonhouse, "Men, Women, War, and Politics: Family and Polis in Aristophanes and Euripides," *Political Theory* 8 (no. 1, 1980): 65–81.

18. Foley, "The 'Female Intruder' Reconsidered," 6–7, writes about how Lysistrata engages in the same fantasies when she "envisions the agora as an enlarged domestic sphere into which the men have inappropriately admitted war." Foley continues: "[A]s the play proceeds the distinction between acropolis and home collapses; the action in the public and private worlds becomes one. . . . The acropolis becomes like a household."

19. Sally Humphreys, *The Family, Women and Death: Comparative Studies* (London: Routledge and Kegan Paul, 1983), 1.

20. I explore the significance of these proposals for the capacity to make normative judgments in Arlene W. Saxonhouse, *Fear of Diversity: The Birth of Political Science in Ancient Greek Thought* (Chicago: University of Chicago Press, 1992), 108.

21. As Foley, "The 'Female Intruder" Reconsidered," 18, notes, "Praxagora can equate domestic and civic management only by eliminating foreign policy and the legislative and judicial functions of the city."

22. Carl Schmitt, *The Concept of the Political*, ed. and trans. George Schwab (Chicago: University of Chicago Press, 2007 [1932]), 67.

6

Aristophanes and the Polis

Stephanie Nelson

Aristophanes' relation to Athens is paradoxical. His comedy subverts nearly all the cultural ideals of the Greek polis, celebrating the old, the ugly, and the physical, not to mention lawless individuality, yet it was written and produced as part of a state festival (or rather two state festivals) that celebrated Athens. As is evident from the ceremonies that permeated the Greater Dionysia—the opening sacrifice made by Athens' most important officials, the generals; the awarding of honors; the display of tribute brought by the allies; the parade of war orphans, given their armor by the city upon their coming of age—the festival was designed to display the splendor and power of the city to its citizens and the international audience that attended.[1] Even more importantly, Aristophanes continually describes himself, in no uncertain terms, as a servant of the city. From his first extant play, the *Acharnians*, to his last fifth-century play, the *Frogs*, the comic poet consistently portrays himself as the city's champion, battling her enemies and benefiting the city as a "deliverer from evil and cleanser of this-here land" (*Wasps* 1043; cf. *Acharnians* 630ff., *Knights* 507ff., *Peace* 759–60, *Wasps* 1017ff., *Frogs* 686–87).[2] Yet his comic heroes abandon Athens (*Acharnians*, *Birds*), celebrate their own villainy (*Knights*), defy all civic restrictions and responsibilities (*Wasps*), infiltrate sacred spaces, including even the Acropolis (*Women at the Thesmophoria*, *Lysistrata*), and defy the gods (*Peace*, *Birds*, *Wealth*).

Scholarship has tended to approach this problem by treating the issues of Aristophanes' politics and of his comedy in isolation. With the exception of Niall Slater's excellent work, considered below, the extensive debate on

Aristophanes' relation to politics has ignored the elements of his comedy that are considered nonpolitical: fantasy, wordplay, inversion of values, defiance of logic, and general subversion. This is particularly true of Aristophanes' use of metatheater, where the playwright breaks through the illusion of the drama and points out that this is a play that we are watching. Similarly, studies that specifically address the dynamics of Aristophanes' comedy, such as the work of Michael Silk or Charles Platter, tend to underplay the question of Aristophanes' involvement with the city or see it as a carnivalesque release, a model ill suited to a state-sponsored festival.[3] The result, I believe, is that a crucial element of Aristophanic comedy has been missed. The center of gravity around which Aristophanes' plays balance themselves is indeed Athens, but it is not the Athens of contemporary politics that is his primary comic concern. Aristophanes does not, like the *Colbert Report*, use comedy as a way to approach politics. Rather, he uses contemporary politics as a way to address his primary subject, which is the irrationality of the city itself.

Aristophanes would not be the first to see Athens, and her democracy in particular, as touched with an element of the irrational. In a rather sardonic comment, Herodotus (a supporter of Athens) describes Aristagoras' success in getting the Athenian Assembly to intervene in Ionia, after he had failed with Cleomenes in Sparta, by saying that "it seems that it is easier to fool many men than one" (5.97). In his speech to the Spartans, his newfound compatriots, Alcibiades describes the Athenian democracy as "an acknowledged madness" (Thucydides 6.89). Plato similarly describes democracy as "the charming constitution, anarchic and motley, that awards equality to equals and unequals alike" (*Republic* 538c), while the Old Oligarch (or pseudo-Xenophon) describes Athens as a place where the advice of rascals is preferred to that of good men (*Constitution of the Athenians* 1.6, 2.19, 3.10), disorder is preferred to order (1.8), and no distinction is made between free men and slaves (1.10ff.).

With the exception of Herodotus, the above are attacks made by opponents of democracy. Similar contradictory impulses, however, crop up in Pericles' praise of democracy, where he claims that Athens allows everyone to pursue his own humor without comment or ill will (Thucydides 2.37) and that she expects everyone to participate in polis affairs (2.40), that Athens obtains friends by granting benefits (2.40), and that her domination is a tyranny (2.63). While the Athenians were horrified by the prospect of tyranny (as *Wasps* 486–89), they were, as above, perfectly willing to be a tyrant over others. The democracy actively encouraged the ambitious and yet feared them, alternately elevating and punishing its leading men (as

Thucydides 2.65, *Knights* 1121ff.).[4] Athens was a city that prided herself on its leisure (Thucydides 2.38, Old Oligarch 3.2) yet never rested (Thucydides 1.70), that saw itself as both tyrant over its league (Thucydides 2.63, 3.37; *Knights* 1114) and its benevolent leader (Thucydides 1.77), and was both astounding in its ability to persist through defeat (Thucydides 8.1, 24) and completely unpredictable in its willingness to alter direction (*Acharnians* 630–32, Thucydides 3.27, Old Oligarch 2.17).

Aside from the particular nature of Athens, there is something inherently contradictory in the idea of democracy itself. As Aristophanes points out in the *Acharnians* or *Knights*, the democratic Assembly, designed to direct the city's officers, is instead directed by them. The very nature of the institution, moreover, places individual citizens in the paradoxical position of being the source of policies they themselves may personally oppose. And, in Plato's favorite irrationality, the citizens together are supposed to be competent to direct matters of which none of them individually has any particular knowledge (as *Protagoras* 319aff.).[5] As in Churchill's famous comment that democracy is the worst form of government—except for all the others that have been tried—there seems to be an abundant source for humor in Athens without ever getting to contemporary politics at all.

The observation that contemporary politics does not in fact lie at the heart of Aristophanes' comedy does not mean, however, that it plays no role at all. Aristophanes' plays are studded with references to contemporary Athenians and current events, an effect that would be all the more noticeable when comedy was viewed, as it was in Athens, against the backdrop of tragedy, which excluded any such reference. Although the issue of Aristophanes' involvement in politics has occasioned extensive debate, the primary fact that Aristophanes himself positions his own plays, and Old Comedy generally, directly in the fray makes it difficult to doubt that the plays were indeed political.[6] But there also seems to be an ulterior motive. The contemporary politics of an Aristophanes play does not analyze the issues at hand; rather, it makes it clear that Aristophanes' topic is the actual city in which the spectators live. Tragedy, in Aristophanes' world, concerned itself with universals. Comedy addressed what was irrational in the here and now of the audience.

This use of contemporary politics also explains the curious fact that Aristophanes, for all his reference to contemporary events, actually offers very little concrete advice. Even in the case of *Knights*, Aristophanes' most clearly political play, the reason for the attack on Cleon is only partially the danger that he posed to the city. A more immediate reason is that Cleon is

Aristophanes' pet target. As Cratinus had Pericles as his iconic political foe, and as Eupolis had Hyperbolus, Aristophanes uses his opposition to Cleon as a defining feature of his poetry from his earliest plays until well after Cleon's death.[7] The relation appears most clearly in an oddity that is not often remarked on: although Aristophanes studs his plays with the names of contemporary politicians, Cleon is the only one whom he attacks in more than passing. The one exception, the attacks on Pericles for initiating the war (*Acharnians* 524ff., *Peace* 605ff.), has limited relevance because at the time that the *Acharnians* was produced, Pericles had been dead for more than four years.

While it is perfectly likely that Aristophanes saw Cleon as dangerous to the city (as did Thucydides), this does not explain why Cleon is the only political figure whom he systematically attacks. Nor is the exclusivity unusual; Aristophanes often uses an actual person as the representative of an entire subject: when he wishes to attack intellectuals he uses Socrates; when he wants to attack militarism he uses Lamachus; Cleonymus represents cowards, Chaerephon the followers of sophists, and so on.[8] In the case of Cleon, moreover, Aristophanes' attacks had as much to do with the intense rivalry of the comic poets as it did with an involvement in politics. In a relationship that is increasingly being studied, just as Cratinus used Pericles as his particular target and Eupolis used Hyperbolus (even poaching on Aristophanes' territory by adopting the *Knights* to attack Hyperbolus in his *Maricas*), Aristophanes seems to have marked out a particular territory, centered in Cleon and the war, as his own.[9] That he also, and in a very similar way, adopted Euripides and the "new education" as a target indicates that the motivation behind his dramatized battle with Cleon was not purely political.

Aristophanes' involvement in contemporary politics, genuine as it most likely was, was clearly also employed for other ends. This may explain why the plays, despite appearances, actually offer very little concrete political advice. In the *Acharnians*, *Peace*, and *Lysistrata*, Aristophanes suggests that the Peloponnesian War is a bad thing. In the *Knights* and *Wasps*, he points out that politicians are self-serving. And in the *Frogs*, he warns that the citizens should look after the good of the state as a whole. None of this is likely to make the headlines. Moreover, with the exception of the *Frogs*, where Aristophanes recommends the recall of the exiled oligarchs, even the parabases of the plays suggest nothing more specific than that the Athenians should recognize true merit (mostly his own) and stop being duped by self-seeking politicians and flatterers (*Acharnians* 633ff., *Peace* 736ff., *Wasps* 1014ff., and so on). The advice, as a number of studies have recently pointed out, has much more to do with metatheater and intertextual rivalry between poets than it does with current politics.[10] What it demonstrates is Aristophanes' involvement with the here and now of Athens and the intrinsic connection of that involvement with his comedy.

Aristophanes' target is not, primarily, the specifics of contemporary Athenian politics. It is instead contemporary Athens itself. As Niall Slater has demonstrated, Aristophanes' overall theme of unmasking bombast marries his politics and his comedy.[11] And as the image of "unmasking" implies, the connection lies in Aristophanes' overall tendency to metatheater. By persistently connecting theatrical role playing with Athens and her democratic processes, Aristophanes teaches the citizens to look beyond appearances to the reality that underlies them. In this way, as Slater has shown, Aristophanes' comedy has an intrinsic connection to politics. The drama of the Greater Dionysia and Lenaia, comic as well as tragic, provided a place where Athens was able to see herself. Given the democratic and hypercritical character of the city, it is not surprising that part of this view would involve a puncturing of the city's own pretensions.

But while Slater's analysis of Aristophanes' comedy reveals a crucial element of its relation to the city, it does not give us the whole picture. Important elements of the comedy, such as its interest in metatheater, role playing, and the theater as such, foster a critical attitude in the demos. But other aspects of the comedy that are just as striking do not seem to be directed toward this end. Primary among these are Aristophanes' delight in defying logic. Again and again, Aristophanes' heroes and heroines drive on their respective plays by contriving and accomplishing a "big idea" whose comic beauty lies in its sheer irrationality.[12] Thus Dikaiopolis in the *Acharnians* solves the problem of the Assembly's self-interested militarism by procuring a private peace for himself; Trugaios in the *Peace* addresses the same problem by stealing the goddess, Peace, from the gods; Lysistrata engineers a Panhellenic sex strike without ever leaving the city walls; and in *Frogs* Athens is saved from destruction by resurrecting a long-dead tragic poet. Similarly, *Knights* saves Athens from the villainy of its political leaders by finding a leader viler than all the rest; *Wasps* addresses the problem of Athens' obsession with law courts by releasing its hero from any sense of lawfulness whatsoever; and *Birds* solves the problem of Athenian "busybodiness" by founding a bird-city that conquers even the gods. In all of these cases, it is exactly the impossibility, and even more, the self-contradictory nature, of the play's comic scenario that Aristophanes calls to our attention. Rather than regarding this aspect of the comedy as a mere framework, as is often done, it is worth inquiring if it also has some relation to the city that Aristophanes claimed to be serving.

The *Knights* and the Absurdity of Politics

The *Knights* is Aristophanes' most immediately political play and, as a result, is usually taken as simply an attack on Aristophanes' traditional enemy, Cleon. To regard the play in this way, however, disregards the comic scenario that Aristophanes has carefully developed and dismisses its irrationality as an amusing sweetener for the edge of the cup. A deeper view of the play, and of the relation of comedy and politics, emerges if we see the scenario as basic to Aristophanes' point. The comic oracles that open and close the *Knights* point out the essential theme: the Athenians are doomed to be ruled by the vilest of the vile simply because the vilest of the vile are who they consistently choose to lead them. The persistent reference to oracles and the divine then takes the idea even further, revealing Athens to be a city grounded in a divine reality that is finally purely its own creation.

On this level, the *Knights*' comic claim that the only way to elevate Athenian politics is by becoming as base as possible parallels the comic devices of the *Acharnians*' private peace, or the *Birds*' city in the clouds. That the point of the device is its sheer irrationality appears in the play's finale, whose focus is precisely its own impossibility. In reversing time and old age and returning a now youthful Demos to the Athens of old, Aristophanes and the Sausage seller achieve a task that is, in Greek literature in particular, paradigmatically impossible. That the ending also creates a celebratory atmosphere of wish fulfillment and audience fantasy is clear. In the world of comedy, however, this is perfectly compatible with a claim that the city itself is irrational, which is the claim that has been built up over the course of the play.

Unlike the idea of a private peace or a city in the clouds, the basic law that governs the *Knights*—that in Athens the viler you are, the more certain you are to succeed—is not on its surface absurd. The absurdity lies not in the idea itself, but rather in its acceptance by Athenians. Just as there is nothing contradictory in the statement that all Cretans are liars, unless it is spoken by a Cretan, to accept the worst possible leader for Athens is fine, except where one is understood to do so for the good of the city. Aristophanes brings out this implicit absurdity by casting his chorus as Knights, enemies of Cleon, but enemies because they hold to the aristocratic standards that he debases.[13] The visual contrast of Knights and Sausage-seller onstage serves as a continual reminder of the play's basic question: What good can arise from actively promoting a bad leader? It is a question kept alive by interjections from the "slave," Demosthenes (359–60, 436–37, 1254–56, and see 948–50, 1201–3), and in Cleon's last, pathetic cry: "But my stealing was for the *good* of the city" (1226).

Aristophanes brings out the inherent irrationality of his comic scenario most vividly in his conclusion. The comic premise of elevating the vilest of the vile to leadership should have painted Aristophanes into a corner. Demos (i.e., the audience) must now suffer even greater hardships because he has now given himself over to an even worse thief and perjurer than before (e.g., 296–98). Instead, in the miraculous conclusion, the old man becomes young again and time itself is reversed.[14] It is now easy to obtain peace because the demos, who now "dwells [apparently literally] in the violet-crowned Athens of old" (1323), is one that never started the war, and easy for Athens to be "defender of the islands" (1319) because she never became their tyrant.[15] Although the repeated epithets "violet-crowned" and "gleaming" (which at *Acharnians* 636–40 Aristophanes described as worthy of sardines) suggest a certain flattery, the only reason why this is not a completely triumphant finale is that it is, like most of Aristophanes' comic devices, by definition impossible.

The absurdity of the *Knights*' conclusion is underlined in the Sausage-seller's announcement that "having boiled Demos down for you, I have made him noble/beautiful (*kalos*) from being base/ugly (*aischros*)" (1321). Alongside the moral implications of *kalos* and *aischros*, the visual aspect, made vivid by the sudden appearance of a young and beautiful Demos, complete with a new mask, recalls the traditional story of Jason's father, Aeson, and Medea.[16] But while Aeson serves as the closest parallel to the "boiling down" of Demos, he is not the point of the myth. Rather, the point is the unsuccessful attempt of Pelias' daughters to rejuvenate him, an aim that is doomed, just as Selene's attempt to preserve Endymion, or any attempt to gain eternal youth, is doomed. This is because to regain youth is tantamount to defying mortality. Hence the impossibility of Asclepius giving life to the dead (*Agamemnon* 1022–24) or Orpheus regaining Eurydice, of Tithonus gaining youth to match his immortality, of the attempts to make Achilles or Demophoon (*Hymn to Demeter* 231–62) immortal, or of Odysseus accepting Calypso's offer.[17] The application to the city is evident. It should be that whereas individuals die, a demos, like the family in Glaucon's account (*Iliad* 6.145–49), can remain immortal. Certainly the city acts, and can only act, as if this were the case. The difficulty is that, as Herodotus knew (1.5), and as Pericles' concern with the monuments Athens leaves behind her suggests (Thucydides 2.41), it isn't.

While the ending of the *Knights* points to an inherent irrationality in the life of the city, it also softens the point, both through the element of simple, feel-good celebration and through a reflection on the role of Aristophanes himself. From the explicit identification in the *Acharnians* (377–82, 502–8) onwards there is a tendency in Aristophanic comedy to link the comic hero and the playwright, particularly at the conclusion of the play, where the victory of the hero is identified with the (anticipated) victory of the poet.[18] In the ending of *Knights*, Aristophanes uses this tradition to unite the Sausage-seller/Aristophanes and Demos/the audience against Cleon, now ejected from the city as a *pharmakos* or scapegoat (1405). To this end, the Sausage-seller is suddenly associated with a catalogue of "wise advice" that the audience would recognize as Aristophanes' stock-in-trade, from a criticism of the new education (1375–83) to the suddenly acquired peace treaties (1388–95). The importance of the identification lies in the claim that Aristophanes had made explicit the year before (in the mouth of his comic hero, Dikaiopolis), that "trugody too knows what is right" (*Acharnians* 500).[19] It is not the greatest, but the least-seeming of men, the ragged comic hero and the comic poet himself who, exactly because they seem least important to the city, are in fact her greatest helper. And, as the *Knights* has shown, it is not despite, but exactly because of, their "baseness" that they are so valuable.

On one level, in accord with Slater's view, the "baseness" or subversions of the comic poet serve the city because they puncture the posturing of the great and mighty. But there is another, and I believe deeper, level on which the comic vision of the *Knights* helps Athens to come to an understanding of herself. In the play's comic setup, the success of the Sausage-seller is brought about by a divine oracle that both opens and closes the play (109–222, 1230–52), and that is made even more emphatic by the oracle contest (960–1099) that brings the competition between Paphlagon and the Sausage-seller to a head. But in this play, as the oracle contest makes clear, the word of the gods is emphatically and purely created by, declaimed by, and fulfilled by human beings.[20] Accordingly, the expulsion of the scapegoat Cleon purifies Athens not because it fulfills a mystic, divine rite, but because he was the cause of the trouble in the first place. If, as in the undertone of tragedy that runs through the play, the divine voice implies that Athens must suffer, the comedy of its vision points out that this is because it is the Athenians who invented that divine voice in the first place.

The point of the *Knights*' comic picture of Athens and humanly invented oracles comes out most vividly in contrast to an image devised by Plato nearly fifty years afterward, the image of the ship in the *Republic*. Here, Plato imagines the Athenian demos as a ship owner who "surpasses everyone on board in size and strength, but is rather deaf and short-sighted, and knows seamanship to about the same degree" (488a). Not knowing anything about seamanship, the owner is unable to judge who should pilot the boat. The result is that the sailors determine who is to be pilot by quarrelling among themselves and making up to the owner, while the trained navigator is completely ignored.

In many ways, Plato's image of the ship resembles, and may even be modeled on, the *Knights*, where "Demos of Pnyx" is master, "rustic in temper, irritable, bad-tempered, old and rather deaf" (40–41), and his "slaves" are, as in Plato's image, the politicians that fight amongst themselves in their self-serving efforts to be chief servant, and so control their master.[21] Accordingly, the Sausage-seller, Aristophanes' ultimate victor, is revealed to bear the significant name (an instance of *nomen/omen*) "Quarrelling in the Agora" (1257–58),[22] and, in what looks like a parody of Pericles' assertion that the Athenians should "by looking every day on the power of the city, become her lovers" (Thucydides 2.43), his competition with Cleon is portrayed as a competition between rival lovers for the affections of a *paidika* (733–946, 1162–63, and see 1340–44, *Gorgias* 481d).[23] The absurdity of casting the crotchety old Demos as the "boy-love" and the demagogues as competing lovers renders the picture ridiculous in itself. The real essence of the comedy, however, emerges in the absence of the element most important to Plato. In Aristophanes' version, there is no philosopher-pilot. Rather, the unreason of the entire political enterprise is summed up in the implicit demand that the leaders of the demos adhere to a higher standard and the simultaneous demolition of the idea that any such standard exists.

Unlike the *Republic*, the *Knights* suggests no access to a wisdom beyond the human. In Aristophanes, there are no divine oracles to guide the city and no divine pattern for the ruler to look to in sketching out its form (*Republic* 501b). The positive flip side is that because all there is are us human beings, it is up to us to do something. We may not be able to escape the cave, but at least we can make life a little more livable inside it. The sooner Athenians realize that the divine meaning of their city is one they create for themselves, the sooner they can make a city that awards the greatest prizes to the "quarreler in the marketplace" into "the monarch of the Greeks," whose actions are "worthy of the city and of the trophy at Marathon" (1333–34). The absurdity of the city is that it grounds itself in a greater reality that is finally purely of its own making. But like the oracles that provide the "tragic" subtext to the *Knights*, this is the reason why exactly that absurdity can also be the city's salvation.

Acharnians, Birds, and the Paradox of the City

Unlike the irrational scenario of the *Knights*, which rests on the impossibility of Athenians actually accepting a vileness in their leaders that they claim to assume is the norm, the absurdity of both *Acharnians* and *Birds* is intrinsic to the central concept. In both plays, the comic hero is able to create a city that is also no-city, and in so doing he uncovers the fiction that is the actual city of Athens.[24] In both cases as well, Aristophanes uses the fluidity of stage space in comedy to demonstrate his point. In the *Acharnians*, this occurs in the "no place," neither inside nor outside the walls of Athens, that is, the location of Dikaiopolis' new marketplace. In the *Birds*, it occurs through the magic power of language, as the similarity of the words *polos*, "sky," and *polis* creates a city (179–86) that instantly appears onstage.[25] In both cases, the comedy makes a fundamental point about Athens. Despite the mammoth city walls of Athens, probably visible from the theater, Athens finally has just as much reality as Cloudcuckooland, and Cloudcuckooland just as much reality as Athens. The only difference is that in comedy, one person, rather than a tradition, creates the community. Other than that, the basis of reality is the same: Dikaiopolis' marketplace, Peisetairos' city in the clouds, and Athens all exist purely because people say that they do.

Dikaiopolis' private peace is an obvious contradiction in terms. As a protection for himself and his family, the peace is, of course, precisely as effective as the bumper sticker declaring the owner's property to be a "nuclear-free zone." Nonetheless, by allowing Dikaiopolis to enjoy its benefits, Aristophanes makes a point similar to the one that he will make later in the *Peace*: war and peace, like the city itself, are not self-subsistent entities. Like the human-made statue that Trugaios snatches back from Olympus, peace is made by human beings, not determined by the gods. That human beings nonetheless have to treat it as divine, as Trugaios founds a cult to his statue (or as the American Constitution has been transformed into a sacred document), is the point of the comedy.

The lesson of the *Peace* appears again in *Acharnians* and *Birds*, but in a negative way. Both Dikaiopolis and Peisetairos demonstrate the human ability to transform reality to their own liking. In creating his own city, Peisetairos does no more than innumerable Greek colonists have done before him.[26] In creating his private peace and Panhellenic marketplace, Dikaiopolis only does for himself what Aristophanes has (loudly) been urging Athens to do for some time. In both cases, however, Aristophanes replays the familiar in a way that makes its absurdity apparent. As in Swift's recreating the affairs of England in Lilliput, the designation of this as peace and that as war, this as the city's limits and that as open territory, becomes absurd when it is undertaken by a single person. In the badly battered Athens for which Aristophanes produced the *Peace*, his emphasis was on human beings' ability to create their own divinely ordained ideals. In the more confident times of the *Acharnians* and the *Birds*, he stressed instead the absurdity of human beings treating their own self-created ideals as sacrosanct.

Acharnians and *Birds* are also similar in that the comic heroes of both plays have occasioned a scholarly debate. Both Dikaiopolis and Peisetairos are regarded by some scholars as purely positive figures whose triumph is to be enjoyed vicariously by the audience. But both have also been regarded as ultimately negative, Dikaiopolis as the play increasingly emphasizes his refusal to share his peace with other Athenians, and Peisetairos as he moves from his search for peace and quiet to the position of a tyrant (1708, and see 1673) roasting his own citizens (1583–86).[27] Comedy, however, does not usually worry much about either–or propositions. As scholars have made clear, there are excellent reasons, in both plays, for Aristophanes to emphasize the triumphant, positive view of the hero, and there are excellent reasons for him to want the cautionary, negative view. The advantage of comedy is that he can have both. For Aristophanes, as for Yogi Berra, when one comes to a fork in the road, the best plan is to take it.

Dikaiopolis, in the *Acharnians*, is appealing largely because he is right.[28] As Aristophanes goes out of his way to demonstrate in the play's initial scenes, war is fostered for the private self-seeking of a few; the only rational goal for Athens is peace. Rationally, as any philosopher would tell you, when a human being clearly and distinctly perceives the correct and beneficial course of action, he or she must take it. That is precisely what Dikaiopolis does. The difficulty that ensues illustrates one of the prime absurdities of democracy: the need to acknowledge as "my" decision a course of action that I may consider radically misguided. In the case of Dikaiopolis, the problem appears in its opposite form: in taking the only rational course for himself as an individual, he also separates himself from his fellow citizens. Having begun the *Acharnians* as the quintessential Athenian, as opposed to the Persians and Thracians, the profiteering ambassadors and the self-interested politicians, and having won over the chorus exactly by being a "decent citizen" (595), Dikaiopolis, by taking the only rational course, isolates himself. Having begun the play as so much one of "us" that he can speak for Aristophanes himself ("we are here just by ourselves holding the Lenaia" [504]), he ends it having celebrated the major festival the Athenians held in December, the Rural Dionysia, and the festival held in February, the Anthesteria, missing only the January Lenaia that the audience was currently attending.[29]

In Plato's *Symposium*, Aristophanes, at least according to Diotima, suggests that what one ultimately pursues is not the good, but rather what is one's own (205d–e and 212c). According to Aristophanes himself, the question seems rather more complicated. It could certainly be argued that Dikaiopolis in the *Acharnians* decides precisely to pursue what is good at the cost of sacrificing what is "his own." If one sees the play as justifying Dikaiopolis, Aristophanes seems to be championing the pursuit of the good over loyalty to one's own. On the other hand, however, to the extent that the play presents a negative picture of Dikaiopolis, it also depicts the necessity of remaining with what is one's own, here the city, rather than pursuing an independent good. What is unique to Aristophanes' comic vision is that he makes us feel the strength of both visions. We readily accept Dikaiopolis' good as the good—that is, until it becomes apparent that it is not a good he seems to be willing to share with us.[30] Positioning oneself in the audience, the point becomes apparent—although the good in and of itself is inherently desirable, we ourselves desire a good that is our own. What we inherently want is what is inherently right, but what we have is the polis, which is in general the best we can do.

In *Acharnians*, the advantage of the positive reading is obvious: as his name, Dikaiopolis, or "just city" implies, Dikaiopolis is taking the course that Aristophanes has recommended for Athens.[31] On the other side, however, the negative view of Dikaiopolis implies that Athenians must act together, even when the action, prosecuting the war, is the wrong one. Accordingly, Aristophanes has it both ways—he explicitly identifies himself with his hero early on in the play, and then, in the *parabasis*, distinguishes himself from him by claiming that peace is not desirable at any cost—at the cost, for example, of giving up one's comic poet (652–58).[32] It is, of course, absurd that Aristophanes would spend the first half of a play demonstrating the evils of war and the self-interested corruption of those who prosecute it only to imply, in the course of displaying the comfort and luxury of peace, that one must follow the city nonetheless. It is, however, an absurdity endemic to political life. In fact, it is a position that our own familiarity with democracy has made to seem even logical.

Aristophanes' paradoxical position in the *Acharnians*, of both championing and undercutting his hero, both points to a fundamental absurdity in the city and furthers the poet's persuasive powers within it. That his main interest is the absurdity, however, rather than the political advice, appears in his use of a very similar approach in the *Birds*, where Aristophanes is not advocating any particular course of action. The reason for a positive reading of Peisetairos is clear: his ability to take over all before him, a quality that rides the crest of Athenian self-confidence in 415 BCE.[33] The fact that that wave was to come crashing down in the Sicilian expedition also clarifies, with all the advantages of hindsight, the negative reading of Peisetairos, which implies a warning against the dangers of human (and particularly Athenian) hubris.[34] Viewed together, the negative and positive views of Peisetairos might be summed up in the observation that although overweening ambition can utterly distort human aims, it also feels very good. Nor is there any indication in the play that overweening ambition is anything less than completely successful. By undercutting his hero in the *Birds*, Aristophanes casts, as he most often does, an ironic light on Athens.[35] But he does not thereby offer the city any particular advice or suggest any particular solution to the paradox.

In examining the *Knights*, we looked at Aristophanes' view of Athenian irrationality as a democracy. In the *Acharnians*, we looked at Athens' irrationality as a *polis*. In looking at the *Birds*, what we see is Athenian irrationality simply as Athens itself. Peisetairos is an ordinary Athenian tired of the *polypragmosyne* or "busybodiness" of Athens (30–45, 109–22).[36] In his quest for peace and quiet he will find a haven, almost a golden age, which he will then rapidly turn into precisely the polis he was attempting to escape.[37] The play's location in "Cloudcuckooland" is as universal, and apparently as traditionally universal, as possible.[38] From here, however, Athenian elements infiltrate: the references to Sophocles' *Tereus*, the sacred robe of the Panathenaea (827), a rocky Acropolis (836), and a *Pelargikon* (832), the wall around the Acropolis whose name recalls the Greek word for a stork.[39] Eventually, a crowd of increasingly Athenian visitors arrives: Meton, who is Athenian (as in the joke of his being known throughout Greece—and Colonus [998]) but has a universal "scientific" approach to city planning; the Athenian Inspector and Decree-seller (1021ff.); the Athenian dithyrambic poet Cinesias (1372ff.); and the quintessential Athenian, an informer (1410 ff.).[40] The theme culminates gloriously when Peisetairos points out to Heracles that his father, Zeus, has never introduced him into an [Athenian] phratry (1668–69). Because even the gods, it seems, need to have their legitimacy verified by Athens, there is nothing remarkable in the "other" that was Cloudcuckooland also taking on a purely Athenian look.

As Peisetairos re-creates Athens it is, not surprisingly, Athenian ambition that is Aristophanes' main target. That there are contradictions involved appears immediately in its origin, an ordinary Athenian's desire for peace and quiet, away from the law courts, the assemblies, and the constant commerce of his native city. As Jeffrey Henderson has pointed out, this desire in Peisetairos to isolate himself from the public life of the city recalls the response of the disillusioned and alienated elite to the radical democracy that was increasingly dominating Athens.[41] But in his attempt to capture the prize at the Greater Dionysia, Aristophanes must have expected to find a sympathetic response to his hero's quest in more than just the elite. As Thucydides tells us, the public enthusiasm for the Sicilian Expedition was so great that those who opposed it kept silent, for fear of being regarded as ill-minded toward the city (6.24). What was still available to them, however, was a good laugh at the inevitability of Athenian ambition. Even supporters of the expedition might find that any quiet qualms they had could find a release in enjoying the comic characters' inability to abandon a world of constant striving. As it is "only" comedy and nothing serious, comedy can allow an indulgence in feelings and responses that are not for public display. And as it is "only" comedy, the audience can also allow the play to bring out contradictions within themselves and their own ambitions for Athens.

As has increasingly been appreciated, the audience for Greek tragedy and comedy was not monolithic.[42] Each play must have elicited many different responses in different spectators, and an awareness of this multiplicity seems an integral part of Greek drama. Comedy, however, can go even further. Like tragedy, comedy may appeal to different spectators differently, and like tragedy, it can elicit different, and even opposed, responses within a single spectator. The most patriarchal and xenophobic Athenian male must have winced at Iphigeneia's death or Jason's perfidy. The most radically antitraditional of the spectators, rooting (if any were) for Clytemnestra or Medea, must have felt some discomfort at the slaughter of Cassandra or the children. Comedy, in this way, is not unique in calling forth contrary emotions in the spectators. What is unique is that comedy makes the contradiction the point.

If the opening of the *Birds* appealed to a very unpolitical sentiment, the desire for a Golden Age of peace and quiet, its end was everything that Pericles could wish, replacing the Golden Age life of the birds with a universal tyranny. The joke is that the very same citizens could appreciate either. In the *Acharnians*, success provides the hero with perfect security, appealing to the individual's desire to leave the intransigence, self-seeking, and red tape of political life behind. But it also does more. By developing this fantasy, Aristophanes also points out an inherent contradiction in being part of a polis—the desire both to be part of the city and to determine one's own fate, to enjoy the collective identity exemplified by being "we ourselves, here conducting the Lenaia" and also to refuse to accept that that "us" determines an identity for each individual "me." In the *Birds*, the same desire for independence leads quite naturally (in comedy, as in Athenian history) to the complete domination of others. It is not that the Athenians are being asked to see themselves as either right or wrong in this progression. It is rather that they are being asked to see, in all their own contradictions, themselves.[43]

The Frogs: Saving Athens through Comedy

Aristophanes' last overtly political comedy is also the last comedy that survives from the fifth century. It is the *Frogs*, produced between the disastrous victory of Arginusae, which occasioned the Athenians' last rejection of an offered peace, and the devastating defeat at Aegospotami, which threatened to put an end to Athens herself.[44] Aristophanes' solution to the crisis is a typically comic one—a proper tragic poet who could return the Athenians to the old days when fighting, not talking, was uppermost on the citizens' minds. As many commentators have noticed, the starring role of tragedy in the play exists at least in part to set off the equally critical role of comedy—because only a comic hero, here the god Dionysus in his comic aspect, could come up with a solution so absurd.[45] One aspect of the comedy, however, that has gone unappreciated is that the solution is unnecessary. As Aeschylus himself reminds us, in pointing out that his tragedies, unlike Euripides', have not died with him (*Frogs* 868–69), the Athenians had been restaging Aeschylean comedy since at least the time of the *Acharnians*, when Dikaiopolis' great opening disappointment is to have been awaiting a tragedy by Aeschylus and encounter one by Theognis instead (*Acharnians* 9–11).[46] The problem, it turns out, is not the difficulty of bringing a wise counselor back from the dead. It is rather getting the Athenians to listen to the wise advice they are already honoring in their public festivals.[47]

As in Aristotle's quotation about the city that does not listen to her own laws (*Nicomachean Ethics* 1152a23, and see *Republic* 557ff.), Aristophanes' point seems to be that there is no lack of wisdom in Athens. The problem is that the Athenians honor the wisdom of the poets and the ancient values of the past at the same time that their actions head in precisely the opposite direction. As often, the idea is brought out through the plot. Although the plot of the *Frogs* has been criticized because its two halves, Dionysus' descent to the Underworld to bring back Euripides and the poetic contest to determine the greatest tragic poet, are only tangentially related, the radical change in direction actually serves to make Aristophanes' point.[48] Dionysus descends to the Underworld ready to face all the perils of Hell. What he discovers is that the only peril involved is the near impossibility of making up his own mind.

Aristophanes emphasizes the *Frogs*' sudden change in direction by making it both as abrupt and as emphatic as possible. Foreshadowed by the unique device of presenting two completely different choruses, the second half of the play begins with its own prologue, complete with slaves discussing the coming plot and a complete elimination of Xanthias and all the ambiguities, between slave and master and mortal and immortal, that had informed the first half. Only at the very end of the play does Aristophanes reintroduce the idea of a tragic poet returning to Athens, using Pluto, in an unexpected fourth speaking part, to underline the surprise.[49] The metatheater, moreover, is pointed. Having battled his way into Hell, Dionysus, the god of the theatrical festival, finds himself judging between Athenian playwrights, with the aim of discovering which can best save "our" city (1083, 1448–50, 1501).[50] Not only in the midst of death are we in life—it seems very much that in the midst of death we are right back in Athens.[51]

In this way, Aristophanes once more points out that in the greatest peril that Athens has faced, her greatest foe is, once more, herself.[52] It is notable that among all the wise advice offered for the salvation of the city, only Euripides' comic plan of dropping vinegar in the enemies' eyes (1437–53) has anything at all to do with Sparta.[53] Instead, the conflict between Euripides and Aeschylus plays out again, in a different key—the theme of the first half of the play—where Dionysus confronts a series of terrors, all of which he himself has ultimately brought about. And just as the conflicts of the first half are all resolved simply by Pluto's and Persephone's ability to recognize their kin (668–71), so the promise of the second half is held out in the Athenians' ability to recognize, if they only will, what is truly their own—the city.[54] The ease of Aristophanes' advice, like the ease with which Dionysus penetrated Hades, lies in the suggestion that salvation for the city requires only that the Athenians see what is directly in front of them. The absurdity lies in the problem that making them do so is as difficult as bringing back a tragedian from the dead.

At the end of *Annie Hall*, Woody Allen tells a joke about a man who goes to a psychiatrist because his brother thinks he is a chicken. When the psychiatrist asks why he doesn't just turn him in, he says he would—but he needs the eggs. Aristophanes' view of the city is not too far removed from the joke. The sheer irrationality of Aristophanic comedy is in itself political, because the very irrationality is a reflection of Athens. Human beings (or at least male human beings) in Aristophanic comedy are generally radical individuals whose main concern is with food, drink, sex, and being as *hybristic* as possible. But they are also, in stark distinction to the satyrs, whose similar values closed the tragic trilogy, citizens, and in a recurrent theme, Aristophanes reminds us that as incompatible as his heroes and the city are, the comic hero is nonetheless every bit as dependent on the city as is the comedy he inhabits. The city, in Aristophanes, appears as a purely human invention, attempting to constrain the inherently erotic nature of man with the spiderwebs of its laws, customs, and propriety.[55] And yet, like the eggs in Woody Allen's joke, we need it nonetheless. This may also be the reason why the comic poet, not despite, but because of his subversion of the city's conventions, is also her greatest champion.

Notes

1. For contrary views, see Malcolm Heath, "The 'Social Function' of Tragedy: Clarifications and Questions," in *Dionysalexandros: Essays on Aeschylus and his Fellow Tragedians in Honour of Alexander F Garvie*, eds. Douglas Cairns and Vayos Liapis (Swansea: The Classical Press of Wales, 2006), 253–82; J. Griffin, "The Social Function of Attic Tragedy," *Classical Quarterly* 48 (1998): 39–61, and in response, Richard Seaford, "The Social Function of Attic Tragedy: A Response to Jasper Griffin," *Classical Quarterly* 50 (2000): 30–44; Simon Goldhill, "The Greater Dionysia and Civic Ideology," in *Nothing to Do with Dionysus?: Athenian Drama in its Social Context*, eds. John J. Winkler and Froma I. Zeitlin (Princeton, NJ: Princeton University Press, 1990), 97–129, and Goldhill, "Civic Ideology and the Problem of Difference: The Politics of Aeschylean Tragedy, Once Again," *Journal of Hellenic Studies* 120 (2000): 34–56; P. J. Rhodes, "Nothing to Do with Democracy: Athenian Drama and the Polis," *Journal of Hellenic Studies* 123 (2003): 111. D. M. Carter, *The Politics of Greek Tragedy* (Bristol: Phoenix Press, 2007), 21–63, and Goldhill, "Civic Ideology and the Problem of Difference," 43, give a survey of views.

2. Greek text is taken from the Oxford Classical Texts; for Aristophanes: N. G. Wilson, *Aristophanis Fabulae*, 2 vols. (Oxford and New York: Oxford University Press, 2007). Translations, unless otherwise indicated, are my own.

3. Michael S. Silk, *Aristophanes and the Definition of Comedy* (Oxford: Oxford University Press, 2000); Charles Platter, "The Uninvited Guest: Aristophanes in Bakhtin's *History of Laughter*," *Arethusa* 26 (1993): 201–16, and Platter, *Aristophanes and the Carnival of Genres* (Baltimore: Johns Hopkins University Press, 2006). See, for example, Mikhail Bakhtin, *Rabelais and His World*, trans. Helene Iswolsky (Bloomington: Indiana University Press, 1984 [1968]), 7: "carnival is not a spectacle seen by the people, they live in it." See also S. Halliwell, *Greek Laughter: A Study of Cultural Psychology from Homer to Early Christianity* (Cambridge: Cambridge University Press, 2008), 204–6, 250; W. Rösler, "Michail Bachtin und die Karnevalskultur im antiken Griechenland," *Quaderni Urbinati di Cultura Classica* 23 (1986): 25–44, and A. T. Edwards, "Historicizing the Popular Grotesque: Bakhtin's Rabelais and Attic Old Comedy," in *Theater and Society in the Classical World*, ed. Ruth Scodel (Ann Arbor: University of Michigan Press, 1993), 90, on Bahktin's neglect of Aristophanes. Jeffrey Henderson, "The *Demos* and the Comic Competition," in *Nothing to Do with Dionysus?: Athenian Drama in its Social Context*, eds. John J. Winkler and Froma I. Zeitlin (Princeton, NJ: Princeton University Press, 1990), 271–313; Edwards, "Historicizing the Popular Grotesque," 89–117; and Simon Goldhill, *The Poet's Voice: Essays on Poetics and Greek Literature* (Cambridge: Cambridge University Press, 1991), 183–84, discuss Athenian drama as city sponsored, rather than as

pure license, while Goldhill, *The Poet's Voice*, 176–88, examines carnival overall and its relation to Aristophanes, with sources. For other non-carnival views, see Silk, *Aristophanes and the Definition of Comedy*, 298–99, and J. M. Bremer, "Aristophanes on his own Poetry," in *Aristophane*, eds. J. M. Bremer and E. W. Handley (Geneva: Entretiens Hardt 38, Reverdin and Grange, 1993), 125–65. For claims that Aristophanes is nonetheless carnivalesque, see Rafael Newman, "Heine's Aristophanes: Compromise Formations and the Ambivalence of Carnival," *Comparative Literature* 49 (1997): 227–40; Helmut Schareika, *Der Realismus der aristophanischen Komödie* (Frankfurt: Lang, 1978); E.-R. Schwinge, "Alte Komödie und attische Demokratie," in *Literatur in der Demokratie*, ed. W. Barner (Munich, 1983), 236–45; and, for a survey of various views, Platter, "The Uninvited Guest," 201–16, and Edwards, "Historicizing the Popular Grotesque," 89–118.

4. See Robin Osborne, "Competitive Festivals and the Polis: A Context for Dramatic Festivals at Athens," in *Tragedy, Comedy, and the Polis, Papers from the Greek Drama Conference, Nottingham 18–20 July, 1990*, eds. Alan H. Sommerstein, Stephen Halliwell, Jeffrey Henderson, and Bernhard Zimmermann (Bari, Italy: Levante Editori-Bari, 1993), 36, and (in the same volume) Rainer Friedrich, "Medea Apolis: on Euripides' Dramatization of the Crisis of the Polis," 219–39; for a similar tension expressed in tragedy, Christian Meier, *The Political Art of Greek Tragedy*, trans. Andrew Webber (Baltimore: The Johns Hopkins University Press, 1993), 133–34 and *passim*.

5. Or, as Churchill put it: "The best argument against democracy is a five minute conversation with the average voter."

6. For the extensive bibliography on this question, see Goldhill, *The Poet's Voice*, 188; Bremer, "Aristophanes on his own Poetry," 128–29. Ian C. Storey, *Eupolis: Poet of Old Comedy* (Oxford: Oxford University Press, 2003), 338–48, summarizes and sees Eupolis as somewhat more inclined to social humor. For the debate itself, see W. G. Forrest, "Aristophanes' *Acharnians*," *Phoenix* 17 (1963): 1–12; Bremer, "Aristophanes on his own Poetry," 125–65.

Among those who see Aristophanes as actively engaged and essentially conservative, see D. Rosenbloom, "From *Ponêros* to *Pharmakos*: Theater, Social Drama, and Revolution in Athens, 428–404 BCE," *Classical Antiquity* 21 (2002): 283–346, with 285n16 for a bibliography; Jeffrey Henderson, "Attic Old Comedy, Frank Speech, and Democracy," in *Democracy, Empire, and the Arts in Fifth-Century Athens*, eds. Deborah Boedecker and Kurt Raaflaub (Cambridge: Harvard University Press, 1998), 255–74, and Henderson, "The *Demos* and the Comic Competition," 271–313; Douglas MacDowell, "The Nature of Aristophanes' *Acharnians*," *Greece and Rome* 30 (1983): 143–62; G. E. M. de Ste. Croix, *The Origins of the Peloponnesian War* (London: Duckworth, 1972); Lowell Edmunds, *Cleon, Knights, and Aristophanes' Politics* (Lanham, MD: University Press of America, 1987), 59–66; David Konstan, *Greek Comedy and Ideology* (Oxford: Oxford University Press, 1995); P. Cartledge, *Aristophanes and His Theatre of the Absurd* (Bristol: Bristol Classical Press, 1990). Among those who view Aristophanes as not political, see Forrest, "Aristophanes' *Acharnians*," 1–12; A. W. Gomme, "Aristophanes and Politics,"

Classical Review 52 (1938): 97–109; C. H. Whitman, *Aristophanes and the Comic Hero* (Cambridge, MA: Harvard University Press, 1964), 4–6; A. M. Bowie, "The Parabasis in Aristophanes: Prolegomena, *Acharnians*," *Classical Quarterly* 32 (1982): 27–40; S. Halliwell, "Aristophanic Satire," in *English Satire and the Satiric Tradition*, eds. C. Rawson and J. Mezciems (Oxford: Blackwell Publishers, 1984), 20; Malcolm Heath, *Political Comedy in Aristophanes*, *Hypomnemata* 87 (Göttingen: Vandenhoeck & Ruprect, 1987), and Heath, "Aristophanes and the Discourse of Politics," in *The City as Comedy: Society and Representation in Athenian Drama*, ed. Gregory Dobrov (Chapel Hill: University of North Carolina Press, 1997), 230–49; Goldhill, *The Poet's Voice*, 188–201; Christopher Carey, "The Purpose of Aristophanes' *Acharnians*," *Rheinisches Museum für Philologie* 136 (1993): 245–63. See also Silk, *Aristophanes and the Definition of Comedy*, 301–11, opposing both Heath and Henderson.

An intermediate position is that of Victor Ehrenberg, *The People of Aristophanes: A Sociology of Old Attic Comedy* (New York: Schocken Books, 1962 [1951]), 8: "It has rightly been observed that the very fact of his being a comedian compelled the poet to be 'against the government'—whatever government it might be." See also Christopher Carey, "Comic Ridicule and Democracy," in *Ritual, Finance, Politics: Athenian Democratic Accounts Presented to D. M. Lewis*, eds. R. Osborne and S. Hornblower (Oxford: Clarendon Press, 1994), 69–84, for the ambivalence of comedy as working with that of political democracy. Nor do I see, as Gomme, "Aristophanes and Politics," 97–109, any necessary conflict between being an artist and being directly involved in politics.

7. See Z. P. Biles, "Intertextual Biography in the Rivalry of Cratinus and Aristophanes," *American Journal of Philology* 123 (2002): 169–204, and Biles, *Aristophanes and the Poetics of Competition* (Cambridge: Cambridge University Press, 2011); Emmanuela Bakola, *Cratinus and the Art of Comedy* (Oxford: Oxford University Press, 2010); K. Sidwell, *Aristophanes the Democrat: The Politics of Satirical Comedy during the Peloponnesian War* (Cambridge: Cambridge University Press, 2009); and for a critique of Sidwell's rather extreme position, I. Ruffell, "A Total Write-off: Aristophanes, Cratinus, and the Rhetoric of Comic Competition," *Classical Quarterly* 52 (2002): 139–40.

8. As Halliwell, "Aristophanic Satire," 10–12 (although I do not take this as implying that Aristophanes is not serious). Alan Sommerstein, "How to Avoid being a Komodoumenos," *Classical Quarterly* 46 (1996): 330, points out that Aristophanes tends to have one each of categories such as butcher, baker, and so on, to ridicule; Kenneth McLeish, *The Theatre of Aristophanes* (Bath: Thames and Hudson, 1980), 91, argues generally against pursuing the "real" figure in Old Comedy.

9. See Biles, "Intertextual Biography," 169–204, and Biles, *Aristophanes and the Poetics of Competition*, 134–66, on Cratinus and Aristophanes; D. Welsh, "The Ending of Aristophanes' *Knights*," *Hermes* 118 (1990): 427. For similar plays (as *Clouds* 551–59), see Eupolis' *Maricas* and Hermippus' *Artopolides* on Hyperbolus, and Plato Comicus' *Peisandros*; Alan Sommerstein, "Platon, Eupolis and the 'Demagogue-Comedy,'" in *The Rivals of Aristophanes: Studies in Athenian Old Comedy*, eds. David Harvey and John Wilkins (Swansea: Duckworth and the Classical Press

of Wales, 2000), 437–51, and on the *Maricas* and this type of play, Storey, *Eupolis*, 197–214. Ruffell, "A Total Write-off," 150–54, argues that the approach also reflects Cratinus' *Dionysalexandros, Cheirones, Nemesis,* and *Ploutoi*; in contrast, Bakola, *Cratinus and the Art of Comedy*, 181–207, argues that the *Dionysalexandros* is not simply political allegory. For the common tradition within which the poets worked, see David Harvey, "Phrynichos and his Muses," in *The Rivals of Aristophanes: Studies in Athenian Old Comedy*, eds. David Harvey and John Wilkins (Swansea: Duckworth and the Classical Press of Wales, 2000), 112, and Malcolm Heath, "Aristophanes and his Rivals," *Greece and Rome* 37 (1990): 143–58.

10. See Biles, "Intertextual Biography," 169–204, and Biles, *Aristophanes and the Poetics of Competition*. R. M. Rosen, *Making Mockery: The Poetics of Ancient Satire* (Oxford: Oxford University Press, 2007), "discusses the tension deliberately created by such poets between self-righteous didactic claims and a persistent desire to undermine them, and concludes that such poetry was felt by ancient audiences to achieve its greatest success as comedy precisely when they were left unable to ascribe to the satirist any consistent moral position" (abstract).

11. Niall Slater, *Spectator Politics: Metatheater and Performance in Aristophanes* (Philadelphia: University of Pennsylvania Press, 2002).

12. See McLeish, *The Theatre of Aristophanes*, 67–78, for Aristophanes' basic plot as involving an alienated hero, a "big idea," and an upside-down world.

13. For a similar view, see Plutarch, *Life of Nicias*, 11 (*PCG* 103), quoting Plato Comicus on Hyperbolus not being worthy of ostracism.

14. As Alan Sommerstein, *Knights* (Warminster: Aris and Phillips, 1981) points out, this is beautifully staged by having Demos reemerge on the very *ekkuklema* on which Paphlagon had just been "wheeled in." A. M. Bowie, *Aristophanes: Myth, Ritual and Comedy* (Cambridge: Cambridge University Press, 1993), 71–72, points out as well that the Sausage-seller's career follows the pattern of the Panathenaea. In contrast, Whitman, *Aristophanes and the Comic Hero*, 101–2, finds the Sausage-seller's switch in character disappointing. On the turnaround, see Douglas MacDowell, *Aristophanes and Athens: An Introduction to the Plays* (Oxford: Oxford University Press, 1995), 106, who argues that dramatic coherence is not the point; R. W. Brock, "The Double Plot in Aristophanes' Knights," *Greek, Roman and Byzantine Studies* 27 (1986): 15–27, who sees a "double plot." P. Reinders, "Der Demos in den *Rittern* des Aristophanes am Beispiel des Amoibaions in den Vv. 1111–1150," in *Griechisch-römische Komödie und Tragödie* [*Drama*, vol. 3] (Stuttgart: J. B. Metzler, 1995), 1–20, and Peter D. Arnott, "Greek Drama as Education," *Educational Theatre Journal* 22 (1970): 39, see Demos' turnabout as gaining the favor of the audience; H. Kleinknecht, "Die Epiphanie des Demos in Aristophanes' 'Rittern,'" *Hermes* 77 (1939): 58–65, sees the reappearance as a divine epiphany, which may be a bit extreme.

15. This change has been prepared by continual references to the great Athenian past, from the slaves' early reference to Themistocles' suicide (84) to references to Marathon, Salamis, Cimon, Themistocles, and Miltiades (407, 781, 785, 812–19, 884, 1040, 1312).

16. See Sommerstein, *Knights*, 215; Ovid, *Metamorphoses*, 7.159–349.

17. A tradition that goes back as far as Gilgamesh's loss of the plant "The-old-man-becomes-a-young-man" (*Gilgamesh* 11.300). See E. Griffiths, *Medea* (London: Taylor & Francis, 2006), 23–25, 45–46, for the popularity of the theme, particularly on vases. Edmunds, *Cleon, Knights, and Aristophanes' Politics*, 43–49, takes the transformation as purely positive, implying not a new youth, but an Ionian domination of Greece; MacDowell, *Aristophanes and Athens*, 104n41, sees the rejuvenation as not literal, although L. M. Stone, *Costume in Aristophanic Comedy* (New York, 1981), 402–3, 406–7, and J. Rusten, ed., *The Birth of Comedy: Texts, Documents, and Art from Athenian Comic Competitions, 486–280* (Baltimore: Johns Hopkins University Press, 2011), 424, see Demos as actually acquiring a new mask as well as a new costume; see also S. Douglas Olson, "The New Demos of Aristophanes' *Knights*," *Eranos* 88 (1990): 60–67. Despite Erich Segal, *The Death of Comedy* (Cambridge: Harvard University Press, 2001), literal rejuvenation is not common in Aristophanes; even Philocleon is "young again" primarily in heart. For visual parodies of rejuvenation, see Rusten, *The Birth of Comedy*, 442; A. Kossatz-Deissmann, *Greek Vases in the J. Paul Getty Museum* 6 (2000): 187–204.

18. For Aristophanes' identification with the Sausage-seller in particular, see Ruffell, "A Total Write-off," 150; for Aristophanes' usual identification of the hero's victory with his own, as *Acharnians* 1224ff., see Sommerstein, *Knights*, 215; Kenneth J. Reckford, *Aristophanes' Old-and-New Comedy* (Chapel Hill: University of North Carolina Press, 1987), 119–20. In the very next year, Cratinus was to trump Aristophanes with exactly this technique by making himself the hero of the victorious *Wineflask*, as Bakola, *Cratinus and the Art of Comedy*, 16–24.

19. Oliver Taplin, "Tragedy and Trugody," *Classical Quarterly* 3 (1983): 331–33; Helene Foley, "Tragedy and Politics in Aristophanes' *Acharnians*," *Journal of Hellenic Studies* 108 (1988): 33–47.

20. See R. Parker, *Miasma: Pollution and Purification in Early Greek Religion* (Oxford: Oxford University Press, 1983), 15: "while in high literature the seer is always right, in comedy he is always wrong"; and see Silk, *Aristophanes and the Definition of Comedy*, 338–42; P. Rau, *Paratragoedia: Untersuchung einer komischen Form des Aristophanes* (Munich: CH Beck, 1967), 169–73, for the oracle parodies. Platter, *Aristophanes and the Carnival of Genres*, 108–42, and 114–23 on *Knights* in particular, surveys Aristophanes' undermining of oracular and epic authority.

21. On the identification of the two slaves as Nicias and Demosthenes, see Sommerstein, *Knights*, 3; Bowie, *Aristophanes: Myth, Ritual and Comedy*, 73; MacDowell, *Aristophanes and Athens*, 87–88; and for a contrary view, Kenneth Dover, "Aristophanes' *Knights* 11–20," *Classical Review* 9 (1959): 196–99; Jeffrey Henderson, *Aristophanes: Acharnians, Knights* (Cambridge: Loeb Classical Library, Harvard University Press, 1998), 222n2.

22. For the delay in naming as emphasizing the joke, see S. Douglas Olson, "Names and Naming in Aristophanic Comedy," *Classical Quarterly* 42 (1992): 304–19; for "Agoracritus" as meaning (despite his own interpretation) "Chosen by the Assembly," Henderson, *Aristophanes: Acharnians, Knights*, 387n108.

23. The contest may also reflect a claim of Cleon's to be a lover of the people, as Sommerstein, *Knights*, 181, and W. R. Connor, *The New Politicians of Fifth-century Athens* (Indianapolis: Hackett, 1992 [1971]), 96–98.

24. For a city that is no-city, see *Eumenides* 457, as well as Sir Thomas More's Outopia/Eutopia.

25. See Nan Dunbar, *Aristophanes: Birds* (Oxford: Clarendon Press, 1998), 16–17. Similar indeterminacies of place appear in *Lysistrata* (J. Vaio, "The Manipulation of Theme and Action in Aristophanes' *Lysistrata*," *Greek, Roman and Byzantine Studies* 14 [1973]: 369–80) and *Clouds* 138, where Strepsiades, who has come from next door, explains that he lives "a long way off, in the country" (similarly 1322). For this tendency in comedy, see Peter D. Arnott, *Public and Performance in the Greek Theatre* (London: Routledge, 1989), 132–45. David Wiles, *Greek Theatre Performance: An Introduction* (Cambridge: Cambridge University Press, 2000), 122–23, uses Bakhtin's *chronotope* (Mikhail Bakhtin, *The Dialogic Imagination: Four Essays*, ed. Michael Holquist, trans. Caryl Emerson and Michael Holquist [Austin: University of Texas Press, 1981], 84–258) to contrast tragedy's closed sense of time and space to comedy's open sense. For other considerations of the fluidity of comic versus tragic space, see P. von Möllendorf, *Grundlagen einer Ästhetik der alten Komödie: Untersuchungen zu Aristophanes und Michail Bakhtin* (Tübingen: Narr, 1995), 112–50; John Scott Scullion, *Three Studies in Athenian Dramaturgy* (Stuttgart: Teubner, 1994), 67, 109; J. P. Poe, "Multiplicity, Discontinuity, and Visual Meaning in Aristophanic Comedy," *Rheinisches Museum für Philologie* 143 (2000): 256–95.

26. Although the tradition of Athenian autocthony further brings out the absurdity of Peisetairos' refounding of the city.

27. Although "tyrannos" may mean simply "sovereign" as in tragedy, as Dunbar, *Aristophanes: Birds*, 12, 511, the negative sense of the word is emphasized at *Birds* 1704.

28. For positive views of Dikaiopolis, see L. P. E. Parker's strident defense ("Eupolis or Dicaeopolis," *Journal of Hellenic Studies* 111 [1991]: 201–8) occasioned by E. L. Bowie's remark ("Who Is Dicaeopolis?" *Journal of Hellenic Studies* 108 [1988]: 183–85) that Dikaiopolis' behavior is not worthy of his name; S. Douglas Olson, "Dicaeopolis' Motivations in Aristophanes' *Acharnians*," *Journal of Hellenic Studies* 111 (1991): 200–203; MacDowell, "The Nature of Aristophanes' *Acharnians*," 143–62, and MacDowell, *Aristophanes and Athens*, 75–77, for further references. Whitman, *Aristophanes and the Comic Hero*, 59–69, sees Dikaiopolis' behavior as the regular *poneria* of the comic hero. For his selfishness, see H.-J. Newinger, "War and Peace in the Comedies of Aristophanes," *Yale Classical Studies* 26 (1980): 223; Kenneth Dover, *Aristophanic Comedy* (Berkeley: University of California Press, 1972), 87–88; Foley, "Tragedy and Politics in Aristophanes' *Acharnians*," 33–47; Carey, "The Purpose of Aristophanes' *Acharnians*," 249–51. The fact that both readings are supported by strong arguments and vehement proponents, and that neither has been able to make the other give way, suggests that the difficulty may lie in our assuming that we must decide for one or the other.

29. It is also worth noting that the Anthesteria's Festival of the Pitchers was unique as the one time an Athenian drank alone. See N. R. E. Fisher, "Multiple Personalities and Dionysiac Festivals: Dicaeopolis in Aristophanes' *Acharnians*," *Greece and Rome* 40 (1993): 42–44; R. J. Hoffman, "Ritual License and the Cult of Dionysus," *Athenaeum* 67 (1989): 98–99; H. W. Parke, *Festivals of the Athenians* (London: Thames and Hudson, 1977), 113–15. Bowie, *Aristophanes: Myth, Ritual and Comedy*, 36–38, sees Aristophanes as using the Anthesteria's ambiguities, particularly in the theme of integrating the stranger, Orestes, through the private drinking.

Although Aristophanes' festivals are not uncommonly displaced in time, like the Thesmophoria of the *Women at the Thesmophoria*, the sequence of festivals here seems pointed, as Lowell Edmunds, "Aristophanes' *Acharnians*," *Yale Classical Studies* 26 (1980): 19. Slater, *Spectator Politics*, 63, as Martha Habash, "Two Complementary Festivals in Aristophanes' *Acharnians*," *American Journal of Philology* 116 (1995): 559–77, sees the sequence as a triumphant move through the full agricultural year. However, the play's explicit declaration that "we are all here at the Lenaia" (504), recalled by the closing references to Aristophanes' hoped-for victory (Sommerstein, *Knights*, 215; S. Douglas Olson, *Aristophanes: Acharnians* [Oxford: Oxford University Press, 2002], 365), reminds the audience that it is still January.

30. The ambivalence that Aristophanes generates toward his comic hero makes a similar point: in appealing to his audience as a social body, he shows up the hero's violation of social norms as the act of a buffoon, but in appealing to them as individuals, he simultaneously invites the audience to delight vicariously in the hero's lawlessness and freedom. See Alan Sommerstein, *Talking about Laughter and Other Studies in Greek Comedy* (Oxford: Oxford University Press, 2009), 204–22.

31. For Dikaiopolis as "Just City," see Cyril Bailey, "Who Played Dikaiopolois?," in *Greek Poetry and Life: Essays Presented to Gilbert Murray on His Seventieth Birthday*, eds. Cyril Bailey, E. A. Barber, C. M. Bowra, J. D. Denniston, and D. L. Page (Oxford: Clarendon Press, 1936), 231–40; Edmunds, "Aristophanes' *Acharnians*," 1n2; Foley, "Tragedy and Politics in Aristophanes' *Acharnians*," 46n52. Bowie, "Who Is Dicaeopolis?," 183–85, argues that the name refers to Eupolis, and Sidwell, *Aristophanes the Democrat*, argues that the entire play is Eupolidean, which seems overelaborate. See Parker, "Eupolis or Dicaeopolis," 201–8 *contra*, and Carlo Ferdinando Russo, *Aristophanes: An Author for the Stage*, trans. Kevin Wren (London: Routledge, 1994), 34–35, 252. On the implications of Dikaiopolis as his own city, seen as positive, see J. F. McGlew, *Citizens on Stage* (Ann Arbor: University of Michigan Press, 2002), 66ff.; Peter Nichols, *Aristophanes' Novel Forms: The Political Role of Drama* (London: Minerva Press, 1998), 60; and as ambivalent, Fisher, "Multiple Personalities and Dionysiac Festivals," 31–47. C. H. Whitman, *The Heroic Paradox: Essays on Homer, Sophocles, and Aristophanes* (Ithaca: Cornell University Press, 1982), 41, renders as "man of public justice"; N. J. Lowe, *Comedy* [*Greece and Rome, New Surveys in the Classics* No. 37] (Cambridge: Cambridge University Press, 2008), 39, as "just-[in-respect-of-his-]city"; MacDowell, *Aristophanes and Athens*, 78–79, gives other explanations, such as "making the city just," "just towards the city," and so forth.

32. Biles, *Aristophanes and the Poetics of Competition*, 56–96, takes the identification of Aristophanes and Dikaiopolis as straightforward throughout the play, while Christopher Pelling, *Literary Texts and the Greek Historian* (London: Routledge, 2000), 147–49, sees a slide. See Foley, "Tragedy and Politics in Aristophanes' *Acharnians*," 37, 45; Carey, "The Purpose of Aristophanes' *Acharnians*," 245–63; Bowie, "Who Is Dicaeopolis?," 184, for the *parabasis*' interest in victory rather than peace; contrary, Biles, *Aristophanes and the Poetics of Competition*, 78–79; Fisher, "Multiple Personalities and Dionysiac Festivals," 38–39, with further references. Newinger, "War and Peace," 219–37, describes Aristophanes as no pacifist; and see Forrest, "Aristophanes' *Acharnians*," 1–12; Gomme, "Aristophanes and Politics," 97–109. The distinction is underlined by the chorus' attack on Antimachus (1150–73), both taking up the theme of exclusion and contrasting Lamachus ("Mr. Very-warlike") to "Mr. Anti-War."

33. As Kenneth Rothwell, Jr., *Nature, Culture, and the Origins of Greek Comedy: A Study of Animal Choruses* (Cambridge: Cambridge University Press, 2007), 176–81; Jeffrey Henderson, "Mass versus Elite and the Comic Heroism of Peisetairos," in *The City as Comedy: Society and Representation in Athenian Drama*, ed. Gregory Dobrov (Chapel Hill: University of North Carolina Press, 1997), 135–48. Dunbar, *Aristophanes: Birds*, 12, argues that "the audience were expected to see Peisetairos as a sympathetic character"; Bowie, *Aristophanes: Myth, Ritual and Comedy*, 166–77, that Peisetairos is a new Tereus; and see Reckford, *Aristophanes' Old-and-New Comedy*, 342, for a balance of positive and negative.

34. Alan Sommerstein, *Birds* (Warminster: Aris and Phillips, 1987), 303 and 2–3, compares the play and the roast birds to *Animal Farm*; similarly, Thomas Hubbard, "Utopianism and the Sophistic City in Aristophanes," in *The City as Comedy: Society and Representation in Athenian Drama*, ed. Gregory Dobrov (Chapel Hill: University of North Carolina Press, 1997), 35 and 45n62, for further references. Henderson, "Mass versus Elite," 144–45, defends the roasting. MacDowell, *Aristophanes and Athens*, 225: "the line is merely a joke which passes immediately" does not consider that Heracles' gluttony is a constant reminder of the birds roasting onstage.

35. See C. W. Dearden, *The Stage of Aristophanes* (London: University of London, Athlone Press, 1976), 42, for comedy as generally about Athens, and, in contrast, Dunbar, *Aristophanes: Birds*, 4–5, for the play (as Hypothesis II 9–14) as utopian. For the play as an escape from war, see E. M. Blaiklock, "Walking Away from the News: An Autobiographical Interpretation of Aristophanes' *Birds*," *Greece and Rome* 1 (1954): 98–111; as a criticism of tyranny, William Arrowsmith, "Aristophanes' *Birds*: The Fantasy Politics of Eros," *Arion* 1 (1973): 119–67; as utopian, Konstan, *Greek Comedy and Ideology*, 3–22, and Thomas Hubbard, *The Mask of Comedy* (Ithaca: Cornell University Press, 1991), 158–82, as a dystopia. F. E. Romer, "Good Intentions and the ὁδὸς ἡ ἐς κόρακας," in *The City as Comedy: Society and Representation in Athenian Drama*, ed. Gregory Dobrov (Chapel Hill: University of North Carolina Press, 1997), 51–74, sees moral ambiguity, and see Romer, "Atheism, Impiety and the *Limos Melios* in Aristophanes' *Birds*," *American Journal of Philology* 115 (1994): 351–65, for the play as *Realpolitik* with piety based

on power. For a survey of views, see MacDowell, *Aristophanes and Athens*, 227–28, and the various interpretations in Gregory Dobrov, ed., *The City as Comedy: Society and Representation in Athenian Drama* (Chapel Hill: University of North Carolina Press, 1997), although cast in the either–or terms of either an escapist fantasy or a satire on Sicily. Hubbard, *The Mask of Comedy*, 42, provides a bibliography.

36. See Victor Ehrenberg, "Polypragmosyne: A Study in Greek Politics," *Journal of Hellenic Studies* 67 (1947): 46–67.

37. The birds' life, particularly as without money (156–57), recalls the Golden Age, an association repeated in Tereus' call to the birds to gather (230–59) and in their various lyrics (737–52, 769–84, 1088–1101). For the golden age theme in Old Comedy, see Cratinus' *Plutoi*, Telecleides' *Amphictyons*, Crates' *Beasts*, Eupolis' *Golden Race*, Pherecrates' *Wildmen*, Archippus' *Fishes*, and Phrynichus' *Monotropos*; Storey, *Eupolis*, 268–69; Paola Ceccarelli, "Life among the Savages and Escape from the City," in *The Rivals of Aristophanes: Studies in Athenian Old Comedy*, eds. David Harvey and John Wilkins (Swansea: Duckworth and the Classical Press of Wales, 2000), 453–71; Dunbar, *Aristophanes: Birds*, 6–7.

38. See Sommerstein, *Birds*, 251, and contrary, Dunbar, *Aristophanes: Birds*, 332.

39. See Sommerstein, *Birds*, 252; Arrowsmith, "Aristophanes' *Birds*," 119–67; Whitman, *Aristophanes and the Comic Hero*, 198; Gregory Dobrov, *Figures of Play: Greek Drama and Metafictional Poetics* (Oxford: Oxford University Press, 2001), 118–20. Slater, *Spectator Politics*, 148: "Divine democracy is represented by a glutton and a dolt, while bird democracy devours its own. It is hard to claim we have come very far from Athens after all." Bowie, *Aristophanes: Myth, Ritual and Comedy*, 175, seeing no escape from Athens, quotes Psalm 139.7-9: "Whither shall I go from thy spirit. . . ." For Peisetairos' continuing sense of his Greek identity, see also *Birds* 1244.

40. For the *episkopos*, who saw that Athenian law was enforced in the allied states (hence his inquiry for the Athenian *proxenoi*, 1021), see R. Meigs, *The Athenian Empire* (Oxford: Oxford University Press, 1972), 212–13, 583–86. Although "Decree-seller" is not an official position, his reference to Athenian judicial penalties (1035–36) and the Athenian coinage decree (1040–41) explains his status, as Dunbar, *Aristophanes: Birds*, 384–87; Sommerstein, *Birds*, 269, who also discusses the reading. In contrast, the sycophant is a purely domestic product, as *Acharnians* 900ff. The lyrics describing exotic lands—that harbor the highwayman Orestes (1491), Socrates (1555), Gorgias (apparently an honorary Athenian), and Phillip (1701)—go on to mock the Athenians' ability to be everywhere, even while still remaining in Athens.

41. Henderson, "Mass versus Elite," 135–48.

42. See Platter, *Aristophanes and the Carnival of Genres*, 37; Christopher Pelling, "Conclusion," in *Greek Tragedy and the Historian*, ed. Christopher Pelling (Oxford: Oxford University Press, 1997), 213–36. M. Griffith, "Brilliant Dynasts: Power and Politics in the *Oresteia*," *Classical Antiquity* 14 (1995): 62–129, and Griffith, "The King and Eye: The Rule of the Father in Greek Tragedy," *Proceedings*

of the Cambridge Philological Society 44 (1998): 20–80, sees audience members identifying with characters of their own class. In response, Carter, *The Politics of Greek Tragedy*, 48–49, reasonably points out that nothing prevents lower-class audience members from identifying with Orestes or Oedipus.

43. See David Konstan, "The Greek Polis and Its Negations: Versions of Utopia in Aristophanes' *Birds*," in *The City as Comedy: Society and Representation in Athenian Drama*, ed. Gregory Dobrov (Chapel Hill: University of North Carolina Press, 1997), 17: "It [Cloudcuckooland] is a complex image of Athens' own contradictions, its communal solidarity and its political and social divisions, the conservatism that looked to the image of an ancestral constitution, and an imperial will to power"; and Henderson, "Mass versus Elite," 136–37: "Like the Assembly debaters of 415, *Birds* was designed to evoke responses to a grandiose vision of Athens that were at once contradictory and equally compelling." For comedy (and tragedy) as showing the city to itself, see Gregory Dobrov, "The Poet's Voice in the Evolution of Dramatic Dialogism," in *Beyond Aristophanes: Transition and Diversity in Greek Comedy*, ed. Gregory Dobrov (Atlanta: Scholars Press, 1995), 88–89; Goldhill, *The Poet's Voice*, 185–86.

44. The victory at Arginusae, so important that the slaves who fought in it were freed and apparently made Athenian citizens, occurred about six months earlier and forms a continuous undercurrent in the play. Cleophon, who was responsible for the Athenian rejection of Sparta's offer of peace, is referred to throughout, most emphatically in the play's last line (678–85, 1504, 1532–33). The execution of the commanders for their failure to rescue the dead and dying (having been prevented by a sudden storm) appears at 1195–96, while both the freed slaves and Theramenes, who was responsible for the commanders' trial (541, 967, 968–70), are referred to regularly. See Peter Hunt, "The Slaves and the Generals of Arginusae," *American Journal of Philology* 122 (2001): 359–80, for an account of the battle and its implications.

45. As Helene Foley, "Generic Boundaries in Late Fifth-Century Athens," in *Performance, Iconography, Reception: Studies in Honour of Oliver Taplin*, eds. Martin Revermann and Peter Wilson (Oxford: Oxford University Press, 2008), 24–26; Dobrov, *Figures of Play*, 155: "it is the Dionysus persona who, from the broadest perspective of *Frogs* as a contemporary performance, demonstrates comedy's ability to manipulate and surpass tragedy to provide a powerful remedy for the city's troubles"; Reckford, *Aristophanes' Old-and-New Comedy*, 436: "Euripides' death brings Dionysus to confront the world of death and corpses with Old Comic clowning, and to renew himself, and Aristophanes with him, at the deepest sources of the Old Comic spirit"; Hubbard, *The Mask of Comedy*, 218–19, sees the dramatic contest as finally between the "high" and "low" elements in Aristophanes himself; and see B. A. Heiden, "Tragedy and Comedy in the *Frogs* of Aristophanes," *Ramus* 20 (1991): 95–111.

46. See Slater, *Spectator Politics*, 308n52; Kenneth Dover, *Aristophanes: Frogs* (Oxford: Clarendon Press, 1993), 23; H.-J. Newinger, "Elektra in Aristophanes' Wolken," *Hermes* 89 (1961): 427–30, and for a different view, Z. P. Biles, "Aeschy-

lus' Afterlife: Reperformance by Decree in 5th C. Athens?" *Illinois Classical Studies* 31–32 (2006–2007): 206–42. Although G. O. Hutchinson, *Aeschylus: Seven against Thebes* (Oxford: Clarendon Press, 1985), xlii–xliii (explaining the spurious ending of the *Seven*), argues that there were no revivals until 386 BCE, when one old play was performed at each festival, the four posthumous victories won by Aeschylus' sons are not adequate to explain the continual reference to his work, or *Acharnians* 10 and *Frogs* 86.

47. G. Wills, "Aeschylus' Victory in the *Frogs*," *American Journal of Philology* 90 (1969): 57, argues that Aeschylus does not reply at 1461: "Athens will live if it desires the resurrection of Aeschylus. The mere willingness to listen to him, to its best self, its heroic past, will effect a salvation that no scheming could accomplish."

48. For the play's two halves, see Rosemary Harriot, *Aristophanes: Poet and Dramatist* (London: Croom Helm, 1986), 115; Charles Segal, "The Character and Cults of Dionysus and the Unity of the *Frogs*," *Harvard Studies in Classical Philology* 65 (1961): 207–8, who connects them through the character of Dionysus; W. B. Stanford, *Aristophanes: Frogs* (London: Bristol Classical Press, 1983 [1958]), xxiv–xxvi, who sees this as usual in Aristophanes. As Oliver Taplin, *Greek Tragedy in Action* (Berkeley: University of California Press, 1978), 148, on the *Ajax*: "It is incredible, and yet typical, that the fact that the *Ajax* is divided into two parts has so often been treated as though it were some accident or miscalculation, when Sophocles has constructed this division so carefully and deliberately, and when the relation between the two halves is so clearly one of his chief artistic concerns." The change has been attributed to the sudden death of Sophocles, to the inconsistency of comedy, or just to Aristophanes' change of mind. See J. T. Hooker, "The Composition of the *Frogs*," *Hermes* 108 (1980): 169–82, for a number of such suggestions; Russo, *Aristophanes*, 198–202; Whitman, *Aristophanes and the Comic Hero*, 230ff., for inconsistencies due to hasty revision. See also Dover, *Aristophanes: Frogs*, 6–9, for a summary and a backhanded compliment: "It is hard on a dramatist if his most striking and successful innovation in plot-structure is to be treated by posterity, because his other plots are not so good, as the unhappy consequence of hasty revision" (9).

49. Dover, *Aristophanes: Frogs*, 105. Nichols, *Aristophanes' Novel Forms*, 149ff., points out that as Aeschylus is never mentioned in the first part of the play, his being brought back is even more of a surprise.

50. See Alan Sommerstein, *Frogs* (Warminster: Aris and Phillips, 1996), 290, for Dionysus speaking of Athens as "we" at 1448–50. Aristophanes further emphasizes the metatheater by having Dionysus appeal to his priest, seated in the front row of the theater (296), and by bringing the critical acumen of the audience into the contest (1099–1118), as also at 1475: "What's shameful, if it seem not so to the audience?" Similarly, Charon charges two obols rather than one (140) because this is the entrance price to the theater, as Sommerstein, *Frogs*, 168; Slater, *Spectator Politics*, 185.

51. From the common Attic form of Persephone's name, Pherephatta (671), to the "maintenance in the Prytaneum and a chair next to Pluto's" (764–65).

52. See, for example, Thucydides 8.1 and 96, and the immortal version of Walt Kelly's Pogo: "We have met the enemy and he is us" (as Reckford, *Aristophanes' Old-and-New Comedy*, 193).

53. For these lines as a doublet, dropped in the play's second production (perhaps after the war), see Sommerstein, *Frogs*, 286ff.; Dover, *Aristophanes: Frogs*, 373ff.

54. The link between community and kinship is reinforced by Aristophanes' persistent and unusual use of kinship words for what is "noble" or "gentlemanly," such as *gennaios* and *gennadas* (as the more usual *eugeneis*, 727). For *gennadas*: 640, 738, 739, 997; *gennaios*: 97, 356, 378, 615, 1011, 1019, 1031, 1050 (twice); and *genos* and *sungeneis* of kinship: 698, 701, 1266. See Dover, *Aristophanes: Frogs*, 46, for the unusual "*gennadas*"; Aristotle, *Rhetoric*, 1390b21–23, for *gennaios* as abiding by *phusis*; and *Hippolytus* 1452 as "legitimate."

55. See James Redfield, "Drama and Community: Aristophanes and Some of his Rivals," in *Nothing to Do with Dionysus?: Athenian Drama in its Social Context*, eds. John J. Winkler and Froma I. Zeitlin (Princeton, NJ: Princeton University Press, 1990), 328: "In tragedy, culture is seen as continuous with nature, in that both are arenas of lawful, comprehensible forces linked by man's submission to the gods. In Old Comedy, on the other hand, the hero need not submit to the gods; neither is nature permanent. The species are not separate or stable: a man could be a wasp or a horse, could converse with frogs or clouds. Amid such universal anarchy, the cultural order must seem absurdly insubstantial."

7

On the Anabasis of Trygaeus
An Introduction to Aristophanes' *Peace*

Wayne Ambler

Aristophanes' *Peace* fits into the larger constellation of Aristophanes' eleven surviving comedies, especially in three ways. Most obviously, it is a peace play and hence is naturally grouped with the *Acharnians* and *Lysistrata*, the other two plays in which peace is achieved through comic means. Second, it is one of three plays in which a mortal hero successfully defies Zeus and the Olympian gods, so it invites study in connection with the *Birds* and the *Plutus*. Third, and thanks to the observations of Leo Strauss, we can see that the *Peace* provides a magnificent "emblem" for reflecting in general terms on the sources and character of the comedy that pervades all of Aristophanes' plays: as Trygaeus reaches heaven on the back of a disgusting dung beetle in the *Peace*, so does the comic poet routinely ascend to his high themes by means of low humor.[1] Our introduction takes up each of these three topics, for they are inextricably related.[2]

The protagonist, Trygaeus, is in anguish over war-caused suffering both beyond and within his own family, but he traces the ills of war to Zeus. How, he wonders, could Zeus allow the Greeks to suffer as he does? Preferring to doubt that Zeus knows what is going on rather than assume that the king of the gods is powerless, callously indifferent to human interests, or actively hostile to men, Trygaeus contrives a ride to heaven to gain a hearing with him. On arriving at the gods' residence, he learns that the Olympians became annoyed at watching men fight and listening to their pleas for help, so they moved farther away and abandoned men to the malignant force of

War, who has buried alive the goddess Peace and is gleefully preparing new tortures for the Greeks.[3] Having now learned that Zeus has actively chosen to send the Greeks to their destruction, Trygaeus decides to defy both War and Zeus by rescuing Peace. After doing so with the complicity of Hermes and the hard work especially of peace-loving farmers, Trygaeus makes a triumphant return to Athens with Peace and her two attendants. Trygaeus thus becomes a hero among peace-loving Athenians for having delivered them from war. Although his pious fellow citizens do not celebrate him in these terms, he is also a model of successful defiance of the gods. In this last respect, he shares much in common with Peisetairos and Chremylus, the heroes of the *Birds* and *Plutus*.[4]

Peace

In the spring of 421, the Athenians and Spartans swore to abide by a treaty that promised to end a war that had already lasted ten years; thus began the so-called Peace of Nicias.[5] Immediately before they did so, Aristophanes' *Peace* presented a comic account of the steps leading to this very treaty. The *Peace* is thus closely tied to an event that gripped the attention of its first audience. While it is naturally grouped with the other two of his plays in which peace is achieved onstage, in neither the *Acharnians* nor the *Lysistrata* does the comic action mirror a peace achieved in real life, as occurs in the *Peace*.[6] Scholarly interest in the rich history of Athens and its long war with Sparta makes it inevitable that the *Peace* be read with close attention to the political events with which it deals, though this is not to say that scholarly interest always carries us most directly to the heart of Aristophanes' comedies.[7]

The causes of the peace as presented in the *Peace* are at first glance wholly comic. Thucydides never mentions that an ordinary Athenian vinedresser somehow succeeded in a mad plan to fly to heaven on the back of a dung beetle, that he discovered the goddess Peace being buried alive by War, that he defied the Olympian gods and rescued her, and that this defiance of the gods was the reason for the coming of peace among the Athenians and Spartans. The historian focused on other matters, such as troops on the ground, shifting strategic advantages, and the personal character and abilities of leaders like Brasidas, Cleon, Nicias, and Pleistoanax. But the gulf between the comic poet and the historian narrows upon reflection, for the success of the madman in Aristophanes proves dependent on political circumstances and is limited by them. Let me trace this observation.

In the first place, Trygaeus' wild scheme does not simply triumph over every obstacle in its path; it triumphs especially when obstacles are removed from its path. Although it may be contrary to all good sense and natural laws for a man to ride to heaven on the back of a bug, the *Peace* is in its own way respectful and illustrative of the human and natural causes of events.

For example, as in Thucydides (5.16.1), so in Aristophanes (234–300) the deaths of Cleon and Brasidas were important conditions of the peace. Aristophanes shows that War is able to terrify both Hermes and Trygaeus, but his ability to work harm is dependent on his possession of a "pestle." Either Cleon or Brasidas would have made a fine pestle for War (259–84), but without a pestle to go with his mortar, his terrors prove empty. Along with Trygaeus, we shudder to think what would have happened if War had found human support for his plan to mash the Greeks into a pulp, but he appears impotent without this support. Trygaeus triumphs over reason in being able to fly to heaven on a beetle, but at least one condition for his success in heaven is that actual conditions back on earth be favorable to peace. In this regard, he does not so much cause the peace as observe from heaven the earthly reasons that make peace possible.

Although the deaths of Cleon and Brasidas were conditions for establishing peace among the Greeks, they were not by themselves sufficient to achieve it. It was also important that the Greeks be hungry for peace, or at least that enough well-situated Greeks were. As the *Peace* teaches, however, the Greeks were not uniformly enthusiastic for peace; nor was their enthusiasm for peace unrivaled by other interests. The *Peace* is a play in part about the achievement of the Peace of Nicias, but its riotous comedy does not keep it from disclosing the serious challenges that stood in the way of attaining a durable peace.

Consider, for example, the scene in which Trygaeus and Hermes defy War and lead the Greeks in the excavation of the goddess. Note in the first place that it is human beings, not gods, who do the work of digging the goddess out of War's pit. Moreover, Aristophanes could have depicted them as all contributing with enthusiasm to the achievement of a common objective. Zeus and War would in this way have been defeated by a Panhellenic movement, and the play would have been not only comic but also upbeat about the prospects for a peace sought after by all Greeks. As it is, however, Aristophanes' Greeks are very much at odds with one another, and not all of them seem interested in excavating the goddess at all. It is true that when first told of the prospect of unearthing Peace, the chorus responds with uncontrollable joy. They sing, shout, and dance: they even seem to lose sight of both their overjoyed limbs and their own best interests, so they fail to keep quiet and thus risk stirring the gods or Cerberus into action (301–60). But once it comes to the challenge of actually excavating the goddess, they slip into dissention and work at cross-purposes. Collaboration proves impossible, and at one point or another, blame for blocking the peace effort is leveled against the Boeotians (464–66), Lamachus (473), the Argives (475–77, 493), some of the Laconians (478–80), the Megarians (500–2), the Athenians (503–7), and even the two leaders, Hermes and Trygaeus (469–71). Surely all parties want peace, but they all want peace especially on their own terms. Nor is the desire for peace sufficient to achieve it: strength is also needed, and the weakness of the famished Megarians is a second reason they contribute little to the cause (481–83). These difficulties remind us that Hermes had indicated well before the excavation began that it is the weaker side that prefers peace (211–19); when one gains the upper hand, the desire for victory trumps the desire for peace.

That not all Greeks seek peace with equal zeal is a problem solved by entrusting the excavation to a class of Greeks deemed especially peace loving, the farmers (508–26). Even if it is not desired by all groups, peace may be achievable if those who favor it are awarded positions of special responsibility, and the *Peace* suggests more than once that Athenian farmers were generally more inclined to peace than the artisans were. What is generally true need not be always true, however, and the farmers' enthusiasm for peace is not a permanent part of their character. We learn this when Hermes explains how it happened that Peace vanished in the first place (601–705). Once they were herded into the city as part of Pericles' policy of not challenging the invading Spartans in the field, their spirit of revenge, as they watched the invaders destroy their farms, overtook their judgment, and the demagogic speakers of Athens were able to turn them into enthusiasts for war.[8] While he assigns special responsibility for the war to Pericles, Hermes indicates that Pericles acted out of fear of the farmers' "natures and biting character." He develops this charge by stressing that "you [farmers]" were angry and "baring your teeth" at one another (607, 619–20).[9] A further complication is that the farmers are ignorant, at least according to Hermes, so they are thus subject to being manipulated by demagogues (632–35). Different Greek cities are differently disposed toward peace, and so are different groups within Athens. Peace may be "dear to all," but she is not durably dearest to any (294).

Lest we be left wondering whether there is any truth to Hermes' criticism of the farmers and the Athenians in general, Aristophanes shows us how his charges are received by the accused. When he hears that the farmers bear important responsibility for the war, that they are *not* inherently peaceful,

Trygaeus does not decry this as slander: he either meekly and apologetically recognizes it as fact (668–69, 685–87) or actually defends (and illustrates) the farmers' militant spirit and readiness to exact revenge (628–29). More broadly, Hermes says nothing about the gods being the causes of the war; rather, he presents a wholly human account—if at least our opinions about the gods are included among all things human—and he does not spare the farmers from having played a decisive role. Neither Trygaeus nor anyone else challenges this new account of the war as being man-made and, in part, farmer made.[10] In the same vein, the generally peace-loving Chorus later promises to be "more gentle" to the allies; they do not promise to liberate them or to be perfectly gentle to them (934–36).[11] I consider below, in the section titled "Gods," how Trygaeus attempts to guide the farmers' piety in such a way that it adds additional support to their growing desire for peace.

Not even our peace-loving hero really loves peace without qualification. He has been beaten down by war and wants peace for all the Greeks, of course, but he wants it even more for the Athenians, still more for Athenian farmers, and most for his own family.[12] He expresses, that is, some generous and sincere sentiments on behalf of the Greeks in general, but he shows no special solicitude for the sufferings of the Laconians, Megarians, or Sicilians (242–50). Only when War indicates that he is planning new horrors for the Athenians is Trygaeus especially moved (252–54). And he is sensitive above all to his own domestic hardships (119–21). More generally, Trygaeus shows some of the spirit that can lead to or aggravate wars; he is not a Cleonymus and does not admire his "peace at any price" approach to war (1301–4), he uses physical force against the prophet Hierocles (1119), and he joyfully adds insult to the injury of having put arms merchants and arms makers out of business (1208–64). At the level of strategy, he is fully aware that peace between Athens and Sparta would allow these two superpowers to dominate the rest of the Greeks (1082). He seeks peace, but he does not seek it as a final and sufficient good. Powerful though it is, his devotion to peace is—like that of other Greeks—at risk of being sidetracked or trumped.

As happens also in the *Acharnians*, *Knights*, *Clouds*, and *Wasps*, so in the *Peace* the action of the play is suspended during the parabasis, while the poet speaks directly to the audience in his own name. When he does so here, nothing he says opposes the view that peace would be good for Athens. Indeed, in the ode following the anapests, the Muse is invited to reject wars and dance with the Chorus in celebration of such peaceful delights as the weddings of gods (775–79). Nevertheless, the anapests show the poet to have a combative spirit, more like that of Trygaeus than of Peace herself. Verbs he uses of his own actions include "do battle," "drive out," "cashier," "make war," and "hold out against"; descriptions of his enemies include "fearsome" and "monstrous." And only here does the play include references to victory (768–69). It is true that the victory referred to is in the comic competition, and much of his combativeness is directed against the bad comedy of rival poets. When he uses "make war," it is against lice, not Spartans! But perhaps even this suggests that peace is not what is dearest: victory is in some cases worth a battle. However this may be, the poet also claims to have done battle not only with rival poets; like an angry Heracles, he took on Cleon himself, a fearsome character if ever there were one. He did this for Athens and for her island empire as well (760). As previous paragraphs have suggested, the *Peace* is measured in its assessment of peace.

Finally, Trygaeus celebrates at the end of the play not only because Peace has come to Athens but also because he was the one who brought her. His special responsibility for this great blessing not surprisingly receives a lot of attention by the Chorus, and Trygaeus is clearly pleased to be the author of such consequential achievements. It is he who will be rejuvenated by his successes (861), he who will receive a new divine bride, he whose happiness will be just (865), and he who is a savior of all human beings (915). To bring peace is a greater good than to merely receive it.

The evidence assembled in the previous several paragraphs shows that, successful as Trygaeus and his colleagues are in bringing Peace to the Greeks, the prospects for a durable peace are not good, whether they keep a firm grip on the goddess or not. This wild comedy can be read as being wholly unbelievable, but its crazy conceit should not obscure a darker reality. The desire to avoid defeat is fully compatible with the desire to obtain victory, and neither is quite the same as the desire for peace. Peace is beautiful, but she is praised especially for the good things she is now seen as bringing or making available for enjoyment: harvests, festivals, sheep, women's breasts, cakes of fruit, wine, olive trees, and more (520–38, 575–81). She is, then, a "gain" (588). Peace surely can bring great blessings and hence can be a reason for joy, but Victory was also a beautiful goddess and no less beneficent.

Perhaps this point can be clarified by stating it as a disagreement with an alternative view, which maintains the following: "[T]he play offers unrealistic and perhaps even misguided solutions to the world's problems," for "the play as a whole is predicated on the hope that we are equally capable of redeeming and saving ourselves and of constructing a new world which will be both more livable and perhaps ultimately more sacred than the old."[13] This might be true if Aristophanes were encouraging the hope that it is possible to visit Zeus, the cause of our problems, and wrest control of the human future from him, thus constructing a new world. But, as I see it, the play shows Zeus to be impotent and, in any event, not the real cause of our mortal woes. Far from being of divine origin, peace and its blessings come to the Greeks in part because of certain chance events, especially the deaths of Cleon and Brasidas, and in part because of the way some leaders took advantage of this opportunity; they come to them also in spite of still-strong differences not only among the Greeks in general but even among the Athenians themselves. At the very same time that the *Peace* shows Trygaeus' triumphant excavation of Peace, it also points to the lingering and inherent difficulties that will have to be overcome if an enduring peace is to be secured. It is true that the main action of the *Peace* is wildly upbeat, and the play ends happily: an ordinary farmer rides a bug to heaven and returns with Peace for the Greeks and a luscious bride for himself, and everyone—or almost everyone—joins in the fun at the end.[14] But there are strings attached to this promising conclusion, so that we really should not take it to mean that the Greeks have won a securely pacific world. The central action of the *Peace* shows a great deed achieved by collaboration, but its examples of discord are far more numerous, even after the goddess Peace is on hand and at the height of her powers.

Gods

As we have seen, the *Peace* is deeply concerned with issues related to the Peloponnesian War—not only regarding the immanent Peace of Nicias but also regarding its conditions and limitations. Nevertheless, the initial focus of the play is on the general relations between gods and men: Trygaeus complains about Zeus, not Spartans or Athenians.[15] This is the main reason the play makes for provocative and enlightening reading for readers unthreatened themselves by war with Sparta. What is the character of the gods, to what extent are they responsible for our sufferings, and what can and should we mortals do about it?

Poets and thinkers supply various and opposed answers to these grand questions, so Aristophanes makes a great (if comic) claim for the authority of his play and his hero to settle them. Although Hercules, Odysseus, and Orpheus all descend to Hades and manage to return, as does Aristophanes' Dionysius in his *Frogs*, I know of no Greek hero who ascends to heaven and returns to file a report, save Trygaeus (if others are willing to join me in calling him a hero).[16] His success is even set in sharp relief by Aristophanes' allusions to the failure of the hero Bellerophon and his famous winged horse,

Pegasus, which was dramatized in an earlier play by Euripides.[17] Bellerophon also wished to carry a protest to the gods, apparently, but Trygaeus succeeds where his tragic counterpart fell to his death.[18] Only the *Peace*, then, can provide evidence that can vouch for, amend, or contradict such reports as are passed down by the tradition, such as those we read in Homer.[19] Nor, of course, is Trygaeus unique only in ascending and returning; he is also distinguished by his victory over Zeus. Socrates' basket rose only a modest height to help him conduct his elementary studies of the gods, and his conclusions even contributed to his defeat and the loss of his Thinkery. On the other hand, Trygaeus' bug ascended to heaven itself, where Trygaeus used what he learned to defy the king of the gods. Surely his unparalleled successes merit attention.

Trygaeus' successful anabasis results in a troubling view of heaven. Rather than finding a holy place populated by gods willing to help mortals end or reduce their war-induced suffering, Trygaeus finds heaven to be dominated by War, to whom the gods have given their blessing to do with men whatever he wishes. War's first act is to bury Peace alive; his next move will be to mash up the Greek cities in his massive mortar. As for the Olympians, they have vacated the premises, save for a temporary skeleton staff in the form of Hermes, and there is no evidence that they give any further thought either to their former abode or to their mortal charges. Indeed, their very purpose in leaving heaven was to get even farther from the Greeks, for men at war annoy them by making noise and bothering them with cries for help. Hermes insists that the gods generally favored peace among men, but even if his claims are true, they did nothing effective to promote it. There apparently was a fleeting moment, we infer from Hermes' report, when the gods' interest in not being bothered coincided with the Greeks' (unrecognized) interest in peace, and the gods offered treaties to them (204–19). Whatever the precise character of the gods' efforts in making these offers, they were easily rebuffed and accomplished nothing. The efforts of Peace herself are similarly lacking in energy and unproductive, as we learn later (635–38, 665–67). The most effective action of the gods in the entire play is their removal of themselves beyond the range of all collateral damage and even collateral noise. When it comes to abdication, the Olympians are champions.

Trygaeus' successful arrival in heaven thus asks us to consider a heaven devoid of Olympians but in the hands of a being that delights in war: heaven now houses only a militant force hostile to humans.[20] This distressing but not entirely unbelievable view of things contains a ray of hope, however: terrible though he appears, War does not prove powerful enough to dictate events. Gods hostile to men would represent a massive problem, but the matter becomes more manageable if their power is limited. As it turns out, there are circumstances beyond War's control. He can mash up the Greeks, apparently, but to do so he needs a "pestle." The best pestles for this purpose, Cleon and Brasidas, happen to have died, however. Their deaths give Trygaeus an opportunity, although he must defy Zeus to seize it. Not believing for an instant that the will of Zeus determines or is a guide to what is good for himself or others, he does not hesitate. But with what tactics does he overcome Zeus and his subordinate, War?

It is to human beings that Trygaeus turns for help in foiling Zeus. He summons the Greeks to dig Peace out of the pit into which War has interred her. That Trygaeus calls to human beings for help does not mean he turns his back on the gods; he is not a "humanist." It is to help a goddess that he calls the Greeks, after all. He must believe both that the goddess is important for peace among the Greeks and that she is so weak that she needs human help. He envisions mutual dependence between gods and men, not the supremacy of one or the other. Moreover, when an angry Hermes shows up and tries to block his rebellious effort to rescue Peace, Trygaeus goes to some lengths to pacify him and secure his collaboration. Along with flattery, another bribe, reminders of past favors, and promises of future honors and benefactions, Trygaeus teaches Hermes that the Olympian gods are dependent on the Greeks for the sacrifices they enjoy and need (403–15).[21] Thus does Trygaeus put together a Greek alliance, aided by one god and in support of another, to defy Zeus and War.

In addition to Hermes, Trygaeus seeks further divine support, or at least the belief in further divine support. Just before the digging begins, when he needs to unite the Greeks in a laborious and risky common effort, he leads them in a public prayer (431–58).[22] He does not pray to Zeus, of course, for it is Zeus' decree that he needs help in evading; nor does he pray to Peace, because she is too weak to help herself, let alone help her helpers. He thus selects from the pantheon those deities who are most likely to be friendly to peace or to his project of promoting it. He includes Hermes first and then mentions the Graces, the Seasons, Aphrodite, and Yearning, while Hermes (or the Chorus) stresses that Ares is not among this prayer's addressees.[23]

To speak more generally, Trygaeus engages multiple divine beings, and their traits differ widely. Well before we meet the gods who are most unlike one another, War and Peace, we hear the servants trying to explain the presence of the monstrous and offensive beetle it is their task to feed. They assume the monster must have been sent by a divinity, but from which one? They are confident that such a disgusting creature could not have come from Aphrodite or the Graces, whose favors are so sweet and welcome, and that it must have come from Zeus (39–42). As suggested here, at least, nothing in Zeus' general reputation suggests he would not send evils upon some or all the Greeks below, even without manifest cause. Although the servants' conjecture proves wrong, it reminds us that Zeus is held to be powerful but not reliably philanthropic.[24]

Because there are multiple divinities, it is possible for Trygaeus to attack Zeus without attacking all of the gods at once. Dividing and conquering, a rebel can seek the assistance of some gods, old or new, to help in the attack against the king of the gods. As Chronos and Uranus were gods dethroned by a god, so might Zeus become a god overcome by gods and men together. Like Trygaeus, Peisetairos and Chremylus also seek divine support in their contests with Zeus; the former enlists Prometheus and the birds, whose divinity he announces and defends, and of course the latter depends on the power of Wealth.[25] At least to some extent, and especially in the case at hand and the case of the birds, these divine allies do not need to do anything but be believed in by men; their power resides in the human actions undertaken by their devoted followers. But as Nietzsche would later indicate in more memorable fashion, the end of belief is the death of a god; Trygaeus sees the corollary principle, that stimulating belief in Peace brings her to life and makes her a useful ally in limiting the primacy of War and Zeus. Put in different words, Trygaeus takes advantage of the Greeks' belief in some gods to help overthrow others. In keeping with this, he never indicates publicly that he is attacking Zeus (although he is pleased by harsh words for Ares [457–58]); he stresses the positive, that he is unearthing Peace.

Zeus does not do much for the simple reason that he does not exist except in and through the beliefs of the Greeks. Because he does not do much, he is at risk of not existing even in and through these beliefs: It cannot be easy, can it, for a god to live on durably even in the absence of vital signs? Belief would be strengthened by vigorous, visible action but need not die in its absence, however, if, at least, it can be supported by other "evidence." Beautiful statues and stories might constitute such evidence, but so too can any utility that might come from such belief. Even gods who are inactive for the reason Zeus is inactive can prosper if belief in them is useful in some way, such as by inspiriting, uniting, or otherwise strengthening followers. But such gods are also at risk of being destroyed if the people who believe in them are destroyed, as the god Hermes came to realize once the mortal Trygaeus explained the point: the Olympians depended on the

Greeks for their divinity, so if the Greeks wear themselves out with war, their gods fall with them (406–15).

Trygaeus effects what might be called a "pantheon shift." He does not explicitly reject the Greeks' current assortment of gods. He ceases to pray to the Olympians once he has gotten Peace aboveground, and he takes great pains to install her as an acknowledged deity back in Athens (922–1038), even over the objections of the oracle-monger Hierocles (1046–1126), but he never disavows the Olympians. He is an innovator, but he does not break openly with the existing tradition. He seeks to adjust the pantheon to favor Peace (in order to favor peace), not reject it root and branch. His goals are more modest than those of both Peisetairos and Socrates, for example. Because the Greeks have already shown by their deeds that the allure of peace is not irresistible, and because Ares himself must be overlooked, it is prudent for him to seek additional support from such established gods as Hermes, Aphrodite, and the Graces (456–58). It is prudent as well that he keep quiet about Zeus' opposition to his excavation. On the other hand, if birds are really much better gods than Zeus and the Olympians—if they can (be believed to) deliver not only peace but also wealth, health, happiness, youth, laughter, choruses, parties, and birds' milk (*Birds* 729–36)—then Peisetairos can do away with the Olympians altogether. The lifelessness or near lifelessness of Peace does not prevent Trygaeus from presenting her as a goddess, but it does keep him from making her the only god. It is good, then, that she emerges accompanied by Harvest and Festivity, who add further attractions to those of peace itself.[26]

Trygaeus must defend his pantheon shift against those who oppose it. On his return to Athens, this opposition is represented by the oracle-monger Hierocles and the son of Lamachus. (The opposition of the seller and makers of weapons is based especially on interest, not a view of the gods or the tradition more generally.) Because he seeks to promote peace, Trygaeus must quiet the son of Lamachus from singing always of war (1270–94). But because the boy's war-glorifying songs are rooted in epic sources, if not ultimately in nature itself, Trygaeus must contend not only against a boy but also against a powerful part of Greek tradition. He does so by emphatic denials strengthened by appeals to Dionysius, whom he can take as favoring his enterprise, and by proposing new subjects for song, such as men eating and drinking rather than fighting. Adultlike, he simply dismisses the boy when he fails to convert him, leaving us to wonder whether songs of eating can fully replace songs of fighting.

In a parallel but more difficult case, the oracle-monger Hierocles opposes Trygaeus' offering of sacrifices to Peace. He is surely a boaster looking for a free meal, but this does not mean he may not have a point. He insists that "[it] is not yet dear to the blessed gods, to cease from the din of battle," and this is precisely true of the Olympians as represented in the play: it was their choice that mankind be surrendered to War. He thus serves as another reminder that fidelity to Zeus and the Olympians can support war, or perhaps even tends to, even if the promotion of Peace cuts in a different direction. Hierocles defends his view in part on the oracular authority of Bacis; Trygaeus trumps him by appealing to Homer, but in order to make use of Homer, he must also falsify him. First, he claims—falsely, so far as I can tell—that Peace was also installed as a goddess in Homer (1089–94); second, he reinterprets other Homeric lines to make them seem to support peace, even though they do not (1096–98).[27] The lines in question are from the speech in which Nestor proposes a council rather than accepting immediately Agamemnon's dramatic proposal to abandon the war and return home (*Iliad* 9.63–64). That is, the lines quoted are part of a speech that supports the continuation of a war that had already raged just as long as the one that is the subject of Aristophanes' comedy. Moreover, this speech prepares for Nestor's next speech, which advises the Achaeans to try to win Achilles back into the fold, the better to prosecute the war. Finally, the lines themselves condemn the man who loves war "among his own people"; they contain no critique of war against foreign enemies. Trygaeus succeeds in making Peace an important goddess at Athens, but he needs to make limited war against the tradition to do so.[28]

To put it in general terms, Trygaeus seeks to unite the Greeks or at least the Athenians in a policy of peace by presenting and celebrating Peace as a divinity. That the Greeks want peace makes this possible, and when he succeeds, they will want peace that much more. The belief that she is a goddess and that she can deliver what the Greeks want makes it easier for them to work together. She is a visible, beautiful, tangible stimulus and focus for their efforts. The most evident reason for peace becomes the goddess Peace, and she becomes the focal point of the efforts of the Greeks; she mobilizes them in a way that the general promise of peace does not.

The power of the goddess is evident also when looking at Trygaeus' own political success. His route to influence stems from his uniting of the Athenian farmers, which he achieves by promoting Peace as divine and her excavation as achievable and worth working for. As a result of his successes, the Athenians celebrate him as "good for everyone," as a "savior for human beings," and as "justly having good things" (910–17, 1333–34). He did not, and perhaps could not, unite them on behalf of peace itself, but he does excite them about Peace the goddess. Even a cause very worthwhile in human terms may win a leader greater acclaim if he can make that cause divine.[29]

If Zeus does nothing to stop Trygaeus, Hermes at least tries to. The mortal, however, is ready for the god, and he wins him over in comic fashion by playing upon his various interests with promises, bribes, and flattery. One lesson is that the gods have needs of their own, and these needs are the key to manipulating them. In addition to reminding Hermes that the existence of the Olympians depends upon the existence of the Greeks, Trygaeus also promises Hermes that all current rites to the gods in Athens will be shifted over to him—including even the Great Panathenaea (then in honor of Athena) and the Mysteries (then in honor of Demeter)—if he agrees to help (418–20). Hermes appears eager for Trygaeus to shift the pantheon in his direction. Of course, the *Peace* comes to a conclusion with no hint that Trygaeus will keep this promise, for Hermes is never mentioned after Trygaeus makes his way back to earth, save only in the oath of a servant as the ceremony for installing Peace, not Hermes, gets under way (963). Trygaeus does shift the pantheon, and secures Hermes' help in so doing, but his shift favors Peace, not Hermes.

The Chorus calls upon Hermes to preside over the excavation, though they do so not so much on the grounds that he is a god as because he is—or so at least they now say—the wisest of the gods and is presumed to possess the craftsmanship necessary for this project (428–30). Wisdom or skill, whatever its source, is valued over divinity itself; this should be no surprise to anyone who has met War or Zeus. Hermes' main contribution, as it seems to me, is negative: he is persuaded not to call for help from Zeus or the other gods. Beyond this, it must boost the morale of the Greeks that a god joins in their labors; and in keeping with this, they include Hermes in their prayer while excluding Ares, of course, as they begin their work (456–57). Hermes also joins Trygaeus in pointing it out when some of the Greeks are not working hard to liberate the goddess (481–83, 500–507), but his reproaches are not enough to induce them to act as Hermes wishes. It is left to Trygaeus to put the job in the hands of those who will work together, the farmers. Even though half of the *Peace* is set in heaven, and gods join mortals on the stage, it is especially Trygaeus' leadership and the farmers' hard work that bring the goddess back to light. Even "the wisest of the gods" is less helpful to men than an Athenian vinedresser.[30] Trygaeus went to heaven to get Zeus to do his job; he ends up using the goddess Peace to get men to do theirs.

Trygaeus is not shocked or discouraged to discover that the gods do not act effectively on behalf of peace or the good of the Greeks. Perhaps he sees a bright side in his discovery: if divine allies are not sufficient to ensure victory, neither are divine enemies sufficient to ensure defeat.[31] To be abandoned by the Olympians is also to be liberated from them. The field is now manifestly open to Trygaeus and men generally. As we have seen, not even War can make war without Cleon or Brasidas.

Having noted that the help of Hermes, and the opposition of Zeus and War, are less determining than we might have expected, let us turn to the goddess who is at the center of Trygaeus' efforts. Peace is the source of great hope, but she is also shockingly weak. She is no match for War, of course, and it takes the mortal Trygaeus—aided by the chance deaths of the "pestles" Cleon and Brasidas—to liberate her. But even prior to her entombment, what did she do? There is no scene in which the goddess actually brought peace to warring men; she never pacified opposed parties.[32] When war broke out, she did not resist; she fled (614). Peace is professedly well disposed to peace among men, but she takes no effective measures to advance either her own cause or that of peaceful human beings. Hermes claims that Peace claims to have brought a basket of treaties to Athens after Pylos but was thrice rejected (664–67). It would be nice if these claims were true, but the fact remains that she failed to establish peace even before being buried by War. She apparently did not even bring the treaties until a circumstance beyond her control—the Athenian victory at Pylos—favored them.[33] So peaceful is she that she cannot threaten men into peace; her way of showing anger is only to fall silent (658).[34] She might be able to make peace when men want to make peace; she shows no such capacity when they do not. Her résumé is blank.

The weakness of Peace is such that she is more like a statue than a living being.[35] In spite of her real weakness, which will surely keep her from enjoying unrivaled supremacy over the Greeks over the long haul, she governs the action of the play from her first introduction to the play's conclusion. Her power lies not in her independent action but in what the other characters feel and do because of her: her beauty and presumed divinity help motivate men to work hard on behalf of peace. Even statues can have power over us. The charms of peace among men are made more visible and alluring by the existence of the goddess, that is, and Trygaeus mobilizes and energizes his troops by invoking and displaying accompanying goddesses suggestive of the pleasures of the peaceful life (456–57, 560–64).[36] Trygaeus bends all his efforts to excavate her, bring her back to Athens, see that she is installed as a divinity (922–1038), and ensure that she is well represented in both sacrifices and song (1039–1136, 1264–94). And to achieve these goals, he must also lead large numbers of Athenians to join in his efforts. Thanks especially to Trygaeus' leadership, Peace gives the Greeks, or at least the farmers, a clear source of inspiration and focus for their actions.

There are three surviving plays by Aristophanes in which a mortal successfully defies Zeus, the *Birds*, *Peace*, and *Plutus*; the hero of each acts for a different reason. Chremylus seeks a just distribution of wealth, Peisetairos seeks tyranny, and Trygaeus seeks peace. In none of them does the king of the gods take effective action to protect his interests. In the *Birds* and the *Plutus*, he fails at everything. In the former, his scout Iris is routed, his fellow god Prometheus betrays him without even being detected, and his divine emissaries foolishly surrender all his power; in the latter, he is forgotten once Wealth emerges, and he must come crawling down to earth to make whatever deal he can.[37] The Zeus of the *Peace* is almost equally ineffective, but he manages here to accomplish at least a little something: he and the other gods successfully vacate heaven. Trygaeus' response gives us an example of how to act in such a situation: rally men with thoughts of gods who will increase human beings' energy and dedication for pursuing their own best interests. Peace will not always be able to stand up to War or Victory, but her prospects are greatest when she is vividly represented as a goddess in the minds of men.

I have suggested that Trygaeus is successful in his battle with Zeus partly because Zeus is less powerful than his reputation suggested and partly because Trygaeus employs the piety of the Greeks, and especially the farmers, to increase their readiness both to work and to take risks for peace. The ease with which he enjoys his comic victory might appear to suggest that it is easy for a clever leader to shift his followers' views of the gods: find or invent a god or divine principle to favor your cause, and you will bring to your side a powerful human ally, namely, the piety of those you would lead. I think there is something to this, but I do not mean to imply that piety or its manipulation is any more reliably beneficent than Zeus himself. The farmers' piety did support their enthusiasm for peace, but this enthusiasm was rooted in the bitter and present experience of war. Not even Trygaeus was especially drawn to peace before he suffered the difficulties brought on by the war. Moreover, before the farmers were ready to be led to peace by Trygaeus, they were easily led to war by Cleon and others. As Hermes points out, and as Trygaeus cannot deny, the farmers' passions—which are partly tied to their views on justice and the gods—help get them into the war before Trygaeus puts them to use in leading them out of it. The *Peace* captures a happy moment, for an impressive statesman leads the Athenians back to peace. But, thanks especially to Hermes (601–92), it does not fail to call attention to the passions that jeopardized this peace in the first place. Its comic depiction of the way the farmers' passions drove Pericles in the direction of war even seems a prescient anticipation of the problems that both Nicias and Alcibiades would face later when engaged by a demos insistent on hearing good news as it understood good news. If the circumstances are not just right, riding the piety of the farmers is no simpler or safer than mounting a high-flying dung beetle.

Comedy

As noted at the outset, one core and related element of the *Peace* deserves attention because, as Strauss helps us to see, it gives us the perfect "emblem" of Aristophanean comedy in general: it is not a noble eagle or Bellerophon's winged horse but the disgusting dung beetle that carries the poet to his great heights. The implicit claim of the *Peace*, then, is that Aristophanes' low humor is even better suited than the moving nobility of tragedy to carry one to such high themes—the gods, philosophy, tragedy, democracy, and the city or family in general—as his plays address.[38] As the *Frogs* features a competition between two tragic poets, so the *Peace* claims a comic victory in a competition with tragedy.[39]

This "emblem" does not explain or defend all of Aristophanes' wide-ranging and raunchy humor. It concerns such humor as enables the poet to address the high themes found throughout his plays. In the case of the *Peace*, for example, this means a view of heaven and how to act in light of it. In the case of the *Clouds*, it means the place of the philosopher in the city. In the case of the *Frogs*, it means the place of tragedy in the city. These are indeed high themes; and because Aristophanes' humor need not defer to the "official" or conventional views of his audience, it allows him to approach them from a novel vantage point. The comic poet need not write on the premise that the gods are powerful, wise, or otherwise worthy of the beautiful temples and solemn ceremonies men give them, for example. He can explore the possibility that they have not really earned their exalted reputations—even that they have abdicated—and because such thoughts can be presented especially (and, apparently, "merely") as amusing, the comic poet can put them on center stage even at a festival dedicated to a god. Had an Athenian Nietzsche simply stood up and solemnly uttered, "Zeus has fled," he would not have been given a prize and invited back. If the preceding section of this chapter has enjoyed any success, it will have illustrated one case in which Aristophanes used humor to address a sensitive issue in a novel fashion.

Similarly, by poking fun at Socrates' views in the *Clouds*, the comic poet can air them and—while looking down from his still-higher perch—make plain how different the philosopher's views are from those of the city, how different they are from both the Just and the Unjust Speeches.[40] And in the *Frogs,* while prompting smiles at the solemnity of tragedy in general, he can bring the moral and aesthetic differences between Euripides and Aeschylus to the city's attention. His humor thrives on challenges to existing conventions, and this enables him to call those very conventions into question. If his humor is sometimes shameless, this is partly because it is shameful to violate established conventions.

It would be wrong to imply that tragedy cannot also challenge conventions. Indeed, that he does so too boldly seems to be a main basis for Aristophanes' criticisms of Euripides. But I wonder whether in tragedy it is not more important for the radicals to fail: threats to justice, the established laws, or the gods exist, but they are generally defeated, thus allowing or forcing protagonists to finally recognize their "tragic flaw." In the *Peace*, Trygaeus is the radical: he dares to defy the king of the gods, and—far from ending tragically—he succeeds. Rather than seeing a tragic flaw punished, we see a comic virtue rewarded, even though this virtue entails radical impiety. Because it appears to be a mere joke, however, it gives no offense. It may also help the comedy to avoid offense that the hero succeeds in an effort that redounds to the benefit of his Athenian audience. He brings them peace, so their own interests lead them not to scrutinize his actions too closely. Similar promises of better lives mask the impiety of Aristophanes' other two rebels, Peisetairos and Chremylus. The ugly picture of a world dominated by an uncaring or hostile Zeus is overshadowed by a comic plot in which defiance of Zeus results in widespread joy. Like the honeyed poetry Lucretius added to sweeten his teaching, comic plots distract viewers and readers from distasteful suggestions.

The example of the *Peace* helps us to see how Aristophanes' humor enables him to take a novel look at more ordinary views, but this does not explain or defend his merely raunchy humor. Although he does use humor to help him address his high themes, Aristophanes also shows no discernible inhibition against using humor of the most vulgar variety (though he also pretends that *he* would never stoop to use the low antics that keep turning up in his plays). Jokes abound about aching erections, garments whose nether regions suddenly turn brown or yellow, and private moments spent plucking or singeing hairs in preparation for sexual contact of every description—not to mention exuberant references to farting. This lower (or lowest) sort of humor might be defended in part as necessary to keep a fraction of his audience entertained; such a requirement could hardly be overlooked, after all. As he indicates in the *Peace*, spectators are different and have different capacities and needs (50–53, 43–49), and it is believable that more than a few of these viewers thoroughly enjoyed being reminded of secret pleasures enjoyed, and embarrassing challenges suffered, by themselves and other ordinary Athenians.

Between these two sorts of humor, the raunchiest humor and the high humor built into the very structure of his plots, lies a third sort. I mean in this case the teasing he gives to selected individuals and classes of Athenians: cowards like Cleonymus, hawks like Lamachus, demagogues like Cleon, greedy sycophants, and angry jurymen. Here, his humor seeks both to amuse and to correct. He satirizes.

Beyond the immediate advantages of these two lower sorts of humor, the very atmosphere of ridiculousness may also serve Aristophanes' higher purposes, for amid such madcap goings-on, everything becomes permissible. The eye-, ear-, and nose-catching raunchiness of Aristophanes' most vulgar humor allows his novel treatments of his higher themes to avoid standing out as singularly obnoxious. In a general comic frolic, who can find fault if even the Just Speech or Zeus himself must endure a dig or two?

The *Peace* presents us with a privileged look at heaven from the inside. Zeus abandons the Greeks to War, and his motives for action—even as described by a fellow Olympian—show barely a trace of concern for the interests of the mortals who look to him for support. Rather than potential allies, Trygaeus finds an indifferent or hostile pantheon, something like what would today be called an indifferent or hostile universe. But for the fact that it is comic, the view in the *Peace* would be a disturbing one. That it is comic ought not keep it from being a view to take seriously, at least in general terms.

Notes

1. Leo Strauss, *Socrates and Aristophanes* (Chicago: University of Chicago Press, 1966), 139–40, 143.

2. For example, the weakness of the Olympian gods is a condition for Trygaeus' success in securing peace, and both the gods and the politics of war and peace are high subjects approached by way of Aristophanes' low comedy.

3. Peace is called a goddess at 974–75, and Trygaeus installs her as a goddess at Athens, complete with sacrificial offerings. He refers to her as "Revered Lady" (520, 657, 975, 1108), as he also refers to Athena (271). War is never put into any particular class of being, like gods or daemons.

4. As we shall see below, Trygaeus also differs in his approach to the gods from the Socrates we meet in the pages of Aristophanes. Rather than simply deny the gods, as Socrates does, he combats some of them with the help of others. And herein lies a key to his victory.

5. Thucydides 5.18–19.

6. Dicaeopolis won only a private peace, enjoyed by himself alone; Trygaeus and Lysistrata won peace for the Greeks in general. In both the *Acharnians* and the *Peace*, a god appears onstage and helps bring about peace. No god or goddess appears in the *Lysistrata*, and no mortal attempts are made to challenge the gods. The revolutionaries do appeal to Aphrodite for support, swearing oaths (208, 252, 749, 858, and 939), praising her (556), invoking her (832–33), and indicating that they need her help (551). But what they mean by these attentions is not that they need miraculous interventions but that they need men to be powerfully subject to sexual desire. There is certainly something remarkable about the power of sexual desire, but given that we have it, "Aphrodite's holy mysteries" are much more in accord with nature than triumphs over it (898–99).

7. Strauss makes it impossible to forget this. See "The Problem of Socrates: The First Lecture," in *The Rebirth of Classical Political Rationalism*, ed. Thomas L. Pangle (Chicago: University of Chicago Press, 1989), 106–7.

8. Thucydides 2.13–17.

9. He may here mean the Athenian people in general, but he addresses his speech explicitly to the farmers (603), so "you" and "your" must refer at least in part to them.

10. All commentators note that the causes of the war as presented here in the *Peace* are not the same as those presented in a parallel passage in the *Acharnians*. To speak broadly, Hermes implicates the Athenian farmers; in the *Acharnians*, Dicaeopolis places most blame on just a few corrupt or wanton Athenians (517–19). As a step toward explaining these differences, note that the speakers are in very different situations. Most importantly, the mortal has his head on the block and is at risk of losing it. The jury that will decide his fate is a chorus of Acharnian rustics, or, as they say, it is "the city" that will decide (491). If he insists and repeats that he will not blame "the city" (515–16)—if he blames the war on the acts of a few rather than on the city that now holds his fate in their hands—why should we be surprised? And in spite of their several differences, the two accounts are similar in tracing the causes of the war to human beings and, in particular, to Athenians. Neither blames Zeus or any other god.

11. The Chorus also concludes the second parabasis with a call not for peace but for revenge against the Athenian leaders who took advantage of them by sending them off to do battle (1187–90). Peace is dear to them, but it is not their

only concern. Accordingly, the Chorus closes the play looking forward to wealth, not peace alone (1321).

12. Although the Chorus once calls Trygaeus a savior for all human beings (914–15), both they and Trygaeus himself more commonly speak of him as benefiting the Greeks (59, 105–6, 302, 867). His concern for Athenians in particular is evident at 252–54 and in his remarks to the audience (150, 244, 276). He shows his concern for his family at 119–21, and one may suspect that he would have been willing to be a Dicaeopolis and seek a private peace had he not found a way to win a public one.

13. S. Douglas Olson, *Aristophanes' Peace* (Oxford: Oxford University Press, 1998), xlii. Olson puts a similar point like this: "Aristophanes' play does not look much beyond an end to the fighting with Sparta, however, and imagines peace as the single thing required to initiate a return to an ideal life of feasting, farming, and fertility" (xxxi). This seems unlikely in view of the many problems his other plays take up, such as the folly of the Athenian demos, the poor distribution of wealth, private property itself, demagoguery, and so forth. But I do not find even the *Peace* itself to be so rosy.

14. The makers and sellers of the weapons of war, of course, are not excited about the coming of peace (545–49), a point driven home when Trygaeus encounters and taunts the arms merchant (1210ff.). Hierocles resists the novel theology involved in Trygaeus' effort, and the son of Lamachus remains attached to songs glorifying war. And when the Chorus announces that the arrival of Peace has been greatly longed for, it is "the just and farmers" who have done the longing, not everyone (556).

15. Contrast Dicaeopolis, whose principal target for blame with regard to the war is his fellow Athenians.

16. Ganymede is carried off to Olympus by force, but he neither returns nor sends information. Heracles invites Peisetairos to heaven in the *Birds* to collect his bride, Basileia (1686–87). Because they are later wed, we may infer that Peisetairos has been to heaven and back, but he never says anything about what he saw or learned there. Thanks to an even greater success, Dante will later be able to claim an even greater authority than that of Trygaeus.

17. Because this play has been lost, a detailed comparison with the *Peace* is impossible. Still, some basic points help show a close connection between these two plays. See Olson, *Peace*, xxxii–xxxiv, and *Euripides: Selected Fragmentary Plays*, eds. C. Collard, M. J. Cropp, and K. H. Lee, vol. I (Warminster: Aris & Phillips, 1995), 98–120.

18. Could the following differences help to explain Trygaeus' success? He rode a disgusting dung beetle, not a noble steed, and he was apparently less ready than Bellerophon to deny the gods' existence. A fragment of *Bellerophon* has the hero saying that "if the gods act shamefully, they are not gods." Trygaeus, by contrast, does not assume that the gods never act shamefully. He thus arrives in heaven equipped with bribes and is quick both to flatter and to threaten Hermes (192, 403–25). As he chooses his mount by considerations of utility—such as how to limit the need for onboard fuel, as NASA would—rather than by thinking of what suits the lofty

dignity of his destination (124–39), so his policies on arrival do not rest on the premise that the gods always act justly, nobly, or for the human good. Could his ability to reach heaven and prevail against the gods be linked to his freedom from attractive preconceptions?

19. For example, see *Iliad* 8.1–52 or 24.22–119.

20. Recall also Gloucester in *King Lear* (4.1.38–39): "As flies to wanton boys, are we to the gods. They kill us for their sport." But the *Peace* levels this charge against War, not against the Olympians. The latter put their own interests first, to the detriment of mankind, but they are not guided by the desire to harm human beings.

21. Although he persuades Hermes, perhaps Trygaeus could be wrong about this. If the Olympians have retreated to remote areas, far from contact with human beings, as Hermes reported, perhaps they do not need human beings. But if they no longer have any involvement with men, would they continue to be gods in any recognizable sense?

22. He does not pray either when he begins his flight on the bug's back or before calling the Greeks to come help him excavate Peace. He does pray once his troops are assembled. This prayer serves to unite and motivate the Greeks, and because it is directed in part to Hermes, it may also help cement his commitment to the venture.

23. The responses to Trygaeus from 433 to 458 are given by the manuscripts to Hermes, but the manuscripts seem to be a less reliable guide to the original attribution of the speeches than to their content. It is far from clear that Aristophanes even indicated the name of the speaker before each speech, as all playwrights now do and as we perhaps wrongly assume they have always done. See J. C. B. Lowe, "The Manuscript Evidence for Changes of Speaker in Aristophanes," *Bulletin of the Institute of Classical Studies* 9 (no. 1, 1962): 27–42.

24. I do not mean to resolve so casually the question of Homer's treatment of the justice of Zeus: the hope that the Olympians exist and punish injustice is expressed at *Odyssey* 24.351–52. But certainly Homer includes evidence that suggests the king of the gods is cruel or indifferent to human interests. Consider Agamemnon's complaint at *Iliad* 9.18–25, for example, or Zeus' preoccupation with relations among the gods, regardless of the consequences for mortals, at 4.30–72. So too with the tragedians, I think; consider Aeschylus, *Prometheus Bound*, 1–11.

25. As Strepsiades understands "him," Vortex could also be placed in this group, but by stressing the connection between vortex and necessity, Socrates appeals to principles that are unable to inspire such devotion as gods can. If religious devotion is more easily shifted than ended once and for all, Socrates' battle against Zeus will have to be conducted with few allies; it lacks all appeal to human needs or longings (*Clouds* 379–82, 405, and 437; see also 1075). See Thomas L. Pangle and Wayne Ambler, *Birds, Peace, Wealth: Aristophanes' Critique of the Gods* (Philadelphia: Paul Dry Books, 2013), 9–13.

26. For a more complete discussion of Peisetairos' overthrow of Zeus, see Wayne Ambler, "Tyranny in Aristophanes's *Birds*," *Review of Politics* 74 (no. 2, 2012): 185–206.

27. Peace, *eirēnē*, is mentioned only three times in the *Iliad* (2.797, 9.403, 22.156) and once in the *Odyssey* (24.486). As it seems to me, at least, peace is never there spoken of as a goddess. Peace was a goddess in Hesiod, however (*Theogony* 901–6 and *Works and Days* 228–29).

28. Aeschylus in Aristophanes' *Frogs* reads the tradition differently. According to him, Homer taught tactics, (military) virtues, and armaments (1034–36). Aeschylus himself takes pride in having made men "full of Ares" and made them in love with being fearsome. He adds that he also taught them to be desirous of being victorious over their enemies. He praises his poetry for adorning the excellent work that was the Greek defeat of the Persians (1019–27).

29. I know that a right is not the same as a god, but rights may bring analogous advantages. Working for better medical care is one thing, but defending the *right* to such care is a still higher and more alluring calling.

30. Zeus often received the epithet of "savior" (e.g., Pindar, *Olympian*, 5.17; Aristophanes, *Ecclesiazusae*, 79, 761, 1045, 1103), but it makes perfect sense that the farmers apply this epithet to Trygaeus, not Zeus (or Hermes or Peace).

31. Bear in mind how common it was in Homer and Greek tragedy for a god to be both hostile and effective. Even the beautiful Aphrodite could show both power and malice, as she did in Euripides' *Hippolytus*, for example.

32. This is in contrast to Wealth in the *Plutus*. Although comically, of course, he is actually credited with bringing wealth to decent Athenians. See Cario at 805–22, the appearance of the newly enriched Just Man (824–42), the plight of the Sycophant (850–950), the lament of the old woman and delight of her former lover (959–1096), the cessation of sacrifices to the gods (1097–1167), the laments of the priest, and the reported defection of Zeus (1171–90).

33. Her weakness is also reflected in the fact that there are frequent oaths to Zeus and other gods, including those by Greeks when they are at war (214, 218), but there are no oaths to Peace, even when the Greeks are seeking to bring her to light. The installation of Peace as a goddess is done less to tap her powers than to increase them.

34. Contrast the view that Poseidon is able to send earthquakes and really punish an adversary (*Acharnians* 509–11).

35. In the *Plutus*, Chremylus has a speech to the effect that Wealth is the most powerful god, more powerful than Zeus (129–98), and the play as a whole confirms this claim. No one claims that Peace is more powerful than anything.

36. Peace comes accompanied by Harvest and Festivity, who are first mentioned at 523, on the emergence of Peace. Perhaps the bonus of getting three divinities instead of one suggests that until there is peace, one thinks especially of Peace. Once Peace is attained, further wants arise. Although Peace will be on hand in Athens, Trygaeus is delighted that he will also keep Harvest as his own wife.

37. *Birds* 1202–61, 1494–1552, 1565–1693; *Plutus* 1172–89.

38. Strauss writes beautifully on this general topic; my thoughts are more elementary. See Strauss, "The Problem of Socrates," esp. 105–12, and Strauss, *Socrates and Aristophanes*, 139–40.

39. One amusing criterion in the competition between Euripides and Aeschylus is "weightiness" (*Frogs* 1364–1410). The *Peace* suggests "loftiness" as a related but different criterion, which also allows Socrates to be entered into the competition (*Clouds* 217–34).

40. Aristophanes here makes jokes in both directions, looking from the philosopher's point of view at the city's preoccupation with money, families, and Zeus, and looking from the city's view at the philosopher's strange obliviousness to law, justice, and the gods.

8

Aristophanes' Herodotean Inquiry
The Meaning of Athenian Imperialism in the *Birds*

Kenneth DeLuca

Aristophanes' *Birds* combines what Athens is known for and what birds are known for. What Athens is known for the play makes apparent in what is said therein of its central character—the Athenian Pisthetairos:

> Come here all you birds so that you can learn new things . . . some sharp old man has come who with respect to his thinking is new and who is an undertaker of new works. Come here, come, come, come, come for all the *logoi*. . . . He is so unspeakably intelligent. . . . Pure fox, wholly sophisticated, wholly resourceful, wholly experienced, wholly subtle.[1]

What birds are known for the play also makes evident in what is said therein, here by Pisthetairos: "Here among us [Athenians] if you ask the flighty types, 'who is this bird?' Teleas will say this: 'that guy's the human being bird, [i.e.,] unsteady, aflutter, obscure, not ever remaining in the same place" (167–70). Evidently, what birds are known for is so well known that "birdness" has become something of a universal, for there are human beings at least in Athens who live in light of the standard birds set. It seems that in combining what Athens is known for and what birds are known for, Pisthetairos is not quite as innovative as Tereus-hoopoe seems to think. As a non-Athenian, how would Tereus-hoopoe know what it means to be a thinker, for does it not take a thinker to know a thinker? In any case, the

161

other quality that Athenians are known for, freedom, has already given rise to a human–bird collaboration; however, whereas this collaboration would result in Athens' depoliticization and loss of empire, Pisthetairos' will result in birds' politicization and the realization of empire. As Pisthetairos says, "Eureka! Now I see a plan for the race of birds and power, too, which would come to be if you're persuaded by me. . . . Don't fly around everywhere, slack-jawed, as this is a deed without honor. . . . You must found one *polis*" (162–66, 172).

In combining Athens (or at least Athens' most fundamental and universalizable trait) and the birds, the *Birds* does not just generate empire but the most universal empire of all time, the most universal empire ever known. For birds will rule heaven and earth, gods and human beings. For the quality that the *Birds* boils Athens down to—logos—was always capable of becoming universal; it merely lacked the physical means to achieve this universality. The birds, in turn, have universality—they not only have the versatility to go everywhere, that is, the means, but they take on every possible form, as the play through Tereus-hoopoe suggests:

> Come this way any of my like-feathered ones, as many of you devour the well-seeded fields of the planes dwellers. A thousand kinds of seed-gathering barley-eaters and the swift-flying races with the soft voice, as many as often twitter there in a furrow on narrow lump . . . as many of you down on gardens on branches of ivy covered pasture. And on hills the berry eaters and arbutus eaters cease flying and come towards my voice. And you who gulp down the sharp beaked mosquito in marshy valleys, and as many as are on the dewy places of the earth and the charming plane of Marathon, and bird of many colored wing, francolin, francolin, and those on the wavy swells of the sea, the kingfisher tribes, fly hither! Come here . . . all tribes of long necked birds. (229–54)

The birds exist everywhere and in every conceivable way and take myriad forms. What Athens has in theory and therefore experiences if only in thought the birds really live, but because they lack theory or thought the birds fail to experience it. Pisthetairos will give the birds the thought they now lack that will enable them to really experience and exercise dominion. What Athens lacks, the birds have; and what Athens has, the birds lack. And what the birds lack is political philosophy. As Aristotle says in the *Politics*, political life supplies the most authoritative and the most comprehensive good.² It articulates virtues to aspire to and that one person may embody more than anyone else, as well as virtues all have in common. Political life aims up and across. It makes a one of many at the same time that it justifies the many's looking up to the one. So, as we see in the *Birds*, the many birds combine in building the wall of Cloudcuckooland but submit to Pisthetairos' dining on fellow birds, for these birds disobeyed the laws and were duly punished. Political life requires walls to be built both on the borders of the city and within the city. In helping the birds found a polis, Pisthetairos enables the birds to exploit their power, but power comes with strings attached. Power requires the birds conform to standards because without standards, their unity and their power would be lost. In order to exercise universal dominion, the birds are forced to relinquish individual freedom. The general good trumps the good of the individual, and because birds are too stupid to know the good, they are forced to accept the unlimited authority of Pisthetairos. This is why in the end, whereas the birds become citizens of the world's most dominating empire, Pisthetairos becomes the universe's most powerful god.

Pisthetairos is Aristophanes' answer to Xerxes, the Athens of the *Birds* his answer to Herodotus' account of the Persians, and his *Birds* his addendum to Herodotus' *History*. In Pisthetairos, Aristophanes shows that it takes an Athenian to do universal empire right. Whereas the Persian attempt at empire is based on a flawed view of logos or reason, the fictional empire of the *Birds* corrects that flaw. The Persians pay lip service to logos, but understand it as an end, not as a means. For the Persians, logos is all bang and no buck. It has no conditions and requires no labor. When Xerxes takes stock of and organizes his myriad troops (in Herodotus Book 7), he abstracts from and makes no effort to fuse into one fighting force the myriad diversity of which his army is made. The Persians do not understand logos as persuasion or dialectic. For them, the truthfulness of the truth fends for itself. Whereas the Persians would not know what to make of a Socrates, Aristophanes' *Birds* presents a city that is home to Socrates-es.³ Socratic dialectic is its animating principle. The name of its founder, Pisthetairos, means "persuasive-companion." Cloudcuckooland is Aristophanes' comic correction of the Persians. It depicts empire Athenian style. Whereas the Persian understanding of logos has no place for reason as a medium toward the understanding of the phenomena and no place for intermediary institutions or habituation, the Athens of the *Birds* understands that logos must be grounded in experience. Truth is not something you get as an end, but is instead a thinking through. Understanding requires mediation. The intermediate is as much a part of logos as the end. The Athenian empire of

Aristophanes, unlike the Persian Empire found in Herodotus, would be the product of persuasion. And because persuasion is a truth we can understand only by thinking it through—as demonstrated by Tereus-hoopoe's inability to explain the intelligence of Pisthetairos, evident in his random series of superlatives pointing to but not explaining the intelligence of Pisthetairos—our next step must be a closer look at the argument of the *Birds*.

In the beginning of the *Birds*, Euelpides and Pisthetairos, guided by their birds, look for and find Tereus, once a man but now a hoopoe, because they hope he knows a city that might be good for them (1–92). After Euelpides receives and rejects Tereus' recommended cities, he asks Tereus what life is like among the birds, and Tereus answers that it is free and easy (144–61). Euelpides' question and Tereus' answer seem to inspire Pisthetairos, for right then Pisthetairos spiritedly announces a plan for colonizing the air (162–63). The city for which Euelpides and he are searching is not in some remote corner of the world, which only a bird who was once a man could identify; it is above ground in a realm only a bird could occupy. The answer to their prayers is to become and live among the birds. At first, birds illuminate. Euelpides and Pisthetairos' guide-birds show them Tereus' location as Tereus-hoopoe will show them a desirable city. Initially, birds just point the way. After Pisthetairos takes over, however, birds become the way. Birds start out as a means, but become the end.

After Pisthetairos announces his plan, he explains its feasibility to Tereus. He tells Tereus that the sphere or realm (*polos*) of the birds is the void above, below, and around him (175–77).[4] Tereus, unconvinced, asks, "In what way is it a realm?" (180). Pisthetairos responds:

> As one might say, it's a place [*topos*], and since it revolves and quite everything traverses through it, it is now called a sphere. If you settle it and at once fence it off, from this sphere a city [*polis*] shall receive a name. So that, on the one hand, you shall rule human beings like locusts, and, on the other, destroy the gods in a Melian famine. (180–86)

The empire of the birds has its origin in settling and fencing off a place through which "quite everything traverses." That is, the prospective location of the birds' empire is purely a medium. Its end is to yield to the ends of things that pass through it. After it is settled, it no longer yields to anything, but instead forces all things to yield. Once again, what was a means is now an end.

A little later in the play, when Pisthetairos is explaining to the birds' spokesman how human beings will worship them, he says the following:

> I order that you send to human beings another bird-herald, so that birds being kings, human beings sacrifice to the birds from now on, and then later in turn to the gods. And to allot as is fitting according to each of the birds whoever matches among the gods. If one sacrifices to Aphrodite, then sacrifice barley to the coot [*phaleris*] bird, if one sacrifices a sheep to Poseidon, then to the duck on a sacrificial fire burn grain; if one sacrifices to Heracles, to the gull sacrifice honey cakes; and if to King Zeus one sacrifices a ram, the king is the wren bird, it is necessary to sacrifice to him before Zeus himself an uncastrated gnat. (561–69)

Pisthetairos not only proposes that birds precede the Olympian gods, but also that the Olympians mediate the human worship of the birds. An Olympian god is associated with a bird, and when one is about to sacrifice to that Olympian god, one instead sacrifices to the bird associated with that god. Aphrodite is associated with the coot because the word for coot is similar to the word for phallus. And so when one has reason to sacrifice to Aphrodite, one instead sacrifices to the coot. The gods may change, but human beings and their concerns will remain the same, and because human beings have come to associate certain concerns with certain gods, human beings know how to worship the Olympian gods. The Olympian gods are intelligible; the bird-gods are obscure. Pisthetairos uses the intelligibility of the Olympian gods as a means of making intelligible the bird-gods. Pisthetairos turns the world upside down. Before, one divined the meaning of the gods by studying the birds. Now, one will divine the meaning of the birds by studying the gods. What was once a means is now an end, and what was once an end is now a means.

The inversion of means and ends is the core of the *Birds*, and this last example sheds light on the meaning of this inversion. The Olympian gods not only have power, but they also stand for something. They animate virtue and serve as human models. In a sense, they are men perfected. They suggest that man is not all that he can be, and they make intelligible goals toward which he should aim. The demotion of the Olympians and their replacement by the birds means that man no longer acknowledges standards toward which he should strive. This is not altogether bad, however. With the Olympians no longer looming above him, man is now free to make his own standards, and, as the *Birds* suggests, absent the Olympians there is nothing to prevent the standards he makes from serving his own happiness. In the divine order of the birds, human beings live for "health, wealth and happiness," and the bird-gods facilitate their realization (see 586–610). The bird-gods are the Second Coming of Prometheus and, like fire, are purely instrumental. They are not a model for man. They are all means and no end; they exist to serve human need. In worshipping the birds, men worship a form of technology; man has in view his needs, not a standard to live up to. Once his technology becomes sufficiently advanced, instead of worshipping the birds man can return to eating them.

Although the inversion of means and ends characterizes the elevation of the birds and the demotion of the Olympian gods, and this inversion coincides with man's demoralization, Aristophanes makes clear that not all men are demoralized. Not all relinquish aspiration. Because the birds are unreliable, in order for Pisthetairos' plan to succeed, he must become a bird. Before everyone else can abandon aspiration, Pisthetairos must fulfill an aspiration (see 648–55). By becoming more than a man, he provides the conditions for everyone else to become less than what they might be. His growth allows others to stagnate; his virtue deprives others of the chance to be virtuous. Aristophanes' *Birds* is about virtue, not vice, pushed to the extreme, and it suggests that the problem of virtue is illuminated by Athens. Aristophanes makes the association between Athens and Cloudcuckooland as strong as that between Aphrodite and the coot.

In the opening lines of the play, Pisthetairos—revealing how lost he is—says, "By Zeus, not even Exekestides at any rate could find the fatherland (that is, Athens) from here" (11). Exekestides, the commentaries say, was a Carian who passed himself off as an Athenian. But even had his background been lost to us, his name would tell the tale: *ek* means away from; *heco* means going or coming; and *estioo*[5] means to found a hearth or home. Literally speaking, "Exekestides" is "the man who goes away (or comes from somewhere) to found a home." And where does he go? Athens.

A few lines later, in a speech describing his and Pisthetairos' situation, Euelpides says, "We are sickened by a sickness the opposite to Sacas" (31). What he means is that Sacas, that is, the tragedian Akestor—Sacas was his nickname—wants to make Athens home, whereas Euelpides and Pisthetairos want to leave Athens. Euelpides and Pisthetairos are citizens in good standing whose experience of Athens, evidently, has generated a desire to leave. Sacas has the opposite "sickness." He is not an Athenian in good standing but wants to become one. As with Exekestides, name reflects nature, not the name he has from birth, but the name the Greeks or Athens, with Aristophanes' endorsement, assign to him. Sacas is the name the Greeks used for the Scythian people.[6] In addition, sacas calls to mind *secos*, which may mean pen or enclosure.[7] Here, the name by which the Athenians know Akestor reflects Akestor's provincialism—a quality for which the Scythians were known,[8] and that his birth name would have obscured. An *akestor* is a healer or restorer and calls to mind Akestor's occupation—making tragedies. Tragedy, whose universal themes are anything but provincial, is a sort of *akestor*. By means of catharsis, it cures human beings of vice. In calling him Sacas instead of Akestor, Aristophanes emphasizes his failure to exemplify the universal, whereas his real name, Akestor, suggests the opposite. Akestor's nickname, real name, and occupation all point to the same thing. Athens is home to and of the universal: those with universal leanings or pretensions flock there, and in Athens, the distorting effect of convention (i.e., one's name) is overcome, and one's true nature is seen.

Athens reminds us of the realm of the birds in that, like that realm, "through it quite everything traverses." When the chorus (composed of birds) is introduced, it does not enter en masse, as is customary in Greek drama, but individually as twenty-eight different bird types. Not only is the high number of varieties brought to our attention, but so is the extent of their variation. The first bird that appears is a flamingo. In response to seeing it, Euelpides says, "what ever is it? Certainly not a peacock." Faced with the exotic, all Euelpides can presently do is call to mind another example of the exotic. Pisthetairos says nothing about Euelpides' comparison or the flamingo, instead recommending that they consult Tereus, who informs them that "[the bird] is not among the customary [*ethas*] that you always see, but is a marsh bird."[9] What Tereus says amounts to: to see you must have seen; understanding *x* requires that you have seen *x*. What Tereus says may seem like common sense, but it contradicts the central plot of the *Birds*: that some experiences prepare one for seeing what one has never seen; Pisthetairos, without ever seeing through the eyes of a bird, sees that it would be good to become a bird. Is the play suggesting that Athens, as the "school of Greece," affords such an experience? Does learning Athenian logoi prepare one for truly anything? Or does the *Birds* expose Athenian logos as the ultimate boaster, and is Pisthetairos as deluded as Exekestides and Sacas? Is the *Birds*, in Platonic fashion, a logos on the limits of logos? Whatever the case may be, right after Tereus' remark Euelpides comes close to arriving at the name of a particular species of bird with unassisted reason and observation.

After Euelpides learns from Tereus this particular species' obscure origins, Euelpides, who still has his mind if not his eyes on the obscure bird, says, "Oh my, how beautiful (*kalos*) and flaming red." Tereus responds, "Fittingly so, for its name is flaming-red-wing" (272–73).[10] In order to get a handle on a thing he has never seen before, Euelpides begins by remarking on a quality he has seen before and that he finds dominant in the bird, the bird's flaming red color, and it turns out that this quality supplies the bird with a name. The flamingo may make its home in the marshes or at the extremes, but its name is conveyed merely by looking at it. What the flamingo is, in a sense, shows up in its name. Convention does not mask but reveals nature. The flamingo suggests that the realm of the birds resembles Athens not only for its openness to the foreign, not only because "quite everything traverses through it," but also because the truth shines through it. What truth shines through the other birds that make up the chorus?

Including the flamingo, the twenty-eight birds that enter during the parodos divide into four groups: birds 1 to 4, Euelpides and/or Pisthetairos do not know but make use of; 5 to 8, Euelpides or Pisthetairos identify on their own, but that is all they do; 9 to 10, Euelpides and/or Pisthetairos know and make use of; 11 to 28, arouse no curiosity and Tereus—one after another—merely names.

Birds 5 to 8, Euelpides and/or Pisthetairos know well, because they are no sooner seen than named. In contrast with birds 1 to 4, the particular features of birds 5 to 8 elicit no comment from Euelpides and Pisthetairos. The particulars are lost in the whole Euelpides and Pisthetairos instantly form, and because Euelpides and Pisthetairos form this whole effortlessly, neither part nor whole illuminates anything beyond itself. Birds 5 to 8 are sterile; they generate nothing in Euelpides and Pisthetairos but their names, unlike birds 1 to 4, which generate an image (bird 1), a philosophic joke (bird 2), a derisive generalization about Athens (bird 3), and a pun and a dig at Cleonymos (both from bird 4). As we suggest above, bird 9, a kingfisher, breaks the pattern established in 5 to 8. Pisthetairos turns it into a metaphor for a barber named Sporgilos. In Greek, bird 9 is *keirylos*, and because *keiro* is a verb that can mean to cut hair, Pisthetairos spotting a kingfisher thinks of Sporgilos the barber. Perhaps more interesting than the metaphor created from bird 9 is the missed opportunity of bird 8, also a kingfisher but with a different name, *alkyon*. The *alkyon* derives from the myth of Alycone, who dove into the sea to fetch her dead husband's body and emerged as a bird, as did her formerly dead husband. The time of the nesting of their chicks—a time of calm winter waters—becomes known as the halcyon days. That the first kingfisher they spot (the *alkyon*) surpasses the second (the *keirylos*) for hooking a metaphor is suggested by its development from a bird to a state of being. The same cannot be said for *keirylos*, whose metaphor is completely dependent on the verb that is its basis. *Alkyon* would seem to be the more obvious choice for a metaphor, and Aristophanes uses it himself at line 1594, but it is passed over for the mundane *keirylos*. The reason has to do not with the bird, but with how it is spotted:

> EUELPIDES: And this at least is an *alkyon*. / But what is behind that bird?
>
> PISTHETAIROS: What is it? A *keirylos*.
>
> EUELPIDES: There is a *keirylos* bird?
>
> PISTHETAIROS: Is not Sporgilos at hand? (298–300)

Whereas the *alkyon* is simply visible, the *keirylos* is at first obscure. It is hidden by the first kingfisher, and the fact that it is hidden generates curiosity. With bird 9, as with birds 1 to 4, what Euelpides and Pisthetairos do not know causes them to become active. It appears that intelligibility comes with a price. As soon as the birds become instantly known—and should Pisthetairos' religious reforms take hold, in time they will be such to all—they cease to provide their observers access to nature. When the highest things are birds, the highest activity will become reciting their names, and each name will point to nothing beyond the bird to which it is attached, for the birds are as high as one can go. The owl, like *alkyon*, will become just another bird. How can it survive as an image of wisdom without the love of wisdom?[11] It is therefore fitting that the last bird that elicits a response is the owl (bird 10):

> TEREUS: And there is an owl.
>
> EUELPIDES: What did you say? Who led an owl to Athens? (301)

Because Euelpides and Pisthetairos are stades from Athens, Euelpides is obviously not referring to the Athens of the play, but the Athens where the play is being staged. The owl results in no poetic leap; there is no ascent. It teaches them nothing they did not already know; it merely reminds them where they are. Evidently, with the appearance of wisdom, the love of wisdom disappears.

We began with the flamingo, which Euelpides associates with beauty and fire, the metaphysical and physical causes of generation. And we end with the entry of eighteen birds of eighteen types, and Tereus making eighteen identifications without a word from Euelpides and Pisthetairos. However, just because Euelpides and Pisthetairos are silent and apparently no longer learning anything does not mean that Aristophanes is no longer teaching. The catalogue helps make intelligible Aristophanes' intention in writing the play.

Almost every bird in the catalogue of eighteen has a name whose origin is a particular characteristic that catches man's eye: the name of bird 12, *trugon*, the turtle-dove, derives from a verb, *truzdo*, meaning "to make a murmuring sound"; bird 13, *kurodos*, the crested lark, derives from *korus*, meaning "helmet"; bird 20, *kokkux*, the cuckoo, derives its name from the sound it makes; bird 21, *eruthropous*, the red shank, has a name that means and derives from "red foot"; bird 25, *kolumbis*, a seabird, derives from *kolumbao*, meaning "dive or swim"; bird 28, *druops*, the woodpecker, derives from *drus*, meaning "wood," and *ops*, meaning "voice." As the catalogue suggests, the names of birds lend intelligibility to what is otherwise fleeting and obscure. Birds are in one spot so briefly or perch so far away that it is all man can do to highlight a superficial but glaring trait. The trait becomes the means by which man identifies bird; in sating man's appetite for intelligibility, man cannot help reducing bird to that trait. In naming birds, man does to bird what Pisthetairos suggests happens when birds name and wall in the sphere of the sky, that is, the *polos*.[12] Like the *polos*, birds are difficult to define. In a manner of speaking, through them all things pass, for in being difficult to define anything can be attributed to them—it is for this reason, at least in part, that birds are able to serve as spokesmen of the gods—and how birds are defined is governed by what man finds important as opposed to what is important to bird. What a bird is easily gets replaced by what a bird seems, and because what a bird seems is lofty or elevated and has a whiff of the divine, the seeming that gets attached to birds is given a status that has nothing to do with its origin. The seeming of birds looks like the *kalon*—the beautiful. It attracts the eye; it arouses and spawns the universal; it sheds light on other things but none on itself. In being reduced and reducible to one feature, birds generate a seeming that acts like the ideas or highfalutin opinion. For birds, like the ideas, are vessels of intelligibility, are detachable from their context, but provide no understanding of their connection to particulars, to their origins, or to one another. The triumph of the birds stands for the triumph of sophistry. "Aquiline" tells you as little about the hawk as the owl does about wisdom.

Before Pisthetairos is shown eating a bird, the *Birds* makes evident the subordination man imposes on the birds; man forces the birds to serve as vehicles of intelligibility. In giving birds the idea to wall in the sky, Pisthetairos reverses things. In walling off the sky, the birds give dimensions to something even more vacuous than they, and in walling it off, in creating Cloudcuckooland, all things will serve as vehicles of their intelligibility instead of the other way around. Before the revolution can take place, however, the birds must be willing to listen to Pisthetairos, and, as Aristophanes suggests, Pisthetairos cannot make the birds listen to him on his own. Contra the Persians, the ignorant must be led to the truth, and in the context of the play, this turns out to mean that Tereus-hoopoe is necessary as a bridge between the birds and man. Evidently, the flip side of spawning universals in the world of man that birds do not authorize, let alone even understand, is that in order to convey arguments to the birds, some form of mediation is necessary in order for the birds to even listen to the arguments supporting the plan. In short, no Tereus-hoope, no Cloudcuckooland. What is so important about Tereus, in particular, that Aristophanes would assign him such an important role?[13]

According to myth, Tereus was a Thracian king who supports Athens in her war against Thebes, marries the Athenian king's daughter, Procne, and takes her back to Thrace. The marriage seems more strategic than romantic, for while escorting Procne's sister (Philomela) to Thrace, he rapes her. To hide his crime, he adds to it: he locks Philomela away and cuts out her tongue. Tereus, in keeping with his nature and name (his father was Ares and his name derives from a word, *teros*, meaning guardian or lookout), vigilantly guards his interests: he uses the occasion of Athens' need in order to extend his influence there (Thrace and Athens were not neighbors), solidifies this with a marriage, and then uses his wife's longing to see her sister in order to satisfy his lust. Does he refrain from killing Philomela because he has in mind some future purpose?[14] Tereus has a ruthless eye. It sees events even before they happen, but it is blind to poetry. He reminds us of Pisthetairos' bird-gods. Both have acute vision and both are technological; everything is a means to the satisfaction of interest, but nothing has a meaning beyond its use. So, when Philomela weaves a tapestry in which she encodes Tereus' crimes, despite the fact that Tereus both cuts out her tongue and imprisons her, it easily finds its way into Procne's hands, who is able to discern its meaning. Tereus takes double precautions against the truth being told directly, but apparently none at all against its being told indirectly through an image. Philomela (her name means song-lover) demonstrates a form of ingenuity in which Tereus is totally lacking. She is good at making a thing serve as her instrument without depriving it of its original use—the tapestry does not cease being a tapestry just because it tells a story, so her presence in her instrument may be concealed, and therefore she is able to escape Tereus' notice. He is good at making any thing serve as his instrument, but in order for it to be of use to him, he must restrict its freedom even to the point of mutilation, as the case demands. Philomela's instrument, like a song, is of use to more than just herself, as her sister will soon prove. It is able to mingle with the intentions of another and does not govern the other's intention, so Philomela's form of ingenuity depends on others. Its success is contingent. Tereus' depends on himself, because other people do not matter, and therefore his form of ingenuity is more certain. However, because he subordinates the other to himself, Tereus must conceal his motives. His ingenuity depends on catching others off guard. Tereus, then, must watch himself as carefully as he watches others.

Philomela personifies Athenian freedom. Despite being tongueless, she speaks. She demonstrates that logos is independent of body. And she shows that two may come together as one by means of crafting an image without either being enslaved to the other. Philomela's ability to weave a message into a tapestry enables her and her sister to overcome the tyranny of Tereus and would not have been possible had Philomela not seen that a thing may stand for something wholly unrelated to its original intention. In other words, man may give to things a meaning. Poetry is the means of freedom's realization and the manifestation of that freedom. Philomela's actions speak to two problems that the *Birds* is very much about—poetry and empire—so it is curious that the play never mentions her. It is also curious, given the fact that Tereus personifies tyranny, that the *Birds* gives him a central role. If we are right about him, Tereus seems to represent Thrace as well as Philomela does Athens, but to see this we need Herodotus:

> The Thracians are the most populous of all people after the Indians. And if they could be governed by or themselves possessed one mind and stuck to it, the Thracians would be unbeatable and the most powerful of all peoples by a long shot—so I think. But this could never happen, for there is no mechanism by means of which to bring it about. For this reason the Thracians are in fact weak. They have many names, as many as regions, but these all use about the same laws in all things. (5.3.1–2)

The Thracians, according to Herodotus, cannot act in concert, despite the fact that their doing so would give them almost unrivaled power and that they observe almost the same laws. In having the same laws, one might think that the Thracians are already of the same mind. Looked at from above, nothing seems more likely than that the Thracians will unite, yet Herodotus suggests that nothing is more unlikely. The problem is that the Thracians cannot look at things from above. They cannot get beyond their names, which are all different, so as to gain access to what they all might have in common, which their shared laws suggest is vast. Tereus seems an individualized version of an individual Thracian people. Like the people of each Thracian region, Tereus sees only himself. Freedom means individuality; reason is a device for preserving that freedom and does not afford access to principles under which different people might live. Tereus' remorseless scheming seems to flow from this understanding. He and the Thracians do not see logos as being able to transcend the particular. They are unpoetic. After Pisthetairos tells Tereus his plan, Tereus says he will go along with it if it seems good to the other birds. When Pisthetairos then asks Tereus who will describe it to them (162–98), Tereus responds, "You. For their being barbarians before, I taught them voice [*phone*] living among them a long while" (198–200).[15] Had Tereus been able to teach them logos instead, he could have described the plan himself. Pisthetairos readily accepts Tereus' suggestion that he describe his plan to the birds but wonders how the birds will be summoned, at which point Tereus discloses that he cannot summon the birds on his own; he will need the beautiful song of Procne (201–62). The Tereus of the *Birds* is as unpoetic as the Tereus of myth. What he lacked as a man, he now lacks as a bird, except that as a bird he allies with Athenians, rather than making them an enemy. He prevents an Athenian mutilation rather than causing one (307–408). He, is, therefore, a subject of comedy rather than tragedy. The alliance between the two Athenians, Euelpides and Pisthetairos, with Tereus, reconciles what the Tereus myth suggests is irreconcilable: the pursuit of meaning and the pursuit of interest, the *kalon* (the beautiful) and the *agathon* (the good).

Above, with Herodotus' help, we were able to see that Tereus is Thrace's representative. It is something he seems to share with the rest of the birds. The parallels between Herodotus' Thrace and the birds are unmistakable. The Thracians have many names; the parodos names twenty-eight types of birds.[16] The Thracians use about the same laws in all things; the birds observe a common law, as their leader suggests in his rebuke of Tereus: "For he who was reared among us a friend and dined with us on the plains, on the one hand, flouted ancient laws, and on the other, flouted oaths of birds" (328–32; cf. 1344–72). The Thracians are an untapped power lacking only the leader or the judgment to unite them, so as to make them indomitable. Although the Thracians could be the strongest, they are in fact weak. All of this is true also of the birds. Herodotus says that what Thrace needs is the government or judgment of one, which is what Aristophanes gives the birds in the person of Pisthetairos, as the chorus leader says:

> Oh most dear to me of old men being once my biggest foe, it is impossible that I ever shall willingly let go of your judgment. Having exulted in your *logoi*, I resolve and swear that if you establish with me same-minded *logoi*,[17] being just, guileless, pious, and you would go against the gods being minded [*phronon*] in unison with me, then not much longer still will the gods hold my scepter. What requires force to do, for that we shall station ourselves; but what requires planning by means of thought, all these things lie in your lap. (627–38)

Herodotus asserts that the Thracians lack the prerequisites of unity and so must remain weak, which might also be said of the birds, which would have remained weak had Pisthetairos not come along. Pisthetairos is the way and the device that would have enabled Thrace to fulfill its potential. The dream of an Athenian is equivalent to the perfection of Thrace. In Herodotus, the Thracians are a savage, uncivilized people, but they are free. Their freedom keeps them from becoming political because this would entail a loss of freedom. The Athenians, by contrast, are not as free, but they possess the arts. In the *Birds*, Aristophanes conducts the following thought experiment: what would it look like if one combined art-loving Athens with freedom-loving Thrace? The answer is Cloudcuckooland.[18]

I have tried to show that the Tereus myth sheds light on Aristophanes' *Birds*. Athens shines through Philomela as Thrace through Tereus, and so we come to understand that the conflict between Philomela and Tereus is necessitated by the underlying conflict between Athens and Thrace. Although, in the *Birds*, Aristophanes presents a partnership, not a conflict, between Athens and Thrace, manifest in the alliance between Pisthetairos and the birds, the conflict depicted in the myth helps us see that the alliance presented in the *Birds* is a great curiosity, and why. Can Athenian freedom be reconciled with the apolitical character of Thrace? In the beginning of the play, Euelpides discloses to us what he and Pisthetairos want: "On account of [the ways of the Athenians], we are walking a walkway . . . roaming the two of us in search of a businessless place [*topos apragmon*] where we two settling could then live" (42–45). Euelpides does not say he is in search of a polis (cf. 48), but rather a *topos*. A polis is a *topos* invested with meaning. It is a place where and about which opinions swirl, even regarding the opinions that invest the place with meaning and also the nature of opinion itself. Controversy is, therefore, inevitable in a polis, which, lest it cause the polis' disintegration, calls for compromise. The polis needs walls; opinion must be hemmed in. *Pragma* are part of political life; a businessless polis is impossible, which Euelpides seems to see when he substitutes *topos* for polis. What Euelpides wants is something like Thrace; what he gets is something like Athens and Thrace combined. It is therefore no accident that after he delivers the idea of living amid the birds to Pisthetairos (155), which Pisthetairos then develops into a plan, he becomes a stage prop. In any case, once Pisthetairos walls in the air and creates Cloudcuckooland, turning a *topos* (180) into a polis (184), it is anything but businessless. From line 863 on, it is visited by a priest, a poet, an oracle seller, a city planner, an inspector, a decree seller, two messengers, Iris, a herald, a father beater, Kinesias, an informer, Prometheus, Poseidon, Heracles, Triballos, and perhaps a second herald. Cloudcuckooland seems a far cry from the life of the permanent wedding feast about which Euelpides fantasizes, and which he thinks Tereus offers (127–35, 155–61). Pisthetairos' first order of business as leader of Cloudcuckooland is to send Euelpides to supervise and assist the building of the city wall, and Euelpides is not happy (837–47).

In the *Birds*, as in the Tereus myth, Athens has two representatives, Euelpides-Pisthetairos and Philomela-Procne, who diverge from one another in the play, and perhaps in the myth, according to the different strains of Athens each represents. By contrast, Thrace, being relatively simpler, needs only one representative, so Tereus can stand alone. It is true that Herodotus, for the purposes of explaining Thrace, needs three tribes: the Getae,[19] the Trausi (5.4), and those beyond the Crestonaei (5.5). But, as Seth Benardete shows, each stands for something similar:

> Death is not a terror for these tribes; they are perfectly willing to quit this life for the sake of immortality, happiness, or honor. Their excessive courage, far from working in defense of the common, makes them oblivious to the needs of the common, as it reduces the private to so low a level that even the body is only by convention one's own.[20]

Thrace boils down to courage. Courage is the virtue toward which those who resent compromise strive. Thracians want virtue in deed; they want to realize virtue. For Thracians, action is everything, logos nothing.

When Aristagoras presents the Thracians with terms, they kill him and his army anyway. Thracian courage and Thracian individualism go together. The one thing the Thracians have in common makes it the only thing they can have in common. It is why Thrace is a *topos*, not a polis. Courage is elevated so high in Thrace that it becomes the criterion of the natural, so that even the body loses that status. Because courage requires putting at risk the body, the Thracians demote the body and nature. Herodotus reports that "they sell their children for export" (5.6.1); they leave virgins unguarded to mix with whomever they want, but they guard their wives carefully and buy wives from their parents for a lot of money. On the one hand, being tattooed is judged high-birth; on the other hand, not being tattooed is judged low-birth. The words high-birth and low-birth in the Greek are *eugenes* and *agennes*, which come from the verb *gignomai*, which means "to become" or "be born." Ironically, in Thrace, being of high-birth means to overcome one's birth. It means to show that one's birth does not matter.[21] The Thracian view of birth abstracts from actual birth; their view of nature abstracts from nature. Through courage, the Thracians poetize birth and nature away. In Thrace has emerged a phenomenon we would expect to find in philosophy-loving Athens: soul divorced from body. So, in order to defuse the birds' anger at Euelpides and Pisthetairos, Tereus-hoopoe says, "If they are enemies with respect to nature, they are friends with respect to mind, and hoping to teach us something beneficial have come here" (371–72). The placelessness of the Thracians gives Tereus a window into the psychology of the birds, for just as Thracian placelessness enables them to abstract from birth, or their origins or past, so the placelessness of the birds enables Tereus to easily persuade the birds to forget the injuries they have suffered at the hands of man.

What distinguishes Thrace from Athens is that the Thracians elevate soul without elevating logos. They will not stand virtue mediated by logos. Logos obscures nature; it does not illuminate nature. They do not see that virtue must be a seeming, or that it can never be more than an opinion. In any case, the Thracian attempt to achieve virtue itself, or to live authentically, makes it impossible to tell if they have succeeded. For the word for Thracian, *Thrax*, is similar to the word for courage, *thrasos*.[22] The words are sufficiently similar as to cause one to wonder whether one gave birth to the other, but it is difficult to know which came first. Perhaps Thracian courage has its roots not in the attempt to ascend toward nature, but in a convention passed down through the ages. In any case, one may be "thrasian" without ever lifting a finger.[23]

Whereas Tereus reflects Thrace's simplicity, Euelpides and Pisthetairos reflect Athens' complexity. They bravely leave Athens for an unknown destination, yet poke fun at one another's cowardice.[24] They act courageously and cowardly at once. They see courage's limits while in the midst of an act of great courage. Their mode of action is distinct from their mode of seeing. They are not reducible to one virtue, and therefore they are not dependent on one virtue. When the birds are on the verge of destroying them (307–63), Pisthetairos uses speech to persuade Euelpides to hold his ground and then gets him to fight back by devising a fortification, armor, and weapons. In contrast with the role of courage among the Thracians, courage is a device as opposed to a mode of being. When running away seems likely to save his skin, Euelpides is ready to do so, but once Pisthetairos reminds him that he cannot outrun a bird, he stops. When it seemed best to run, he ran; when it seemed best to stay, he stayed. With Euelpides and Pisthetairos, courage is inseparable from speech. After Pisthetairos gives Euelpides a device for protecting his eyes, Euelpides calls him "wisest," not bravest, and then he tells him he surpasses Nicias with respect to devices. Courage comes in more than one form.[25] Aristophanes makes clear that Euelpides and Pisthetairos differ from Tereus and the Thracians but also from one another. In keeping with the city from which they spring, they stand out because of their logoi, but their logoi are very different. Aristophanes makes this immediately apparent. Euelpides opens with a question, Pisthetairos with a command. Euelpides again asks a question in lines 3, 10, 20, 21, 23, 24, 27 to 29, and 49. Although he speaks in the declarative at line 7, he is aping Pisthetairos. He again speaks in the declarative in his speeches at 14 and 28, but here he is speaking as Aristophanes' spokesman. In lines 1 to 59, Pisthetairos almost never asks a question, and when he does he is not really asking one (25–26, 54). At line 25, Euelpides asks Pisthetairos, "What does (your crow) say about the road?" Pisthetairos responds, "But what other thing, at any rate, than that he says by biting he will gnaw away my fingers?" Pisthetairos says not only what his crow means, but that his crow can mean nothing else. Although Pisthetairos here asks a question, it is meant to close, not open, inquiry. Pisthetairos' sarcastic answer negates Euelpides' question just as his profound answer, Cloudcuckooland, will later negate Euelpides. In the beginning of the play, beset by doubt, Euelpides asks Pisthetairos whether he knows his way back to the fatherland (10), and when Pisthetairos tells him this is unknowable, Euelpides responds, "*Oimoi*," which means something like "woe is me" but with a change of accent means "roads." Pisthetairos then says, interpreting *oimoi* in this other sense, "You, sir, take that road!" (12). Euelpides wonders about turning back, as he will later advocate fleeing from the bird attack, and Pisthetairos chastises him with sarcasm. Although Cloudcuckooland is Pisthetairos' idea, Euelpides' inquiry about life among the birds precedes it. Moreover,

Euelpides handles the entire interview, while Pisthetairos remains silent. In addition to the announcement of his discovery, Pisthetairos' one comment is the result of Tereus' solicitation (128–42). During the entry of the birds, when the flamingo enters, something neither has ever seen before, Euelpides is moved to reflect; Pisthetairos wants an answer, and he immediately turns to Tereus. The unknown evokes Euelpides' curiosity; from Pisthetairos it evokes *praxis*. Euelpides is flighty; Pisthetairos wants to nest. You would not trust Euelpides with a founding, but you would not trust Pisthetairos with the truth. To Euelpides, not Pisthetairos, Aristophanes assigns the duty of informing the audience (13–22, 27–48).

We learn in Plato and Aristotle that there are speeches to the ideas and from the ideas. Euelpides brings to mind the former, Pisthetairos the latter. The former requires hope, because it relates to the pursuit of something that one can perhaps only vaguely see or not see at all. The latter requires trust, because it relates to the application of something about which one does not know to be true or good, but which one can at least identify. Because the latter results in establishing an authority or giving someone power, and because one must be persuaded to choose one thing rather than another and persuade others one is worthy to make choices, it would also require persuasiveness. Accordingly, Euelpides means Mr. Goodhope and Pisthetairos either Mr. Trusty-companion or Mr. Persuasive-companion. Their names correspond to their roles in the play. Euelpides inquires; Pisthetairos acts.[26]

A similar dichotomy is found in the Tereus myth, which sheds light on the one in our play. Euelpides was as lost as Philomela, and like Philomela he serves as a vehicle of understanding. Without Euelpides' inquiry, Pisthetairos may not have hatched his plan. Without Philomela's tapestry, Procne would not have known the nature of her husband. Euelpides reveals the truth to Pisthetairos, as Philomela reveals it to Procne, and as a result of what they learn, they both act. There is a difference, however. Procne learns that her marriage to the Thracian Tereus was a mistake. Pisthetairos learns that an alliance, a marriage of sorts, with Tereus would produce the most glorious revolution imaginable. Procne wrests herself from Tereus and does an unimaginable deed, which her name somehow reflects. Of all the characters in the myth, and seemingly in our play as well, her name is the only one that does not easily resolve into an applicable meaning.[27] It is as if her marriage produced an alliance, or offspring, which she must take back, and in taking it back it becomes as incomprehensible as her deed. In the *Birds*, she twice makes known her presence but never speaks (cf. 201–62, 658–84). Whereas Procne thoroughly divorces herself from Tereus, Pisthetairos instead converges on him. Both, for example, eat their own kind.[28] Pisthetairos and Tereus make such a happy pair that one can stand for two. After Tereus summons Procne at line 655, Tereus is not heard from again (658–74). Once Pisthetairos brings logos, or persuasiveness, to Thrace, Tereus becomes superfluous. As Pisthetairos' name suggests (643), he is quite able to digest him. Whereas Procne's name and her character defy intelligibility in her separation from Tereus, in Pisthetairos and Tereus' union, Pisthetairos' name becomes easier to decipher. Pisthetairos could be rendered "Pisthetereus," the persuasive-Tereus, or a Thracian subjected to an Athenian logos. To shed light on what this means, let us once more return to the myth.

After Tereus learns that Procne, with Philomena's help, has fed him his own son, he chases after the fleeing women, and as he is about to catch them, they all become birds: Procne becomes a nightingale, Philomela a swallow, and Tereus a hoopoe. In Greek, hoopoe is *epops*. *Epops* brings to mind *epopsios*, which can mean overseeing all things; *epos*, which can mean word, song, prophesy, or story; *epi + ops*, which can mean last word or epilogue; and *epi + opse*, which can mean beyond late. *Epops* is winged, but no matter how it is construed, it describes Tereus. The gods do to Tereus what Tereus does to the world. He takes things apart to suit his interest, so the gods take him apart to suit theirs, which is to serve as a vehicle of illumination. He becomes a pure medium. In order to serve this function, we must not do what Tereus does in the parodos. Upon seeing him, we cannot just say "hoopoe." We must look beyond the name, to where the name points, and to how its various meanings fit together. Like Philomela, the ingenuity of the gods is transcendent. Unlike the bird-gods fostered by Pisthetairos, the hoopoe into which the gods transform Tereus points beyond him. And in having Tereus passively announce the last eighteen birds as they enter during the parodos, providing a last word of sorts, it seems Aristophanes does, too. Aristophanes' punishment rivals that of the gods. Tereus took Philomela's tongue but could not prevent her from speaking; Aristophanes takes from Tereus everything but his tongue and shows that he still has nothing to say.

Notes

1. Aristophanes, *Birds*, ed. Peter Burian, Bryn Mawr Greek Commentaries (Bryn Mawr, PA: Bryn Mawr College, 1991), lines 252–59 and 428–31. The speaker is Tereus-hoopoe. All translations are my own.

2. Aristotelis, *Politica*, ed. W. D. Ross (New York: Oxford University Press, 1988), 1252a5–6.

3. At 1282, Aristophanes turns Socrates into a verb. In the city of the *Birds*, Socrates has been replaced by "socratizing," so at least in theory there now could be more than one Socrates. In practice, there would be none.

4. Aristophanes has Pisthetairos pun on the Greek word for city. In Greek, city is polis; sphere or realm is *polos*.

5. A form of this word appears at 864.

6. According to Herodotus, the Persians called all the Scythians Sacae. Herodoti, *Historiae*, ed. Carolus Hude (London: Oxford University Press, 1975), 7.64.

7. It is where our word "sack" comes from.

8. See Book 4 of Herodotus' *History*. Also see chapter 4 of Seth Benardete's *Herodotean Inquiries*, which provides an analysis of Book 4 (South Bend, IN: St. Augustine's Press, 1999), especially 114–15.

9. *Ethas* is related to ethos.

10. The bird is, of course, a flamingo.

11. The birds of the *Birds* bring to mind the ideas of Plato's *Republic*. Both are aloft but provide no means of ascent.

12. See lines 180–86, where Pisthetairos advises Tereus to make a polis out of *polos* by fencing in the sky. Naming a bird is like putting boundaries or "walling in" an area of the sky.

13. Clearly, Aristophanes had alternatives to Tereus if all he needed, as Euelpides says at 16 and 114, is a bird who was once a man. For example, there is Ceyx, who along with his wife, Alcyone, was transformed into a bird. Perhaps, in part, to remind us of this, Aristophanes has an *alkuon* enter at 298 (cf. 251). If it suited his larger intention, we might have had Ceyx and Alcyone instead of Tereus and Procne. Furthermore, Aristophanes makes clear that the particulars of the Tereus story were known, enabling him to use Tereus without being forced to provide every detail. See lines 100–1, where Sophocles' tragedy the *Tereus* is mentioned. All this suggests that Aristophanes uses Tereus with some purpose in mind.

14. It is not reported that Tereus raped her again.

15. See Tereus' invitation to the birds at 227–59. He refers to birds as having a "soft murmur" (*gyrus*) at 233 and a "pleasurable voice" (*phone*) at 236, and, more significantly, he refers to his own activity as the uttering of a sound (*aude*) at 241. But note what he says about Pisthetairos: "For here is some sharp old man, new in his understanding and a manipulator of new works, but come, here, here, here, here, for all the *logoi*" (255–59).

16. Again, see Tereus' invitation to the birds at 227–59, and the emphasis given to the diversity of the birds: "As many as live on the well-seeded fields of farmers" (230–31); "myriad tribes of barley-eaters and the races of seed-gatherers" (231–32).

17. *Homophrones logoi*. Compare this with the parallel phrase in Herodotus: *Hypo enos . . . phoneoi kata touto* (5.3.1). *Homophrones* and *phroneoi* have the same root.

18. Book 5 of Herodotus is on Athens, but it begins with Thrace. In order to illuminate Athens, both Aristophanes and Herodotus turn to Thrace. See also chapter 5 of Benardete's *Herodotean Inquiries*, in particular, 132–37. My understanding of Thrace comes from here.

19. At 4.93, Herodotus calls them the bravest and most just of the Thracians. See also 4.94.

20. Benardete, *Herodotean Inquiries*, 133.

21. In a way, then, Tereus is the ultimate Thracian. If donning an unnatural skin pigment is regarded as reflective of high-birth, what about donning feathers? He takes the death of his children hard, but there is a difference between selling your children and countenancing their murder by one's wife. If wives count for a lot, then the fact that the one he picked murdered her own children would be unforgivable.

22. In some of their cases, these words are very similar.

23. The Thracians remind us of the Scythians. Both are free but uncivilized. Herodotus illuminates the contrast. He regards the Thracians as stupid if not the stupidest. For example, at 4.95.2, he says the Thracians "live badly" (*kakobion*) and are "rather mindless [*hupaphronesteros*]"; and at 4.46.1, Herodotus calls the peoples of the Euxine Pontus (the Black Sea), which includes Thrace, "the most unlearned [*amathestata*]." Because this area also includes Scythia, Herodotus goes out of his way to except them: "For one of the greatest of human *pragmata* and the wisest of all we know has been discovered by the Scythian people, their other things I don't admire." This discovery turns out to be that they do not build cities and therefore are unconquerable. Both the Thracians and the Scythians are apolitical. They differ as to its cause. The Thracians are apolitical because of an unreflective opinion they all share. The Scythians are apolitical because of a discovered *pragma*. Like courage among the Thracians, it prevents the Scythians from having anything else in common. However, because it is discovered, should the day arise that it no longer serves its purpose, the Scythians have the capability to change it. The Thracians, in lacking self-consciousness, would seem to lack this capability.

24. See 85–91. Euelpides closes this exchange by sarcastically saying to Pisthetairos, who because of fear has just let his crow fly away, "My good man, how courageous [*andreios*] you are." See also 65–68. Euelpides identifies himself to Tereus' servant as a "superafraid Libyan bird," and when the servant accuses Euelpides of speaking nonsense, Euelpides tells him to notice what's between his own legs. Euelpides is "scared shitless." Pisthetairos says practically the same thing, identifying himself as a "shitterling from Phasis."

25. Note that all of Pisthetairos' preparations are irrelevant. Tereus' cunning, not Pisthetairos' generalship, causes the birds to relent. See 364–405. In other words, the scene is important not for its effect on the action, but for what it discloses about Euelpides and Pisthetairos.

26. Note their different aspirations. Euelpides' can be found at 128–34; Pisthetairos' at 137–42.

27. Even her father and son have names of significance. Her father's name is Pandion, which might mean many gods, which fits Athens' status at the time of his rule. It had not yet taken form. Pandion was pre-Theseus. Procne's son is Itys, who brings to mind Atys, whose name means "doom." At 1.34.2, Herodotus

has "*Atun*"; at 212, Aristophanes has *Itun*. Atys was the son of Croesus, killed by Adrastus, a suppliant of Croesus. See Herodotus, 1.34–46.

28. See 1574–86, where Pisthetairos is cooking a stew of rebellious birds.

9

Learning the Lesson of Dionysus

Aristophanes' Tragicomic Wisdom and Poetic Politics in the *Frogs*

Christopher Baldwin

In his brief discussion of comedy in the *Poetics*, Aristotle raises the question of how comedy came to be called comedy. Did comedy, as seems most likely, derive its name from the Greek verb meaning "to revel" (*komazein*)? Or could its name be derived from a somewhat obscure Doric word for village (*komai*), because comic poets were forced to wander from village to village since they were "banned from the city?"[1] Now, Aristotle may well have doubted the soundness of this alternate etymology of comedy; he might, appropriately enough, be having a bit of fun and joking around in his discussion of comedy. His playful humor, however, also makes a serious point and raises an interesting question. Aristotle's playful discussion of comedy points out that comedy and its revels were not, at least in their original form (Old Comedy), simply or easily compatible with the city. If we consider the only complete examples of Old Comedy that have come down to us, Aristophanes' comedies, we can easily understand why this might have been so. For Aristophanes' comedies question and lampoon things that the city cannot have, or would prefer not to have, questioned and lampooned. Aristophanes' comedies raise questions, for example, about whether we are necessarily subject to the will of the gods of the city (*Birds*) and even whether such gods exist (*Clouds*); they question the most fundamental purposes and policies of the city (*Peace*) and its leaders (*Knights*); and they even question the most basic social and moral conventions governing the family (*Clouds*) and the relationship between the sexes (*Lysistrata*). It is little wonder that comic poets were banned from the city. The real question—the question Aristotle helps us recognize and raise—is not why comic poets were banned from the city but how comic poets like Aristophanes ever came to find a place in the city. With this question in mind, I turn to a reading of Aristophanes' *Frogs* where Aristophanes reflects, perhaps more fully and completely than in any of his other plays, on the question of what makes a poet a truly great poet and the relationship between such a poet and the city.

In the *Frogs*, we find Athens in a state of decline. Once the "school of Greece" and a city whose great politics were to leave "eternal monuments" to its glory, Athens finds itself beleaguered by the long and devastating Peloponnesian War, now in its twenty-seventh year.[2] Although the city has just won an important naval battle at Arginusae, it is still hard-pressed by Sparta and in grave danger of losing the war; what is more, the commanders' failure to recover the bodies of the lost and fallen at Arginusae because of bad weather has caused considerable political upheaval and strife in the city, leading to the execution of six of the city's best naval commanders.[3] While Dionysus, the hero of the *Frogs*, claims to have been present with the Athenians at Arginusae, he does not seem much concerned with the commanders' impious failure to recover the bodies of the fallen or with the increasingly dire military situation and politically divided character of the city. Dionysus is concerned not with great politics and the political decline of the city but only with great poetry and the poetic decline of the city, particularly the sorry state of tragic poetry in Athens now that Euripides and Sophocles have died. At the start of the play, Dionysus is the god of the theater and only the god of the theater, not at all a god of the city. This, however, changes over the course of the play. By the end of the play, Dionysus claims that his primary concern is "to save the city so it might celebrate the choruses and drama" (*Frogs* 1419).[4] Over the course of the play, without in any way abandoning or lessening his concern for poetry, Dionysus learns also to care for politics and the city, becoming a god of the city even while remaining most fundamentally the god of the theater. The *Frogs*, then, shows us how those most concerned with great poetry—like Dionysus and Aristophanes himself, who claims Dionysus as his teacher (*Clouds* 518–19)—might learn to care about politics and come to find or forge a place for themselves, even a respectable place, in the city.[5]

A Divine Comedy: Contesting Divinity

The drama of the *Frogs* is set in motion by Dionysus' love of Euripides. Having recently read again Euripides' *Andromeda*, Dionysus was struck by the greatness of Euripides' poetic genius, a genius that none of the remaining Athenian tragic poets even comes close to matching. So Dionysus decides to descend to Hades to steal Euripides away, intending to bring him back to life to revitalize tragic poetry in Athens. Thus imitating in some ways Heracles' descent into Hades to steal away Cerberus, Dionysus, god of the theater, decides to play the role of Heracles more literally, disguising himself as Heracles. Hilarity then ensues, as we would of course expect of an Aristophanic comedy. The first half of the play especially presents us with the sort of humor in which Aristophanes typically delights. Dionysus' servant, Xanthias, tries to amuse Dionysus and the audience with original (even if somewhat crude) bodily humor, and we are treated to the comic banter between master and servant. We watch the incredibly effete Dionysus attempting to imitate the incredibly manly Heracles, cutting so ridiculous a figure that Heracles cannot help but simply laugh at the sight of Dionysus when he visits to learn what he can expect to encounter in the underworld. After a comical exchange between the two, and between Dionysus and an unexpectedly reanimated corpse, Dionysus and Xanthias enter the underworld, where the disguised god is not recognized even by those who worship him, a chorus of frogs (with whom he engages in a ridiculous croaking contest), and a chorus of Mystery novices. After a series of costume changes between Xanthias and Dionysus, who is atremble at the thought of being punished for Heracles' previous misdeeds in Hades, the god, whose identity is now greatly in doubt, is whipped and beaten repeatedly by a lowly servant to test his divinity by seeing if he is superhumanly immune to pain, a test Dionysus manifestly fails and a spectacle that surpasses in both hilarity and impiety even the beating of Strepsiades by his own son Pheidippides in the *Clouds*.

Aristophanes' humor, however, is not only funny, but also deeply thought provoking. According to Aristophanes himself, he is concerned not only with presenting us with "many laughable things," but also with provoking us to think about "many serious things" (*Frogs* 391–92; cf. *Clouds* 518–62). Indeed, simply by depicting comically Hades and the gods, Aristophanes prompts us to laugh at and think differently about sacred things we are perhaps not supposed to laugh at or think about in heterodox ways. The very laughter Aristophanes provokes is in itself liberating and thought provoking. Yet Aristophanes does more than merely provoke us to thought; he also guides and directs our thoughts. In the first half of the *Frogs*, I would suggest that Aristophanes particularly provokes and guides our thoughts to questions about the afterlife, divine justice, and the nature of the gods.

Aristophanes, of course, never denies the existence of Hades or the afterlife. In fact, by presenting the action of the play as taking place in Hades, he could be said to affirm, albeit comically, the existence of Hades and the afterlife. Aristophanes does, though, provocatively question whether the most sacred and authoritative accounts of the afterlife and our continued existence after death are entirely accurate. For example, no less an authority than Heracles confirms the conventional belief that in Hades the just are rewarded and the unjust are punished terribly (*Frogs* 136–64). Yet when Dionysus and Xanthias enter the underworld, they (and we) never witness the punishment of the unjust. In fact, in precisely that place where we have been led to think we would witness the most terrifying punishments of the most horribly unjust, just as Dionysus and Xanthias pass over into Hades, we encounter nothing at all; the utter silence that we would otherwise encounter as a result of the utter absence of divine punishment of the unjust is broken only by the comical croaking of the chorus of frogs (205–84). Could it actually be, Aristophanes prompts us to wonder, that the gods do not punish the unjust in this life or the next? The comical croaking of the frogs and the ridiculous croaking contest between Dionysus and the frogs cannot help but distract us somewhat from this troubling question. Yet Aristophanes' decision to name his play after the chorus of frogs also provokes us to wonder about the importance of this strange chorus, never to be heard from again, that wholly takes the place of the spectacle of the punishment of the unjust and thus leads us back to the question of whether the gods actually might not punish the unjust.[6] We *hear* of the punishments and terrors that await the unjust in the afterlife, but we never *see* them for ourselves and altogether lack any credible evidence of the truth of the stories told of the punishments and terrors that await the unjust in the afterlife. It is true, of course, that Xanthias, Dionysus' servant, affirms the existence of one of the terrors of Hades, the monster Empussa (285–306). Yet we never see Empussa ourselves and have good reason to think that she is nothing but a figment of Xanthias' apparently rich and fertile imagination; he seems to be playfully pretending to see Empussa in order both to please and play with Dionysus when he says he would like to encounter one of Hades' fabled monsters. Could it be, as Aristophanes seems to provoke us to ask, that all the rich and vivid stories of the punishments and terrors said and believed to await the unjust in the afterlife are ultimately nothing but the imaginative musings of Dionysus' other servants, the poets?

The troubling possibility that the gods do not punish the unjust is further suggested by questions that Aristophanes raises about the character or nature of the gods themselves. Just as Aristophanes affirms the existence of Hades and some form of life after death but questions the conventional accounts of these things, so too does he seem to affirm the existence of the gods but question the conventional accounts of them. The gods exist—we see them onstage—but they are not entirely as they are said or believed to be. To begin with, the gods seem far from wise. Heracles, for example, might well be many things, but certainly not wise, and neither is Dionysus particularly wise. For example, his clever plan to disguise himself as Heracles to enter Hades and steal away with Euripides proves to be most unwise; his plan proves unnecessary because Pluto is entirely willing to help him return to Athens with Euripides, and it serves only to lead him into a situation where he is repeatedly whipped and beaten in an effort to test his divinity. What is more, the gods' integrity is, no less than their intelligence, called into question. Both Heracles and Dionysus seem to be controlled more by their passions and whims than in control of them—Heracles controlled by his physical passions and whims and Dionysus by his more intellectual passions and whims, such as his love of Euripides and great poetry. Even more troubling, though, is the fact that neither Heracles nor Dionysus seems particularly honest or just. Heracles, for example, lies about the terrors of Hades in order to make his own exploits there seem greater than they were (277–82). Worse still, Dionysus disguises himself as Heracles, lying about his true identity so that he might unjustly steal Euripides away from one of his fellow gods, Pluto, in a way that will not only allow him to escape all responsibility for his injustice but also place the blame squarely on the shoulders of his own brother, Heracles. Might not many of the stories told of the gods lead us to wonder, Aristophanes suggests, if such is the true character of the gods? And could such gods, lacking in both intelligence and integrity, truly be thought to govern this world and the next wisely and justly, ensuring that the just are rewarded and the unjust punished?

Not only does Aristophanes call into question the gods' wisdom and justice, but he also calls into question perhaps the most fundamental or defining quality of their divinity, their immortality and immunity to suffering—thereby provoking us to wonder if any beings are truly immortal and immune to pain and suffering. Heracles, for example, suggests that Dionysus might try to enter Hades by committing suicide, implying that not even the gods are simply immortal (117–35). Most prominently and comically, however, the whipping contest between Dionysus and Xanthias reveals that Dionysus and the gods are not immune to pain and suffering and calls into question Dionysus' divinity. By showing us Dionysus and Xanthias exchanging costumes and roles multiple times, their bantering and bickering more as friends and equals than as master and slave, and the fact that both seem equally susceptible to (but also capable of enduring) considerable abuse, Aristophanes provokes us to wonder about Dionysus' divinity and the relationship between Dionysus and his servant. In the end, who is the god, or more godlike, and who is the servant? Does Xanthias serve Dionysus' purposes, or does Dionysus serve Xanthias'?

In the first half of the *Frogs*, then, Aristophanes raises comically and explores radical questions about the afterlife, divine justice, and the nature of the gods; it is, in a manner of speaking, a divine comedy. Over the course of the rest of the play, Aristophanes might seem to retract or withdraw his radical questions and instead offer and affirm more or less conventional answers to these questions. He suggests that the gods of the city, like Dionysus, are in fact gods. Dionysus' divinity, so provocatively questioned in the first half of the play, is confirmed when he is recognized as a god by his fellow god, Pluto, the ruling authority in Hades.[7] Realizing that his existence and security, let alone his well-being and flourishing as a god, depend decisively on his fellow gods, Dionysus seems to learn "a political lesson": he is necessarily part of, and dependent upon, a larger group or community.[8] As a result, he learns to respect the community of which he is a part and its needs; he learns to be more politically responsible and even to serve the needs of his community. Accordingly, in the second half of the *Frogs*, Dionysus willingly serves in a civic or quasi-civic capacity, as a judge in the poetic contest between Aeschylus and Euripides that takes center stage, and he reveals his concern with upholding a more conventional understanding of justice; he seems to reward the more conventionally just and pious Aeschylus by bringing him back from death to Athens and to punish the heterodox and dubiously sophisticated Euripides by leaving him behind in Hades, and he does so in no small part because he thinks that Aeschylus can better serve Athens given its current political needs. Aristophanes thus seems to suggest that the gods of the city exist and that they care for the city and for justice in this world and the next.

A Political Tragedy: Contesting Great Poetry

I would suggest, though, that Aristophanes does not simply withdraw or retract the sort of radical questions he raises in the first half of the play, but instead continues to explore these questions in the second half of the play, albeit more subtly. For as the second half of the *Frogs* begins we learn that those who excel in the various arts, such as tragic poetry, are honored in death just as in life, or perhaps even more so, but that there has been a dispute over who should be and will be the most honored tragic poet, Aeschylus or Euripides (755–813). The contentious dispute seemed to admit of no just or adequate resolution until Dionysus' chance and fortuitous descent to Hades. But now that he is there, who better to judge who is the best tragic poet than Dionysus himself, god of the theater? He can decide who deserves to be honored as the best tragic poet and return to Athens with that poet, seeing to it that poetic justice is done. The poetic contest between Aeschylus and Euripides that comes to take center stage during the second half of the play provides us, however, not only with a rich and insightful discussion of the nature of great poetry, but also with a vivid and thought-provoking example of and case study in the possibility (or impossibility) of divine justice. For by presenting us with the spectacle of Dionysus judging a poetic contest between Aeschylus and Euripides in Hades, Aristophanes shows us—and invites us to reflect upon—an example of divine justice in action. Aristophanes thus continues to explore the sort of questions he has raised in the first half of the play, focusing especially on the question of divine justice, even as he goes on to consider and highlight the question of what makes a poet a truly great poet. As perhaps befits a consideration of such serious questions and a dispute over who is the greatest tragic poet, the second half of the *Frogs* is somewhat less ridiculously comic and more serious than the first half of the play; it is somewhat more tragic. Of course, being an Aristophantic comedy, the second half of the play is hardly simply serious or tragic. It is still deeply, even if more subtly, humorous.

Much of the comedy of the second half of the *Frogs* results from Aristophanes' comical presentation and exaggeration of the differences between Aeschylus and Euripides, who initially could not seem to be more different. Aeschylus is nothing if not traditional. He prays to the gods of the city, like Demeter, and he both embodies and defends the belligerent and martial civic virtue of the Athens of old, of the fighters at Marathon. Euripides, on the other hand, is the very model of novelty and sophistication. He prays to new and strange gods, like Ether—to things believed in by sophisticated and morally dubious philosophers like Socrates (*Clouds* 263–66)—and he embodies and represents the sophistication and rationality of contemporary Athens, of Aristophanes' audience.

Still, as different as Aeschylus and Euripides are, they also turn out to share a deep, even if more subtle, kinship. To begin with, both men are deeply concerned with honor and are willing to struggle and risk loss to acquire the honor each believes he deserves and clearly desires, particularly in contrast to Sophocles, who seems able to accept both his life and his death for what they are with an impressive and unshakable sobriety (*Frogs* 78–82, 786–94). Both men also obviously care deeply about tragic poetry and even agree, at least in broad outline, as to the fundamental standards by which great poets should be judged. They agree that great poets must, of course, be poetically skilled; they must be able to express themselves in poetically original, appropriate, and inspiring or pleasing ways. Even more important, though, Aeschylus and Euripides agree that truly great poets must, first and foremost, be wise; they must be able to educate and improve their audiences (954–1097, especially 1008–10). Aeschylus and Euripides disagree, however, over the particulars of what exactly constitutes poetic skill and especially over what constitutes genuine wisdom, over what it means to educate and improve their audiences.

Aeschylus contends that truly great poets, wise poets, should teach people to be dutiful citizens and warriors, encouraging them to be courageous and just, eager to punish injustice and to harm their enemies. Like the great poets of old, going all the way back to Homer, they should teach people to respect the more traditional rustic and martial virtues and to be pious and worship the gods. They should obscure any unwholesome truths, the existence of which Aeschylus concedes, and instead inspire their fellow human beings to aspire to lofty goals by using appropriately lofty language. Euripides, however, disagrees. He finds Aeschylus' language and (especially) the goals he sets for his fellow human beings to be unbearably lofty. Aeschylus' goal or image of human excellence is, Euripides implies, unrealistically high and inhuman; he has forgotten about Aphrodite and eros, about a fundamental (even if imperfect and sometimes unlawful) aspect of our humanity. Accordingly, in a conscious break with Aeschylus, Euripides tells us, he chose to speak to his fellow human beings as human beings and to be more rational, realistic, and honest than Aeschylus. Truly great poets, wise poets, Euripides argues, should teach people to be more intelligent and thoughtful citizens and human beings and how to deal with the world as it in fact is. They should teach people how to be free, self-governing citizens and human beings, able to manage both the affairs of the city and their own private affairs with intelligence and humanity, aware of both our tremendous capacities and limits as human beings, perhaps especially when facing the sometimes seemingly overwhelming and irresistible power of eros. Yet just as Euripides denies that Aeschylus has improved his fellow human beings, so too does Aeschylus deny that Euripides has improved his fellow human beings; instead of improving his fellow human beings, Aeschylus argues, Euripides has debased them. What Euripides considers virtue or excellence, Aeschylus regards as debased; what Aeschylus points to as virtue or excellence, Euripides finds unbelievable and inhuman. The two poets disagree fundamentally as to what constitutes genuine virtue or excellence.

It is little wonder that Dionysus is unable to say which of the two poets is wiser. For whereas in the *Clouds* we are presented with a contest between the Just Speech and the Unjust Speech, in the *Frogs* we witness a contest between two Just Speeches, as it were. Both Aeschylus and Euripides make a compelling case that they genuinely sought to educate and improve their audiences and did in fact do so. Broadly speaking, Aeschylus sought to make them good citizens, while Euripides sought to make them good human beings. Now, Euripides, it could be argued, is insufficiently mindful of the needs of the city and of the dignity and excellence of citizenship, but one could also argue that Aeschylus fails to appreciate fully our humanity and the dignity and excellence of being a truly free and self-governing human being. It is hard, though, to blame either poet for failing to do full justice to the other poet's impressive conception of human dignity and excellence or for failing to reconcile the two different conceptions. It is hard to imagine how one might do full justice to both conceptions, and one might well doubt whether anyone could ever reconcile the two different conceptions, doing full justice both to the demands and the dignity of being a good citizen and to the demands and the dignity of being a good human being. One, it seems, must simply choose between the two. But how? In particular, how can Dionysus justly choose between these two conceptions of human dignity and excellence, between Aeschylus' and Euripides' wisdom, without doing injustice to the other?

Like Aeschylus' and Euripides' tragic presentations of the choices faced by characters like Agamemnon, Orestes, and Oedipus (1119–97), Aristophanes' presentation of the choice Dionysus must make between Aeschylus and Euripides points to the possibility that we face a tragic choice as human beings, a choice between different and irreconcilable conceptions of virtue or excellence. We cannot choose to be virtuous in one way without *necessarily* failing to be virtuous in another way. As a result, we cannot help but do wrong even while genuinely trying to do right. It is *impossible* to be simply or altogether virtuous and do the right thing. Dionysus, it thus turns out, simply cannot justly judge between Aeschylus and Euripides on the most important ground of their poetic excellence, their wisdom, without doing injustice to the other.

Hoping to extricate himself from an impossible situation and avoid the tragedy of having to choose between Aeschylus and Euripides on the grounds of their wisdom, Dionysus turns to a consideration of their technical skill as poets and the manner in which they express their wisdom. Yet the consideration of Aeschylus' and Euripides' technical skill as poets, while quite funny, no more allows Dionysus to declare a just victor than did the consideration of their wisdom. Aristophanes' Aeschylus and Euripides parody and criticize one another's plays in insightful and witty ways. Each, for example, points out certain formulaic or predictable aspects of the other poet's art. Aeschylus, Euripides observes, always and somewhat ridiculously opens his plays in the same way, with a solitary and silent protagonist, letting the dramatic tension build until he or she finally speaks to great and dramatic effect (907–20). Euripides, though, Aeschylus points out, is comically predictable in his use of meter and rhythm (1198–1248). Still, while each wittily parodies, criticizes, and disapproves of the other poet's poetic skills and choices, it also becomes clear, upon reflection, that each is also a skilled and accomplished poet. Each is original and writes in a way that is appropriate to his subject and inspiring or pleasing. Aeschylus and Euripides both express themselves in remarkable and beautiful, even if different, ways; each employs different, but equally impressive, poetic means ideally suited to achieve his different poetic end, conveying and inculcating his different conception of human virtue or excellence. Aeschylus makes use of his great dramatic skill and the power of his language to overwhelm his audiences, leaving them in a state of awe and reverence for the obviously weighty and serious subjects he treats and thereby inspiring them to be better and more serious citizens. Euripides, however, employs his equally impressive poetic skills in a different way, writing with a kind of clarity and realism that leads his audiences to become more thoughtful and compassionate or humane in their own lives, able to appreciate and enjoy the lightness with which he is able to treat and discuss even the weightiest of subjects.

Both Aeschylus and Euripides possess great, even if imperfect, poetic skill and wisdom. Both are great poets and both deserve, even if for different reasons, to win. Dionysus simply cannot justly prefer one poet to the other on the grounds of poetic excellence without also at the same time necessarily committing a great injustice against the other. Like so many of Aeschylus' characters, Aristophanes' Dionysus finds himself in a seemingly impossible or tragic situation and in need of more-than-human help (1264–76). Accordingly, Dionysus prays, as it were, for help to his fellow god, Pluto, but to no avail (1411–14). Dionysus learns he is on his own, and on his own he finds a more or less adequate solution to his dilemma. Unable to judge justly between Aeschylus and Euripides on the basis of their poetic excellence, Dionysus presents service to the common good of the city as the criterion on the basis of which he might justly judge between them. Somewhat disingenuously claiming that he has always cared about the city, that he came to Hades with the intention of "sav[ing] the city so it might celebrate the choruses and drama" (1419), Dionysus declares that he will judge in favor of whichever poet is best able to offer sound political advice to the city.

In order to assess Aeschylus' and Euripides' ability to give sound political advice to the city, Dionysus asks them about both the city's leadership, particularly whether it should make use of the brilliant but dangerous Alcibiades, and about the sort of general policies the city might do well to pursue. The sophisticated Euripides proves to be politically cautious and moderate. He advises that the city not make use of the sophisticated and morally dubious Alcibiades, a view with which Dionysus seems to sympathize (1427–30). When asked further what sort of general policies the city might do well to pursue, Euripides is reluctant to answer at first; his first response is comical, as though he finds the idea of poets offering political advice, and of the city looking to poets for political advice, more than a little laughable (1437–42). Dionysus' disapproval of his treating politics as simply comical prompts him to offer a somewhat more serious response. He proposes that the city replace its failed leaders with other, better leaders, a moderate and sensible enough policy endorsed if not directly by Dionysus himself, then by his just and civic-minded admirers and worshippers, the chorus of Mystery novices (1443–50 with 686–737). The traditional Aeschylus, on the other hand, offers rather bold and daring political advice. Although he does not approve of the morally dubious Alcibiades, Aeschylus suggests the city might need to make use of him (1431–33). While Aeschylus is as reluctant to offer more general political advice to the city as Euripides, the reasons for his reluctance differ from those of Euripides. Aeschylus does not find it laughable that poets offer, or be expected to offer, political advice; rather, given the sorry state of affairs in Athens, he laments the possibility of anyone being able to help the city, even himself (1458–62). He perhaps thinks that a good poet can be of use to a healthy city, but cannot make an unhealthy city healthy again. Still, at Dionysus' insistence, Aeschylus intimates that Athens might do well to return to the bold and daring policies and strategies of Pericles, or perhaps especially to the even bolder and more daring policies and strategies of Themistocles, although Dionysus suggests that doing so might prove quite difficult (1463–66).

As the contest between the poets draws to a close, we might well expect Dionysus to favor Euripides. After all, he regards both Aeschylus and Euripides as great poets, but he expresses a personal fondness and love for Euripides and a general sympathy for his politics that he never expresses for Aeschylus. Yet Dionysus chooses Aeschylus, immediately after the heterodox Euripides unbelievably enough urges Dionysus to remember the oaths he swore to the gods to bring him back to Athens, thus reminding Dionysus of his rather obvious heterodoxy just as Dionysus is making his decision. Dionysus, it seems, concludes that Euripides simply lacks sufficient political wisdom to be able to offer the city sound political advice. He, too, obviously fails to take seriously enough those things the city needs its citizens, especially its leading citizens and advisors, to take seriously: the political affairs of the city and the gods of the city. Like Dionysus at the beginning of the play, Euripides, too, obviously cares much more for great poetry than for politics and the city. As a result, he cannot easily present himself as a part of the city, let alone as a leading citizen and advisor to the city. Euripides cannot help but be regarded with suspicion and even some animosity by a considerable part of the city, as Aristophanes comically suggests in his *Thesmophoriazusae*, and his political advice will therefore quite possibly go unheeded, even if it is sensible. Aeschylus, on the other hand, clearly cares not only for great poetry but also for politics and the city; he is an eminently respectable citizen and advisor whose advice the city might well take. Moreover, while Aeschylus' advice might well be daring, dangerous, and difficult to carry out, it may also be what the city needs to do. Making use of a man like Alcibiades is surely dangerous, but he is also an extremely capable military and political leader and perhaps the only man capable of saving the city in its current dire situation.[9] In such a situation, daring action orchestrated by a capable leader, even if difficult to implement and of uncertain success, might well be the city's last and best hope of salvation, much like the Athenians' daring action under the leadership of Themistocles at Salamis. Most of the time, under ordinary circumstances, Dionysus might prefer Euripides' politics to Aeschylus'. Athens, however, finds itself in extraordinary circumstances that seem to call for extraordinary measures. In these circumstances at least, Dionysus suggests, a dose of Aeschylus' intense political seriousness and his more martial, hard-nosed politics might be what the city needs and help to save the city, and with it the possibility of great poetry continuing to survive and flourish in the city. Accordingly, Dionysus chooses Aeschylus over Euripides.

Dionysus cunningly avoids his seemingly—but, it turns out, *only seemingly*—tragic fate, having to judge between Euripides and Aeschylus on the grounds of poetic excellence. Favoring Aeschylus over Euripides as the greater poet is something Dionysus simply could not do as the god of the theater. Instead, he favors Aeschylus over Euripides as a god of the city on the grounds of Aeschylus' superior political wisdom, not his superior poetic excellence. Doing so might, of course, seem to involve him in yet another tragedy, having to obscure somewhat both his great admiration for Euripides' poetic excellence and his great personal fondness for Euripides, as well as hurting his friend by publicly siding against him and with Aeschylus. Yet one could well wonder if this situation is simply or altogether tragic. Aeschylus and the chorus of Mystery novices certainly do not seem to think it is; they regard the ending of the play as a happy one. Euripides is punished for his lack of sufficient concern for politics and the city by being left in Hades, while Aeschylus is rewarded for his superior concern for politics and the city. Dionysus has affirmed the gods' concern for the city and for seeing to it that justice is done in both this world and the next, and the city and great poetry have at least some chance of survival. They are not tragically doomed.

What is more, neither is Euripides' situation simply tragic. He is, it is true, left dead in Hades, but he was already dead to begin with. He is not actually harmed or punished in any real or additional way. While Euripides' situation is certainly not enviable, neither is it perhaps as tragic or lamentable as it might initially appear. After all, as Euripides himself has suggested, death is perhaps not what people think it is or as bad as people think it is, as Dionysus, partly comically and partly consolingly, reminds his friend (1477). Indeed, Dionysus even cryptically intimates that Euripides might actually fare well in death (1478), perhaps even better than Aeschylus. The revival of Aeschylus and his poetry is due to the current needs and preferences of the city, but it will not last forever; after hopefully helping the city and the cause of great poetry, Aeschylus must inevitably die again and return to Hades. When he does so, he hopes and expects that he will continue to be honored in death as the greatest tragic poet and that Euripides will never be so honored (1515–23). His hopes and expectations, however, are left unacknowledged, and no such guarantees are made. In the long run, Euripides, to say nothing of Sophocles, might well be honored in death as a greater poet than Aeschylus. As the *Frogs* ends and Dionysus silently witnesses, without any apparent jubilation, Aeschylus' victory over Euripides and revival, one cannot help but wonder if he serves the cause of political justice in the short term as a god of the city must, but hopes in the long term, as the god of the theater, to see the cause of poetic justice prevail. Both political justice and poetic justice might ultimately be done. It is a more or less happy, even if imperfect, ending, as produced and directed by Aristophanes' Dionysus—and ultimately, of course, by Aristophanes himself.

Aristophanes' Tragicomic Wisdom and Poetic Politics in the *Frogs*

In the *Frogs*, we learn much about the nature of great poetry through the poetic contest between Aeschylus and Euripides. Truly great poets, we learn, must possess not only great poetic skill but also great wisdom, including political wisdom. I would suggest, though, that the *Frogs* does more than simply present us with a rich and thought-provoking discussion of great poetry. Aristophanes does not merely *tell us* about great poetry in the *Frogs*, but he also *shows us* great poetry. That is to say, the *Frogs* itself is meant to serve as an example of truly great poetry, an example that suggests an additional, unstated criterion for being a truly great poet. In addition to being poetically skilled, wise, and politic, truly great poets, Aristophanes suggests, must also be able to write both comedy and tragedy, but perhaps especially comedy.[10]

In the *Frogs*, Aristophanes lets us see, perhaps more so than in any of his other plays, the full and impressive range of his skill as a poet. What his other plays repeatedly demonstrate, Aristophanes again confirms in the *Frogs*; as a comic poet, he is a genius without equal. His humor is always novel and original (*Frogs* 1–18; cf. *Clouds* 534–62) and expressed in ways that are comically appropriate, hilariously pleasing, and both poetically skillful and delightful, often even quite enchanting and beautiful. In the *Frogs*, though, Aristophanes reveals not only that he is a master of the art of comedy, but also that he possesses a deep understanding of tragedy. He obviously knows the plays of Aeschylus and Euripides intimately and understands thoroughly the art or craft of writing tragic poetry. Otherwise, he would not have been able to parody so brilliantly and insightfully Aeschylus' and Euripides' plays, playfully bringing out each poet's own unique style and tremendous (even if sometimes humorously predictable) skill as a poet. Indeed, Aristophanes proves to understand the art of writing tragedy so well that he can practice it himself. Before our very eyes, he deftly transforms Dionysus, the comic hero of the first half of the *Frogs*, into the tragic or quasi-tragic hero of the second half of the *Frogs*. Aristophanes thus proves himself able to write not only great comedy but also tragedy, and he does so with great poetic genius and skill. He writes a wholly new and original type of tragedy: a tragedy with a happy ending, which masterfully and appropriately combines both tragic and comic elements in unfailingly delightful and charming ways that subtly reveal his tremendous skill as a poet.

Not only, though, does the *Frogs* reveal to us Aristophanes' great skill as a poet, but it also reveals to us his great wisdom, a wisdom arguably even greater than Aeschylus' and Euripides'. For in the *Frogs*, Aristophanes helps us to raise and explore provocative questions about the afterlife, the gods, and especially divine justice, and he proves able to do what neither Aeschylus nor Euripides could. He proves able to help us begin to appreciate and understand both the dignity and excellence of citizenship, as suggested by Aeschylus, and the dignity and excellence of being a truly free and self-governing human being, as suggested by Euripides, while also tragically pointing to the troubling and disenchanting thought that we—like Dionysus—cannot possibly judge justly between these two competing and ultimately irreconcilable conceptions of human dignity and excellence. Yet Aristophanes also ultimately suggests that our situation—again, like Dionysus'—is not simply tragic and thus reveals to us his tragicomic wisdom. As human beings, Aristophanes implies, we might well find ourselves, like Dionysus, in a situation that is lamentable and difficult in many ways, but it is not simply tragic, for if we learn from and follow the example of the cunning Dionysus, we too can find our way to a more or less happy ending, an ending more comic than tragic. It is perhaps for this reason above all that Aristophanes suggests that a truly great poet must be able to write both comedy and tragedy, but especially comedy. For only such a poet can adequately reveal to us both what is ridiculously comical and what is lamentably tragic or quasi-tragic about the human situation as well as the possibility that we might, like Dionysus, live lives that are, even if not entirely without their lamentable aspects, still more the stuff of comedy than of tragedy. Only such a poet can reveal to us the truth about the human situation in its entirety and point to its highest possibilities. Only such a poet can help us come to see, as Nietzsche would later put it, that "there are heights of soul," Dionysian heights, "from which even tragedy ceases to look tragic."[11] Yet if we truly hope to learn from and follow the lead of Dionysus, Aristophanes suggests, we must also learn, as Dionysus learns, that none of us fares particularly well entirely on our own; we depend on the communities of which we are a part for our well-being. This is true, Aristophanes indicates, even (or perhaps especially) of Dionysus and those most like him, such as truly great poets. The city is the necessary precondition for great poetry; for truly great poets and their poetry to survive and flourish, they must find or forge a place for themselves in the city. As a result, even while remaining most fundamentally concerned with great poetry, truly great poets must, like Dionysus, learn to be politically responsible and to respect the city and its most basic needs—for example, the familial, moral, political, and religious conventions that constitute and support the city. Moreover, if they hope to find or forge not only a place for themselves in the city, but also a comfortable and respected place, then truly great poets must learn not only to be politically responsible but also politically respectable and wise, able to give the city the sort of political advice it might well expect from a prominent citizen, advice that hopefully will contribute to the well-being of both the city and great poetry.

Not only, though, does Aristophanes suggest in the *Frogs* that truly great poets should thus learn the lesson of Dionysus; he also puts that lesson into practice himself. For while Aristophanes raises many provocative questions in the *Frogs*, he does so in a politically responsible manner, in the guise of a mere comic poet. He allows us to think that his questions are only jokes and not meant to be taken seriously—that they are part of a comedy that is merely meant to entertain. Aristophanes even seems to affirm the eminently respectable wisdom of the extremely civic-minded Aeschylus, whose edifying views are so useful to the city in general and to Athens in its particular circumstances. Yet Aristophanes also simultaneously pokes fun at Aeschylus, thereby moderating or correcting the potential extremism of his views and leaving much of his audience in a largely, but perhaps not entirely, Aeschylean frame of mind; they might even feel a bit of sympathy for Euripides and his way of looking at things. Aristophanes thus benefits the city by producing better and more thoughtful citizens, the sort of citizens who benefit the city in general and might even be able to save Athens in its current troubling and dire (but not tragically doomed) circumstances. Aristophanes, however, benefits and prudently advises the city in such a way that he simultaneously manages to benefit the cause of great poetry. For by helping to preserve the city and its general well-being, he also helps to preserve the precondition of great poetry, and, what is more, by helping to preserve and shape a city that is moderately Aeschylean in character—and hence not simply Aeschylean, and perhaps even somewhat Euripidean in character—he helps to create a city that is open to truly great poetry of all sorts, even Aristophantic comedy.

The *Frogs*, then, helps us come to understand much about the nature of great poetry in general and Aristophanes' own particular greatness as a poet—a greatness that certainly rivals, and perhaps even exceeds, that of the greatest tragic poets. It also helps us come to understand the relationship between truly great poets and the city and how such poets, even comic poets like Aristophanes, might come to find a place in the city. The *Frogs* helps us come to understand—and shows us—how truly great poets like Aristophanes might learn to care about politics and the city, and even engage in a sort of poetic politics by shaping public opinion, in such a way that they might find and forge a place, even a respected place, for themselves and great poetry in the city even as they reveal to us their great skill and wisdom. And for so revealing to us Aristophanes' Dionysian wisdom, to say nothing of the Dionysian laughter it provokes and helps us to delight in, the *Frogs* is, I would suggest, well worth the price of admission.

Notes

1. Aristotle, *Aristotelis De Arte Poetica Liber*, ed. Rudolf Kassel (Oxford: Oxford Classical Texts, 1965), 1448a30–b4.

2. Thucydides, *Thucydidis Historiae*, 2 vols., ed. Henry Stuart Jones (Oxford: Oxford Classical Texts, 1942), 2.41.

3. Xenophon, *Historia Graeca*, ed. E. C. Marchant (Oxford: Oxford Classical Texts, 1922), I.6.29–7.35.

4. All references to Aristophanes are cited parenthetically by line numbers as indicated in Aristophanes, *Aristophanis Comoediae,* 2 vols., eds. F. W. Hall and W. M. Geldart (Oxford: Oxford Classical Texts, 1906).

5. That the dramatic unity of the *Frogs*, sometimes disputed by scholars, is to be found in the development and education of Dionysus from an apolitical admirer of poetic excellence to a more politic admirer of poetic excellence has also been argued (in different ways) by Charles Paul Segal, "The Character and Cults of Dionysus and the Unity of the *Frogs*," *Harvard Studies in Classical Philology* 65 (1983): 207–42; Cedric H. Whitman, *Aristophanes and the Comic Hero* (Cambridge, MA: Harvard University Press, 1964), 228–58; Leo Strauss, *Socrates and Aristophanes* (Chicago: University of Chicago Press, 1966), 236–62. My own reading of the *Frogs* is particularly indebted to Strauss's subtle and provocative reading.

6. As Leo Strauss observes, "The title of the play draws our attention to this possible impossibility" (*Socrates and Aristophanes*, 241).

7. Cf. Strauss, *Socrates and Aristophanes*, 245 with 179 and 182.

8. Strauss, *Socrates and Aristophanes*, 246.

9. Cf. Thucydides, *Historiae*, 6.15.4 and 8.86, especially 5–7; Xenophon, *Historia Graeca*, I.4.13–23, 5.10–17; II.1.21–26.

10. Cf. Plato, *Symposium,* ed. John Burnet (Oxford: Oxford Classical Texts, 1901), 223c4–d6.

11. Friedrich Nietzsche, *Beyond Good and Evil*, trans. Walter Kaufmann (New York: Vintage, 1966), 30.

10

Wealth and the Theology of Charity

Paul W. Ludwig

Of all the comedies, the *Wealth* plays with ideas most closely resembling modern liberalism in three of its founding pillars: 1) that the pursuit of property or wealth leads to happiness; 2) that poverty alleviation decreases crime; and 3) that God, if He exists, is identical to pure giving or charity. Perhaps this last claim, that modern liberalism has a theological foundation, is surprising.[1] Admittedly, a great deal of work remains to be done on the Christian presuppositions of modern democracy, as well as on the cooptation of recognizably Christian ideas by early modern philosophers, who sometimes made them serve a new political morality that was not entirely Christian.[2] What is clear is that an ideal of love stemming from the Gospels and Epistles introduced nonclassical assumptions into the philosophies that they influenced, such as Neoplatonism. The arduous attempts of great minds such as St. Augustine to reconcile the classical heritage with these new Christian assumptions left intellectual fissures, fault lines that were later attacked by the reformers, particularly, in the case of Christian charity, by Martin Luther.[3] A new spirit of benefaction or magnanimous generosity can be seen to inform the philosophies even of such early moderns as rejected Christianity root and branch. The most remarkable example is the belief that philosophy itself ought to become charitable or helpful to the society around it—a new idea that would have found little purchase in the Greek classics. Classically, philosophers had largely left benefaction to political actors, noble men active on behalf of their polis; benefaction formed little part of the contemplative life per se.[4] By contrast, early moderns envisioning political as well as philosophical reforms, such as Bacon and Descartes, placed their philosophizing at the service of humankind, generously enlightening and "relieving man's estate." This sea change in philosophy's purpose and role is only one example of the long finger of influence exercised on modernity by "charity" or, as it is sometimes called in popular theology, agape.

Paying attention to this ideal of love makes us aware of a radical break not only between ancient and modern philosophers but also between ancient and modern citizens. Chremylus and Blepsidemus in Aristophanes' play might scarcely recognize modern citizens, for whom charitable contribution is private and not a political act. Ancient benefactions, such as equipping a warship for the city at one's personal expense, or sponsoring a chorus for the public drama contests, were, in part, ways of seeking honor and office in the city. The idea that one should give and get nothing in return was less salient to the average Athenian than it is to us, although an analogous morality, restricted in its application to friends and loved ones, did exist.[5] The vast differences between Aristophanes' world and ours, which may appear to render comparison impossible, in fact present rich opportunities for excavating the assumptions and theoretical underpinnings of these very different moralities. A comedy such as the *Wealth* is a rich resource for reconsiderations about who we are as liberal democrats.

For reasons comparable to early modern theological innovations, *Wealth* creates a revolutionary or reformed theology, in which the chief or highest deity's (perhaps by the end of the play he is the only or monotheistic deity) essential function is to care for humankind. Crucially, the god Ploutos or "Wealth" lacks the fearsome or terrible aspects of traditional gods: his power, though absolute, stems from his goodness and his gift giving. Divine retribution is limited to the withholding of wealth. To anticipate the comparison, a part of the modern project was to defang or defuse fanatical religious passions such as those that had been awakened during the wars of religion. A God such as Spinoza's, who demanded only obedience to civil authority and charity toward neighbor, was the next best thing to no God at all.[6] For a paradigm, early moderns could refer to the accepted stories about Jesus, who was not vindictive, did not defend himself and his prerogatives out of self-interest (in stark contrast to Greek gods), and whose very being was a pure gift or philanthropic act. This was a radical reconception of divinity, one made possible by Christian doctrine but also aided and abetted by philosophers who intended to prevent God from making demands on us politically.

Thus, to dismiss Aristophanes' gods as vulgar jokes—though they also function successfully at that level—or as theological machinery, quaint and mere background for the plot, is to miss a stratum of intellectual humor in the plays. The *Wealth* depicts the dethronement of Zeus in favor of a new god, universally beneficent to mankind: Wealth. Formerly (i.e., in the real world), the blind god of wealth bestowed his gifts on the unjust and left many honest citizens destitute. In the counterfactual or escapist world created by the play, Chremylus helps Wealth regain his sight in order to begin bestowing wealth on the deserving. At last, justice is rewarded, and all humankind begins acting justly because there is now no incentive to do evil. But, as so often happens in the comedies, dystopian elements intrude upon the fantasy in *Wealth* (although in this play they are more muted than usual). The *agōn* or central debate of the play questions whether the banishment of poverty is an unmixed blessing, because need is the mother of invention. Undercurrents in the play make us wonder: If incentives alone can produce justice, what becomes of the view that justice is a noble action that must be performed despite reward or punishment? Finally, though humans may desire the chief or only god to be a kind of sugar daddy, it is unclear whether such a god possesses all the attributes necessary to sustain divinity's status. In particular, the all-benevolent god may not be able to evoke fear and awe sufficient to maintain allegiance.

Chremylus and "Charity"

Chremylus, an aged Athenian farmer, has not prospered in life, despite his avowals that he has always been god-fearing and just (28–29; cf. 104–5). His worries about his son's poor prospects cause fissures in his own piety: with amusing forthrightness, he asks the oracle of Apollo if it would not be more advantageous for his son if he raised him to be unjust (32–38). The god, failing to answer the impious question directly, instead commands him to latch onto the first person he meets upon exiting the holy precinct and persuade him to come home with him. That first person is an old blind man, dirty and ragged. When they reach home, Chremylus and his slave Carion force the old man to reveal his identity: he turns out to be Wealth, the god of wealth. The reason for his miserable condition is that Zeus has struck him blind to prevent Wealth from carrying out his avowed wish to confer wealth only on the deserving; this is all due to Zeus' begrudging humankind, specifically begrudging useful or dependable people, Wealth says (87–94). Bereft of sight and the power of discernment, Wealth confers himself randomly, but this ends up meaning he confers wealth on worthless people (because there are so many more of those), who then either bury him underground or dissipate him, hence his dirty and shabby condition

(95–99, 234–44). Wealth has acquiesced in his fate to the extent that he believes *all* people are bad (107–11)—a view that will have rather large ramifications for the success or failure of the eventual project to improve the lot of humankind by making wealth generally available.

Chremylus contradicts Wealth's pessimistic view of humankind, countering it with a claim that there are moderate people like himself, who treat wealth right; he adds with charming sincerity that people like himself really do love their loved ones—second only to their love of money (110, 245–52). Chremylus quickly hatches a plot to repair the damage wrought by Zeus' perfidy: healing Wealth's blindness. Chremylus arguably crosses the line into outright impiety with his sudden and explicit challenge to Zeus' kingship or tyranny.[7] Money, he argues, is omnipotent because it measures—and in a way equals—all good things, indeed all things simply (144–46, 182–83). As in *Birds*, Zeus can be starved into submission by withholding sacrifices: money is needed to purchase the sacrificial animals, so Wealth can start a boycott that will bring Zeus to his knees and effectually make Wealth the supreme god (136–42). Crucially, Wealth's omnipotence relies, in part, on the fact that no one is ever satisfied with his current wealth—unlike romantic love or so many other goods of which people eventually get their fill (187ff.), everyone always wants to be richer. Even if they have thirteen talents, they want sixteen, or forty, another indication that Wealth might be correct in his assessment of the universal evil character of humankind.[8]

But Chremylus seems to be a living counterexample to this dismal claim. He wishes to think well of other people. His slave Carion is his foil in this: for example, when demonstrating that everything is at the beck and call of money, Chremylus mentions that Corinthian courtesans disregard poor men but eagerly offer themselves to rich customers (149ff.). Carion tries to strengthen his master's argument, drawing an analogy between courtesans and boys with pederastic suitors or lovers: "And they say boys do the same thing, not for the sake of their lovers but for the sake of money."[9] Chremylus is quick to disagree: "Not the worthy boys but only the male prostitutes [*pornous*]; since the worthy ones don't ask for money." The slave is at a loss, or pretends to be: "How's that?" Chremylus explains: "One will ask for a good horse, another for hunting dogs." The slave then suggests what sounds like the truth: "Since they're ashamed to ask for money, maybe they cover their baseness with a name" (159). Chremylus seems incapable of seeing the implicit prostitution in the ordinary conventions of pederasty. By contrast, his lowlife slave sees through the facade immediately. Chremylus shows himself to be more conventionally just or pious than his slave, a piety that extends to how he views the world and people around him.[10] He will soon show an even more moral or generous side.

Chremylus' willingness to share Wealth with his friends (Blepsidemus and the chorus of his fellow farmers and demesmen) is the closest a human comes in the play to charity in the later, modern or Christian sense. It is the god who is charitable in *Wealth*; the concomitant Christian command that humans must imitate God's charity by being charitable to one another (e.g., 1 John 4:7–8) is absent from the play. With no one telling him to practice charity, Chremylus is charitable naturally and spontaneously. Of course, Chremylus may share only because he wants something in return: the succor and general support of his friends as he undertakes a dangerous mission (namely, curing Wealth's blindness against Zeus' will [cf. 348–51]). What the play makes clear, however, is how rare it is to call friends together to share *good* fortune. So unusual and contrary to the custom of the country is his charitable behavior that it makes his actions seem suspicious (339–45, 352–55; cf. 239–40, 804–5). Blepsidemus' suspicions are perhaps more justified than he knows, because Chremylus is indeed contemplating a crime vaguely analogous to the more ordinary guilty plan of temple robbing (stealing "gold or silver from the god"): Chremylus intends to unseat the same Zeus by whom he swears he has done no such thing (356–59). Chremylus now progresses in his thinking to the claim that, by making his friends wealthy, he will make them good or dependable, smart, as well as temperate or moderate (*sōphronas*, 386–88)—this last was a signal Greek moral virtue. Apparently the virtues, too, are dependent on wealth, just as he argues that all crafts and methods owe their discovery to wealth (160ff.). The latter theory would explain the current dearth of physicians in impoverished Athens: no wages means no one has an interest in doctoring (406–7). But can virtue and the arts—even the philanthropic art of healing—truly be at the beck and call of money?

Just as the friends are about to spirit Wealth away to Asclepius, the patron god of healing, to cure his blindness, they are prevented by the appearance of Wealth's evil counterpart, a hideous old crone named Penia, or "Poverty." She resembles a Fury and, though they do not recognize her, she has been these poor men's constant companion for many years (423, 437). She calls their plan unholy and lawless. They commit injustice against her by driving her from the land (*sc.* by inaugurating the reign of Wealth [427–30, 457]). She also appeals to their self-interest: by attempting to benefit humanity, they actually are doing humankind the greatest disservice. Poverty, she claims, is the cause of all good things (460–70)—a thesis she is willing to defend with arguments. The stage is set for the characteristic *agōn* or debate.

The Counterclaims of Poverty

Chremylus begins by laying down a supposition he supposes is shared by all and sundry: virtue should be rewarded, and base and godless men should get punished (489–91). As was earlier foreshadowed, it now emerges that his scheme is a self-fulfilling prophecy: it will bring about the justice that it rewards. By cohabitating only with the good, Wealth will make everyone universally into dependable, wealthy, and god-fearing people (494–97). Although Wealth will withhold himself from the wicked at first, clearly the scheme foresees a time when the wicked will be brought—by the incentive of wealth—back into the fold (otherwise not all could become virtuous [cf. 496–98]). This tacit assumption justifies the assumption behind Poverty's counterclaim: universal wealth actually removes the incentive to care for arts and skills (510ff.). Her assumption is that Wealth will eventually be distributing himself universally and equally, even though no one has yet claimed this (when all are equally good, all will get wealth equally).[11] Because no one will have less than anyone else, no one will have incentive to better himself through struggle and invention.[12] The big assumption shared by both Chremylus and Poverty is that everyone has equal abilities to *become* good (otherwise, even perfect incentives would not be universally effective).

Her incentive argument counters the earlier claim that wealth causes the arts and sciences. In fact, poverty causes them. There will be no arts in the reign of Wealth. Chremylus never thought of that; he says that he assumed slaves would do all the work (in the new dispensation). But even the slave trade will have no practitioners, Poverty counters, because there will be no incentive to practice it. Chremylus and Blepsidemus will end up having to do all their work themselves; hence they will not profit from their scheme (509, 517ff.). At least now Chremylus has a slave, Carion. It appears that both Poverty and Wealth (with Chemylus as the latter's spokesman) exaggerate their roles in causing human labor and invention. Obviously, without poverty, no one would need to work for wealth; but equally, without at least the possibility of becoming wealthier, there would likewise be no reason to work. Either alone would be insufficient to create the incentive. Only a mixture (of both wealth and poverty) really motivates labor and invention. Wealth and Poverty are actually synergistic, but neither of the principals notices this.

Chremylus senses a weakness in Poverty's argument when she claims that, because of her, there is a good supply (*eupora*) of everything: "Could [poverty] be able to *supply* any good thing?" (*porisai*, 532, 535). Poverty is forced to make a distinction: there is a difference between poverty and beggary, or utter penury (*penia* vs. *ptōcheia*, 548ff.). Beggars have nothing; poor men, by contrast, are thrifty and pay attention to their work. She thus seizes part of the middle ground: if beggary and wealth are the extremes, poverty suddenly becomes a point somewhere in the middle of the continuum. That is, poverty may be the best word to describe the synergy of wanting and having.

Perhaps Poverty's strongest claim is that wealth leads to hubris, while poverty leads to *sōphrosunē*—the very virtue on which Chremylus' scheme prided itself (563–64, 387). Here again, both sides of the argument have merit: poverty alleviation removes the incentive for one type of crime, as Chremylus says. But luxury creates a new incentive for a different type of crime, like hubris, as Poverty says. So both sides are right, or wrong in equal measures. As we saw, however, Poverty may now occupy some of the middle ground in between the extremes that cause crime. A moderate poverty is, unbeknownst to many, a good thing. People simply do not know what is good for them (578). She is driven to extravagant claims, however, by the theological question of whether Zeus, too, does not know what is good for him—after all, he does keep Wealth to himself. She is forced to counter that, contrary to what everyone thought, Zeus is actually poor. The alternative is unthinkable: that the chief god should be wealthy but so illiberal as to hoard it like a kind of profiteer (*philokerdēs*, 591). Poverty is on Zeus' side and perhaps is even his emissary (cf. 580). Let us assume that Poverty is correct: a moderate poverty is best for humans. Then it would appear possible that Zeus blinded Wealth in order to prevent good men from being corrupted.[13]

The conclusion of the debate is clearly an intellectual victory for Poverty: Chremylus is reduced to violence and to shouting irrationalities such as "You won't persuade me—not even if you persuade me!" Threatened, if not beaten physically, the old woman reluctantly retires, with the parting shot that they will repent and send for her to come back sometime in the future. Chremylus, in the face of contrary evidence (that moderate poverty has been good for him), concludes, "It's better for me to be wealthy" (611).

Carion the slave relates secondhand the scene in Aesclepius' temple where Wealth gets his cure. With a good deal of what can only be called blasphemy (e.g., 705–6), Carion narrates how the god of healing came to cure the god of wealth. Because of the darkness and Carion's shiftiness and general unreliability (668, 713–15), much remains murky in the account. In the aftermath of the cure, tacit assumptions in Carion's pronouncements provide more food for thought about the general question of the human penchant for evil or selfishness. A preternaturally large crowd, he says, is accompanying the triumphant god home from his healing. The just men, who previously had little livelihood, welcomed him. By contrast, as many as had grown wealthy in the former dispensation, because they gained their livelihood through unjust means, did the opposite (751–56). But why *do* all just men have little livelihood? And why does he assume the wealthy always gain it by unjust means? Is there no such thing as a just wealthy man? Carion implicitly assumes not. His seems like a slave's morality, motivated by *ressentiment*. Marxist critique would make a similar assumption, as might Luke's version of the Beatitudes: "Blessed are the poor" (Luke 6:20). Elsewhere in the Gospels, it is easier for a camel to pass through the eye of a needle than for a rich man to enter the kingdom of heaven (Mark 10:25; Matthew 19:24). But such assumptions, if true, are grist to Poverty's argument, not Wealth's: these moralities assume that wealth corrupts; only the poor are righteous. Thus, Poverty is being vindicated by one of the reforming party, Carion himself, though perhaps he does not realize it. Chremylus' reform would then be in the process of universally corrupting humankind. As if to highlight the new belief that money can buy everything, including health and happiness, Chremylus' wife goes inside to get sweets to shower on Wealth and his "new-bought eyes" (769). The inherent evil of humankind is about to receive further corroboration: Chremylus returns from the temple, complaining about how difficult it is when so many friends come out of the woodwork and crowd around when you are successful, all wanting to show off their goodwill toward you (782–87). The fair-weather aspect of these friends comes sharply into focus in what follows.

Visitors to the New God: The Results of the Reform

A number of people now come to call on Wealth, illustrating the effects of the new dispensation. The first is a "Just Man" who used to be wretched but now has good fortune; he comes to give his due or just prayers of thanksgiving to Wealth (840–41). His is one of the few examples of gratitude we see in the play. Like Chremylus earlier, he too had been charitable in his former life (it is important that his misfortunes all occurred before the reform). Contrary to the modern or Christian ideal of charity, he had hoped for a return on investment: having inherited sufficient property from his father, he spent it to help the needy among his friends—thinking that his generosity would prove useful in life (829–31). The low-minded Carion immediately guesses that his money ran out quickly. The Just Man admits this was the case but explains: "And I thought: whomever I benefited up to that time, when they were needy, I would have as really firm friends, if ever I became needy." But in the event, he says, his expectation was totally overturned: his fair-weather friends turned away and pretended not to see him. They even mocked him (834–48). The friends' behavior (back then) seems to present the flip side of the (current) behavior of Chremylus' friends in this early stage of the reform. Humans are naturally friendly when they can get wealth, but they are unfriendly when called upon to give it. Once again, Wealth's original belief has been borne out: by any ordinary standards of morality, humankind is evil. Only now, Chremylus' assumption—that money alone causes virtue—is illustrated: justice and friendship are at the beck and call of money. Or, as Poverty might say, need alone motivates people to do anything, including being just or friendly.

Yet even if altruism or pure charity is no longer to be expected, it is still the case that vast differences in the manner of self-seeking exist. Chremylus' calling his friends together to share in the danger and the reward, and the Just Man's calculation that he would reap benefits if he sowed them, contain very real elements of self-interest. But their self-interest is moderated or channeled in such a way that they help rather than harm their friends. The Just Man sought his own interest by benefiting others. This turned out to be an irrational way of seeking his interest, but only because of human nature. Chremylus' fulfillment of his desires is hampered by the glut of new "friends" who have come out of the woodwork. Had he thought twice about his initial offer to share, he might have fewer obstacles now. Is, then, Wealth's original belief correct only about *rational* humankind: we are evil? That is, does ignorance alone save Chremylus and the Just Man from falling into the evil behavior characteristic of the general run of humankind? On this dismal view, bad people are smart, and good people are just ignorant. Alternatively, the ignorant behavior of the latter category would sometimes make them look good, but at bottom they would be like everyone else. We note that Chremylus, too, modified his piety when it ceased to be in his interest. But if all humans act, by their own moral standards, in substandard fashion, does this not say more about humans' standards than anything else? If everyone is bad, why not call bad the new normal and reserve "bad" for those who fall below this new norm? Would it not perhaps be more realistic to "define deviancy down," in Daniel Moynihan's phrase?[14]

An Informer next comes to call on Wealth. He is the very opposite of the Just Man—formerly he made his wealth by accusing other people and prosecuting them in law courts and reaping part of the settlements

(Athens had no public prosecutors; only private individuals could prosecute). The tables are now turned: he has become poor while the Just Man has prospered. In his railing against Wealth, he corroborates Poverty's earlier assumption. "Where O where is the one who promised that, if he regained his sight, he alone would make us all wealthy right away?" All? Did Wealth ever promise this? Certainly, not in so many words: the whole point was to take money away from the evildoers. The Informer is evil and hence has been robbed of his wealth. Yet the assumption rings true when we consider the reformation's incentives to reform one's character. All will become honest; therefore all will be rewarded. The Informer no doubt thought himself one of the good men before ("dependable and patriotic" [900]). He sees his prosecutions as public benefactions (911–12). He is mistaken, but it is certain that he will become good in the new dispensation. He will have to if he is to continue to seek his own interest. All the incentives are now on the side of good behavior. The Informer is merely caught in the transitional phase, when the bad get their comeuppance but also recognize their mistakes and begin to mend their ways. Surprisingly, however, it soon becomes doubtful that he will ever mend his ways.

In his debate with the Just Man, the Informer gets the better of the argument in one crucial regard. Under the economic assumption we have been entertaining, all human intention is the same (viz. self-seeking), so the difference between "good" and "bad," if one still exists, comes down to different actions on behalf of self. The Just Man benefited his needy friends. The Informer "benefited" the whole city, at least in his own mind (*polin euergetein*). The very different scales of these benefactions are summed up, by the Just Man, as "officiousness" (*polupragmosunē* or minding other people's business) versus "living an inactive life in peace" (913, 921–22).[15] The Just Man clearly prefers the latter. To the Informer, this looks like the lazy—and presumably unenviable—"life of sheep." It appears to him to be no "way of life" at all (922–23). No adequate response to this argument is made.[16] It now appears that, if we want to persist in calling self-seeking "evil," there is a further distinction to be drawn: between actives and inactives. Needless to say, the inactively evil cause less harm than the actively evil (the very existence of the Informer bears witness to this). But does justice amount to nothing more than doing no harm? If all are evil, it is hard to say that activity alone makes one more evil. The harm to others might be offset by the benefit—to the active one—of being active. If activity is a good thing, it is even possible that the actively evil are better, in a rarefied sense, than the lazily or inactively evil. What is clear is that Aristophanes is willing to play one morality off against another, entering into the assumptions now of one, now of the other. To follow him, we must do likewise. No one in these debates, least of all ostensible villains or evil characters such as Poverty or the Informer, are mere stooges, set up to convey some obvious truth. Or, rather, a shallow reading (in which these two are mere villains driven out) does seem to vindicate conventional truths, while a minimal attention to the arguments points us to deeper levels of wonder and delight in ideas.

Love and Money

The next to come to complain is an Old Woman who tries to sound more youthful than she is (963). As a result of the new dispensation, her young boyfriend has broken up with her. He was poor but handsome. She sets much store by the couple's former willingness to do anything for each other, but it emerges that theirs was a mercenary relationship (cf. 1009, 1019). The erotic desire was entirely on her side, and she paid for his sexual services by giving him monetary gifts to help him buy, say, a cloak for himself or necessities for his mother and sisters, even food (982–86). Under cover of the "friendship" he pretended they shared, he would ask for these gifts, alleging they were mere mementos to remind him of her when she was absent (989–91).

Now, the boyfriend has totally changed toward her. He is no longer willing to perform services, returns her gifts, and even adds insult to injury. Upon hearing the Youth's humorous insult, Chremylus immediately offers his own judgment: "Obviously he wasn't a wicked type, in his character. Rich, he is no longer pleased by a poor soup, whereas before he ate up anything, under the influence of poverty" (1003–5; a bawdy pun that could be translated "went down on anything"). Chremylus gives the boyfriend high marks for breaking off the relationship as soon as he could, perhaps because there is something simply wrong about the sexual subjection of youth to age.[17] Oddly, though, the insulting way he broke it off is the proximate cause of Chremylus' admiration (1002). Could Chremylus admire his chutzpah? Yet why not equally condemn the Youth for the time when he did prostitute himself? At the very least, the Youth would appear not to have had much self-respect, or to have let poverty drive him to immoral behavior. Chremylus seems to give the Youth a break on the grounds of economic necessity, à la the argument of economic reform. Poverty compels people to do evil; the alleviation of poverty permits them to be virtuous again. The literal sense of "under" poverty (cf. 1093), together with the Old Woman's age, reminds us of the old crone Penia or Poverty herself—it is as though the Youth were working under or servicing that old crone, as well. Again, on the assumptions of Chremylus' own reformation, wealth gives the Youth the opportunity to become good, and he avails himself of it. "His character" (*tous tropous*, 1003) remained good while he was doing bad because, when wealth permits his true colors to shine through, his character shows itself as good—it must have been good all along.

Surprisingly, however, not merely the boyfriend's underlying character but also his mercenary and duplicitous behavior was good—it must have been good because in the new reign of Wealth, the boyfriend has been rewarded with wealth. He is one of those honest men who finally get what they deserve. That is, not only does Chremylus vouch for his underlying character, but the reward structure of the new dispensation vouches for his actual prior behavior as well. How can this be? It seems a case of vice rewarded—or else a very alien sense of virtue. Alan Sommerstein brilliantly expounds the aristocratic morality that can be assumed of any self-respecting Athenian male. As a courtesan herself, the Old Woman is the Youth's social inferior, though wealthier than he. Justice per se is required only among peers, which the Old Woman is not. As such, any justice the Youth might have shown toward her would be considered by the original audience to be a superadded bonus, a magnanimous gesture. By contrast, if the Old Woman were a female citizen of good reputation, the Youth's injustice toward her then really would blacken his character.[18]

This argument relies on the Old Woman's being de jure a prostitute (as the Youth is only a de facto one [cf. 149ff.]). The evidence that she is a prostitute is slender: it is her overly familiar method of addressing the Chorus as "friends" and Chremylus as "dearest" (cf. modern English "darling") in her first meeting with them (959, 967).[19] Chremylus later, at 1063, likens her cosmetics to the tricks of salesmen; one implication could be that she is selling herself. Yet we have already seen that even young gentlemen "sell themselves" in a sense, so this usage again may be de facto rather than de jure.[20] Modern scholars may be exaggerating the female modesty expected by the Athenian male sexual ethos. Particularly in the free-swinging genre of comedy, it is very difficult to know where to draw the line between acceptable and unacceptable female behavior. In comedy, we might expect a feminine analogue to the no-holds-barred behavior of male protagonists.

Because Sommerstein's case is only probable, then, it might be useful to examine what happens under the opposite assumption, viz. that the Old Woman is not a prostitute but a female citizen in good standing. As the Old Woman herself tells Chremylus: "Darling, what the god is doing is not correct, when he says he always helps those who suffer injustice. . . . Justice, by Zeus, should compel [the Youth]—who received good—to do good to me in turn; or else he justly should not receive any good whatsoever" (1025–30). On the assumptions that her boyfriend really has treated the Old Woman unjustly (cf. 1071–85, also acknowledged by Sommerstein) and that, additionally, he has done it in a way the original audience would perceive as unworthy to reward with wealth, the original question returns. Why is vice rewarded?

Perhaps we are intended to define deviancy down, making use of the economic assumptions we have seen in so many places in the play. The boyfriend's mercenary and duplicitous behavior was neither more nor less evil than the general run of humankind. He merely sought his self-interest as best he could, according to his lights. Now he continues to do so: he now has wealth, so he no longer needs the Old Woman. She is an unfortunate casualty of the process, but everyone does what he must. Had the Youth been ignorant, he might indeed have refrained from using the Old Woman, but then his sisters and mother might have gone hungry. Chremylus' own focus on character (cf. *tous tropous*) seems to cherish some noneconomic assumptions, somewhat in tension with his economic scheme of reform. What would have constituted a bad character, according to Chremylus? Perhaps a man of bad character would be a sexual deviant, although this particular fetish is not a popular one. Perhaps a weak character might have simply acquiesced in sexual slavery, perhaps even growing—or attempting to grow—to enjoy it. Such a slavish character would then be unable to reform himself, even when the incentives changed. By contrast, for this Youth, the reformation was immediate.

However, if we apply the economic thinking to moral character itself, the question arises of to what extent the Youth is responsible for his character. If everyone does what he must, then everyone's character becomes what it must. The Youth is fortunate, to be sure, to have such a character as would rebel against subjection. The good still exists in the economic worldview. But nobility does not seem to. The prior choices that produced his character were simply instances of his pursuit of self-interest, according to his lights. He did what he had to do, no more and no less. He can no more be praised for the resulting character than a racehorse can be praised for the genes and nutrition that made him swift. On this extreme view, no one deserves to be rewarded. Or, alternatively, everyone deserves it equally. We saw earlier that the reform simply assumed that all humans have equal abilities to become good: only the incentive structure was needed for reform.

Now the presumed equality of ability appears in a worse light: if incentives really are all that matters, then character loses its moral significance.

Earlier we saw how Poverty assumed, surprisingly, that Chremylus' new scheme intended to give wealth to everyone. Now perhaps we see a deeper reason why she thought that—and why, perhaps, she thought this was the greatest of evils for humankind. The assumptions of the economic reformation remove any possibility of praise or blame, of moral virtue and vice.[21] Morality itself is done away with. Harms and benefits (as opposed to injustice and justice) still exist, but the incentives will manage these in ways to maximize benefits and minimize harms. Something in the human psyche rebels against such a possibility. Would we not prefer a world with more harm in it, if only justice and the possibility of praise could also be preserved? One would almost prefer doing evil for its own sake, rather than acquiesce in this inhuman system. Suddenly the Informer's words take on greater weight and meaning: it appears to be "a life of sheep" and no "way of life at all."[22] In a similar way, the cruelty of the boyfriend's parting insult to the Old Woman, which Chremylus appeared to appreciate, might even stop looking gratuitous and start looking like the kind of self-assertion that might be necessary to reinvigorate moral agency or reinject some life into this amoral new economic world.

The Old Woman is either a prostitute or a respectable female citizen. A third possibility would combine these assumptions. Let us assume the Old Woman was a prostitute in the old dispensation. In the new demimonde created by the fantasy, she can no longer be regarded as one.[23] There is no moral praise or blame here, no categories of reproach. Presumably, the reform takes account of such facts of human nature as the de facto prostitution of Athenian boys (149–59). The reform perceives that de jure prostitutes were never really much different from the rest of humanity. The old, aristocratic morality in which they could be blamed has by now certainly gone by the boards. Surprisingly, however, Chremylus will proceed to encourage the Youth to make good on his promises.

The Youth now appears, on a bender, presumably celebrating his newfound independence. He heaps many fresh insults on the Old Woman, in which fun Chremylus joins. Amid the jokes, Chremylus states that he will not allow the Youth to hate her and that (despite all the arguments on the Youth's side) "since you deemed the wine worth drinking, it is necessary for you to drink up the dregs with it" (1071–72, 1084–85).[24] *Pace* Sommerstein, this necessity of justice—to which Chremylus calls the Youth—appears to be more than a magnanimous gesture to a social inferior. The implication is that, in the new dispensation, the Youth is going to have to sleep with her again, at least one more time. By an expedient that amounts to putting a bag over her head, Chremylus claims to render this possible (1087).

A kind of justice, then, apparently exists in the new dispensation. It is an economic-style justice: if you dance, you pay the piper. Exchange seems to be its basis. Citizens cannot follow naked self-interest without harming one another. They must follow a modified self-interest, modified by proper incentives. Self-interest can work through the incentive structure. Punishment is a "cost": it consists of deprivation of wealth. But "paying" also seems like a kind of punishment, especially in the case of the Youth, where the payment is extra-monetary. Chremylus invites the Youth indoors, but he balks when the Old Woman appears to accompany him. Chremylus calms his fears: the Old Woman will not force or rape him (1091–92). The Youth seems to take this as assurance that he will never have to service her at all (*sc.* because without force, he will never do it [1092–93]). They all go indoors, the Old Woman claiming, and Chremylus confirming, that she is sticking to the Youth. What happens inside?

Like the *Assemblywomen*, but in an infinitely gentler way, the upshot of the reform seems to be that old people get to sleep with young people against their will. The rape of the young lover by old women at the end of *Assemblywomen* was an ugly, dystopian scene showing rather clear undesirable outcomes of Praxagora's reform movement. In a much more muted way, Chremylus seems to be engaged in making sure that, in the exchange between the Old Woman and the Youth, both get what they want or get what is coming to them. But the task appears to be like squaring the circle.

Religion and Charity

The visitor scenes—and the play itself—culminate in the religious consequences of the reform: the last two visitors are a god, Hermes himself, and finally a priest of Zeus. Hermes appears diffident at first but soon announces his errand, as messenger of the Olympian gods. Zeus' intention is to kill Chremylus and his whole household, right down to his dog and pig. Carion the (former?) slave treats the god with immense hubris throughout the scene (e.g., 1110, 1133). Zeus' rage stems from the fact that, as anticipated, no one is sacrificing to the gods anymore. When people are liberated from economic necessity, religion goes by the boards.[25] Hermes confides that he could care less about the other gods; he is starving to death (1118–19).

Carion says that Hermes' and the other gods' woes are justified because they used to accept sacrifices without delivering the care mortals expected in return, sometimes even inflicting a damage (1116–17, 1124–25). Trying to call in a favor, Hermes reminds Carion how he used to protect the slave from getting caught when he stole small items from his master, Chremylus. Carion retorts that Hermes helped only on the condition that he share in the loot, calling him a burglar or housebreaker. The charge is curious because the sacrificial system itself called for reciprocal exchange. The gods were never expected to act on mortals' behalf from motives of pure charity or selflessness. Rather, gifts and tokens of respect were repaid (or not, as Carion asserts). The ideal was a win–win situation for both god and man. Now Carion has moved to a stricter standard: had Hermes ever given him anything gratis in the past, he would owe him now. As matters stand, he implies, Carion owes him nothing. They had a reciprocal relation; Hermes scarcely honored it even when it existed; and they no longer have that relation. Hermes clearly has nothing to offer now, so there is no question of further barter. In the course of this exchange, one cannot help but think of Wealth, a god who does not enter into exchange relations with his people, but simply gives to them without asking for anything in return.

Unable to call in a favor, Hermes begs for charity or mercy—the generosity or magnanimity shown by the victor. He asks for something gratis, even though he himself never gave anything gratis. He offers to abandon his fellow gods and become a fellow householder with Carion. Hermes is a turncoat (1151). Sticking strictly to economics, Carion asks what profit (*ophelos*) Hermes would be to them. Hermes tries on a number of his former roles and cult titles, none of which is needed in the new dispensation: twisting or "turning" away thieves is useless where there are no tricksters or twisters anymore (1153–54). Again, the assumption is that everyone has now become good (including even the tricky Informer?). "Marketer" is equally futile: everyone is wealthy, so who needs them? "Trickster," least of all: Carion reiterates that there is no job for trickiness, only for a "simple character" (*haplōn tropōn*). Carion seems to fall in with Chemylus' moral way of thinking.[26] Nor do mortals any longer need a "Guide." In desperation, Hermes comes up with the role of being god of *agōnes*, contests for prizes. While it would be nice to think that humans in the new dispensation will pursue excellence now that they are free from economic need, as Greek aristocrats had done in athletic competitions or the Athenian *dēmos* saw fit to institute in drama competitions (such as the one in which *Wealth* was competing), Carion strangely does not quite assent to this last suggestion. Instead, he accepts Hermes on board as a servant to servants, giving him a menial task. It is by no means clear that competitions for excellence—or indeed excellence itself—will survive in the new dispensation.

The final visitor is a priest of Zeus, particularly Zeus under the cult title "Savior." Needless to say, Zeus the Savior was not much of one, and is no longer needed after the reformation. The Priest is starving, because he regularly ate the sacrifices people brought to the god. In two of his three examples of the good old days (1178–84), people used to sacrifice to Zeus the Savior retrospectively in gratitude for the bounty they had received. Apparently, though all humans were (are) self-interested, they did know gratitude. The question arises of whether gratitude, too, will be a casualty of the new economic dispensation.[27] People are now literally using the holy precinct as a giant toilet (1183–84). The Priest does not hesitate long before declaring his intention to defect from Zeus and join Chremylus. Chremylus informs the priest, and us, of the most surprising development: Zeus the Savior himself has already jumped ship and come over to the rebels. He is, Chremylus says, inside with them; he came spontaneously (*automatos*). This could mean that Wealth (aside from Hermes, the only god who we know is with them) is the real Zeus the Savior and perhaps was so all along. Or it could mean literally that the erstwhile chief or supreme deity has come over. The alternatives amount to the same thing. Wealth is—perhaps always was—the chief or supreme deity.

The Great Installation of the new deity is now about to take place. Wealth will be installed in the rear chamber of the temple of the goddess Athena, where he allegedly was before (1191–93). Ostensibly, his function is to guard that chamber, which was the treasury. But because two gods, including the greatest, have already been overthrown, one cannot help speculating that Wealth will be overthrowing Athena as well. Will Athens be Athens, and will Athenians still be Athenian, after giving up on Athena?

The ex-Priest agrees to join in the parade. The Old Woman comes back out, to play the role of a virgin basket carrier. Virginity is not what it used to be in the old regime. She still has not gotten what she came for from the Youth (1200). Chremylus reassures her: everything will be accomplished for her. "The young man will come to you this evening" (1200–1). This answers, but in another way raises again, our question at the end of the Old Woman's scene. The reform does imply the Youth will have to sleep with the Old Woman. But because he has not done so yet, this is an intentional loose end in the play—the reform has not yet succeeded in doing what it must. But there is hope that it will be accomplished. He did it before, so presumably the Youth can do it again. As if to give one last fillip to Poverty's argument, a parting shot against the reform, the Old

Woman is given a line in which she agrees to be the virgin basket carrier only on one condition: that Chremylus *promise* that the Youth will come to her this evening. She is the one character left with a desire not yet met, and she is motivated to join the public procession by that desire. Only need motivates anyone to perform any public good, Poverty might say. In lieu of promising to make good on his claim that the Youth will come, Chremylus instead tells a joke at the Old Woman's expense. Apparently eros is a loose end of the economic reform; it really is the case that money cannot buy love. The parade prepares to set off as the play ends.

Charity Undermines Justice

If we look more closely at Chremylus, the reformer clearly does not anticipate the amoral consequences of the reform. His emphasis on moral character is only one small part of his strong beliefs about justice.[28] A window into Chremylus' justice opens when he ceases to respect Zeus upon hearing of his ill will—as though an envious god were no god at all, or did not deserve to be a god. Theologically, this is odd. As Sommerstein points out, "a basic principle of ancient religion" was that reverence is "obligatory not because the gods were good, but because they were powerful."[29] This is certainly a side of Greek religion to which Judaism and Christianity blind us.[30] Yet it may be another case of scholars veering too far to the other side, overcorrecting for differences between ancient and modern mores. Chremylus does not fit the ancient pattern: he ceases to revere Zeus not because he has heard something that leads him to doubt Zeus' power but because he has heard something that leads him to doubt Zeus' justice. Leo Strauss gets deeper into Chremylus' psychology with his insight that, for Chremylus, "Zeus lacks the power stemming from justice."[31] Chremylus believes in the might of the right. In the Sophistic tradition represented, for example, by the debates in Thucydides, the right has no might. The expectations of the Melians, that fortune will favor just men over unjust, are utterly overthrown.[32] Sophisticated people, like Thucydides' Athenians, have a tendency to believe that justice is powerless; the opposite belief is naive. Yet even if the sophisticated position were true, one would still have to take into account the power of the beliefs of people like Chremylus, who do believe in the power of justice. Chremylus is willing to act on his belief. His reverence for Wealth—after he finds out that all of Zeus' power stems from Wealth—might seem to follow the pattern of ancient religion, but that pattern may mask a deeper reason: namely, Chremylus finds it simply meet and right that Wealth—who has professed such just intentions toward humankind (88–90)—should also possess great power, omnipotence even. Might ought to go along with goodness.

His evident justice makes it all the more intriguing that Chremylus says, at the commencement of his great scheme, that Wealth must enrich his house today "by fair means or foul" (literally "both justly and unjustly" [233]). How can this just man permit himself to use such a phrase? One is tempted to say that the benefit emanating from his scheme is so great that it overrides minor injustices. Other plays by Aristophanes do indeed privilege the good over the right.[33] Chremylus is about to confer a benefit upon his friends—a benefit to end all benefits. We also saw how he had begun to doubt justice, at least as regards the upbringing of his son (32ff.). Yet his embrace of the just god Wealth would seem to have ended his internal debate decisively in favor of justice. How, then, can Chremylus believe he—or Wealth—could ever get away with acting unjustly? It is as if he thinks there is something here greater than justice.

Charity certainly transcends justice in the New Testament parallel. The benefactor in the Gospels is God Himself, often figured in the parables as a human master. His gift throws all considerations of justice and injustice into the shade. The workmen of the last hour receive the same wages as those who toiled all day. If the Master chooses to reward them equally, can he not do what he will with his own money? The early workmen are merely envious because he is generous (Matthew 20:1–16). The Pharisees, no matter how close to perfect rectitude they may come, have no hope of earning their way into the Kingdom on merit. Instead, they must accept the gratuitously given largesse of God. People with pretensions to righteousness understandably balk: no merit of mine counts for anything? Justice is not rewarded; only charity counts. The New Testament insouciance toward righteousness paradoxically generates a new concern for righteousness, or at least for charity. To whom much has been given, much is expected. Gratitude toward the benefactor issues in a change of heart. It would be like spitting on the gift not to use it well. Charity makes us want to "pass it on," or "pay it forward." Jesus commands charity toward others; we noted earlier that this is a great difference between Christian charity and *Wealth*. This difference now leads to a further ground of comparison between *Wealth* and modern liberalism. Though we do witness cases of gratitude in *Wealth* (at least initially), it is really the incentive system that causes Chremylus' fellow citizens to start behaving well. It is in their interest to behave justly. The abundance provided by Wealth gives everyone the means to be just. Would not, then, any residual charity or benefaction, in the new dispensation, be precisely "giving of their abundance"—a practice specifically singled out by Jesus as failing to attain the standard of charity he set (Mark 12:41–44, in the story of the widow's mite)? Chremylus confers a godlike benefaction, but then the system stops needing great benefactions—or perhaps any "charity" at all. Something analogous happens in liberal capitalism.

In modern liberalism, greed, which might have seemed a private vice, becomes a public benefit through non-Christian mechanisms, indicated by Mandeville and Smith, such as the invisible hand. By contrast, success in *Wealth* is a direct reward and is entirely dependent on the miraculous or supernatural. No natural mechanism is evident that would create wealth and thus perpetuate the new system under its own steam. Rather, the god of wealth just keeps on giving, no one needs to work, and everyone becomes just—or conforms to what vulgar justice used to look like: doing no harm.[34] Like capitalists, Chremylus' citizens may be as greedy as they please. The greedier they are, the more justly they will behave. Their "justice" is predicated on their greed.

Doing no harm has no greatness about it; it lacks the glamour of Chremylus' original daring benefaction. No one needs to benefit anyone else handsomely or generously—because everyone is already getting exactly what is coming to him. If a neighbor deserved more, or better, he would already be receiving it from Wealth. Hence the original generosity or giving—both Chremylus' and the god's—marks the end of giving or generosity. The original divine charity paradoxically leads to a drying up of charity. At least in Christianity, God refrains from making everything right all at once; He sets a distant day of judgment, leaving work to be done by those still on earth. Charity toward others thus remains possible in the interim. In *Wealth*, it becomes impossible. We might speculate that the invisible hand of liberal capitalism (which actually generates the wealth), together with its welfare state, partially fulfills the escapist fantasy of *Wealth*: a system of perpetual abundance. The wealthier the society, the less need there is for charity. Confronted with a beggar, the modern citizen is liable to wonder: Can he really have fallen through the safety net? Is it not more likely that he willfully refuses to work? The thought is a little too close for comfort to the belief of some religious people that poverty is a punishment for bad behavior. The welfare state together with general abundance paradoxically hurts those who remain in poverty, because their poverty looks like their fault. The traditional "blindness" of wealth—the unpredictability of who will be wealthy and who will be poor—which both Chremylus' and our systems reverse, turns out to be crucial to sustaining a charitable attitude. In these several ways, the ideal of charity undercuts justice, and too much charity undercuts charity itself.

The Theology of Charity Is Secularizing

The *Wealth*'s theology of charity shows signs of doing away with gods entirely. We have seen how Chremylus believes a god must be good in order to be a god at all. Zeus moves, when deprived of his goodness, from the chief or highest deity to a being deprived of all power, essentially a person of no account. The converse also occurs. Wealth first appears as a powerless person, utterly destitute. Like Jesus' divinity, Wealth's is initially disguised.[35] Wealth moves, when his goodness is made clear, to the position of the chief or only deity. In the Gospels, Jesus admonishes the evil spirits (who sense his power and therefore recognize him) not to tell anyone, presumably so as not to rob ordinary people of their chance to recognize his divinity, a recognition tantamount to seeing that power will no longer be the defining mark of divinity: goodness replaces power (e.g., Mark 1:23–27, 34; cf. 1:43–45). In *Wealth*, the god himself is ignorant of his power and must come to recognize it. A mortal, Chremylus, is needed before Wealth can find that he has any power at all, that he is in fact omnipotent. So needy is this god that Chremylus exhorts his friends to become "saviors of the god" (327).[36] In Hegel, God is in the process of becoming and needs man as a means of self-discovery as much as man needs God. In recent theologies such as process theology, too, God changes based in part on interactions with people. Process theology is of course heretical from a traditionalist point of view. Obviously, conceiving God as Becoming runs the risk of reducing God to a part of nature, or to Nature itself, as Spinoza had already done. But the insights of process theology, of Hegel, and of Spinoza are implicit, or at least prepared for, in the fundamental Christian paradox of the god who becomes a mortal. The greatest gift God can confer is to give Himself; charity somehow entails mortality. In each of these theologies, the emphasis gets displaced from "Godness" to goodness. The insight that God is no God unless he is good thus appears to be a move toward secularism, toward leaving gods behind.

Wealth punishes in only one way: the withholding of wealth. Many modern Christian theologies likewise deemphasize divine retribution. In particular, eternal punishment has come to seem incompatible with God's goodness; more precisely, Hell is uncharitable.[37] Modern theologians propound an all-good God, too good to be vindictive. But vindictiveness is different from vengeance. Such beliefs as "Vengeance is mine, says the Lord" prevented people from taking vengeance into their own hands at the same time that they refrained from other bad behavior through fear of divine vengeance. In a similar way, Chremylus' new god makes few demands on people. It is far from clear that many people will be sacrificing to him in the future. Certainly there will be no right or wrong way to sacrifice, no orthodoxy. As the play reaches its climax, Wealth increasingly seems a merely titular god. His handler, Chremylus, controls him. He ends up similarly to the birds in *Birds*, though they are supplanted explicitly by their handler, Peisetaerus, while Chremylus is arranging a parade for Wealth's installation as the play ends. Still, the parade to establish him in a kind of storeroom may well lead to an out-of-sight-out-of-mind situation. Unlike the birds, who are ensnared by their self-interest, which Peisetaerus turns to his own advantage, Wealth seemingly has no self-interest. He cannot help but be kind and giving to humans. Humans thus do not need to go out of their way to make use of him; they already in effect use him.[38] There is no need for explicit control by a handler, like the birds suffer in *Birds*, because Wealth effectually places himself under the control of humans.

But this lowliness (his ultimate lack of control fits a pattern with his initial lowliness) sorts ill with the ability to inspire the awe or respect traditionally deemed necessary in a god. The Olympians whom he defeats have many vices, including the greedy interest in sacrifices through which Aristophanic heroes so successfully attack them. But at least their selfish interest keeps them aware of, and protective of, their prerogatives. Is not a "jealous" God, a God who may sometimes withhold His favors, necessary for keeping human beings in line? That is, precisely because of the scarcity of goods that leads to competition and injustice among humans, we may need a god whose withholding of favors both explains that scarcity and at the same time preserves the peace among rival claimants to the scarce resources. The abundance coming from Wealth wishes away the problem of scarcity, thereby doing away with the need for a watchful, begrudging god. Of course, in the initial stages of Chremylus' plan, Wealth does punish evildoers like the Informer. Later, after everyone has become good, no retribution occurs, but only because it is no longer necessary. The reform is internally consistent. As analogues go, Wealth's ultimate stage answers to heaven, or the afterlife. The moral and political consequences of such a vision are questionable only if the transitional period is protracted, or if we doubt that such a boundless source of good things exists. In modern liberalism, for example, the abundance really is limited, as times of recession bring home to us. An undemanding God is fine during the good times. But what happens when times get tough? Traditionally, citizens strove to behave better than they otherwise would in hopes that their behavior might be rewarded. Charity, as we have seen, already removes some of the theological underpinnings of this hope. Traditional citizens also strove to behave better because of their fear of punishment. Newer Christian theologies remove that pillar of good conduct, as well. Charity-based theologies tend toward secularism because they make it impossible to believe in a god who is not "on our side." The extreme anthropocentrism of the theology of charity thus comes back to haunt it.

Notes

1. See Michael Allen Gillespie, *The Theological Origins of Modernity* (Chicago: University of Chicago Press, 2008), especially 10–15, for the debate between Karl Löwith and Hans Blumenberg. On the identity between the Christian God and charity, see 1 John 4:8, *ho theos agapē estin*, translated in the Vulgate Bible, *Deus caritas est*.

2. On Machiavelli's "spiritual warfare," see Harvey C. Mansfield's and Nathan Tarcov's introduction to Niccolò Machiavelli, *Discourses on Livy*, trans. Harvey C. Mansfield and Nathan Tarcov (Chicago: University of Chicago Press, 1996), xxxv. An example of charity being co-opted can be found in Francis Bacon's Essay 13, "Of Goodness and Goodness of Nature," in Francis Bacon, *Essays or Counsels Civil and Moral*, ed. Brian Vickers (Oxford: Oxford University Press, 1999).

3. See the Lutheran account of Anders Nygren, *Agape and Eros*, trans. Philip Watson (Philadelphia: Westminster, 1953), e.g., 468–562, 709ff.

4. Benefaction is a productive activity, whereas contemplation does not produce anything beyond itself (*Nicomachean Ethics* 9.7, 1167b34–1168a10; 10.7, 1177b1–26).

5. *Nicomachean Ethics* 9.8, 1168a30–35.

6. Benedict Spinoza, *Spinoza's Theologico-Political Treatise*, ed. Martin D. Yaffe (Newburyport, MA: Focus, 2004), preface and, e.g., 13.1.10, 14.1.44.

7. *turannida* (124); the word is ambiguous but sometimes had the pejorative sense "tyranny."

8. Obviously, if the human desire for wealth is truly insatiable, then no redistributive reform, such as Chremylus', will be feasible.

9. All translations are my own renderings of the Greek text in Alan H. Sommerstein, *The Comedies of Aristophanes, Vol. 11: Wealth* (Warminster: Aris & Phillips, 2001).

10. Chremylus is, of course, quick to think ill of Zeus; he takes Wealth's word for it that Zeus is unjust. However, reality manifestly backs up Wealth's claim: there are honest men everywhere who are poor, like Chremylus himself, while the unjust often prosper.

11. See, e.g., 1178. Scholars have worried that the Wealth has "two plots": in the first plot, rich and poor exchange places; in the second plot, everyone is rich. Matthew Dillon and David Konstan, in David Konstan, *Greek Comedy and Ideology* (New York: Oxford University Press, 1995), find that the first plot is predicated on social injustice, the second on universal scarcity. Penia introduces the second,

new idea into the play, and Aristophanes "masks the distance" between disparate conceptions in order to be "conservative, or at best apolitical" (83–84, 89–90). S. Douglas Olson, "Economics and Ideology in Aristophanes' *Wealth*," *Harvard Studies in Classical Philology* 93 (1990): 223–42, especially 237–38, takes this idea further, suggesting that the second plot defuses resentments built up in the audience by the first. The play thus functions as a social control on revolutionary tendencies. Edmond Lévy, "Richesse et Pauvreté dans le *Ploutos*," *Ktema* 22 (1997): 201–12, especially 211–12, concludes that the ideology of the play is reactionary, like the Old Oligarch's, in favor of old money against the "nouvelle richesse." But as Sommerstein, *Wealth*, 14, points out, the alleged "two plots" are reconciled in the long-term effects of the reform. Sommerstein's note 70 quotes the medieval commentator Thomas Magister, on line 497: "For when the wicked see that because of this [*sc.* the healing of Wealth] the virtuous are faring well, they will wish to abandon their previous life and change to better ways, in order to benefit thereby." This overall consistency in Chremylus' scheme of course does not rule out the possibility that Aristophanes agrees with Penia's arguments. E. David, *Aristophanes and Athenian Society of the Early Fourth Century B.C.*, Mnemosyne Supplement (Leiden: Brill, 1984), 41–43, compares Penia's arguments with *Republic* 421c–422a, but believes the playwright could not deny a fantasy to the majority of his audience who did not wish to think too hard.

12. This ignores the insatiable desire for money that was a pillar in the argument for Wealth's omnipotence. See note 8 and accompanying text.

13. Similarly, Zeus might permit the very wealthy their luxury in order to test them, thereby driving the wicked among them to ruinous acts. Zeus' uncharitable thought about the human penchant for evil would not, then, be envious but just or benign. Cf. Leo Strauss, *Socrates and Aristophanes* (Chicago: University of Chicago Press, 1966), 285, 294. Strauss calls attention to the excluded middle in the debate: middle-class people might be immune to both causes of vice, luxury and deprivation. He points out Aristotle, *Rhetoric*, 1391b1–3: "more overweening and irrational on account of good fortune they are, but one best character trait follows upon good fortune: that they are lovers of god and are in a certain condition toward the divine, trusting on account of the things that have come to be from fortune."

14. Daniel Patrick Moynihan, "Defining Deviancy Down: How We've Become Accustomed to Alarming Levels of Crime and Destructive Behavior," *American Educator* 17 (Winter 1993): 17–30.

15. On *polupragmosunē* see, e.g., Plato, *Republic*, 433d–434a, 369b–370b; cf. Thucydides 2.60.2, 2.63.2. See also Victor Ehrenberg, "*Polypragmosyne*," *Journal of Hellenic Studies* 67 (1947): 46–67.

16. The Just Man counters that the Informer could retool himself, learn (*sc.* a new skill, other than informing). But this ignores the fact that there will be no work, no skills, in the new order. Perhaps to confirm our (lazy?) assumption that the Informer is simply evil, Aristophanes gives him this line in response: "Not if you were to give me Wealth himself" (or wealth itself [924–25]). The Informer is lazy and bad: he does not want to work. Or does he? We know he works hard at his successful prosecutions because, of course, he profits from them. And if we have

been paying attention to the play's arguments, Poverty has already established that people only work for profit. If the Informer were given "wealth itself," he would have no incentive to learn a new skill. The Informer is hardly lazy: he is the one arguing for activity, while the Just Man is arguing for inactivity. Perhaps, then, the Informer is just evil: he wants to harm others above all else, even if offered a better way. But evil, in the play so far, has not consisted of harm for its own sake, but only harming others to gain wealth: our fellow human beings get in the way of our pursuit of wealth, and the evil among us are willing to ride roughshod over them in the pursuit of it. Now, however, it appears that the Informer would stay busy (rather than lazy) even if he were already wealthy, that is, had all the wealth in the world (cf. Sommerstein, *Wealth*, on "[all] the silphium of Battus" [925]). The Informer would choose to harm others rather than become inactive. Though he thereby appears to fall to a worse stratum of evil than has heretofore been broached, another way of looking at him is to stress the good of activity over inactivity. For all his misunderstanding and ill will, the Informer harmonizes with that part of Poverty's philosophy that emphasized the way neediness forces us to be active, invent arts and sciences, and even virtues. In this twist on Poverty's argument, the neediness itself would be merely instrumental to the true goods that are these various activities or activity per se.

17. Compare the three old women's legally sanctioned rape of the young man in the *Assemblywomen* 1014–1111.

18. Sommerstein, *Wealth*, 201–2.

19. Sommerstein, *Wealth*, 199. Stephen Halliwell, "Aristophanic Sex: The Erotics of Shamelessness," in *The Sleep of Reason: Erotic Experience and Sexual Ethics in Ancient Greece and Rome*, eds. Martha C. Nussbaum and Juha Sihvola (Chicago: University of Chicago Press, 2002), 120–42, especially 141n42, makes a similar point about *Assemblywomen* 953, citing David Konstan's authority. Allegedly, only courtesans speak to strange men in so familiar or friendly a fashion, even in comedy. But of course, if the Old Woman of *Wealth* is not a courtesan, and the girl in *Assemblywomen* is not a courtesan either, then we have two instances of non-courtesans speaking like this.

20. The Youth, when he appears, casts such aspersions on the Old Woman's virtue as could seem to apply only to prostitutes, in a pun implying that she has slept with thirteen thousand men. But again, insulting a woman by calling her whore is not the same as a calm assertion of fact that she is a prostitute.

21. For a modern version of this extreme view that only incentives matter in politics, see Kant's famous dictum that a nation of devils could solve the problem of setting up a state: Immanuel Kant, *Perpetual Peace*, ed. Hans Reiss, trans. H. B. Nisbet, *Kant: Political Writings* (Cambridge: Cambridge University Press, 1991), 112.

22. The inhumanity of this purely economic vision of morality may also shed light on the Informer's final rebellion, if such it is, in which he appears to seek evil for its own sake, rather than become inactive. See note 16.

23. Demimonde: the term is Halliwell's to describe a similar topsy-turvy world in which all citizens are prostituted to one another in *Assemblywomen*; see Halliwell, "Aristophanic Sex: The Erotics of Shamelessness," 127, 131.

24. The lees or dregs (*trux*) Aristophanes especially associates with comedy, which he sometimes calls *trugōidia*, "winesong" in parody of *tragōidia*, tragedy (e.g., *Acharnians* 499–500). *Trux* here, however, is also—or merely—a setup for *trugoipos*, the bag or filter of 1087.

25. In a modern example, Soviet communism could not stamp out Russian Orthodoxy by direct persecution, whereas Roman Catholicism in Europe has scarcely survived the prosperous post–World War II welfare state.

26. On character, see also 630, 365.

27. Certainly the Just Man and others have come to sacrifice to Wealth in gratitude. But we have already seen that the Just Man's morality may be the result of ignorance (an ignorance that will be less likely to prevail in the new incentive system). In any case, these are early days in the reform: just as vice will eventually be stamped out, virtue and its concomitants, like gratitude, will probably disappear as well.

28. For example, back in the initial debate over how to interpret the oracle, even when considering unrighteousness for his son, Chremylus thinks righteous thoughts: Carion is beside himself with frustration that his master could subscribe to a literalist interpretation of the oracle (45ff.). "The first person you meet leaving a temple," the slave thinks, clearly means any old person from around these parts; hence the god is saying, "Conform to the custom of the country," that is, be evil. The god is saying what Carion already knows is true by reason alone: even the blind can see that "in the present generation" (50) it is advantageous to be bad. But Chremylus sticks to his right-thinking literalism and is rewarded, whether by luck or divine will.

29. Sommerstein, *Wealth*, 17.

30. E.g., Leviticus 19:2: "You shall be holy; for I the Lord your God am holy."

31. Strauss, *Socrates and Aristophanes*, 286.

32. Thucydides 5.84–116, especially 103–104; they also mention a fond hope that the Spartans will come to their rescue.

33. Reversing the Kantian "priority of the right over the good." See especially Paul W. Ludwig, "A Portrait of the Artist in Politics: Justice and Self-Interest in Aristophanes' *Acharnians*," *American Political Science Review* 101 (no. 3, 2007): 479–92.

34. The opposite of *polupragmosunē*, usually called *apragmosunē*. See note 15 and accompanying text.

35. There are a number of intimations that Wealth is mortal, e.g., he is called "human" and "man" at 118 and 654, respectively.

36. A line with overtones for the cult title later used of Zeus: "Zeus the Savior." Sommerstein, *Wealth*, 161–62, notes the Orphic resonances of the phrase, but another god, Apollo, is Dionysus' savior in the mystery rituals, whereas the play envisions human saviors.

37. Contrast Dante's inscription over the gateway to Hell, in which Hell speaks of itself (*Inferno* 3.5): "I was made by . . . primal love" ('*l primo amore*).

38. Cf. Strauss, *Socrates and Aristophanes*, 303–4.

Part III

11

Anger in Thucydides and Aristophanes
The Case of Cleon

Timothy W. Burns

No two writers appear to be more different in their fundamental concerns and teachings than the madcap comic poet Aristophanes and the austere historian Thucydides. The one bombards us with domestic affairs, private gossip, lewd and scatological jokes. The other's work is pervaded by an oft-noted sadness. Yet Aristophanes himself suggests a possible common ground between the two: laughter presupposes suffering (*Frogs* 1–15),[1] or the comic presupposes and builds on the tragic—on the inevitable burdens and sufferings to which nature and law subject human beings and from which comedy affords us relief. If we want even just to laugh with Aristophanes, Thucydides can help us with the preliminary knowledge of the sufferings of his many Athenians. Thucydides is, moreover, as much a lover of peace as is Aristophanes (2.8.1), so there is an indication of a wide common ground, especially because they were contemporary Athenian citizens. In the *Peace*, for example, set at the time of the peace of Nicias, the piety and the sufferings of the rustics are more intelligible on the basis of Thucydides' description of the move, caused by Pericles' strategy, of Athenians from the countryside to the city (2.14–18), and we know from Thucydides what Aristophanes means when he calls Cleon and Brasidas the "pestles" of war sought by the god Polemos (War) (*Peace* 238–85; cf. Thucydides 5.16).

Such examples could easily be multiplied, but—invaluable as they are—dwelling on them would reduce Thucydides to an extended footnote to Aristophanes' plays. We move to a more substantial ground of comparison and contrast when we realize that Aristophanes' plays open themselves up to serious readings, and this occurs as soon as we see that his comic presentations have non-comic equivalents.[2] And while each author restricts himself to a specific literary genre, Aristophanes no less than Thucydides is in search of the serious reader. The latter famously distinguishes his useful, eternal possession, which aims at the truth, from works composed to please the ear in contests, but the former similarly distinguishes the laughers from the wiser, that is, serious, readers.[3]

As one makes these realizations, one finds oneself wondering where to begin the daunting task of examining the many rich fields that open up. One path toward an introduction to them—which is all that we attempt here—is to focus on Cleon, whose speeches and deeds play such a crucial role in the first half of the Peloponnesian War and who, as it happens, officially attacked both Thucydides and Aristophanes.[4] Pitted against Nicias in both Thucydides' work and in Aristophanes' plays (most explicitly in the *Knights*), Cleon may be said to represent a distinct direction for political life.[5] The theme that the two thinkers introduce through him proves, moreover, to be comprehensive, enduring, and further explored in their respective works. It is the angry demand for justice over and against natural, compelling erotic longing.

The Comic Boastfulness of Cleon

Thucydides' Cleon is the post-Periclean leader of the war party in Athens. Between the eulogy of Pericles (2.65) and Cleon's first speech (3.36.6ff.) we hear no speeches at Athens. He is the first Athenian leader to appear after Thucydides has warned us of the decline in leadership at Athens that followed the death of the manifestly public-spirited and intelligent Pericles, a decline marked by more self-interested and pandering attempts to lead the demos, that is, by its more democratic, less de facto monarchic character. Cleon manifests the civic vices of those he would lead. He is introduced before his first speech both as violent and as the foremost man among the demos in Athens. He demonstrates that violence by calling for the death of all citizens of Mytilene, the first "allied" city to revolt from Athens during the war. While Cleon is unsuccessful in his motion, he subsequently moves and carries the decree for the slaughter of one thousand Mytilenaian captives at Athens (3.50.1).

Cleon is later reintroduced (4.21–22) as "a demagogue and the person at the time most influential among the people" during the peace negotiations offered by the Spartans after Demosthenes had trapped their men on the island of Sphacteria, off Pylos. He demands of the Spartans the surrender of the men on the island and the giving back of four cities ceded to Sparta before the war. The Spartan ambassadors offer to negotiate even about these, but in private (because public failed negotiations would disclose their intention to capitulate to Athenian power and become now-junior partners with Athens). Hearing this, Cleon drives the ambassadors away with the charge that he knew all along that the ambassadors' intentions were unjust, and now it is clear to everyone; by accusing Sparta of conspiring unjustly *against its own allies*, he deprives Athens of a de facto victory and forces the war to continue.

This prepares the way for Cleon's greatest humiliation, followed by his greatest triumph: the capture of the Spartans who are trapped at Pylos (4.27–49). The Athenians receive news from messengers that their forces have been unable to capture the trapped Spartans, and so they begin fearing that the Spartans will escape, especially because Sparta has ceased sending peace ambassadors. They now regret having rejected the Spartan offers of peace. Cleon knows their blame for this rejection is directed at him and seeks a way out of it: he publicly accuses the messengers from Pylos of lying! The messengers reply by calling him out on this calumny: let him go to Pylos and see for himself. The Athenians then elect Cleon and another Athenian as fact finders. Trapped, but realizing the Athenians are more inclined now to send an expedition, Cleon declares that if the situation at Pylos is indeed as reported, then not a moment can be wasted on any fact-finding mission. A force must be sent immediately, he declares, and, pointing to Nicias, who was an enemy of his, he impugns his honor and his bravery: real men, he declares, would find it *easy* to bring a force to Pylos and achieve a victory, as he himself would were he a general. Nicias does not rise to this bait, but instead—seeing that the Athenians are beginning to clamor against Cleon's boastful calumnies—publicly offers to turn over his generalship to Cleon, with any powers he wishes. Flummoxed, Cleon declares that he is not a general. But to Cleon's horror, Nicias—who does not wish to go—insists on turning over his command. And the members of the demos, now enjoying Cleon's humiliation, shout for this boaster to go as general, so in the end he is compelled to take up the command. He promises to kill the trapped Spartans or to return with them as captives within twenty days, and to do so with no Athenian hoplites but only allied light troops and archers

(4.31–32). This final boast provokes the Athenians to laughter—the only instance, so far as I have noted, of laughter in Thucydides' work. The rather short-sighted moderates (Nicias' friends) are delighted, thinking that Cleon will either die or obtain a victory "for them."

But Cleon has the last laugh. The specific troops he has called for have in fact been requested by Demosthenes, whom Cleon has chosen as his colleague and who has careful and detailed plans for their use (4.30.4). With these, Demosthenes succeeds at Pylos, and Cleon returns to Athens with his promise, "insane as it was," fulfilled (4.30–39). He returns like an impossibly successful hero in one of Aristophanes' comedies. But the results of his impossible victory are not uniformly desirable. True, the surrender of the men at Pylos, particularly the 300 or so Spartans (4.36.3 with 38.5), astonishes the Greek world and brings Sparta to the depths of despair. But Cleon's victory also contributes not a little to the Athenian demos' own mad thinking that it can accomplish *anything*, with or without power or resources, and thereby to its fury and punishment of generals who fail to accomplish what the demos wishes.[6]

Thucydides makes it abundantly clear that the victory for which Cleon claims credit belongs to Demosthenes (4.32.3, 4; 4.33.2); the latter is, as it were, Cleon's deus ex machina. The victory overthrows the reputation Spartans had obtained through their "great" action at Thermopylae (4.36.3)—the reputation for defiance of necessity: a Spartan would die rather than submit to any necessity (4.40.1). This overthrow, together with the details of the battle, suggests that Cleon's boastful theft of the victory entails a boast of something still more significant. For Thucydides had drawn in his archeology a parallel between the poetic magnification of ancient things, including above all the attribution of divine intervention in the Trojan War that hides the necessities that moved the war's participants, and the magnification, in the present, of things known by hearsay, including the existence of a picked company of Spartans "which never at any time has come into being" (1.20.3). The overthrow of Sparta's reputed virtue—of virtue induced by awe or reverence—is of the same nature as the overthrow of the gods. Now, Demosthenes' plan was designed especially on the basis of what he had learned from his earlier defeat at Pylos, in which he had led his troops into ambushes by an enemy that was seeing yet unseen. A chance forest fire had this time stripped the land of its clothing of trees, so that the enemy was no longer seeing yet unseen (4.29.2 with 4.30.1–2 and 32.2). His planned indirect assault on the enemy by light troops is assisted by the "nature" of the place, which Demosthenes had noticed (4.32.2–33.3 with 4.3.2 and

4.4.3), while his enemies are, by contrast, commanded from start to finish in strict accord with Spartan *nomos* (38.2). And Demosthenes' troops' initial fear of the "terrible things" in fighting against Spartans, due to their grand reputation, is dispelled when they have direct experience of their enemy's weakness.[7] In the end, the Spartans retreat to a strong "ancient" fortification not far distant (35.1 with 31.2), where the grand Spartan reputation is overcome by some of Demosthenes' Messenian troops—members of the people whom Sparta had enslaved and whom Demosthenes' guerilla warfare was designed to liberate. They, unseen, discover a difficult path to a height in the rear of the Spartan troops, left unguarded because of the Spartans' trust in the strength of their position (36). Demosthenes' victory over the Spartans, we suggest, was preceded by his liberation, through his discovery of nature over and against law, from the terrors induced by Sparta's reputation and the trust in the divine upon which that reputation rested. Cleon's pretense not to fear the Spartans and what they stand for (4.28.4) succeeds only by relying on Demosthenes' genuine liberation from that fear (cf. *Knights* 21–83).

Now a well-reputed general, Cleon carries the decree for another bloody deed, the complete destruction of Scione, which had revolted to Brasidas (4.122.6, carried out at 4.129–132, 5.18.78, and 5.32.1), and then leads an expedition to Thrace against Brasidas, in which his men contrast his cowardice with the manifest courage or manliness of Brasidas, and in which both he and Brasidas are killed—which eliminates the two chief opponents of peace (5.2–10 with 16.1). Thucydides describes Cleon's long-standing opposition to peace as motivated by a belief that "peace would make more manifest his base deeds"—in contrast to Brasidas, for whom peace would end his great success and the honor he derived from the war.[8] In short, with his towering moral indignation and its accompanying boastfulness, bloodthirstiness, calumnies, lies, pretense, theft of the deeds of others, and cowardice, Cleon is the least attractive Athenian in Thucydides' work. He is, we might say, a perfect subject for comedy.

Law, Anger, Necessity, and Eros

Yet the episodes we have described come after the second introduction of Cleon. By far the most revealing episode—which Thucydides sets apart from the rest—is Cleon's inaugural attempt to have the Mytilenaians put to death. By introducing him in this way, Thucydides pairs Cleon's one-

and-only recorded speech with an opposing speech by Diodotos, an otherwise unknown Athenian whose name means "Gift of Zeus." And in their debate, the question of moral responsibility for crime is examined explicitly and most penetratingly. Cleon claims to speak and act strictly with a view to compelling interests but is in fact moved by a belief in justice and its corollary, human freedom. Diodotos, who persuades the Athenians to spare most Mytilenaians, does so with appeals to their sense of justice but slips in an argument against human freedom that is the most far reaching in Thucydides' work, one based on an understanding of eros. The debate suggests that—and why—those who understand the argument against justice are, for that very reason, least likely to make that argument publicly, while those who argue explicitly against justice and human freedom usually disclose an abiding attachment to it. Archrealists like Cleon, who pretend to easily dismiss the demands of justice, evince a deep confusion on this issue. His speech shows us how claims concerning the compelling power of interest are susceptible of being twisted into a harsh and inhuman lesson. Deliverance from the hopes that haunt and pervert men like Cleon issues in a gentleness manifest in the speech of Diodotos. By examining their debate, we stand to gain a clear insight into the deliverance from hope that Thucydides offers, and what it is that is being faced in that deliverance.

The circumstances leading up to the debate were as follows. In the fourth year of the war, Mytilene, an ally of Athens, revolted from the Athenian alliance, taking advantage of the plague at Athens to do what it had long desired to do. Betrayal of the Mytilenaians' plans to the Athenians forced them to revolt before they were fully prepared, however, and, as suppliants of the Olympian Zeus (3.14.1), to seek aid from the Spartans, whose customary dallying helped to seal their fate. An Athenian blockade eventually forced the Mytilenaians to capitulate (3.2–19, 25–36). The revolt was the clearest case of injustice thus far in the war, and the Athenians were angry about it chiefly because the Peloponnesian fleet had dared to move over to Ionia to assist the Mytilenaians—something that caused the Athenians to think that the revolt was long premeditated or deliberate (3.36.2). They voted to condemn to death all of the male citizens but decided on the following day that such a harsh punishment was unjust, and another assembly was called. In the ensuing debate, Cleon argues for the retention of the decree of blanket capital punishment that he had succeeded in getting passed on the previous day. Diodotos, however, argues successfully that only the oligarchs ought to be put to death. The setting for the debate gives us an example of both the quick temper of democratic human beings and their ability to get over their anger quickly.[9] Cleon, who speaks first, means to make sure that they quickly regain it.

Like all populists, Cleon talks tough. He presents himself as both knowing the ways of the world and having the true interest of the people and their laws at heart. The problem, as he presents it, is that the regime of the people is inherently naive about the ways of the world. The people think that they can rule an empire by saying "please"; the trust that marks their domestic regime, and that depends on deference to a common good, leads them to believe that there is a community of cities as well. They accordingly attempt to rule an empire as if it were a democracy, sacrificing their own advantage in the expectation of a grateful deference to their leadership. Echoing what Pericles had dared to tell the Athenians only when forced to by the plague, Cleon loudly proclaims at the start that their empire is a tyranny, held not through the goodwill of their subjects but by superior Athenian strength (3.37; cf. 2.63.2). As members of a democracy, they are not sufficiently steadfast in their anger, so they fail to inspire in their subjects the necessary fear. If time blunts the edge of anger, anesthetizing the pain of injustice, it thereby removes us from our only access to reality. Punishment must accordingly be swift and certain; the quicker the action follows upon the injury, the less blunted the anger is, and so the closer the punishment will be to the desert.

Yet clever speakers, moved by vanity or bribes, threaten to lure the Athenians away from the concern for the city, to which their anger would direct them. Anger, deaf to smooth talkers, is the just man's protection from their beguiling blandishments, preventing him from becoming a traitor to his own cause. It brooks no exceptions, and forestalls the efforts of clever speakers to pull the wool over the eyes of the simple and just, who make no pretense to be wiser than the city's laws. Those laws, laid down in anger, recognize the harsh truth about the world, and the Athenians shouldn't allow a man who seeks honor for being wiser than the laws to dissuade them from the punishment of the Mytilenaians, which the lawful decree of the previous day had meted out. The Athenian people need to cease gratifying their vain desire to appear clever,[10] to cease applauding every newfangled proposal. To wean the people from the wise guys and back to their own good, Cleon attempts to renew their anger.

He does so by recalling to their minds the facts, not as they seem now but as they seemed at the time, and the fact is—he claims—that the Mytilenaians have done more harm to Athens than to any single city. Their action was deliberate, it was unprovoked, and they would surely do it again.[11] They weren't compelled by Athenian violence or by Athens' enemies; they were strong, free, and held in the greatest honor. And yet they freely conspired to rebel. They even neglected the warning examples of others who had rebelled and been punished, and their prosperity, far from making them cautious, caused them to become hubristic, to put strength before right, and so as soon as they thought they would prove stronger, they attacked Athens. If Athens is blameworthy, it is for having spoiled the Mytilenaians rotten by sparing the rod, forgetting that it is man's nature to despise servility and to be awed by firmness. The Mytilenaian people, moreover, took what they thought was the safe course and bet on the oligarchs against the Athenians. If they are not all punished in an exemplary way, the going price of revolt will be a mere fine; what subject city wouldn't then revolt on a slight pretext? The Athenians will be forced to risk lives and treasure putting down other revolts and will recover for their labors ruined cities, with the source of their strength—tax revenues—thereby being lost. In short, the Athenians caught the Mytilenaians red-handed in a cold-blooded, treacherous attempt to destroy Athens, and it would be both unjust and disadvantageous to let them off the hook.

After this passionate indictment, Cleon turns to address what he calls the three greatest enemies of rule or empire: compassion, pleasure of words, and decency or equity (40). Concerning the first, he asserts that the Mytilenaians must be given no hope that they will be excused on the plea that their transgression was human, for it is only the unintentional that is excusable. Nor should the Athenians be led by a clever speaker to feel compassion, for this should be felt only for those likely to feel it in return, not for those compelled, like the Mytilenaians, to be enemies; it is given to induce a change, but, being irredeemable, the Mytilenaians must be annihilated. Decency, too, should be reserved only for those who will change to fidelity, not for those who are enemies forever. In sum, anything short of a blanket capital punishment would win Athens no gratitude, but would instead indicate—how could it not?—that the Mytilenaians acted justly in revolting, and hence that the Athenians act unjustly in ruling. But be it just or unjust, they must punish the Mytilenaians or give up the empire. Finally, lest the Athenians become soft at the present distress of the Mytilenaians, Cleon describes the harm they intended: voluntary, premeditated, unprovoked crime is crime without limit. They flouted justice, and nothing would have restrained such unscrupulous men. Had they succeeded, they would have brought about the utter destruction of Athens in an attempt to destroy all witnesses to their injustice. To ensure that they don't now weasel out, Cleon bids the Athenians to imagine how, when they heard the terrible news of the revolt, they would have given *anything* to pay the Mytilenaians back for such a blatant attempt to destroy their city, and to now punish them accordingly. If the Athenians feel their anger again, they will do the right thing; the Mytilenaians' death will be both just and expedient.

What Meletus is to Socrates, Cleon is to Thucydides; as mentioned above, we learn from other sources that Cleon was responsible for Thucydides' banishment. All the more remarkable is the fact that on a number of points, Cleon's professed tough mindedness resembles the oft-noted realism of Thucydides' himself. His praise of moderation as law-abidingness, for example, concurs with Thucydides' praise of the Spartans generally and of their king Archidamos in particular (1.18, 3.37.4–7, 1.79.2, 84–85; 8.24.4). His claim that the Mytilenaians' hubris is but one example of the common experience of prosperous cities, especially those who experience it unexpectedly, concurs with Thucydides' findings.[12] Again, Cleon's blame of the people for being overpowered by the pleasures of the ear, and so unable to grasp even what goes on before their eyes, recalls Thucydides' own statements about poets and their audience (1.20–21). Above all, Cleon's blame of the Athenians for mistakenly expecting that generous or gracious sacrifice of their own good will produce goodwill in return, and thus secure them the good that they seek through rule (3.37), seems to reflect Thucydides' own strong if less obvious critique of the Athenians on this score.[13] Yet in spite of this apparent agreement, readers of Thucydides are almost unanimous in their opinion that Thucydides loathes Cleon.[14] And rightly so. For a look at Diodotos' speech shows us why the two men could not be further apart.

To Cleon's charge that his listeners desire, as spectators of speeches, a world different than it is, Diodotos answers with equal force that the anger that is deaf to debate is itself captive to the hope for a world different than it is.[15] It is deaf to reason (*logos*), and there is no other way to know what will be in the dim and distant future than by speech or reason.[16] Deliberation is thus a source of strength, while anger betrays a weak mind and shortsightedness. This is not to say that Diodotos is unaware of the problem in deliberative assemblies to which Cleon referred. On the contrary, he concedes Cleon's point that there is always a conflict between public good and private ambitions and paints an even bleaker picture of its resolution. The envy of a successful speaker's individual honor works against the city's good, but since to agree with someone is to honor him, the problem is not resolvable.[17] But to grant this, as Cleon does, should move one to see that there will be no manner of end to it and so to see the foolish nature of the demand that human beings cease injustice once and for all. Instead, Cleon remains angry, and the angry demand for the law's punishment of alleged injustice likewise leads men like him to reject what is advantageous to a city. Angry punishment is for the sake of the crime, not for the sake of deterring witnesses to the punishment. It looks back at the crime to determine what it deserves, rather than looking forward to determine what is advantageous.[18] On account of these and other difficulties, Diodotos claims, he will have to deceive the angry Athenians in order to serve his city's advantage (43.1–3).

Accordingly, by speaking of the impossibility of deterrence, Diodotos appears to direct his argument strictly to the question of interest. He begins with the claim that the death penalty has not stopped men from attempting to commit crimes. In support of this claim, he presents to the Athenians a brief but important speculative history of punishment, arguing that while there were probably fewer crimes punished capitally in the remote past, the hope, in the face of persistent transgressions, of making transgressions less frequent through punishment has caused capital punishment gradually to be extended to still more crimes. Yet transgressions persist, and persist of necessity. For human beings are, he argues, ever compelled by their needs and passions, including and above all the erotic desire for freedom and empire, to hope against fear that the impossible is possible. The manifest terror of laws is powerless against the compelling passions of human nature; the death penalty will deter neither cities nor individuals in the way that Cleon had promised (3.45).

If, moreover, the Athenians leave the Mytilenaians no hope of repenting, other cities will simply prepare more thoroughly before revolting and hold out to the bitter end when they do revolt, leaving Athens with ruined cities. Dead men don't pay taxes, and as Cleon himself had observed, money is the source of Athens' strength. As an alternative to such disadvantageous punishment after the fact, Diodotos proposes putting all their subject cities on probation: he would have the Athenians practice close surveillance of all of them and, against those who do revolt, swift punishment of as few of the culprits as possible. Finally, by blaming only the few guilty oligarchs, the Athenians can ensure that the people in all subject cities will remain friendly to Athens. Even if the Mytilenaians are guilty, then, the Athenians should pretend not to notice. Neither should they be moved by pity or clemency, but strictly by advantage, which, he claims, cannot be combined with justice (3.46–47).[19]

Now, the success of Diodotos' appeal to interest rests in part on its surreptitious appeal to justice.[20] The brief history of punishment that he sketches, which purports to be merely the final stage of successive efficiency analyses of punishment, in fact exculpates all crime, as had the Athenians' argument at Sparta, which was also marked by a freedom from anger (1.74.2–76.4). For it indicates that the condition that would have to obtain for justice to be possible, the possibility of free transgression, does not obtain. If human beings are compelled by nature to transgress, then they cannot be blamed for transgressing. For justice does not ask the impossible, and it is impossible for human beings to overcome the compulsion to pursue what appears great to them. By speaking in this context of the compulsion to transgress, especially to transgress in the name of freedom and empire, Diodotos puts the imperial Athenians in a milder mood and prepares them not only for his argument concerning Athens' present interest, but also for his subsequent appeal to the justice of punishing only the few "guilty" Mytilenaians. That he does so suggests the judgment on his part that the moral indignation of most human beings, while without any genuine ground, nonetheless cannot easily be removed from men's souls.

Diodotos accounts for such indignation in a manner that ties it to eros and that spells out what eros entails. In addressing the efficacy of the death penalty, he addresses not only the mistaken hopefulness of subjects like the Mytilenaians, but—more emphatically—the mistaken hopefulness in the power of deterrence on the part of the ruling Athenians. Hoping in the death penalty, the Athenians, too, like unsuccessful criminals, are making a mistake that is due to an erotically driven hope in an impossibility and denying the evidence of their eyes. To grasp the specific character of this mistaken hope in punishment, we must observe that his claim concerning the failure of capital punishment to deter all crimes is not meant to establish that fear is simply of no effect on anyone. In fact, Diodotos affirms, though he does not wish to stress, that human beings do indeed fear punishment for alleged injustices and can be deterred by fear from what they might otherwise attempt (42.3–4 and 47.1–3 with 48.2). The mistaken hope that he addresses is not the hope that punishment deters crime, but rather the hope that the punishment will deter *all* future transgressions, or put an end to them. And this explains why Diodotos had presented Cleon's speech as an attempt to discern without reason what will be in the dim and distant future: Cleon's appeal is to his listeners' belief that *all* future transgressions can be avoided through the death penalty.

Diodotos' history of punishment would at first seem to suggest, then, that the hope in punishment represents a grossly mistaken hope in the power of fear. The progressive extension of capital punishment appears to have been due to hopeful but repeatedly mistaken calculations that are made strictly in an effort to deter crimes. Yet a continuous intention to deter, or to compel others to act in accordance with their own interest, cannot possibly explain what he presents as a progressive blindness, against ever mounting evidence, to human compulsions to transgress laws. The inefficacy of punishment, which should be ever more manifest, would not be so progressively immanifest were not something else at work, and increasingly at work, in the hearts of rulers. As Diodotos' exculpation of all wrongdoing suggests, that something is anger—angry faith in law. Besides, as he himself has told us, when it comes to punishment, it is the angry demand for strict justice that obstructs recognition of what is most advantageous (44.4; cf. 46.4). Above all, as he implies in his description of the present Athenian practice of continually expecting their allies *freely* to submit to their rule,[21] and continually punishing them harshly when they do not, the hope for an empire or rule that is eternally secure, without need for care or vigilance, betrays a perpetually disappointed hope in *justice,* rather than in fear, to fulfill this desire. Diodotos' argument may thus be said to disclose the mistaken hope, attending our anger, that just punishment will put an end to unjust action once and for all, that it will finally set things right. The hope of those who punish is thus not in the power of fear; it is not a hope that a wrongdoer will be moved to attend to his interest. It is rather a hope in the power of justice, of that justice that mistakenly assumes a freedom to transgress. But whence comes such hope?

Punishment belongs to rulers, and the hope that punishment will put an end to all crime belongs, according to Diodotos, even more to rulers of his own time—such as the Athenians—than to those of the remote past, in which punishments were milder.[22] But this suggests that the hope generated by eros is both behind the Athenians' own quest for empire, as he says explicitly, and (as we can now see) at the bottom of their angry desire to punish (3.45.5–6). As he indicates, it is the character of erotic longing to believe that what is beyond and against the necessary things is possible (cf. 5.99), or to be averse to strict calculation of the possible and impossible (cf. 2.40.4–5 with 40.3, and see again 4.65). Eros, we may say, generates hopes against the possible, or longs for what is in fact not possible. It arises, then, from an initial *awareness* of the inevitable, ever-pending disappointment with our lot and the consequent need to believe that we can be worthy of overcoming our lot by our self-sacrifice. Above all, as Diodotos' condemnation of both anger—thwarted eros—and the Athenians' existing, negligent imperial practices suggest, the erotic longing for freedom and empire breeds hopes of surmounting decline or decay itself and thus of enjoying an end to all troubles, including the troubling awareness of our mortality. The human awareness of decay or death prompts the longing for something that can overcome the limits of our mortal nature. What the Athenians want from their rule is an eternal, trouble-free life, and reason tells them that it isn't available. Reason recognizes the need for constant vigilance over subjects because of the very compulsions of which Diodotos speaks. Avoiding the hope for an end to all troubles, Athens could steer clear of much evil. It instead turns to lawful justice, which promises to benefit us in the most important or final way, overcoming our strongest discontent. This promise, which Diodotos addresses directly, is visible when it is thwarted, yielding the angry accusation that others have failed voluntarily to neglect their interests for the sake of justice.

The demand, to which Diodotos alludes, for a punishment more terrible than death (45.4; cf. 38.1) is thus the reverse side of the erotic hope for something more splendid or greater than our trouble-filled lives. And in general, as the reaction against what threatens or thwarts such hope, anger continues to embody it, expecting, in its desire to punish, to set things right once and for all. It results from a perceived threat to or disappointment of the hope for that ultimate security from sorrows and trouble that was to be obtained by just self-sacrifice and seeks a punishment that will end the threat permanently. To preserve this hope, anger must blame the (inevitable) disappointment of these hopes on an immediate obstacle, who is held to have freely chosen an ungrateful defiance or contempt of one's worth. Finding someone to blame for the disappointment, anger allows the hope for the deserved life without pain to persist against the ever-contending evidence. In attributing blame, it reaffirms the sense of worth that promises to be rewarded either by unseen fortune (cf. 3.45.6) or by other human beings. Anger therefore prepares one to bear the loss of a manifest good so that the initial hope in justice—the hope that through self-sacrifice, through obedience to law, an end to troubles will be found—need not be abandoned.

If we now turn back to Cleon's speech, we notice that it is just such hope that leads him to think that capital punishment will deter future aggression. Though he claims to have known from the beginning that the allies couldn't be trusted, his anger betrays this as a boast. His apparent hardheadedness bespeaks in fact the pain of ingratitude. For Cleon does not, as he had first claimed, attempt to free the Athenians from a misguided hope for gratitude earned through self-sacrifice, but rather attempts to have them act on the basis of a bitter disappointment of this hope in order to restore and cherish it. The free reign he would have the Athenians give to their anger betrays his abiding hope in permanent, trouble-free security obtained through justice.

This is perhaps most clearly manifest in his denunciation of the Mytilenaians for not having subordinated their interest to justice (39.3). They dared to put strength before justice, he exclaims, and it is a just strength that has now brought them low; *their* hopes were in themselves; they were self-reliant: Cleon is more willing to forgive allies who rebel in a foolish, noncalculative or arbitrary way—without any allies—than to forgive others. Similarly, his single argument in favor of killing all of the Mytilenaians rather than the ruling oligarchs alone is that the people and oligarchs alike took the *safe* course rather than risk themselves for Athens' sake. And what he says of pity and equity—that it should be reserved only for those who will freely[23] be devoted to Athens—betrays the same hope. The generosity that the powerful Athenian city displays toward its allies, the Mytilenaians, leads him to believe that Athens deserves an equally generous response from them despite the harm this would mean for them.

While calling for a tyrannical rule, Cleon in fact wishes for subjects who freely show gratitude to Athenian rule. The usual Athenian practice of generosity, which he decries, in fact helps to assure him that Athenian rule has been and is fundamentally just, that Athens deserves to rule and hence deserves to have no more trouble from her subjects. Cleon's hope that the Mytilenaians will be once and for all an example to others is, then, not a view that is strictly attentive to interests. It rests on a view of interest that is suffused by the hope that there can be a "once and for all." The hindsight that suggests the error of a too-lenient policy likewise reflects his hope for a trouble-free empire. The punishment of Mytilenaian hubris that is to deter all future hubris betrays an abiding hope in an empire without revolts, an empire in which the Athenians' just claim to rule is duly acknowledged by all. He blames the Mytilenaians for thwarting this hope, and the Athenians, *not* for having had it, but for now abandoning the punishment that it demands. The Mytilenaians have violated the trust and friendship shown them, the trust that is the bond of a community whose members are expected freely to obey the laws. If Cleon now demands tyranny, it is out of indignation at this breach of trust: the revolt has unmasked secret unjust aims, a conspiracy to rebel. The allies cannot *now* be trusted with so much freedom. Since they involuntarily submit to justice, they must be reeducated by strength. Harsh laws will make Athens' hubristic subjects moderate. As he indicates, the firmness he calls for is to elicit not a devious and contemptuous servility (39.5), but an awe of those dedicated, come hell or high water, to law. For the call for harsh punishments reflects the desire that Athens, too, subordinate her interests to justice; although Cleon knows that greater severity in general runs the risk of causing more rebellion (39.2), he nonetheless demands it. He in fact wishes the Athenians to act in a reckless manner in punishing, "giving everything" to punish, a wrongdoer,[24] especially the greatest of wrongdoers, who would, he claims, have destroyed Athens forever. He demands a deed that squares with their imagined deed, one that puts justice before advantage, restoring the supremacy of right and thereby securing Athenian rule.

For all of his complaining about the Athenians' tendency to hear of deeds and gaze at speeches, then, it is Cleon's own argument that changes in speech what genuinely did occur in order to argue what ought to be done. The Mytilenaians have destroyed Athens (40.5–6) only in his mind. In the end, the greatest harm that has been done is the pain of an apparent injustice: the Mytilenaians' betrayal of Athens' trust. It is the pain of having their cherished hopes in their justice disappointed, and the desire for the gratification of inflicting punishment that would cure that pain reflects a continuation of their hope to be permanently secure by being worthy of it, and hence promises even more pain as it grows. Believing that the Athenians deserve permanent security, Cleon is able to look forward to it with hope. But, as Diodotos' speech indicates, that is an illusory hope.

Recognizing the depth and ubiquity of the hope Cleon feels and to which he appeals—the hope in a trouble-free life obtainable through freely chosen self-sacrificial deeds—Diodotos does not attempt to persuade the Athenians by an appeal to interest alone. Like Cleon, he appeals also to justice. But while Cleon had appealed to interest out of a concern for justice, Diodotos appeals to justice out of a concern for interest. Free of unfounded hopes and imaginary fears, Diodotos is free of the anger that looks to the past and free to consider those permanent necessities and present circumstances by which alone our future advantage can be known. By softening the people's anger and appealing to their sympathy for longings like their own, Diodotos raises the Athenians to an act of gentleness that makes their empire worthy of remembrance. His speech shows us political rhetoric at its peak: he pretends, as he advises the Athenians, not to notice injustice when he sees it and—as he does not tell them—to notice some limited injustice where none exists.

Of all Thucydides' speakers, Diodotos alone applies the teaching of necessity to individuals, examining the basis of our attachment to justice and nobility, to running risks for the sake of something splendid.[25] He presents "freedom and empire" as the greatest things, but, as we have seen, they are to his mind objects of a *deluded* ambition. The erotic passion that leads to empire is not, strictly speaking, compulsory, but rather represents an extravagant longing, which gives rise in turn to extravagant demands and ambitions. Political ambition arises out of a specific error—a specific hope.

Diodotos raises doubt, then, about the genuinely compulsive or inevitable character of these ambitions.

While Diodotos' argument about anger and justice directly answers the arch-realist Cleon, his disclosure of their source, in the Athenians' thwarted erotic longing for empire, also recalls to the reader's mind Pericles, the most outstanding leader of Thucydides' day and one who is likely to be more attractive to non-realists than is Cleon. In his funeral oration, Pericles exhorts the Athenians to become erotic lovers of Athens, freely dedicating themselves to the city, subordinating their interests to the common good of Athens in the promise of eternal or deathless glory (2.43). The late, brief Periclean admission that it is the nature of all things to decline or give way (2.64.3) seems, in the light of Diodotos' speech, not to have been genuinely accepted by Pericles, but rather to have provoked a rebellion against nature, an erotic rebellion, which found expression in the quest for "eternal glory."[26] Diodotos, we may say, sees through the false character of the experience of that quest—the false hope on which it rests—a quest that Pericles had done his best to make the lodestar of Athens. The hope for life without troubles, or at least an eternal compensation for troubles, animates the Athenians, including those who long for glory, and that is a hope that is mistaken. The lack of wisdom in the pursuit of empire, the lack of attention to what is possible, does not mean that empire is unjust, but that it rests on unfounded hopes, on a spurious experience. Empire is not the way to the human good.

Diodotos' critique of erotic longing thus moves the reader to doubt the wisdom of Pericles' call for the Athenians to become erotic lovers of their city's power, and the hopes that that love spawns. Pericles had jettisoned the old, pious Athens and encouraged the adoption of a whole new politics. In the best case, the new politics gives rise to a Diodotos, who brings his fellow citizens to do what must be done to serve their interests, or keeps them from self-destructive acts. But what emerges from his speech is a critique of Pericles' devotion to the everlasting glory that would come through service to the common good of Athens. Pericles' own love of glory was not an adequate response to a fully grasped insight into his own and his city's mortality. It was rather a diversion from the truth about his own death, a diversion that evinces an inability to see clearly or accept fully, both in his own case and that of his city, what was and was not possible. Through the speech of Diodotos, Thucydides does his best to ensure that we overcome the need for such diversion, but that we likewise avoid the false freedom from delusion claimed by the likes of the brutal Cleon.

Justice and Necessity in Aristophanes: Our Split Nature

The debate in the *Clouds* between Just and Unjust Speech—Pheidippides' preparation for an indoor Socratic education—affords us the most obvious starting point for Aristophanes' attention to the theme of natural erotic necessity over and against lawful justice. The debate is initially about two kinds of education: the Just Speech's ancestral education in reverence for antiquity, shame, justice, and sexual modesty versus the Unjust Speech's education in their opposites. But the Unjust Speech wins only when he turns explicitly from education to "speak of the necessity of nature (*phuseos anagkas*): you err/transgress (*hemartes*), you fall in love (*erasthes*), you commit adultery, and you are caught" (1075–76). The only necessity of nature to which the Unjust Speech refers is eros leading to adultery, that is, to lawless sexual pleasure. Here, as elsewhere in Aristophanes, eros is used to designate sexual eros; it is never used to describe a longing that can be satisfied by or in political life. The Unjust Speech almost implies, in this account of natural erotic necessity's overcoming of a strong sense of shame—and of the need to overcome shame by thinking, as he does, that nothing is shameful or unjust (1077–82)—that this sense will appear to one who has it to be present as it were by nature, or that the education in shame championed by the Just Speech corresponds to something in, or some part of, the nature of his addressee, just as he assumes, like the Just Speech, that the gods live better lives than humans but that this includes—even for Zeus—being overcome by erotic necessities (904–6 and 1047–68 with 1080–82). The recognition of Zeus' powerlessness against nature, we may say, frees the Unjust Speech from the law-supported sense of shame that would otherwise (and once did) direct him.

But does Aristophanes himself agree with the Unjust Speech? The debate taken by itself would seem to suggest that he does. The Unjust Speech and not the Just Speech favors, after all, the kind of bawdy comedy Aristophanes writes, and Aristophanes allows the Unjust Speech (shockingly) to win this debate. Moreover, the young, intelligent Pheidippides appears to be won over quite dramatically to the Unjust Speech's way of thinking. His erotic longings appear to be no longer directed, if they ever were, toward procreation and the rearing of offspring—a fact that is crucial in refuting the teaching of his father, Strepsiades, on the injustice of father beating. Still, Strepsiades returns to "Zeus," to divine law, in disgust at Pheidippides' teaching on mother beating and incest, a teaching that would deprive him of Pheidippides as his son and only his son. That is, his return to the law has its cause in a concern for a private, familial orderly erotic relation protected by law, not in any devotion to law as good in itself. And return to the law he does; the play ends with his defeat of Socrates in the name of "Zeus," or divine justice (1452ff.). We therefore cannot say that the victory of the Unjust Speech unambiguously discloses Aristophanes' agreement with the argument concerning the erotic necessities of nature over law. To gain some clarity on this issue, we need to turn to the *Acharnians*, where Aristophanes, thinly disguised as the rustic Dikaiopolis, presents *himself* as daring to give the true just speech at Athens (496–501).

Set in the sixth year of the war (266, 890), the *Acharnians* begins to bear out our suspicion that the Just and Unjust Speech are representative of two parts of man rather than (only) two different educations. Dikaiopolis first appears to be a member of the same political party as the chorus of old Marathon fighters who hate Cleon (1–8 with 300, 509–11, 659–64, 692–702). He similarly seems to be a lover of the poetry of Aeschylus (9–10). He claims to seek a separate peace for himself, his wife, and his children (131; cf. 241–62), and allegedly the god Amphitheos miraculously obtains one for him (44–203; see, however, 238–40 and 280). But when Dikaiopolis faces stoning at the hands of the raging and patriotic Acharnians, who have borne the enemy's destruction of their crops and who, in the name of Zeus, angrily seek vengeance upon him (225–33), he stops them cold with remarkable ease: he takes a basket of their *livelihood*, coals—the amusing spoken pretext, which he does not dispel, is that the coals are "fellow citizens"—as hostage, and they immediately drop their strong vows to stone him to death (302–46). All are initially won over by Dikaiopolis' threat to the source of their livelihood, which causes them to put their patriotic zeal and anger on the back burner (while pretending to be concerned for their captive comrades). But to make them steadfast in their desire for peace, Dikaiopolis makes additional appeals justifying his action.

With his head voluntarily placed on the chopping block, yet clinging to "life," Dikaiopolis calls time-out to prepare a defense of himself. He fears the anger of the Acharnians and of Cleon, who had attacked him because of his comedy the previous year and so has a need to appeal to compassion (357–84). That is, Dikaiopolis discloses now unambiguously that he is in truth the comic poet himself, who recognizes a need—learned from hard experience—to appear compassionate rather than as a clever comic poet in order to fight anger. And he refers to the steps he will now take to justify his deed before the Acharnians as a manifestation of his "strength of soul" (393; see also 480–89). Aristophanes seems then to share a common ground, manliness or courage, with the fearsome Acharnians, whom the alleged

Amphitheos was too terrified to fight. Just what that ground truly is appears in the sequel. He removes his rustic garb—his initial disguise—and with the assistance of Euripides, the novel tragedian of compassion (384 with 394ff.), he re-dresses as a pitiable beggar. The poet turns out not to be a follower of Aeschylus but, like the Socratically educated Pheidippides, to be a lover of Euripides' poetry (394ff. with *Clouds*, and 959–60, 1353–76 with 988–1024), and like him stands in favor of nature and opposed to the veneration of antiquity that his initial disguise had suggested.

Armed with the new, piteous guise supplied by Euripides, Aristophanes/Dikaiopolis splits his bellicose opponents into two groups, by means of two successive and different types of appeal. Half of the chorus of Acharnians is won over by his initial appeal to justice—by the argument that they, the Athenians, and not the Spartans, are guilty of having caused the war and all its sufferings (509–65); the members of this group experience guilt or blame themselves. But the other half, the angry followers of the fierce and dreadful warrior Lamachos, does not feel guilt; they are neither surprised nor moved by the argument that the war is unjust (560–63). This half is won away from Lamachos and what he stands for only with an angry, demagogic appeal to its self-interested envy of the well-paid muckety-mucks like Lamachos, whom Dikaiopolis accuses of unjustly leading the impoverished demos in war (595–627); they are won over by the blame and accusation of others who have secretly harmed their collective self-interest and exploited them.

In the second half of the play, we learn to which of these two groups of formerly angry men Dikaiopolis is closer: he makes a guiltless, self-interested use of his separate peace (719ff., esp. 1018–46). He purchases, for example, two little piggies[27] for a meal in Aphrodite's honor and a great deal of food from the enemy Boeotians. And he shares not a morsel of his delicious meal with the hungry members of the chorus. Unlike the heroes in other plays, Dikaiopolis (shockingly) saves or cures no one but himself, and while he turns the fierce Acharnians themselves into objects of pity, he does so for his own ends. But despite this ruthless, guiltless pursuit of his own good, Dikaiopolis manifests compassion for a young bride and her erotic needs (1047–69). The one who clear-sightedly obtains his good in accordance with the necessities of our erotic nature, as the Unjust Speech had put it, becomes—no less than Thucydides' Diodotos—on that account not cold or misanthropic. And while he leads a life like that of the Unjust Speech, telling lewd jokes and enjoying a festive meal with dancing girls and two buxom prostitutes, it is clear that his message, no less than Diodotos', is somewhat deceptive. For Dikaioplis is the comic poet *in disguise*; the non-comic equivalent of the pleasant social activities in which he engages, as the chorus makes clear, would be the poet's own activity of writing and performing comedies (393–489 with 628–58). We might even say that these are his erotic activities, since he presents himself in the *Clouds* as having given "birth" to his comedies even while constrained by *nomos* to appear as a "virgin," and since the god who raised him and by whom he swears, Dionysos, speaks in another play of his own longing for a dramatic poet as something resembling an erotic longing.[28]

Dikaiopolis' victory, which he acquired through his "strength of soul," appears thus to represent the victory of a radicalized version of the half of the chorus whose members were unmoved by an appeal to justice, were fierce to help with a collective good, and were won from devotion to war by evidence that their good was being sacrificed for the private benefit of their alleged leaders. We recall that the other half had consisted of men who are or can be made to feel guilty, to be dissatisfied with their lawless participation in an unjust war, or, as Plato's Aristophanes presents it, who suffer from the "wound" that law inflicts on our formerly strong and lawless souls.[29] Both halves of the split chorus are moved, once they are won over and reunited, to sing of the happiness that Dikaiopolis enjoys, thanks to the many good things his prudence and wisdom have won him, and of which he will not, as they put it, be cheated. They sing especially of how Aphrodite and Eros go together with his peace (836–59, 971–99).

We conclude from the *Acharnians* that the guilt that law induces, and (to a lesser extent) a spirited, manly devotion to the bellicose pursuit of a collective good, hold humans back from the true goods of their nature, and that the "strong soul" of Aristophanes succeeds in freeing itself altogether from the law to enjoy its own good, including above all the goods of Eros and Aphrodite. Aristophanes thus confirms in the *Acharnians* our suspicion that the Just and Unjust Speech represent two sides of a split nature, one of which seeks with a manly spirit what seems to be beneficial for ourselves even when it runs contrary to the other side of our split nature, the side that expresses itself in lawful, spirited devotion, in the stern sacrifice of our good that the law demands, and that experiences guilt in the enjoyment of certain goods, especially sensual goods and goods that come at the expense of others. Dikaiopolis makes the latter side fall by appeals to compassion and interest in order to give himself a life conducive to his own interest, with some compassion for the erotically desperate. Yet to achieve victory over his angry opponents—both the Acharnians and Cleon—Aristophanes has also had to use the very anger that had characterized them (see esp. 319–27), an anger that included an inducement of guilt in half the chorus. Does Aristophanes, in contradistinction to Thucydides, consider anger, then—righteous indignation—to be a part of a healthy, manly soul? And if so, how and to what extent?

With this question in mind, we turn to the Cleon plays, the *Knights* and the *Wasps*, both of which allow us to understand more fully the split in human nature we have observed.

Anger/Waspishness in the *Knights*

The *Knights* opens with Demosthenes and Nicias, two slaves in the household of Demos, attempting to find a way to defeat a third slave, Cleon (the Paphlagonian tanner), who has succeeded in winning over to himself the affections of their master, Demos, and thereby made their own lives more miserable. Cleon's ascendency over the demos is, no less than in Thucydides, based on demagogic flattery, calumny, bribery (45–59), an opposition to orators (60 and 880, with *Symposium* 191d6–192b5), and brutality. But Aristophanes makes it clearer than Thucydides did that these go together in Cleon with an appeal to stateliness of a certain kind, that is, with (comic) appeals to his own majesty and to the majesty of state and of empire (consider 340, 415–16, 475–76, 624–76, and so on). The chief means by which he achieves these is a large stash of oracles (61, 110ff.). In the most important of these oracles, he is compared with the punitive Zeus as the third of four predicted rulers, and he is similarly Zeus-like in that nothing escapes his notice (*Knights* 74–75, with *Acharnians* 435; see also *Knights* 338, 410, 863). When Demosthenes reads this oracle—which he has obtained by ordering Nicias to steal Cleon's stash—he interprets its description of the fourth predicted ruler to mean that a sausage seller will succeed (and hence defeat) Cleon, and when a humble and pious sausage seller happens to walk by at that moment, Demosthenes convinces him to overthrow Cleon, with the help of the knights, and become a great ruler of Athens (110–230). It thus comes about that Cleon is defeated by a man who uses the same calumnies, accusations of bribes, embezzlement, perjury, theft, shouting, and so forth that are Cleon's stock-in-trade (235ff.).

What becomes clear, in other words, is that the oracle had expressed Cleon's deep fear that Athens will be further degraded by the rule of a guttersnipe like the sausage seller as his successor (cf. 950). Cleon is, we can say, caught up in the grand and stately Themistoclean project of empire and in Pericles' extension of that project through the presentation of the *city* as superhuman (cf. 284 with 810–21). And he is indeed eventually defeated by the sausage seller in a manner that goes beyond what he had feared: the sausage seller appeals to the simple bodily needs and private comforts of Demos—Demos the human being. Even when the fight between Cleon and the sausage seller is moved from Demos's household to the Council, to a public forum—in which shame or a sense of dignity is operative—where Cleon fully expects to win, the sausage seller defeats him. He does so by offering the Council members an opportunity to buy low-priced sprats rather than by refuting Cleon's stately charges against the knights (362, 395, 475–76, 624–90). That is, because he doesn't even pretend that the Council members act public-spiritedly, the sausage seller wins them over. It turns out, finally, that because the sausage seller has a genuine, filial love for Demos, he despises Cleon, who in turn actually despises Demos (716–19, 1215) and merely uses him as the means to a stately, grand leadership of the city far above his humble, leather-tanning origins. The sausage seller has a son's fears that he will lose should father Demos decide between him and Cleon at the pynx—in an official assembly—rather than by his reasonable self at home (746–55). But even at the pynx, the sausage seller wins: Cleon again proves unable to think of Demos as individual human beings with individual, private needs. Cleon will indeed fight for Demos, as he claims, or rather for the city, even "alone" (741–43, 763, 773–76, 790), but he will do so in accord with an oracle predicting Demos's eventual empire over all Greeks (797–98). And as the sausage seller successfully counters, Cleon merely uses war to hide his own knaveries as in a mist; he has no compassion for the sufferings, brought on by his stately pursuit of empire, of Demos's simple, rustic needs—like a cushion for his seat, which the sausage seller now provides (781–959, esp. 792–804; cf. Thucydides 5.16). Cleon, who considers such things "petty" (e.g., 788), is dumbfounded to discover that Demos finds such attentions to his body to be *just* (875).

The sausage seller finally defeats Cleon decisively in two steps. First, in an oracle contest with Cleon, he twists and openly invents oracles (960–1099). That is, by showing the fraudulent nature and political uses to which alleged oracles are easily put, he causes Demos to abandon his oracle-supported longing for universal empire and to place himself in the sausage seller's hands (cf. Thucydides 8.1.1–4). He then outdoes Cleon in serving up dishes for Demos, robbing Cleon of a dish, and convincing Demos that Cleon has, as ever, kept most of the food for himself (1110–1225). When Cleon objects that he has done so "for the good of the city"—drawing a distinction between the city and the demos—Demos demands the crown of him (1226–29). Cleon then learns that the sausage seller is the successor predicted by the oracle, or at least the oracle as the sausage seller guesses it to read and claims to fulfill it (1229–49, esp. 1243–47 with 1257–58). The crown is given to the sausage seller, who proceeds to boil Demos down for the sake of his rejuvenation, that is, to a return to Demos's old, rustic way of life, including its erotic delights (1316–1408). Members of the demos are, we may say, much less naturally inclined to the grandeur of empire than Cleon or other allegedly high-minded, that is, "boastful," men believe them to be. The demos finally realizes that it does not need democracy and its imperialism; it needs only natural, that is, economic, and erotic goods, and one of its own directing things. The sausage seller will readily provide these. When the poor have cried, the sausage seller hath wept. He is a natural ruler of the demos, attending to and scrappily fighting for its genuine, natural needs; the demos had been unhappily seduced from these natural needs by the stately appeals of proponents of empire like Cleon. The sausage seller, with none of Cleon's stately pretentions, has also none of his fury; he is angry on behalf of his father, but the rest is as feigned as the oracles he invents on the spot.

The rejuvenation of Demos—his being cured of the delusory hopes for grandeur and great pay so that he may enjoy life in the country—is a rekindling of Demos's original and raging desire to live his life, as in the past, by ancestral custom (see esp. 1316–34 with 805–9). It is a liberation from Cleon's Zeus-like anger, but not altogether from the rule of Zeus. The sausage seller was in fact assisted in his victory by the manifest gratitude, which, in stark opposition to Cleon, he showed to Athena: where Cleon had taken for himself the credit for all he had done for Demos, the sausage seller attributed his benefits to the goddess. Cleon had to learn from the sausage seller—too late—to thank the goddess, and even then Cleon, hopelessly stuck on grandeur, had seized on her warlike rather than gracious aspect (1166–90 and 1202–3; cf. 903 with 763–68, 810–19). But when speaking to the chorus of knights, the sausage seller attributes his victory not to (even a warlike) Athena but to Zeus (1253). The rule of Zeus is the common ground between the sausage seller and the knights, to whom the sausage seller also defers and whose own belief in Zeus is the ground of his deference (341, 366, 500, 577, 581–94).

But the knights—these alleged gentlemen—had been driven in their partisan hatred of Cleon recklessly to approve of the shamelessness that characterized the sausage seller's original refutation of Cleon and to become, like Cleon, genuinely savage (399–407, 421, 427–28, 454–60). In deed and even (quite ridiculously) in speech, they declare worthless the very education in moderation that distinguishes them (333–34) and are lowered to what we see of them in the Corcyrean civil strife, in which words change their meaning and the pretense of their party to moderation is exposed as just that (Thucydides 3.82.6–8). The knights' vaunted education in moderation and divine law does not run very deep, and their belief in Zeus merely makes their own desire for vengeance more terrible. They prove to be, moreover, unmanly in their hope for salvation from the manly sausage seller (see 1300–15). And while they profess to be "noble" in their self-sacrificial deeds for the city (565–81), this appears to be pure artifice. The sausage seller, educated in neither their education nor that of the (sophisticated) Unjust Speech but in the agora, the streets, the school of hard knocks (185–90, 293–98, 411–14, 1236–44), proves to be their superior, in manliness and in knowledge of what the demos needs.

It thus becomes apparent that Aristophanes' desire for peace and for an end to the rule of the angry Cleon is not one with the knights, who not only lack a firm grasp of human nature in its division, but also are under the spell of Zeus. Aristophanic anger, whatever its provenance, is not informed by divine law. And it is only because of the impossibility of actually boiling down the demos that rule by the "moderate" knights appears to be a reasonable choice over rule by a Cleon. That is, it is no more than a second-best political order. The best order appears to require a return to the age of the Peisistratids. But both political orders clearly rely on the continued adherence to law, to "Zeus" or his Athena. Just how far Aristophanic anger is from the spirit animating the gentleman is made most clear in the *Wasps*.

Anger/Waspishness in the *Wasps*

The names of the play's main characters, Philocleon (Lover of Cleon) and his son Bdelycleon (Hater of Cleon), would seem to point to another political play about Cleon. And the members of the chorus of wasps are indeed followers of Cleon; they are piteously impoverished, and Cleon has been using for his own benefit their need to feed themselves and their families (230–59, 291–315; cf. *Knights* 50–51, 255, 797–804), which has required training them, as we will see, in political suspicion and anger. But we learn from the prologue that the play will not be another attack on Cleon (62–63), who never appears, even when his help is called for against Bdelycleon (197, 409). The play is instead about a private issue between the father and the son. The father, a malicious juryman who insists on going to court each day to condemn defendants without pity (88–135), turns out to be not a follower of Cleon, but someone whose natural disposition to inflict harm is merely fed by Cleon's calumnies and accusations. Philocleon is the harsh, irascible father of a nouveau riche son with pretentions to importance. He has no economic need to attend the court, yet no desire to share in the life of luxury offered by his son (508–11). He is driven to condemning by something else: on account of an oracle of Apollo delivered to him at Delphi, he is haunted by the fear that he will be killed by Zeus should he allow a defendant to escape him (158–60 with 278–80, 323–33).

Bdelycleon, who thinks little of this oracle's effect on his father, attempts to keep him home to enjoy himself and do no one harm (340–41, 504, 720). But he must first convince the wasps, who in their spirited defense of Philocleon persuade themselves that the son is plotting a conspiracy to end the courts and establish a tyranny, that he has no political intentions (403–507). And the wasps are captivated by Philocleon's description of the juryman's life as possessing a Zeus-like grandeur and power (512–641, especially 624–29). But Philocleon agrees that he would not continue to inflict harm as a juryman if it could be proven by his son to be foolish. And Bdelycleon easily shows him and the wasps that it is indeed foolish: far from helping the waspish jurors, men like Cleon are taking for themselves the lion's share of Athens' imperial wealth, rather than using it to pay jurors (650–733). As in the *Acharnians* and the *Knights*, this kind of appeal is fully effective upon the impoverished old wasps, who are deprived by it of their desire to sting; here, as in those two plays, the waspish members of the demos lose their anger with surprising ease. (They belong in particular with the second of the two types of Acharnian chorus members.) The wasps find perfectly reasonable Bdelycleon's offer to his father to provide comfort and pleasures for his father in exchange for the father's abandonment of jury service, especially because they see that the son intends no political change—which would be economically disastrous for them—but would merely stop his father from attending the courts.

But the passion of the "bee" (366) Philocleon to condemn defendants abides. Having heard his son's argument, he is indeed with fear and trembling moved to abandon his professed desire for the stately grandeur of jury service and even to condemning Cleon, whom he now regards as his enemy. Yet he does not abandon the desire to condemn defendants. In accordance with the oracle and the fear it evokes in him of Zeus' punishment, he is simply made utterly miserable by his new situation (696–97, 713–14, 740–42 with 750–63). Yet the chorus had spoken of the manifestation of the presence of a god who is offering to protect him and load him with benefits (734), and he therefore is able to accept his son's offer to forego jury service for the private pleasure of judging and condemning at home (764–98). His fear is further mollified when he recalls another oracle that reassures him that he does not transgress the original oracle by condemning defendants at home (799–804). His son then tricks him, however, into putting his vote at the domestic trial (of dogs) in the acquittal box (891–994). Philocleon faints upon hearing the verdict, deeply troubled in his conscience for acquitting an accused man, and begs the god's forgiveness rather than death (999–1002). Yet Philocleon's pious guilt—his guilty conscience—proves in the end to be no more than a fear of Zeus; it leaves him completely when he fails to suffer any bad consequence for his action (1122ff.). The awesome presence of a god, it seems, is felt by human beings when and only when fear moves them and it vanishes with that fear. It is only "fear" (of what Hobbes would call "powers invisible") that prevents men from acquiring without guilt those things to which nature would otherwise incline them.

Philocleon, much to his son's chagrin, subsequently pursues sensual pleasures with no loss of what turns out to be a natural maliciousness or dissatisfaction that attends his vigorous pursuit of Aphroditic pleasures. The life of the stately, dignified pleasures of the would-be gentleman proves to remain unattractive even to a Philocleon cured of his fear of Zeus. Bdelycleon thus succeeds only partially in curing Philocleon. Aristophanes' point in presenting us with this partial victory begins to become clear when we recall that Bdelycleon's claim to be up to the great task of completely curing his father and the wasps had been accompanied by the claim *not* to be a comic poet (650–51). Over and against what this professed non-comic poet believed, there prove to be limits to converting men waspish by nature to gentleness and compassion with the offer of a life of uppity refined pleasures. As for the comic poet himself, he closes the play with what the chorus announces as the unheard-of feat of a play's hero leading it away in a festive dance. And Aristophanes helps to ensure that we understand the meaning of this—his own final use of the (liberated but still malicious) Philocleon—by having his chorus claim, in the parabasis, that with a kind of Heraklean fury the poet had previously engaged the monster Cleon.[30] That is, unlike Bdelycleon, to whom his father's guilt was unintelligible, Aristophanes—who understands that guilt—is able to take on or use for his own ends a version of the malice of a Philocleon, of malice free of any religious component, of natural malice or anger. He turns to comic use—to a genuinely high end—a version of the anger that, as his chorus also indicates, he considers to be necessary for the city's defense against foreign enemies but to spill over regretfully—in a manner that needs his correction—into the judicial function of citizens.[31]

Aristophanes no less than Thucydides discloses in his plays the possibility of making human beings gentler by appealing to some of his readers to acknowledge the superiority of that side of our (split) nature that seeks what seems to be beneficial for ourselves, especially the pleasures of Aphrodite, over and against the spirited devotion to stateliness and law induced by fear of Zeus. But as genuinely free of anger as he turns out to be, Aristophanes also considers anger to be needed for the city's defense, while indicating that the demos is at its best when it is under the (admittedly mild or sexually lax) rule of ancestral law. The needs of the family, too, and its devotional loves have proven (in the *Clouds*) to be generative of a deep opposition to liberation from Zeus. How far and how widely he considers it possible and desirable to dispel the fear of Zeus, and hence anger, is made clear in a number of plays, including above all the *Plutos* and the *Birds*, and in his attention to the desire for other, more peaceful, golden, festive gods with whom his work abounds.

Notes

1. I wish to thank Fred Baumann, Devin Stauffer, and Stuart Witt for their comments on an earlier draft of this essay, which is the first of a three-part study. The second and third parts, on Nicias in Thucydides and in Aristophanes, appear in the journal *Polis* 29 (no. 2, 2012) and 30 (no. 1, 2013). References to Aristophanes' plays are by line numbers. Parenthetical references to Thucydides' text are in the standard notation of book, chapter, and line. All translations from the Greek are my own.

2. Leo Strauss, in *Socrates and Aristophanes* (New York: Basic Books, 1966), examines the plays with this principle in mind (see especially 50–52). What Strauss achieves in this book is altogether remarkable. He carries the attentive reader on a relentless, carefully worded investigation of the serious, non-comical teaching of Aristophanes, bringing to bear enormous learning with deft and subtle references that imitate the poet himself and so only unobtrusively disclose the full argument that Aristophanes makes through the corpus of his extant plays. My interpretation owes an enormous debt to his pathbreaking work. Errors are of course my own.

3. *Clouds* 518–62; cf. *Wasps* 1049, and consider also *Acharnians* 496–501. In the parabasis of the *Clouds*, Aristophanes, by referring to the play's failure to win the prize when it was performed, makes clear that he has reworked the play—that it was not simply intended as an ephemeral dramatic performance.

4. We learn of the attack on Aristophanes from the poet himself (*Acharnians* 377–82, 502–3). The claim concerning Cleon as the author of Thucydides' banishment is made by Plutarch, *On The Malice of Herodotos*, and repeated by Marcellinus, *Life of Thucydides*, sec. 46. See Timothy Burns, "Marcellinus' Life of

Thucydides, Translated, with an Introductory Essay," *Interpretation: A Journal of Political Philosophy* 38 (no. 1, 2010): 21.

5. Aristophanes presents the dead Cleon as even a leader of the rabble in Hades; he is called to the assistance of angry, low-class hostesses in Hades, though he never shows up (*Frogs* 569–78ff.).

6. See 4.65 and cf. 4.108.2–6. Brasidas' victories have a similar effect on the Peloponnesians, but in his case, the victories have been attributed to "Athena" (see 4.116, 5.10.2), and the fate of the two men (5.11.1, 5.16–17) corresponds to this different attribution of credit for their victories. Compare *Knights* 1166–90 and 1202–3, and see the discussion below.

7. 4.34.1–2; compare *Peace* 233–90.

8. See the striking parallel of this judgment of Cleon at *Knights* 792–804.

9. Cf. Aristotle, *Nicomachean Ethics*, 1126a13–15.

10. 4.37.4–7. Cf. Hobbes, *Leviathan*, ed. C. B. Macpherson (Baltimore: Penguin, 1968), chap. 17, 225–26.

11. The Mytilenaians would thus meet all of the usual criteria of the post-Furman statutes for jurors deciding on the death penalty. Cf. Walter Berns, *For Capital Punishment* (New York: Basic Books, 1979), 181–82.

12. cf. 4.65, 4.108, 8.24.4–5 and 40.2. See also Jacqueline De Romilly, *Thucydides and Athenian Imperialism*, trans. Philip Thody (Oxford: Basil Blackwell, 1963), 322–27.

13. See Christopher Bruell, "Thucydides and Perikles," *St. John's Review* 82 (no. 3, 1981): 24–29; Christopher Bruell, "Thucydides' View of Athenian Imperialism," *American Political Science Review* 68 (1974): 11–17; David Bolotin, "Thucydides," in *History of Political Philosophy*, eds. Leo Strauss and Joseph Cropsey, 3rd ed. (Chicago: University of Chicago Press, 1986), 7–34; Clifford Orwin, *The Humanity of Thucydides* (Princeton, NJ: Princeton University Press, 1994).

14. Thucydides' low opinion of Cleon has been observed and speculated on at least as far back as Marcellinus' *Vita*. The one scholar whose opinion of Cleon is high, and who sees Thucydides as sharing that high opinion, is Laurie M. Johnson, *Thucydides, Hobbes, and the Interpretation of Realism* (DeKalb: Northern Illinois University Press, 1993).

15. Thucydides is of course not alone in exposing the illusions that attend anger. It is true that both Aristotle and Plato present the angry man as such, concerned above all with punishing wrongdoers in a manly defense of just citizens, as possessing the virtue that makes him worthy of leading or ruling others (Plato, *Laws*, 730d5–7; Aristotle, *Nicomachean Ethics*, 1109b17–19, 1126b2–3; cf. Xenophon, *Oeconomicus*, 11.22; 12–13). Yet classical thought in general had grave reservations about the ability of anger and of angry men to direct human beings to what is best for them. Consider Aristotle, *Nicomachean Ethics*, 1110b25–28, 1111a6 and a16–20, 1114a31–b12, 1115a2; Plato, *Laws*, 860d–862c; and see Thomas L. Pangle, "The Political Psychology of Religion in Plato's *Laws*," *American Political Science Review* 70 (1976): 1062–65.

16. Compare Thucydides' praise of Themistocles, 1.138.3.

17. Cf. Clifford Orwin, "Democracy and Distrust, A Lesson from Thucydides," *The American Scholar* 53 (Summer 1984): 318–20.

18. 43.1.5; 44.2–4. Cf. Aristotle, *Rhetoric*, 1358b1–20; Thomas Aquinas, *S.T.* II–II qu.107 a 6 ad. 3.

19. Diodotos' not appealing to compassion is striking, and not only in light of Cleon's indication that he expects such an appeal. Consider, for example, Nicolaüs calling for mercy and compassion for the Athenian captives in Syracuse: Diodorus Siculus XIII 19.6–28.1.

20. Cf. Clifford Orwin, "The Just and the Advantageous in Thucydides: The Case of the Mytilenaian Debate," *American Political Science Review* 78 (no. 2, 1984): 485–94, and *The Humanity of Thucydides*, 142–62.

21. As Thucydides tells us (3.1), the Athenians' first reaction was in fact a refusal to accept the revolt of their major ally. Had the Athenians acted more promptly, they would not even have had to fight (3.3.5–3.4.1). As goes without saying, the Spartans were likewise soft or cowardly in coming to the aid of Mytilene, where quick action would have yielded great opportunities either to obtain Mytilene and/or force other revolts (cf. 3.13, 3.16).

22. In 3.45, Diodotos points to a time before there was law, to a time when necessity, the ground of the possible and impossible, was less obscured by hope in just laws, and hence to a time when there was less vengeance or greater mildness (cf. 1.9.2, 2.102.5). Similarly, Diodotos, as opposed to Cleon, refers to the daring that the compulsion of poverty induces (3.45.4; cf. 1.2.2, and contrast Cleon's hopeful account at 39.4). It was in fact the compulsion of hunger that was behind the capitulation of Mytilene (3.27), a fact that Diodotos must cover over in order to elicit Athenian sympathy for the free and just act of the Mytilenaian demos (3.47.3). Law or justice denies and hides, or blinds us to the truth by denying or hiding, compulsion.

23. Cleon's four references to necessity (3.39.2, 39.7, 40.3, 40.6) uphold rather than question this freedom.

24. In this respect, the Cleons come into their own during civil strife (3.82.5, 83.3).

25. In making their more famous argument about compulsion, the Athenians at Melos speak only of cities. The closest they come to speaking of individuals is in their distinction between the two classes in the city, the few and the many, and here they assume as a matter of course that the few leaders (whom they address) need no deceits.

26. Thucydides suggests that human beings cling to stories or speeches that promise some kind of immortality or life without evils to all who prove themselves worthy of it. These are the (poetic) products of the soul-in-rebellion-against-death. While Pericles appears to believe that he and his fellow Athenians are no longer in need of such poetic stories (2.41.4), Thucydides suggests otherwise. He characterizes Pericles' final speech, in which he re-exhorts the Athenians to pursue glory and discloses to them the boundless character of their empire, as an attempt to "divert their minds from their present ills" (2.65). The Athenians own half the

world already; their eternal glory will redeem the misery and death they have suffered from the plague. But Pericles himself had described the function of religious "festivals" to be a diverting of the mind from sadness (2.38.1). Glory, like religious festivals, offers something beyond everyday cares of ordinary life, a good beyond the goods that require such care. The whole funeral oration, we may say, depends on an obscuring of the individual deaths of each citizen, a forgetting of their deaths, by making those deaths meaningful as service to a noble cause. The deaths of each become deaths in common, and each is offered the prospect of ageless glory as part of the commonly beloved city (2.43.2) The glorious power of Athens hides the annihilation of each particular citizen from himself by fostering hopes in an ageless glory. Even Pericles' own individual death is, it seems, obscured from him by the prospect of the everlasting glory that will come from leading a city with everlasting memorials of good and evil.

27. 835. The Greek word is *choiros*, which means both "little pigs" and "female genitalia." A modern equivalent that captures the extended pun (and pretense) of the scene would be "pussies."

28. *Clouds* 518–36. Aristophanes admits that he had his first "children"—composed and produced his first plays—while he was still legally a virgin. At *Frogs* 53–59, Dionysos' mention of his longing (*pothos*—for Euripides) causes Herakles to assume that he means a sexual longing. Dionysos explains that, no, his longing is like a sudden eros for soup, and the notoriously voracious Herakles (see, e.g., *Frogs* 549–60, *Birds* 1577–1639, *Wasps* 60) understands immediately (*Frogs* 60–66).

29. *Symposium* 190b4–191a4. For this reading of Aristophanes' speech, I am indebted to Daniel Burns, "Aristophanes' Speech in Plato's *Symposium*," paper presented at the Northeast Political Science Association Annual Meeting, Philadelphia, Pennsylvania, November 19, 2009. On Dikaiopolis' "splitting" of his opponents, see Strauss, *Socrates and Aristophanes*, 66 with 234.

30. *Wasps* 1030–51, and see *Acharnians* 319–27 with 645–58. The chorus of the Acharnians defends Aristophanes from the calumny of Cleon with the claim that he has combatted the boastfulness and susceptibility to flattery of Athenians; he turns anger or indignation into something comical, and can do so because it is, or is ever on the verge of being, boastful. He thereby teaches justice.

31. See *Wasps* 1075–1121, and cf. *Acharnians* 346–61. Aristophanes' adopted, purged anger is close to but a bit stronger than the Socratic impatience with stupidity: see Strauss, *Socrates and Aristophanes*, 313 and note 4.

12

The Comedy of the Just City
Aristophanes' *Assemblywomen* and Plato's *Republic*

Peter Nichols

I. Introduction

It seems reasonable to read Book V of the *Republic* (*Politeia*), in part, as responding to Aristophanes' *Assemblywomen* (*Ecclesiazusae*).[1] Upon that premise, the writings taken together would evince Plato's debt to Aristophanes. These observations, of course, offend the body of scholarship that denies a connection between the works or even suggests that the *Republic* came first.[2] We, nonetheless, rely upon the consensus of learned authorities, establishing the earlier publication of Aristophanes' comedy and the unmistakable allusions to it in the text of the dialogue. Though Plato modified or perhaps even improved Aristophanes' argument, his treatment of what seems so nearly the same dramatic topic still would demonstrate how seriously he took the comic poet. The relationship between the authors is palpable in other Platonic dialogues. In the *Apology* (18a–e), Socrates mentions Aristophanes' *Clouds*, attributing to its influence the "first false charges"—the accusations that had been circulating informally for years before his trial. The comic depiction of Socrates apparently was so influential as to require a response. In the *Symposium* (212e), Plato allows the character of Aristophanes to make his speech in praise of Eros. He then circumvents any Socratic refutation of his argument (such as that visited upon Agathon) by the boisterous entrance of Alcibiades, just as Aristophanes is about to address Socrates on the issues between them. The *Republic* in its entirety seems to

259

be at least in part a response to the portrayal of Socrates in the *Clouds*.[3] But it is the plot of the *Assemblywomen* and the argument of the *Republic* in Book V that represent the most striking similarity between works by the two authors. In both, there is a scheme to devise a perfect city—one altogether just and harmonious. Each scheme entails abolition of private property throughout the city, or at least in its ruling part, as well as the elimination of the family and private life. Each "perfect city" regulates the coming together of men and women. In both works, the political ascendancy of women is contemplated, though more emphatically in Aristophanes' play, where he makes a young housewife the protagonist. The result in each case is a "new world order" that is at once comical and chilling. This is especially so because the modern world has witnessed revolutions leading to "social experiments"—the French Directory, communism, fascism—not as literary contrivances but in reality.

Of course, none of the foregoing implies that Plato merely adapted Aristophanes' idea, and Book V is but one section of the *Republic*. We merely observe that the authors treat a similar theme in two literary forms, and so are connected, for all that separates them. The comparative analysis undertaken here must necessarily comprehend the difference between those forms as vehicles of wisdom. It must extend to the issue of poetry (or drama) and philosophy, so famously addressed in Book X of the *Republic*.

II. Praxagora's Design

The *Assemblywomen* tells of a woman's plan to revolutionize society. The opening soliloquy, in which Praxagora addresses her lamp, seems to convey that this comic design must be promulgated by women. It is Praxagora's plan, to be executed by the wives of Athens. It is not that the scheme directly concerns the sexual relations between the women and their husbands, as in the *Lysistrata*, or the poetic portrayal of women per se, as in the *Thesmophoriazusae*. Rather, Praxagora's plan is inherently feminine, first of all, because of its objective. The idea is to make of the city a public embodiment of the domain in which the women have previously held sway: the household. The objective, in that sense, is to feminize the city. Socialism, it seems, represents an ascendancy of the feminine aspect of humanity.[4] Socialism—the satisfaction from the common fund of all material wants and the relegation of every citizen to the status of public charge—denudes the manly impulse to fend for oneself, lead the family, and earn a living. It will not be a matter of women merely stepping into the men's roles, of being the same sort of public officials that their husbands were, of conceiving the city's purpose as they conceived it. War and foreign policy, for example, are not mentioned by Praxagora, except that the follies of the men in that regard will end.

The one instance in which the women are forced simply to emulate the men is in accomplishing the peaceful revolution itself. The surreptitious packing of the Assembly briefly commits the conspirators to a specifically male function (by the lights of their society). They have to emulate men physically and rhetorically to do this. But the planning itself, beginning with Praxagora's soliloquy, reflects what the women esteem as their virtues. Praxagora admits her lamp to the planning conference because it has silently witnessed their private lives, including their ordinary deceptions. Instead of siphoning off the wine when their husbands are not looking, the women will siphon off the men's political power. In Praxagora's rehearsed speech, moreover, the deceptive domestic practices of the women are incorporated into the list of their credentials for governance—those practices embody feminine virtue. Their consistency in practicing trivial machinations accompanies their adherence to household routine. According to Praxagora, women are better suited to rule than men because of their conservatism. That is, they maintain all of their customs and proclivities—dying wool, sitting down to roast meat, carrying things on their heads, holding the Thesmophoria Festival, committing adultery, buying themselves presents, and drinking their wine neat. They eschew innovation. They will not repeat the debacles of the men, debacles that spring from impetuosity. Every new idea rashly adapted turns out badly. The list of male foibles begins with paying citizens for attendance at the Assembly, which guarantees a mercenary rather than a civic-minded motive for attendance. Then came all of the frenetic and contradictory foreign policy decisions, those that perpetuated Athens' decline after its defeat at the hands of the Spartans. Besides consistency, the women, as wives and mothers, will be most devoted to the well-being of the soldiers, including, first and foremost, their nutrition. The women excel their husbands in business sense as well. They know every cunning artifice by which money is acquired, and so are hard to cheat.[5]

Now it must be added that Praxagora herself, in hatching the plot, is more innovative, radical, and unpredictable than any man. She uses the argument that women are conservative and inclined to do what they have always done to effect a revolution, albeit a peaceful one. When she is through, women will do what they have never done—rule the entire city, which means rule over the men. Praxagora, as befits her name, introduces (in Machiavellian terms) a "new order and mode." In the course of rehearsing the presentation to be made in the Assembly, Praxagora actually upbraids her subordinates (she treats them as such) for doing precisely that which she praises. The women have always sworn by female deities—goddesses—and continue to do so, much to the displeasure of Praxagora, who is training them to impersonate men. They have always combed wool and propose to continue doing it during the Assembly session. They have always imbibed and expect to do that at the session as well. Praxagora does not react well to this failure to comprehend the newness of the situation and the necessity of changing rather than maintaining female behavior.[6] She is not really such an admirer of the feminine propensity to follow the same customs and ways. Nor is Praxagora's outlook circumscribed by the mundane and practical. Praxagora, like the makers of modern social revolutions, has a certain theoretical bent. She plans a new society on the basis of how she calculates human beings will behave, given the proper new set of incentives or disincentives, or because she deems a certain new law regulating relations between the sexes democratic. The policy innovations of the men that she denounces—making an alliance against Sparta, declining an opportunity to make peace, dispensing with the services of Thrasybulus—seem incidental compared to her enterprise. It envisages the complete and immediate transformation of the city—the effective creation overnight of a new city. In the conceit of the drama, furthermore, the transformation actually is carried out rather than merely contemplated in speech, as in the *Republic*.

Aristophanes' assessment of his society and particularly the state of its public affairs we discern from the ease with which Praxagora's scheme is accomplished. It is not the French or Russian Revolution—no force is required. There is no explicit indication that violence is necessary to preserve the new regime or to prevent a subsequent election reversing the change, though there are perhaps intimations of that in the play's later scenes. The men, so far as Praxagora's legislative gambit is concerned, are completely supine. Our first glimpse of Athenian manhood is Praxagora's husband, an older fellow wearing his wife's nightgown, squatting in the alley, and discussing his constipation with sympathetic neighbors. At the moment when his wife is legislating the birth of a new world, he is "giving birth" in the least exalted sense conceivable.[7] He and his friend—another husband who lives next door—are clueless. So is Chremes, who comes running breathlessly from the Assembly to tell of the historic vote. None of the men in the Assembly, according to Chremes' account, had any idea that women were present in the Assembly or that one was addressing them. Two men (authentic members of the sex) did address the Assembly before Praxagora. The topic of the day was how to save the city. The first man to speak,

Neocleides, had impaired vision (a problem figuratively shared by all of the men) and was hooted down before he could say anything. The next speaker, Eudaeon, actually suggested a form of socialism: the compulsory distribution by the clothiers of cloaks in the winter and accommodations for the homeless at the furriers. Blepyrus concurs in this proposal and adds his wish that merchants be forced to distribute free barley to the poor. Chremes heard everything, but didn't actually participate in the business of the Assembly because he was late. This tardiness also denied him remuneration for attendance. That appears to have at least figured in his reason for going, as reflected in his exchange with Blepyrus at 380–81. The citizens of this participatory democracy are singularly unsuited to self-governance and ripe for the dependent existence that Praxagora has in mind for them. They are not especially manly men. They are much the same demos that in the *Knights* acquires virtue only after being boiled in a pot.

Describing Praxagora in the Assembly and ignorant of her identity, Chremes likens her to Nicias (the pious, moral, and gentle personage portrayed by Thucydides). Praxagora's argument in the Assembly, as related by Chremes, actually differs from the practiced version. The version given in the Assembly does not include the women's conservatism—their tendency to do things the same way without innovation. There is no mention of their being the mothers of soldiers. Instead, when Praxagora rose before the Assembly, says Chremes, she extolled female intelligence, discretion, and honesty. Women keep secrets (specifically those of their festivals) and conduct their business dealings in private, without the formalities of the law but with scrupulous honesty. They have none of the public vices of the men, either—they are neither informers nor conspirators against the democracy. Of course, this utterance occurs as part of a successful conspiracy to overthrow and supplant the existing regime. The details of Praxagora's new city are imparted first indirectly by Chremes and interpreted by Blepyrus. The women have been given all of the men's roles. Blepyrus immediately places this in a domestic context. His wife will have to get up and go to work in the morning while he will inherit the status of housewife. She also will now have the male role in sexual relations. The initiative will be hers, and Blepyrus wonders if, at his advanced age, he will be able to comply with her demands. That is the significance of what has occurred in the apprehension of the new "First Man" of Athens.

Praxagora's arrival, ostensibly from assisting a girlfriend in childbirth, marks the effective commencement of her rule. She has, in reality, midwifed the birth of a regime, though she feigns ignorance that anything has changed. She acts as though her paramount concern is disabusing Blepyrus of the notion that she was with a lover. The fictitious baby, Praxagora says, was masculine. Does she see the new regime as in some sense masculine? She sees herself that way, inasmuch as she continues to swear by gods rather than by goddesses (631). When she "learns" of the Assembly's revolution, Praxagora proceeds from acting surprised to expounding upon the wisdom of the new circumstance. This is the third instance in which she articulates the superiority of women. The regime of the women will be upright and honest—no more of the feigned evidence, informing, and other iniquitous behavior that characterized the society dominated by men. Furthermore, all social ills will be abolished, beginning with poverty. Street crime, aggressive collection practices, and slander (presumably for money) will vanish.

Spurred on by the chorus, Praxagora once again delivers an oration in defense of her innovation. The chorus exhorts her to prepare something new, in the name of successful comedy, not social progress. Audiences warm to the new. Praxagora hopes that the audience of male characters onstage will be open to new ideas, for she has a few to impart. And she will brook no interruptions or contradictions until she has finished. Socialism is the new way—everyone must share equally in the world's goods, and none may be rich while others are poor. All property—land and monetary wealth—will be placed in a common fund, to which everyone will be required to contribute one hundred percent of their worth. The women will manage this common fund with the same practical wisdom that they have employed in the management of their own households. Praxagora is confident of the citizens' compliance with her communitarian edict. All citizens surely will relinquish their private property because they now will have no need of it. Everyone will own everything—the socialist contention that became so familiar in the twentieth century—so of what use is private wealth?

Blepyrus' thoughts (once again) turn to the erotic desires—money can buy their object. Wouldn't that be an incentive to retain private funds? But now Praxagora unveils the most astounding aspect of her plan—the communism of women and children. A man can have a woman he desires without payment or courtship. The only legal limitation on his promiscuity is the provision that he have intercourse with an unattractive woman before he enjoys the pretty one. By the same token, the fair young maiden must service an ugly man (quite possibly an old one) before the handsome one she desires. This idea is defended before the incredulous Blepyrus as democratic (*dēmotikē ge hē nōmè*) (631). This will abolish not only the natural distinction between attractive and ugly, but also the class divisions that have at times affected amorous relations. The affluent playboy no longer will have an advantage over the common working stiff.[8]

Praxagora is one of two Aristophanic characters to defend his or her endeavors in the name of democracy. The other is Euripides in the *Frogs*, who, like Praxagora, swears by Apollo (a god associated with law) when so holding forth (952).[9] The character of the dead tragedian, speaking in Hades, proudly recounts bringing women (and, it seems, their erotic desires) to the fore. He made the formerly private female beings public, as does Praxagora in her sense. Euripides' reward for this artistic venture is to be condemned to death by the women in the *Thesmophoriazusae*—they prefer to remain private.[10] No punishment is visited upon Praxagora other than imminent failure, suggested by the encounter between Chremes and the Citizen.

We then come to the subject of children. They also will be held in common—the ordinary connection with biological parents will be obscured. No child will know who in the older generation begat him. He will regard every male member of that generation as his father. He will now be deterred from the inclination toward father beating by his putative siblings, who will object to the beating of one who may be their biological father. Praxagora is the supremely confident social reformer—very much devoid of conservative restraint. The litigiousness of the Athenians, she affirms, will end with the private property. Once no one owns anything outright, there will be no debtor–creditor relationships and no resulting lawsuits. Theft itself will be a thing of the past. Everyone will be the owner of everything and will be able to replace anything taken from him out of the common store. Punishment for any misbehavior that does occur will consist in withholding the wrongdoer's ration from that same public till. Gambling also will cease, as there is no point in trying to win your own money. The law courts will be converted to dining halls, and the women will cook for the men and weave their clothes, as before. All walls separating houses will be obliterated and the whole city converted to one giant communal household. The lists formerly used to select jurors will now be used to summon different groups of citizens to dinner. There will be enough for all, Praxagora assures her credulous husband, and after dinner the sated throng will proceed to the fulfillment of their amorous desires, according to the "affirmative action" plan. This will permit closing the brothels, because no one need pay for sex and the ladies of the night need not sell themselves. They can act like free women. Slaves may sleep with slaves, says Praxagora, and they also will harvest the crops. The new egalitarian order still does not include them.

Our first and only glimpse of the workings of the socialist economic scheme occurs before the house of Blepyrus' friend Chremes. As a dutiful subject of the new regime, he is preparing to contribute his possessions to the city. He is accosted by a character identified only as *polites* ("Citizen"). The Citizen is astonished by Chremes' abject obedience and not a little disdainful. Like one of the peasant farmers annihilated by the Bolsheviks in the early days of the Soviet Union, the Citizen sees no reason why he should surrender the property for which he has labored simply because the new government so decrees. He requires some further explanation before he does anything so rash. The Citizen would appear to be the only intelligent male character presented by Aristophanes in the play, though he remains comic because of his dishonesty. To Chremes, blind obedience seems perfectly reasonable. He is certain that everyone else will comply. Chremes is only afraid that if he does not hurry, there will be no reason for his contribution. This concern elicits a guffaw from the Citizen. The state will have room for Chremes' property, all right, wherever he brings it. The Citizen is not so sure that very many Athenians actually will turn in their things. They are always passing resolutions and then refusing to follow them. He makes much the same criticism of Athenian men as Praxagora. There are examples adduced: the law authorizing copper coins, in reliance upon which Chremes sold his grapes for the coins, only to have the law changed to require silver at the last minute. The same sort of thing occurred when a tax was enacted that was supposed to raise millions. Only a fool relies upon his compatriots to comply with every legislated innovation that comes along. There is also a glint of the role that force must play in inducing obedience to laws such as Praxagora's. In response to the Citizen's prodding, Chremes says that if the other citizens refuse to turn in their property, those who do will fight them (unless they prove too strong). This is the clearest suggestion of violence that is appropriate to comedy, but the methods by which socialism is enforced upon unwilling populations are more familiar to us today than they were in Aristophanes' time (not that he understood any less what would be involved).[11]

The acrimonious colloquy between Chremes and the Citizen is interrupted by the Town Crier, announcing in essence that dinner is served. Now, this is an edict with which the Citizen is prepared to comply. Chremes suddenly is made to feel very much a fool, as one who has not made the lawful contribution to the community races ahead to grab the benefits. In a parody of the Citizen's interrogation of him, Chremes demands to know what the Citizen will do if he is found out in his contrivance. Learning that the Citizen is utterly shameless and undeterred by the threat of legal sanction, Chremes hurries to turn in his property. He declines the Citizen's offer to help him with it out of a most reasonable fear that the Citizen would claim to be turning in his own property. The scene, in fact, closes with the Citizen exclaiming that he has a plan, which is never disclosed, to reap the benefits of the new system without forfeiting his property. Praxagora did not reckon on the aspect of human nature so well illuminated in the exchange between Chremes and the Citizen. Like all social planners of her ilk, Praxagora ignores and underestimates the human desire to keep what is one's own. She determines that private wealth is wisely sacrificed and expects others to submit to the decision.

The consequences of the sexual "affirmative action" law are laid bare, so to speak, in the next scene. The hags vie with the fair young girl, intruding upon the natural affinity of the young for the young. The newfound happiness of the old and ugly is the enemy of the youthful and lovely. And as with the economic plan, force is required to obtain compliance. Here, the element of coercion is brought forward explicitly, as the hags make a wishbone out of the young man, pulling him in different directions. The hideously unromantic character of the scene is heightened by the hags' citation of law to justify what is essentially a rape.

The play closes with a scene in the house of Blepyrus and Praxagora, which still exists, along with their marriage.[12] The new law has not taken effect. The maid encourages Blepyrus to go to the dining hall to partake—he, it seems, is the only man in Athens who still has his dinner to anticipate. He, in turn, invites the audience and judges to accompany him. The chorus, not for the first time, implores the judges to award the play first prize because of the novelty of the work and the fun it has provided. Even if it appears that Praxagora will not succeed, her male creator still can.

III. The Platonic Adaption of Praxagora's Design

Book V is the most sustained and memorable comic episode in Plato's *Republic*. Elsewhere in the work, certainly, Socrates says outlandish things, not believing them, we suppose, but uttering them for some purpose in the drama.[13] It is in Book V, nonetheless, that Socrates envisions the notorious and fantastic society, thought by many in our time to be a prototype for modern totalitarianism.[14] Emphasizing the radical quality of his proposals, Socrates calls each of them a "wave" (*kuma*). This word also means "foetus"—Socrates, like Praxagora, presides over the birth of a new regime.[15] He likens his predicament, and that of his interlocutors, to floating in the sea—they are compelled to swim and to withstand the three great waves. These are, respectively, the equal opportunity afforded women to perform any role for which they are qualified, the communal sharing of women (really spouses of both sexes) and children, accompanied by a eugenics program and the kingly rule by a philosopher. The entire plan in the *Republic* is proposed by a man, who occasionally swears by goddesses (e.g., *Gorgias* 449d5) much as the scheme in the *Assemblywomen* is contrived by a woman who swears by gods (even after her male imposture is over). The obliteration of the family that constitutes the second wave is in furtherance of strict meritocracy, the essence of justice in Socrates' discourse. The same rationale and moral objective demand that individual capacities be employed regardless of sex. Hence, women shall be soldiers, generals, and rulers when they are qualified. Socrates and his young friends make this provision even while acknowledging that, empirically, not many women will be qualified for the top rank (455c–d). Not content with allowing equality of opportunity (or, as we say, "gender neutrality") in hiring, Socrates extends the reform to having men and women wrestle nude as part of their physical training. It is here that Socrates makes reference to jokes and laughter, not unreasonably anticipating that coeducational naked wrestling would be viewed with humor. Socrates' observation that the "women guardians must strip, since they'll clothe themselves in virtue instead of robes," and must wrestle with men similarly attired, virtue preventing the exercise from becoming a sex orgy, will be unlikely to staunch the laughter (457a). Perhaps even less a protection against derision is Socrates' attempt to equate the differences between men and women with those distinguishing a bald from a long-haired man (454c). There is the further provision that women not only partake in combat but actually bring their infant children onto the battlefield with them (467a). This last notion, however, Socrates introduces as part of the "second wave," which bears the greatest resemblance to Praxagora's regime.

The communism of property, women, and children in the *Republic* is part of the perfect justice of Socrates' new city. In it, virtue and aptitude alone determine each citizen's position. The family must be abolished, because it entails the arbitrary ties of blood and the attendant prejudice in favor of loved ones. We benefit our children, parents, siblings, and spouses not out of objective assessment of their merit. It is in the furtherance of meritocracy that Socrates suggests a eugenics program by which the most gifted are to be bred with their like. The mating of the best men with the best women to produce the best offspring is to be facilitated by a "throng of lies and deceptions," including rigged lotteries. There is not a specific rule that the young must sleep with the old—indeed, the ages of procreation for both sexes will be strictly regulated. It is nonetheless apparent that the rigged lotteries will force people to sleep with those whom they find physically unappealing.

The similarities between Praxagora's account of her new regime at 583–709 and Socrates' of his at 458–466a have been elsewhere noted.[16] In both instances, the connection between biological parents and their children is severed—the children don't know their actual parents (*Republic* 461c–d, *Assemblywomen* 634–39). In a striking reprise of Praxagora's account, Socrates maintains that no one will abuse a member of the older generation, because that older person could be his parent and because another member of the younger generation, considering the possibility that the victim is his parent, might intervene (*Republic* 465, *Assemblywomen* 636–37). Praxagora and Socrates each asserts that with private property abolished and everything shared in common, there will be no crime and no lawsuits (*Republic* 464a–e, *Assemblywomen* 640 et seq.).

Certainly, the idea of the *Assemblywomen* is continued and taken up in Book V of Plato's dialogue. Socrates refers to the first two "waves" as the "female [drama]," succeeding the "male drama" (451c). Praxagora's plan is, however, radically transformed. The most portentous aspect in Socrates' revision of Praxagora's scheme is the "third wave"—the rule of philosophy. It is an implication of political justice as now defined: everyone occupying the position to which he or she is suited. The philosopher is the only person, by that standard, who is qualified to rule. He (or she) perceives the ideas, the categories of beings, including the virtues, comprising reality. He (or she) alone genuinely "sees" the world—that is, finds definitions of all the species of things, actions, and moral qualities, rather than merely reacting to the individual examples that life presents (473d *et seq.*). From the foregoing, it is apparent that democracy and its animating principle, political equality, have nothing to do with Socrates' regime. There are no ballots and the philosopher is king, not an elected prime minister. The city is founded in speech, and only in speech, on the basis of the founders' reasoning, not the consent of the governed. Quite apart from the argument of Book V and the continual theme of philosophy after that, democracy is taken up and ranked unfavorably in Book VIII. It is worse than timocracy and oligarchy and superior only to tyranny (557a–565c). It is a regime in which virtue is set aside in favor of equality. Students have no awe of teachers, nor children of parents. The veneration of commonality dismisses all distinction between admirable and shameful and implies an indifference to moderation of physical pleasure. Democratic man, moreover, is susceptible to tyranny when offered material benefits in exchange for liberty.

Praxagora is a self-professed democrat. That is the basis upon which she introduces the "equal access to sex plan." And her ascent to power does result from a democratic vote in the Assembly, if one leavened by fraud. There is, of course, a question of whether Praxagora's democratic devotion will survive her own assumption of power. Will the Assembly ever again be convened, now that the new regime has taken hold? Praxagora stipulates that there will be no need for law courts, because censorious conduct and pecuniary disputation will vanish. The society proposed by Socrates shares this characteristic—the absence of law courts (425b). What need would Praxagora have for additional laws or elections, either, since she claims to have brought the city to perfection by what she has done? In other words, does Aristophanes in the *Assemblywomen* show us the descent of a democracy into tyranny, albeit with comic mildness? Even if he does, the animating spirit expressed by Praxagora at the outset is the democratic principle of equality. Aristophanes has it lead to disaster.

Praxagora's egalitarianism is actually flawed by sexual privilege. Her design contemplates the role of women as the politically superior sex. It does so even as Praxagora herself, assuming the role of ruler, adopts such masculine characteristics as we have noted. Socrates' pure meritocracy is paradoxically more egalitarian—it leaves open the possibility of anyone ruling if he or she is qualified, regardless of sex or other status. The rule of pure reason excludes all distinctions of class, title, and family and is in that sense equalizing.[17] At the same time, its enforcement of every adjudged disparity in virtue is what makes Socrates' perfect regime antiegalitarian. The eugenics program perpetuates the disparity. It is indeed the mathematically predictable failure of this program that will cause the descent to inferior regimes (546a–c). Socrates does go into the foreign policy, and specifically the war-making policies, of the just city. While women will join the men on the battlefield, nothing is said about the traditional female role of homemaking. We know that separate homes are to be abolished, at least for the rulers and soldiers (auxiliaries).

IV. Aristophanes and Plato

If, then, Aristophanes and Plato agree on the folly of seeking perfect political justice, and on the unwisdom of democracy, what most deeply separates them? The ostensible means of achieving political justice in the *Republic* is allowing, or rather forcing, the philosopher to rule. It is observed that Socrates' philosopher is compelled by the city to rule in the same way that the young man is compelled to sleep with the hags at the end of the *Assemblywomen*.[18] In making the philosophic presentation of political utopianism, Socrates conjures a deeper version of such than Aristophanes. In the society of the *Republic*, wisdom is made to govern, and a wholly objective standard of virtue to be enforced. The manifestly intolerable character of the regime belies most fully the notion that "communism is a system that looks good on paper." Beyond this, the philosophic presentation of the utopia does not depict its undoing, or at least not its immediate undoing. The drama of the Platonic dialogue consists in the story of a conversation. Within the conversation, the perfectly just regime is described in speech. The example of a character actually implementing the plan and failing, or being about to fail, requires the complete drama of a play.

Aristophanes omits the presence of philosophy as the ruling authority of the city, perhaps because he proceeds from the conclusion that Socrates effectively adapts: the impossibility of marrying philosophy to power. The satire of the *Clouds* presents the philosopher as too imprudent, indiscreet, and unfamiliar with human nature even to get along in the world, let alone to rule. Instead, Aristophanes tells the story of a political plan to eradicate all of the ills of society by social engineering.[19] Looking back from our time, the plot has an eerie prescience, as we have intimated. Aristophanes elucidates the madness and tyranny attendant upon abolition of the private life and the affront to human nature associated with the abolition of private property. Millennia before Burke, Aristophanes shows the destructive error of theorization in politics. The apparent failure of Praxagora's enterprise suggests the necessity of limiting government so as to permit the private life to thrive, and the resulting human happiness. Perhaps it indicates the need for a greater public virtue and public spiritedness at the same time. It is, after all, the utter failure of male leadership that precedes the design of Praxagora.

The Platonic adoption and improvement of the *Assemblywomen* may be summarized as follows. Aristophanes illuminates the error of trying to achieve political perfection on the basis of two faulty premises: rank materialism and egalitarianism. Praxagora looks no higher than seeing to it that everyone enjoys equal food, shelter, and sexual opportunity. Plato takes the idea and applies it, changing the notion of political perfection to something more profound. Socrates' city is based on the full analysis of wisdom and human happiness. The absurdity of the scheme that results suggests that even the deepest notion of perfection, one that is anything but crass and materialistic, one that is scrupulously meritocratic, is not the basis for governance or social innovation. It is the basis, instead, for the most admirable individual. The philosopher is at the center of the philosophic quest for justice because the philosophic life, not any attainable political system, exemplifies justice. The philosophic life is, of necessity, the subject of philosophy. It is not a subject of tragic drama—the story of a man living the contemplative life, without inner conflict or worldly ambition.[20] It is evidently a subject for comic drama, as the *Clouds* so memorably demonstrates. But that is debunking philosophy and not, Plato urges us, showing its actual essence. To enunciate the truth of something requires knowledge of the forms—analysis and definition of the categories of being. On behalf of drama, it can be said that no generalization articulated philosophically will ever account for life's complexity, for all of its nuance and contradiction. Only the dramatic depiction of life can do that, the artistic replication of particular cases, particular examples. The Platonic dialogue emerges, in this context, as a kind of synthesis.[21] It is the drama of a philosopher, an actual character with a name, and shows him philosophizing. Hence we learn what philosophy says and we see what a philosopher does.

Aristophanes, we have said, demonstrates the folly of pursuing political perfection and of taking democratic folly for perfection. This leads ineluctably to the conclusion that people are better left to dwell in the imperfect but tolerable world of private prerogative interspersed with public duty. In itself, the *Assemblywomen* does not portray a superior human being. It might be said that the comedies as a whole suggest such an individual by ridiculing all of the failings that stand between man and his perfection. There is an old joke in which two friends are standing before Michelangelo's most famous statue. The more emotional friend exclaims, "How could a mere mortal have created such a thing?" The somewhat philistine friend replies, "It's really quite simple. You just get an enormous piece of white marble, take out a hammer and chisel, and knock away all of the parts that don't look like David." The exalted human being sculpted by Aristophanes' comic chisel would not be Praxagora or any character in the plays. They are all ridiculous, or they would not be Aristophanic characters. Obviously, that includes the hapless figure of the philosopher in the *Clouds*. It also includes Aristophanes himself as a comic character and the tragedians portrayed in the *Frogs*, although, according to the argument of that play, the hope of Athens' salvation lies in the legacy of its dead poets.

Notes

1. In general, I have used the translation of the *Assemblywomen* by David Barret (Middlesex: Penguin Books, [1978] 1982), making occasional reference to

the Oxford Classical Text. I have relied upon the Allan Bloom translation of the *Republic* (*infra*, note 3).

2. See the discussion in Holger Thesleff, "Platonic Chronology," *Phronesis* 34 (no. 1, 1989): 1–26. At 11–13, in particular, Thesleff affirms "some kind" of connection between the utopian scheme presented by Praxagora (esp. *Assemblywomen* 571ff.) and Plato's *Republic* (esp. Book V). He goes on to criticize "those who deny the possibility of Aristophanes' having Plato in mind." He does so, however, acknowledging that the publication date of the *Republic* followed that of the *Assemblywomen*. The reason for supposing that the influence went from Plato to Aristophanes is that "Plato had a distinct political philosophy before 388, long before the *Republic* received its final shape" and that "a comic parody is likely to exaggerate and disfigure to the point of sheer nonsense." These observations can hardly obscure the fact that the *Assemblywomen* was probably published not less than twelve years before the *Republic*—392 BC and 380–370 BC, respectively. *The Oxford Classical Dictionary*, 2nd ed. (Oxford: Oxford University Press, 1970), 113; Plato, *The Republic*, ed. Paul Shorey (Cambridge: Harvard University Press, [1930] 1994), xxv. Still less can they counterbalance Socrates' apparent adaptation of arguments from the *Assemblywomen*, his reference to the "female drama" (451c), and his repeated allusions to comedy. See Allan Bloom, "Response to Hall," *Political Theory* 5 (no. 3, 1977): 315–30. At 324 Bloom notes, "It [the fact that Socrates refers to the *Assemblywomen*] is too evident to need discussion, and only lack of attention or the desire to quibble can cause one to deny the relation." Furthermore, "[t]o support the denial one has to invent schools of thought the existence of which has no basis in historical fact, or to invert all probabilities based on dates as well as capriciously to neglect the text." In this category of commentator, Bloom presumably would place Helene P. Foley, "The 'Female Intruder' Reconsidered: Women in Aristophanes' *Lysistrata* and *Ecclesiazusae*," *Classical Philology* 77 (no. 1, 1982): 1–21. Though she affirms that, according to most scholars, the play precedes the dialogue, she insists that the authors had different thematic concerns (15–16). Similarly, R. G. Ussher, *Aristophanes: Ecclesiazusae* (Oxford: Oxford University Press, [1973] 1986), xvi–xviii, recognizes that Aristophanes' comedy came first and criticizes speculation that the order may have been reversed in much the same terms as Bloom. Ussher, nonetheless, insists that nothing Socrates says need have related to the *Assemblywomen*. See also Kenneth S. Rothwell, *Politics & Persuasion in Aristophanes' Ecclesiazusae* (Amsterdam: E. J. Brill, 1990), 9–10, to the same effect as Ussher.

3. Allan Bloom, ed. and trans., *The Republic of Plato* (New York: Basic Books, [1968] 1991), 307–8.

4. Cf. Nietzsche, *Twilight of the Idols*, "Skirmishes of an Untimely Man," sec. 38, in which "females" are included in the category of "democrats."

5. See Kenneth M. DeLuca, *Aristophanes' Male and Female Revolutions* (Lanham: Lexington Books, 2005), 87. "As Praxagora's presentation makes clear, women are most unlike Athens. Women are practical."

6. See Lauren K. Taaffe, *Aristophanes and Women* (London: Routledge, 1993), 110. Praxagora's "comments emphasize the fragility of an actor's disguise"

and that the women need to learn the "rules for behavior in the assembly" as well as for "behavior as an actor."

7. See Leo Strauss, *Socrates and Aristophanes* (Chicago: University of Chicago Press [1966] 1980), 266. Blepyrus is the only character in this comedy who swears by Dionysus, connecting him to Aristophanes. The comic poet himself is absurd.

8. In fact, the notion of affirmative action for the ugly finds serious expression in Daniel C. Hamermesh, "Ugly? You May Have a Case," *New York Times Sunday Review*, August 28, 2011.

9. See Peter Nichols, *Aristophanes' Novel Forms: The Political Role of Drama* (London: Minerva Press, 1998), 168.

10. Strauss, *Socrates and Aristophanes*, 269. Euripides brought out the women's foibles. Praxagora is actually opposed to him.

11. See Leo Strauss, *The Rebirth of Classical Political Rationalism*, ed. Thomas L. Pangle (Chicago: University of Chicago Press, 1989), 108.

12. See Strauss, *Socrates and Aristophanes*, 277. See also Niall W. Slater, "Waiting in the Wings: Aristophanes' 'Ecclesiazusae,'" *Arion* 3 (no. 5, 1977): 97–129, 117. "The old man . . . revels in the new state of things" under Praxagora's laws.

13. Attributing philosophic inclinations to a dog in persuading Polemarchus that the guardian must be properly educated as well as warlike (Book II) would be one example. See Bloom, *The Republic*, 350.

14. Most recently, conservative commentator Mark Levin in *Ameratopia* (New York: Threshold Editions, 2012), 23–26, commits this error. He thereby joins such a leftist academic as Richard Rorty, who makes at least a tentative reference to Plato as a "power freak." *Essays on Heidegger and Others*, vol. 2 (Cambridge: Cambridge University Press, [1991] 1997), 31.

15. Bloom, *The Republic*, 459n16.

16. E.g., Bloom, "Response," 324.

17. See Nietzsche, *Twilight of the Idols*, "The Problem of Socrates," secs. 5–7; *The Gay Science*, Book V, sec. 348. "Nothing is more democratic than logic; it is no respecter of persons. . . ." The rest of the sentence consists of a nasty physical reference to Jews.

18. Bloom, "Response," 327.

19. Cf. Martin Holtermann, *Der Deutsche Aristophanes* (Gottinger: Vandenhoeck & Ruprecht, [1999] 2004), 255–56. Certain intellectuals in Wilhelmian Germany recognized the relevance of the *Assemblywomen* to the fight against social democracy ("*für den Kampf gegen die Sozialdemokratie*").

20. Thus, even in Shakespeare's *Timon of Athens*, a tragedy, the character of Apemantus is presented comically, as a "churlish philosopher" (*dramatis personae*).

21. See Leo Strauss, *The City and Man* (Chicago: University of Chicago Press, 1964), 136–37.

13

Peisetairos of Aristophanes' *Birds* and the Erotic Tyrant of *Republic* IX

Matthew Meyer

In *Republic* X, Plato has Socrates refer to an ancient quarrel between philosophy and poetry (607b).[1] Although some have questioned the extent to which there actually was any sort of quarrel between philosophy and poetry prior to Plato, it is generally acknowledged that this quarrel runs throughout much of Plato's own works and the *Republic* itself.[2] Specifically, the quarrel seems to be at its height in what are often referred to as Plato's "middle dialogues": the *Phaedo*, *Symposium*, *Phaedrus*, and *Republic*. Although the defining feature of these dialogues is the introduction of and appeal to a rather simplistic theory of the Forms, another, less noted feature is that they all refer to Dionysus and the figures, festivals, and mysteries associated with the god.[3] Such references are important for understanding the ancient quarrel between philosophy and poetry because there are four poetic genres—tragedy, comedy, satyr-play, and dithyramb—that were performed at annual festivals in honor of Dionysus, and one can find in each of the aforementioned middle dialogues ideas, techniques, and structural features that Plato seems to have appropriated from each genre. Specifically, one finds dithyrambic elements in the *Phaedrus*, a kind of satyr-play in the *Symposium*, a full-blown philosophical tragedy in the *Phaedo* and, I would argue, a philosophical comedy in the *Republic*.[4] If this is right, then one can understand Socrates' claim at the end of the *Symposium* that an author should be capable of writing both tragedy and comedy as a reference to Plato's own poetic activity (223d).

Understanding the middle dialogues in this way certainly undermines any straightforward reading of Plato's participation in the ancient quarrel.[5] Simply stated, Plato cannot be opposed to all forms of poetry because he composes his own poetry. Nevertheless, one can argue, as I want to do, that Plato employs his poetic talents to attack the understanding of nature, life, and politics that he thinks the poets of his time, either implicitly or explicitly, espoused. The idea is that in each of the aforementioned works, Plato is consciously seeking to replace the vision of nature, life, and politics expressed in each of the poetic genres listed above with his own understanding of these matters. On this reading, the *Phaedo*, for instance, is Plato's tragedy in which Socrates qua tragic hero presents and dramatizes Plato's views about nature, the soul, and the afterlife that contrast sharply with the views of these matters that are either implicit or explicit in the tragedies performed in honor of Dionysus.

Although I cannot defend such claims within the scope of this chapter, they do provide a framework for the point that I want to pursue here. Specifically, I want to generate at least some evidence for thinking of the *Republic* as Plato's comic response to Old Comedy. On the one hand, this means that Plato himself is taking on the role of a comic poet by consciously borrowing and incorporating techniques from the genre as he defends the just life of the philosopher.[6] On the other hand, this means that Plato is consciously opposing the understanding of nature, life, and politics that is either implicit or explicit in the plays of a comic poet like Aristophanes. In this chapter, I focus my efforts on highlighting Plato's opposition to comedy rather than on the way in which he borrows from the genre, and I do so by arguing that Plato's portrayal of the erotic tyrant in *Republic* IX is modeled on the comic hero of Aristophanes' *Birds*, Peisetairos, and then use this point to argue that *Republic* IX should be read as a direct attack on the vision of the good life that the *Birds* seems to endorse.

There can be little doubt that Plato's portrayal of the erotic tyrant in *Republic* IX at least resembles the comic hero of the *Birds*. The fact that Peisetairos refers to himself as a tyrant while donning the wings of eros at the end of the play is enough to establish such a resemblance. However, showing that Plato's portrayal of the erotic tyrant in *Republic* IX resembles Peisetairos is not the same as the stronger claim that Plato's sketch of the erotic tyrant consciously draws from Aristophanes' portrayal of the hero of the *Birds* and therefore that Plato is attacking a vision of the good life put forth in at least one of Aristophanes' comedies. Although the lack of explicit references to Aristophanes and the *Birds* in the *Republic* makes it impossible to prove this stronger claim, I use the speech that Plato attributes to Aristophanes in the *Symposium* to bridge the gap between *Republic* IX and Aristophanes' *Birds* and so further substantiate my thesis. Specifically, I locate the tyrannical eros of *Republic* IX in Aristophanes' account of the hubristic behavior of the original circle-people in the *Symposium* and then, following Paul Ludwig,[7] link the latter account to the action and the main character of the *Birds*. What emerges from this analysis is that Plato is very much cognizant of an Aristophanic or poetic eros that resembles, in significant respects, the eros portrayed in *Republic* IX and that he consciously replaces, in works such as the *Republic*, *Phaedrus*, and the *Symposium*, this understanding of eros with the kind of eros that animates the philosopher. If this is right, then there is reason to read the opposition in the *Republic* between the erotic philosopher and the erotic tyrant as an opposition between Platonic philosophy and Aristophanic comedy, respectively, and therefore to think that the quarrel between philosophy and poetry is at its height in the opposition between these two figures, a fact already suggested by Plato's claim in the *Apology* that Aristophanes is Socrates' oldest and most serious accuser.

I. The Erotic Tyrant of *Republic* IX

The erotic tyrant of *Republic* IX is a curious figure, so much so that his appearance has left some commentators at a loss as to what to make of it.[8] As Julia Annas has noted, there seems to be little, if any, substantive connection between the portrayal of the tyrant in *Republic* IX and any tyrant that Plato might have encountered in his own life, such as Dionysius I of Syracuse. For Annas, the most curious feature of Plato's account is his attribution of erotic fantasies or, what she aptly calls, the "riot of the id" to the tyrant. As she notes, successful dictators like Lenin and Stalin often had very dull imaginations because of their narrow focus on political power. In the end, it seems as though Plato's portrait is designed, and unfairly so, to show how the inner corruption of the tyrant's soul makes him incapable of attaining and preserving the power that he so desperately craves.[9]

Despite such concerns, the fact that Plato's account of the degenerative regimes concludes with a depiction of the tyrant and a comparison of his life with the life of the philosopher comes as no surprise. This is because the theme of psychic and political tyranny runs throughout the *Republic* and appears in various guises at the beginning of the work.[10] For instance, the dialogue starts with Cephalus explaining the peace of old age as a liberation from the savage mastery of the sex drive (329b–d). Tyranny is present not only in *Republic* I as a drive that can master the individual psyche, but also as an individual capable of mastering an entire city. This occurs when Thrasymachus, who enters the conversation portrayed as a savage beast (336b),[11] lectures Socrates on the nature of the relationship between the ruler and the ruled. Specifically, rulers rule their subjects for their own advantage, just as a shepherd fattens his sheep for his own benefit. On this model, the most perfect ruler is the tyrant. Like a criminal, he takes away what belongs to others by stealth and force; however, he does so all at once and without punishment (344a).

In *Republic* I, there is no explicit mention of eros or an erotically charged tyrant. Again, sex is mentioned, and insofar as one equates eros with sexual lust, one can find both eros and tyranny at work in the opening portions of the text. However, there is reason for thinking of the kind of eros that animates the tyrant as something more than just sexual lust, and once one does, one can begin to make the case that eros is already at work in *Republic* I in the form of *pleonexia*, the very drive that animates Thrasymachus' tyrant (344a). This is because the straightforward translation of *pleonexia* is to have more, and wanting to have more is a process of making what is not one's own, one's own. Similarly, the tyrant's eros is marked by its acquisitive nature. On the one hand, possession is a necessary means to satisfying the tyrant's insatiable appetites. On the other hand, possession and the activity of taking possession become ends in themselves, where the tyrant takes pleasure in the activity of acquiring more as well as in the consciousness of having done so.

Republic IX opens with a description of the tyrannical soul. This follows upon the discussion of degenerative political regimes and their corresponding characters in *Republic* VIII. The tyrant falls in the same group of psychic constitutions as the oligarchic and the democratic souls of *Republic* VIII insofar as all three are defined by their respective interest in satisfying appetitive desires. In order to differentiate the three psychic constitutions, Plato has Socrates first distinguish between necessary and unnecessary desires (558d) and then further identify two species of unnecessary desires, lawful and lawless (571b). Necessary desires are those whose satisfaction sustains or benefits us, such as the consumption of food for the purpose of maintaining health (558d–e). In contrast, unnecessary desires are those that can be eliminated from one's psychic constitution through proper training and whose presence can be harmful to the individual (559a). As a subspecies of unnecessary desires, lawless desires are those whose satisfaction is forbidden by law or custom (*nomos*). For this reason, the waking individual often seeks to repress these desires from entering into consciousness (571b). As a result, lawless desires tend to reveal themselves in dreams, when the ruling or rational part of the soul slumbers (571c). Whereas the oligarch only satisfies necessary desires, the democratic soul pursues in equal measure both necessary and unnecessary desires (561b–c). The tyrant, however, differs from the democratic man in that he allows unnecessary desires, both lawful and lawless, to rule his psychic constitution.

According to Plato's account, the tyrant emerges as the son of the democratic man, and there are two elements that seem to complete the transition from the latter to the former. The son of the democratic man grows up refusing to distinguish between good and bad pleasures. For Plato, this equality among pleasures opens the door to the mysterious "enchanters" (*magoi*) or "tyrant-makers" (*tyrannopoioi*) who begin to wage a war for the soul of the son of the democratic man (572e). Specifically, the tyrant-makers encourage in the young man a certain hostility to law under the banner of complete freedom. This effectively creates a spiritual anarchy within his psyche, as he no longer differentiates right from wrong. To complete the transition to tyranny, these enchanters then implant an eros so that the life of the tyrant-to-be is consumed by the pursuit of unnecessary and presumably lawless desires (572d–573a). According to Plato, once this tyranny has been "established by love, what he had rarely been in dreams, he [becomes] continuously while awake" (574e).

The introduction of eros in *Republic* IX is shrouded in mystery.[12] On the one hand, it is far from clear just who these enchanters and tyrant-makers are. On the other hand, we are given no clear sense of what eros is or what it seeks. It obviously has little, if anything, to do with the eros of the final mysteries described by Diotima in the *Symposium*, where eros, as a mixture of poverty and resource, stems from lack and ultimately strives to contemplate beauty itself. Moreover, it does not seem to be any single desire or drive among the various appetitive desires already within the soul precisely because eros is something implanted by the tyrant-makers so that the idle desires insist that all available resources be distributed to them (*Republic* 572e–573a).

What does seem to be clear is that the eros under discussion is bred through the stimulation and intensification of appetitive desire. Specifically, we are told that incense, myrrh, crowns, and wine not only swell the erotic longings of the individual, but also sting him or her into a frenzy of madness (573a–b). Although some might understand such madness (*mania*) to be a state of psychological instability that results in the breakdown of personality,[13] it is better to think of this madness in terms of a singular desire for an object or a set of objects that results in a lack of concern for goods that most people care about and the willingness to ignore or even break conventions that would otherwise prohibit the satisfaction of such a desire.[14] In this sense, Plato thinks of the madness he attributes to the tyrant as the opposite of moderation (*sophrosyne*) (573b). On this understanding, to be madly in love with someone might mean a willingness to break with the wishes of one's immediate family or even to risk one's life to be with that person. Similarly, to be mad about money might result in a willingness to break laws in order to obtain it, or to be mad about wisdom and the contemplative life might mean a willingness to live in poverty and a corresponding unwillingness to involve oneself in the affairs of others.

In the case of the tyrant, his madness comes from an intense longing to increase his sphere of power and control, and it results in a cavalier disregard of others, a willingness to violate legal prohibitions, and a shamelessness with regard to social mores. On Plato's account, the erotic soul will go hunting for feasts, revels (*komoi*), parties, courtesans, and everything else of this sort (573d). Such feasts and revels, however, require resources, and the young tyrant will seize anything available to satisfy his cravings. Eventually he turns on his parents, not only seeking to get the better (*pleon echein*) of them, but also thinking he deserves to do so (574a). In other words, the young tyrant is now convinced that he has a right to their property, and if they refuse to hand it over willingly, he is ready to beat them.

The tyrant's antinomian behavior, which includes parent beating, the robbing of temples, and the desire to attack and have intercourse with the gods, represents only part of the transition to tyranny. This is because there is a difference between anarchy and tyranny, and what the tyrant wants is not merely lawlessness, but ultimately to be the law. Although one is forced to speculate at this point, it seems that the eros implanted in the tyrant's soul is what effects this transition. Specifically, the tyrant is not only willing to break the laws to satisfy his desires, but he is also described as believing that he *ought* to get what he wants such that he has the *right* to run roughshod over anyone or anything that stands in his way. What generates this latter belief cannot be appetitive desire alone. Instead, it must be something in addition to appetitive desire, and I want to suggest here that it is eros as a form of self-love[15] that convinces the tyrant that anything hindering the satisfaction of his desires is bad and ought to be eliminated and anything facilitating the satisfaction of his desires is good and ought to be pursued.[16] Thus, in the workings of the tyrant's psyche, it is eros as self-love that sets out to replace any opinions about right and wrong that might restrain him from satisfying his appetites with opinions about right and wrong that simply reinforce his insatiable quest to have more (573b).

In the tyrant's confrontation with his parents, it is eros as self-love that convinces him he *deserves* to get the better of them when they resist. In the world beyond the home, it is eros as self-love that convinces the tyrant-to-be that he deserves to rule, and it is this mentality that sets him on a course that generates a conflict not only with the ruling political authorities, but ultimately with the gods (573c).

Admittedly, my understanding of eros as a form of self-love goes beyond a strict reading of *Republic* IX. Although portions of the text do license such speculations, my claim is supported most by the reading of the *Symposium* that I develop in the next sections. Indeed, it is the tyrant's interest in attacking the gods that suggests a turn away from real-life politics and a turn toward literary and mythical accounts of human ambition,[17] and Plato's subtle references to the tyrant's fellow symposiasts as well as his lust for revels or *komoi* point directly to the *Symposium* and the literary genre most intimately associated with the symposium and the *komos*, namely, comedy.[18] However, before delving into Aristophanes' speech on eros in the *Symposium*, I want to develop a framework for interpreting Plato's *Symposium* by first distinguishing between two types of eros in Plato's thought.

II. Plato on Two Kinds of Eros

There is one prima facie problem with trying to locate the kind of eros that animates the tyrant of *Republic* IX within the speeches of the *Symposium*. Quite simply, the slanderous presentation of eros in *Republic* IX seems to have little, if anything, to do with a series of speeches in the *Symposium* that are designed to praise something that is introduced as a god. Moreover, the eros of *Republic* IX seems to be diametrically opposed to the final understanding of eros that Plato places in the mouth of Diotima. The key to understanding how Plato's treatment of eros in *Republic* IX can be reconciled with the *Symposium* is to note that there are, in the *Republic* and in a text like the *Phaedrus*, at least two competing forms of eros that can be found in Plato's works, one that is endorsed as a proper, philosophical eros and one that is presented as a corrupting, tyrannical eros.[19]

In the *Republic*, eros appears most prominently in Plato's discussion of the tyrant; however, there is another sort of eros present in the work. Indeed, one can read the *Republic* as an attempt to direct both eros and *thumos* away from a potential alignment with appetitive desire and to associate these psychic forces with reason, learning, and knowledge. The contrast between an eros animated by the appetites and an eros directed toward learning and knowledge occurs most vividly at the beginning of *Republic* VI. There, those of a philosophic nature are described as being erotically disposed toward learning. To explain this sort of eros in a way that Glaucon can understand it, Plato has Socrates compare it to the care that a lover might bestow on a young boy (*Republic* 485c). Of course, Socrates is not endorsing pederasty, but using it as a way of making intelligible a kind of eros that is directed to objects of a different sort. Indeed, Socrates' later remarks suggest that these are two mutually exclusive objects of eros. This is because we are told that eros is like a stream that can be diverted one way or the other, and the more water that rushes toward one object, the less water will flow in the other direction (485d).

What these remarks show is that although most of the discussion of eros in the *Republic* is devoted to condemning the possessive sort of eros that animates the tyrant, a philosophical eros is nevertheless present. Indeed, one might say that just as the *Republic* focuses on and ultimately slanders tyrannical eros and only references a philosophical eros in passing, the centerpiece of the *Symposium* is an extended discourse on philosophical eros, with only brief references and intimations of the tyrannical eros from *Republic* IX. In contrast to both works, the dialogue in which the two forms of eros are discussed and contrasted at relatively equal length is the *Phaedrus*.

The first sort of eros discussed in the *Phaedrus*, which is initially presented as the only understanding of eros, is the harsh kind of love that can be linked to the erotic tyrant of *Republic* IX. Here, eros is opposed to moderation (*sophrosyne*) and understood as a desire (*epithumia*) (*Phaedrus* 237d). Whereas the temperate man acts according to right opinion even when his desires tempt him to do the opposite, the erotic man allows desire to overthrow reason and compel him to act contrary to what reason judges as best. Thus, Plato has Socrates claim: "The irrational desire which has gained control over judgment which urges a man towards the right, borne towards pleasure in beauty, and which is forcefully reinforced by the desires related to it in its pursuit of bodily beauty, overcoming them in its course, and takes its name from its very force—this is called love" (238b–c).

As one can see, Plato is freely employing vocabulary and distinctions from other dialogues. Not only does Plato have Socrates distinguish between reason and desire, but he also has Socrates speak of erotic desires overthrowing the rule of reason. This, of course, is a central theme of the *Republic*. Moreover, Plato begins to reformulate traditional concepts such as hubris in terms of his own philosophical views. Specifically, Socrates characterizes this sort of eros not as hubristic vis-à-vis other persons or even the gods, but rather as hubristic vis-à-vis what is divine in us, namely, reason.

In his discussion of hubris, Plato also explains the way in which our appetitive desires can tyrannize us (*Phaedrus* 238b). Although little was said about this above, the psychic distinctions of the *Republic* allow Plato to identify our true selves with reason or the rational part of the soul and then to speak in terms of this part being enslaved by appetitive desire or the part that makes us most akin to animals (*Republic* 589c–d). Also taken from the *Republic* is the idea that the desires that tyrannize the best part of us tend, in turn, to tyrannize the objects they desire. That is, these desires want to control, possess, and even consume the desired object. Although this is most obvious with desires for food or drink, as we literally make these things our own by consuming them, the desire to control and possess others can also play a significant role in sexual relationships. In the *Phaedrus*, Plato describes the attitude and behavior of the lover possessed by this sort of eros as tyrannical. Specifically, the lover seeks to make the beloved as pleasing as possible to himself, all the while making sure that the beloved does not equal or surpass his own standing. As a result, the relationship is most harmful to the soul of the beloved (*Phaedrus* 241c). Similar to the political tyrant of *Republic* I, who molds his subjects so that they serve his own interests, the goal of the lover is not to cultivate excellence in the young man, but rather to make him into something that the lover can possess and use as a means to satisfying his appetitive desires. As Plato explains, "as wolves love lambs, so is lovers' affection for a boy" (*Phaedrus* 241d).

For my purposes, the description of this kind of eros is valuable because it brings together a number of themes from Plato's portrayal of the tyrant in *Republic* IX that are also present in both Aristophanes' speech in the *Symposium* and Aristophanes' *Birds*. Specifically, passages from the *Phaedrus* associate this sort of eros with the satisfaction of appetitive desires and further associate the quest to satisfy these desires with both hubris and tyranny. Moreover, this eros is then sharply contrasted with a different sort of eros that is now understood as a god or something divine (*Phaedrus* 242e). The reference here to the *Symposium* is clear, and it is in Socrates' palinode that we find an understanding of eros that roughly corresponds to the theory placed in the mouth of Diotima. This is because Socrates speaks of an eros that leads the erotic individual to a divine feast in which the soul beholds realities such as justice, temperance, and knowledge as they are in themselves (*Phaedrus* 246d–247e).

In the *Phaedrus*, these two forms of eros are not merely contrasted in theory, but are also said to be at work within the soul itself. This is because Socrates portrays the human psyche as constituted by a chariot driver and two horses—one white and one dark—that can pull the chariot in different directions (246a–b). Whereas the white horse is a friend of honor, temperance, and modesty and willingly obeys the commands of reason, the dark horse is full of hubris and boastfulness and therefore must be beaten into submission (253d–e). The difference between the two horses is most notable when the individual approaches a beautiful boy. The white horse knows that sexual contact with the boy is contrary to nature, and so there is a sense of shame for desiring such contact. In contrast, the dark horse pulls shamelessly (*anaideia*) toward the boy (254e). As a result, the charioteer must restrain the hubristic horse with force and pain. When this is done repeatedly, the horse is eventually tamed so that he is overwhelmed with the fear (*phobos*) of punishment every time he encounters a beautiful boy thereafter (254e). As I suggest below, Plato's description of the taming of this shameless and hubristic horse through fear and punishment has close parallels to the eventual taming of the original circle-people in Aristophanes' speech in the *Symposium*. It is to this work that I now turn.

III. Tyrannical Eros in the *Symposium*

The literature on eros in the *Symposium* is immense.[20] However, much of the writing devoted to the issue has focused on working out the details of what is thought to be Plato's understanding of eros as it is articulated in Diotima's speech. In contrast, there has been relatively little attention paid to the other speeches in the *Symposium* and to the possible presence of a tyrannical eros within the work. In this section, I want to identify the various areas where I think tyrannical eros is present in the *Symposium* and then argue that its presence is most prominent in the speech on eros that Plato attributes to Aristophanes.

One reason why the presence of tyrannical eros in the *Symposium* goes largely unnoticed has to do with the stated goal of the speakers. Specifically, they have been asked to sing the praises of eros rather than to slander it. Thus, the harsher elements of eros, when mentioned at all, are either downplayed or ultimately rejected so that eros may be depicted in the most edifying light possible. The praise of eros begins immediately with Phaedrus' speech, where the god is said to be the cause of our greatest blessings (*Symposium* 178a–c), and it reaches its apex in Agathon's speech, where eros is effectively purged of its harsher nature when he eliminates the stories of Hesiod and Parmenides that implicate eros in the castrations, imprisonments, and father beatings of the gods (195c). Although Socrates rejects elements of Agathon's praise—most notably his claim that eros is a god (202d)—Agathon has nevertheless made it possible for Socrates to describe eros as a *daimon* who bridges the gap between the human and the divine (202e).

Hints of an ugly side to eros emerge at the beginning of Pausanias' speech when he modifies Phaedrus' account by claiming that there are two sorts of eros (180d). Specifically, there is a "heavenly" eros associated with an Aphrodite born of Uranus and a "common" (*pandemos*) eros associated with an Aphrodite born of Zeus. The latter sort of eros is an indiscriminate love for both women and boys that can strike anyone at any time and is most interested in sexual intercourse. As such, this sort of love is focused more on the body than on the soul (181b). In contrast, the heavenly sort of love is for young boys only and is supposedly focused more on the virtue of the soul than on sexual gratification. Important for my purposes is that the heavenly sort of love, presumably in contrast to the vulgar sort of love, is *not* hubristic (181c).

Commentators have also noted the appearance of a lower sort of love elsewhere in the *Symposium*. Specifically, Richard Kraut has argued that Plato's portrayal of Alcibiades near the end of the work gives expression to a confused eros that very much resembles the description of the erotic tyrant of *Republic* IX.[21] On one level, Alcibiades' drunken entrance, along with his attempt to seduce Socrates, shows that his eros can be readily linked to the pleasures of the body. On another level, Plato describes Alcibiades' love and his behavior vis-à-vis Socrates as jealous, violent, and even mad (*Symposium* 213d). As Kraut notes, this is not the philosophical madness described in the *Phaedrus*, but rather the madness of a violent tyrant who seeks to rule over other humans and even the gods.[22]

In his analysis, Kraut also probes deeper into the ultimate object of the tyrant's appetitive longings, and he speculates that what is really at stake for the tyrant is the replication of his life for eternity.[23] Although such a desire is not attributed to Alcibiades in the *Symposium*, Plato explicitly attributes such a longing to Alcibiades in *Alcibiades I*.[24] Specifically, we are told that Alcibiades wants his reputation and influence to saturate all of mankind (*Alcibiades I* 105c). Thus, the kind of eros attributed to a figure like Alcibiades seeks to extend infinitely his own name or self across space and time.[25] That is, the individual driven by this sort of eros wants to have his name imprinted on all things, through possession and rule, for all time, through offspring and fame.

If this is right, one can also find the tyrannical eros of *Republic* IX in Diotima's description of the lower forms of eros in the *Symposium*. According to Suzanne Obdrzalek, there are good reasons for sharply distinguishing between a properly directed eros that aims at the contemplation of beauty and goodness themselves and a misunderstood eros that aims at personal immortality.[26] In the lower mysteries, Diotima reveals that humans suffer terribly from their love for immortality, and that even acts of apparent self-sacrifice have been performed "for the sake of immortal virtue and this sort of glorious reputation" (*Symposium* 208d–e). For Obdrzalek, these lower mysteries are contrasted with the higher or final mysteries (210a). In the higher mysteries, the quest for *personal* immortality falls away.[27] The genuine aim of eros is not the extension of the self through space and time, but rather the contemplation of beauty itself. Here, the erotic individual does not seek to grasp or possess the object of his longing, as the tyrant would, but rather to behold it as an object of philosophical contemplation.

Just as one can establish a plausible link between Plato's portrayal of Alcibiades and the lower forms of eros that Diotima associates with the sophists (208c) and the poets (209d), one can also connect the figure of Alcibiades and the lower forms of eros in Diotima's speech to both the account of eros in *Republic* IX and the account that Plato places in the mouth of Aristophanes in the *Symposium*. On this point, three features of Alcibiades' entrance are significant. First, Alcibiades' dress and behavior recall descriptions of the tyrant in *Republic* IX. Second, Alcibiades is engaged in a traditional revel or *komos* when he bursts onto the scene (*Symposium* 212c–e). As noted above, not only is the participation in *komoi* attributed to the tyrant in *Republic* IX (573d), such revelry also points to the genre of comedy and thus the art of Aristophanes. Finally, Alcibiades' entrance interrupts what would have been Aristophanes' response to Socrates' account of Diotima's understanding of eros (*Symposium* 212c). The reason Aristophanes wanted to respond is that Diotima explicitly rejects elements of Aristophanes' account (205d–206a), and the distinction that Diotima makes between her own account and that of Aristophanes is crucial for the argument here. Specifically, Diotima rejects the story that people unconditionally desire their other halves. Instead, they only desire something that belongs or should belong to them if that thing is also *good* (205e). The problem with Aristophanes' account is that it conflates these two, effectively making whatever is (at least originally) one's own (*oikeion*) the object of desire or the good. This view, however, is precisely what is implicit in Diotima's account of the lower mysteries. As Obdrzalek puts it, these lovers "mistake themselves for the good."[28] Although these are Obdrzalek's own words, the phrasing here is both apt and important. It is not that these lovers believe that they *are good* in the sense that they measure up to some objective standard of goodness; instead, they think that they are *the good*, and therefore they see themselves as the source and measure of value.

In my mind, it is this Protagorean notion that each individual conceives of him- or herself as the measure of goodness that underlies Aristophanes' account of eros in the *Symposium*. I say underlies because explicit references to eros only emerge in Aristophanes' speech once human beings have been sliced in half by Zeus for their impious behavior (191d), and so one might argue that eros and feeling oneself to be a measure of value are mutually opposed. The idea is that Zeus splits the original circle-people precisely because they see themselves as measures, thereby refusing to recognize Zeus as the standard of justice. As a result, each individual now experiences eros for his or her lost half. Once they find their other halves, eros is supposedly extinguished and they feel themselves, again, to be the measure of things.

Even here, however, it is clear that Aristophanes' account of eros has little to do with a standard of goodness that exists independently of the lover. For Aristophanes, we love the part of ourselves that we lack and therefore long to become our original, whole selves. Only if we conflate the self and the good can we say that eros is a love of the good. Even if we do, it is still right to say that, for Aristophanes, this sort of love is self-love,[29] and, in this sense, the Aristophanic lover parallels the lover of the lower mysteries who mistakes himself for the good. The difference is that in the lower mysteries, the self-lovers are trying to attain immortality and so an infinite extension of the self through time, whereas, in Aristophanes' account of eros, present-day humans are simply trying to recapture their original sense of self-love.

There is, of course, more to Aristophanes' story, and it is in probing the additional details of his account that one begins to see further parallels between it and the lovers of the lower mysteries, on the one hand, and the erotic tyrant of *Republic* IX, on the other hand. Specifically, the story informs us that we humans are now lovers of our other halves because Zeus has divided us into two, and the reason Zeus divided us into two is that we, in our original condition as spherical beings with four arms and four legs, decided to mount the heavens and attack the gods (*Symposium* 190b–c). However, the fact that we were motivated to do anything in our original condition signifies that we must have been motivated by something more than the simple quest to establish or reestablish a sense of self-love, as is the case with the post-lapsarian lovers. For this reason, Ludwig has argued that there is a more primitive eros or Ur-eros that motivates the original circle-people in Aristophanes' account,[30] and it is this Ur-eros that can be sharply distinguished from the philosophical eros found in the *Republic*, *Phaedrus*, and *Symposium* and equated with the tyrannical or bad eros in the *Phaedrus* and *Republic* IX. On this model, the original circle-people, as self-lovers, are both self-satisfied and self-sufficient. Nevertheless, they are motivated by the desire or an eros to spread or expand their selves across space and time, and it is this ever-expanding self-love that motivates their ascent on the gods. On the one hand, they want to be like the gods insofar as the gods are immortal. On the other hand, they want to replace the gods as the standard and measure of all things; thus, their quest for divinity results in a conflict with the reigning deities.

Of course, one cannot simply infer from the fact that because the original circle-people are motivated by something that they must be motivated by a form of eros. Nevertheless, the fact that the ascent on the gods in both *Republic* IX and Aristophanes' own comedy, *Birds*, is described in erotic terms gives us reason to infer that the anabasis of the circle-people in the *Symposium* is also motivated by a form of eros. However, the difference between Aristophanes' speech in the *Symposium* and Aristophanes' comedy is that the main character of the *Birds* actually succeeds in overthrowing the gods, and so rather than being tamed by the fear of punishment, as the dark horse in the *Phaedrus* and the circle-people eventually are, the main character of the *Birds* is ultimately hailed as a god.

IV. Eros *Tyrannos* and Aristophanes' *Birds*

Aristophanes' *Birds* was produced in 414 BC at City Dionysia during the time of the Sicilian expedition. Thucydides (6.24) describes the excitement surrounding the expedition in erotic terms: "all alike fell in love with the enterprise." However, such excitement was mixed with ominous signs. One night, all the stone Hermae in the city were mutilated, a clear act of hubris vis-à-vis the gods (6.27). At the center of the controversy was Alcibiades, the figure most responsible for convincing the Athenians to undertake the expedition. Alcibiades himself was known for his eroticism. As Plutarch reports (16), Alcibiades lived a life of prodigious luxury, drunkenness, debauchery, and insolence, and he had a golden shield emblazoned with the figure of Eros armed with a thunderbolt. All this, according to Plutarch, smacked of the habits of a tyrant.

Although it would be wrong simply to equate Peisetairos with Alcibiades, there are certainly reasons for thinking that Aristophanes is drawing from the person of Alcibiades and the events of the time in his construction of Peisetairos and the play as a whole. This is significant not only because Plato links the figure of Alcibiades to Aristophanes' speech in the *Symposium*, but also because Annie Larivée has argued that Plato's sketch of the erotic tyrant in *Republic* IX is meant to recall the life and ambition of Alcibiades.[31] What to make of these connections is certainly open to debate. However, what should be clear is that the eroticism, ambition, imperial politics, and even hubris that surrounded the figure of Alcibiades are not only present in the accounts of eros in both *Republic* IX and Aristophanes' speech in the *Symposium*, but also on full display in the fantasy politics of the *Birds* and the action of its main character, Peisetairos.

Birds tells the story of how a pair of disgruntled Athenians, Peisetairos and Euelpides, leave behind their city in search of comfort and freedom among the birds only to hatch and execute a plan to conquer the skies and overthrow the gods. Motivating this attack on the gods is eros, a theme that runs throughout the play. Eros makes its first appearance in Aristophanes' descriptions of Peisetairos and Euelpides, where the two characters are portrayed as lovers (*Birds* 323) of and as having a love (412) for the lifestyle of the birds. This lifestyle is largely characterized in terms of comfort and freedom. Specifically, the birds live free of laws or *nomoi* and therefore represent a superior alternative to an overly litigious Athenian society (40–48).

Nevertheless, one could argue that the eros of Peisetairos and Euelpides is at work even before the theme is explicitly introduced. Although they want a city that is "warm and woolly" like "a big soft blanket" (120–22), they also want a city that can satisfy their intense desires for food, sex, and drink. Whereas Peisetairos wants a city where he is forced to attend the wedding feasts of his neighbors, Euelpides longs for a place where fathers will scold him for not kissing and fondling their sons as they exit the gymnasium (128–42). Similar to the dynamic at work in *Republic* II (372a–373e), where the desire for luxury leads Socrates' initial city of health and peace to war, the desires Peisetairos and Euelpides have for such goods ultimately motivate Peisetairos' grand plan for power (*dunamis*) (162–63). Specifically, Peisetairos thinks that the birds could win power by privatizing the otherwise free space of the sky and, in so doing, lord their global city over men and starve out the gods, just as the Athenians did in the siege at Melos (185–86). In other words, Peisetairos' desire to preserve and enhance his "bridegroom life" (161) transforms him into a busybody or *polypragmon* (471)[32]—the opposite of Plato's notion of justice as minding one's own business (*Republic* 433a–b)—and puts in motion a plan to make what is not his own, his own by using this newly colonized territory to achieve control of everything.

The power politics of Peisetairos is first met with resistance and threats of violence from birds suspicious of human designs. Peisetairos, whose name means "persuader of companions," meets this opposition with the rhetorical powers of the most refined sophist (429). He does this by concocting a story in which the birds are said to be far older than Kronos, the Titans, and even Earth and therefore were once kings of everything (469–70). Similar to the mysterious enchanters of *Republic* IX who convince the young tyrant that he deserves nothing less than to rule, Peisetairos' story appeals to the sense of honor or pride of the birds such that they can no longer be satisfied living as anything else but the reigning deities that they once were.[33]

At the same time, Peisetairos leaves out some significant details that are only revealed in the parabasis, where we learn that the birds themselves are offspring of Eros and Chaos and that "the universe contained no gods, till Eros mingled all" (699–700). These details are significant because they not only place Eros at the center of the comedy, but also indicate that Eros stands above all the gods, even the birds. Thus, Eros, rather than the birds, ultimately deserves to rule. The view that Eros is the god of all gods has its roots in the poetry of Hesiod's *Theogony*, and, as noted above, Phaedrus articulates a version of this story in the *Symposium* (178a–b) only to have Agathon reject it (195b–c).

The parabasis of the *Birds* also links an understanding of the good life characterized in hedonistic terms to a general sense of shamelessness that the bird-life encourages.[34] On the one hand, the chorus leader proclaims that if the birds are treated as the gods they are, they promise to provide "great wealth-and-health, long lives of peace, with youth and laughter, dancing, feasts" (*Birds* 730–35). This "eternal drunk" of the symposium is precisely the characterization of the good life that Plato associates with both poetry and the poet's praise of the mere appearance of justice (*Republic* 363c–e) and then condemns in *Republic* IX (586a–b). On the other hand, this life of pleasure (*Birds* 754) is one that abandons or inverts what humans count as shameful: "All the things that human beings count as shameful and deter, We consider splendid and encourage birds to practice them" (*Birds* 755–56). In *Republic* VIII, Plato details a similar reversal of attitudes about shame as the soul slides toward tyranny. There, the individual is initiated in great rites as a "numerous chorus" urges him on "by calling insolence good education; anarchy, freedom; wastefulness, magnificence; and shamelessness, courage" (*Republic* 560d–e).

In *Republic* IX (574b–c), the shamelessness of the tyrant is symbolized by his willingness to strike his own parents. In Aristophanes' comedy, parent beating is the first example of the birds' approbation of shamelessness: "If, on earth, the law decrees it's wrong for fathers to be struck, in the sky we think it's good for someone to accost his dad" (*Birds* 757–58). A potentially puzzling feature of the *Birds*, however, is that once Peisetairos has come to power, he quickly seeks to restrict this sort of behavior. This occurs when a father beater comes to Peisetairos professing his eros for the ways of the birds and the newly founded Cloudcuckooland (1347ff.). Although Peisetairos admires his aggressive attitude, he nevertheless discourages the father beater by informing him of another ancient law (*nomos*) that sons must also feed their fathers (1353–57).

Here, some might accuse Aristophanes of having constructed a confused and contradictory character, as Peisetairos is first attracted to the *nomos*-free society of the birds only to do an about-face by appealing to a law that dampens the excitement a father beater might have for such a life. What appears to be a contradiction, however, is simply an instance of the relativism that runs throughout the *Birds* and, I would argue, Aristophanic comedy in general.[35] Although Peisetairos may have endorsed father beating when he lacked any sort of father-like authority, he advises against it once he rises to power. Similar to those lovers of sights and sounds in *Republic* V (476a–d) who deny the existence of beauty itself, it is wrong to speak of something as good or just in itself in the world of the *Birds*. Instead, one must always ask and answer these sorts of questions by situating the issue in terms of some context and in relation to some person. So as Peisetairos' position changes, his attitudes about such matters change accordingly.

The relativism implicit in the *Birds* also explains Peisetairos' shifting attitude toward law or *nomos* in general. At the beginning of the play, Peisetairos and Euelpides sought to flee the laws of Athenian society in search of freedom. As the play develops, Peisetairos—Euelpides mysteriously drops out of the play (846)—begins to see the law as a means to satisfying the very desires that drove him away from Athens. In short, he begins to see the law as an instrument for power. Such a view of law is made explicit when Peisetairos defines justice in terms of Zeus handing over power to him and the birds (1599–1601). Thus, the very laws that once worked to control and suppress the longings of Peisetairos now become the very means by which he can guarantee their satisfaction.

Of course, one can readily see the parallels between the understanding of justice that is both implicit and explicit in the *Birds* and Thrasymachus' claim in the *Republic* (338c) that justice is the advantage of the stronger; and just as Thrasymachus' definition of justice goes hand in hand with his praise of tyranny, Peisetairos puts forth his definition of justice in the midst of his attempt to become a tyrant or ruler of the Greek universe by overthrowing the gods. Nevertheless, Peisetairos' quest to rule over everything does not come without resistance from the gods, and it is his response to this resistance that reveals the hubristic nature of his tyrannical eros. This is on full display when Zeus sends Iris to warn Peisetairos of the disastrous consequences he will face for waging a war against the gods (*Birds* 1189–92). Impervious to such threats, Peisetairos responds by comparing himself to Porphyrion, the king of the giants,[36] and threatening to rape Iris (1248–55). Although Iris storms off with accusations of hubris (1259), Peisetairos continues with his plans unhindered.

The play culminates with Peisetairos achieving what he would call a just city or his *kallipolis*.[37] That is, after some negotiating with the likes of Herakles and Poseidon, Peisetairos is given both the scepter and Zeus' princess as his bride. It is the latter acquisition that occasions the wedding feast that concludes the play. Such a feast recalls the appetitive longings that initially drove Peisetairos and Euelpides away from Athens. More important is the fact that Peisetairos appears onstage carrying Zeus' thunderbolt and wearing the wings of eros as the chorus hails him as a blessed and triumphant ruler (*tyrannos*) (1708). Peisetairos, as the erotic tyrant, has replaced Zeus as the most honored and revered figure in the Greek world and has effectively been transformed into a god.

V. Interpreting the *Birds*

On a straightforward reading, the *Birds* provides us with evidence for Plato's claim at the end of *Republic* VIII that poets "extol tyranny as a condition 'equal to that of a god'" (568b). Peisetairos has secured through force and persuasion a blessed state of peace in which all opposing forces have been subordinated to his rule, just as an Olympian victor would bask in victory after having defeated all his competitors. Moreover, just as poets such as Pindar would honor the Olympian victor with songs to glorify his name, the chorus now salutes Peisetairos as "brilliant victor, highest of gods" (*Birds* 1764–65). In the language of the *Symposium*, Peisetairos' accomplishments and the praise that the chorus heaps upon them have made him immortal. No longer a wingless creature-of-a-day and a pathetic, dreamlike human (*Birds* 686–89), eros has provided Peisetairos with wings to live among the birds as their blessed, divine, and immortal ruler.

There can be little doubt that the *Birds* ends on a jubilant note. However, not all readers of the play have held that Aristophanes sought to glorify

Peisetairos' ascent to absolute rule. Specifically, Ludwig has followed William Arrowsmith in holding that Aristophanes designed the play as a reductio ad absurdum of the imperial eros of his Athenian audience.[38] Because I am arguing that Plato has an Aristophanic hero like Peisetairos in mind with his portrayal of the erotic tyrant in *Republic* IX, such a reading of the *Birds* would mean that Plato and Aristophanes agree that there is something unsatisfying, if not altogether disturbing, about *eros tyrannos*. As a result, Plato and Aristophanes would have to be considered allies with respect to this issue in the ancient quarrel between philosophy and poetry. In contrast, I think that the divide between Plato's philosophy and Aristophanes' poetry could not be more acute, and this, in part, is due to the fact that I think the straightforward reading of the play is correct.

At the heart of Arrowsmith's reading is the idea that Aristophanes intended his Athenian audience to identify with the birds. As such, the Athenians are portrayed as gullible suckers who are taken in by Peisetairos' erotically charged rhetoric of empire only to find themselves subjected to a new tyrant even more monstrous than Zeus. In terms of the politics of the day, Aristophanes is warning the Athenians that Alcibiades has duped them into setting out on a Sicilian expedition that will end only in disaster. Evidence for this reading can be found near the end of the play when Peisetairos is having birds, and so members of the Athenian demos, chopped and cooked for his wedding feast (1583–85, 1687–88). Thus, the celebratory feast at the end should be read ironically. Aristophanes does not want the audience to celebrate with the comic hero but rather to recognize the potential consequences of their own corrupt mind-set, one that has lost its sense of community, common purpose, and connection to the earth in falling in love with empire.[39]

Following Arrowsmith, Ludwig develops a similar reading: "Aristophanes presents a *reductio ad absurdum* of human desires, first getting his audience to identify their own desires with Peisetaerus' and then showing the folly to which such hopes really lead."[40] For Ludwig, the primary reason for reading the *Birds* in this way is the fact that Peisetairos reintroduces *nomos* as the play unfolds. On this reading, the *Birds* is initially about a return to nature, and this return to nature means getting away from the *nomoi* that have domesticated and denatured man. Because the gods, in particular Zeus, are the ultimate guarantors of the *nomoi*, getting back to nature means overthrowing the gods. This, of course, is what Peisetairos sets out to do. As Ludwig sees it, the problem is that Peisetairos' quest to eliminate *nomoi* in a return to nature "transforms itself into the conventional city once more."[41] And just as Peisetairos' escape from the city results in a return to the city, his rebellion against the gods results in the creation of a new god, namely, himself. In terms of the *Symposium*, Peisetairos' hubris has caused him to commit the very sin of the circle-people, and thus Ludwig concludes that "Peisetaerus becomes a circle-man, but then he only stands in need of surgery again."[42]

Perhaps the most problematic aspect of such readings is that they transform Aristophanes' comedy into a tragedy. For Ludwig, it is Peisetairos' monstrous overestimation of his own greatness that "sets the tragedy in motion."[43] In this way, their Aristophanes becomes something like Nietzsche's Euripides. That is, Aristophanes provides us with a comedy that kills the comic spirit of victory and celebration by showing how the egotistical shamelessness characteristic of Old Comedy leads to disastrous results. Thus, the *Birds* is hardly an occasion for celebration and revelry. Instead, the audience members who grasp the true meaning of the play are left with a horrifying vision of their own selfish and imperialistic ambitions. However, this would indeed be a strange sort of comedy and contrary to the comic spirit. As Jeffrey Henderson remarks, "a comic poet's job was to win a prize by creating reassuring laughter, not gloomy foreboding."[44]

Moreover, the textual evidence that supports such a reading is rather thin. Much of Arrowsmith's case depends on the significance of Peisetairos roasting rebellious birds near the end of the play. There are potential concerns here, but hardly enough to warrant a reading that transforms the comedy into a tragedy. The worry is that this is a kind of cannibalism, either because Peisetairos is seen as a bird who is now eating birds or because the audience sees the birds as Athenians, and so themselves, now being eaten by a fellow Athenian. Such worries, however, are ameliorated by the fact that Peisetairos is eating traitorous birds, and this is likely a comically exaggerated way of dealing with such characters. As Henderson notes, Peisetairos is not acting much differently than the Athenians did in 415 when they condemned a number of traitors to death.[45] Finally, it is the chorus of birds that celebrates Peisetairos' ascension to divinity, and in so doing, they sing of the "great prosperity" that "awaits the race of birds because of this man" (1726–28). So if this comedy has turned into a tragedy for the birds, the birds themselves are unaware of it. Indeed, what such comments suggest is that the birds, or at least the loyal ones, are the direct beneficiaries of Peisetairos' rise to power, and this is the reason why he is celebrated as their savior (*soter*) (544).

On my reading, the audience is supposed to be equally jubilant about the rise of Peisetairos. Although the audience may identify with the loyal birds and therefore delight in the benefits that the ascension of Peisetairos will bring, it is more likely that the play is designed for the audience to identify directly with the comic hero himself. Similar to the way in which sports fans identify with and vicariously experience the joy of victory through their favorite sports teams, the *Birds* allows each member of the audience to imagine himself boldly and successfully scaling the walls of heaven in the quest for absolute power.[46] Thus, Peisetairos' willingness and ability to dispose of anyone or anything that stands in his way, including traitorous birds, simply adds to the pleasure of identifying with him. Indeed, the laughter that Aristophanes' play produces seems to derive from the feeling of superiority that the audience vicariously experiences through the exploits of the hero.[47] Once these obstacles are overcome and the gods are overthrown, the audience members can now experience, via the comic hero, life and the world as if they were gods. On this reading, the victory of Peisetairos is a victory for all who identify with him, just as the victory of a sports team is a victory for an entire city, state, or nation, and therefore the victory and apotheosis of Peisetairos is indeed an occasion for a communal celebration befitting of the spirit of comedy.

So construed, the true longing of Peisetairos is not for a return to a nature free of *nomos*, but rather a desire to bridge the gap between nature or *phusis* and *nomos* by constructing a city according to nature or eros. What irks Peisetairos and Euelpides at the beginning of the play is not law as such, but rather an Athenian law that places restraints on their erotic yearnings and therefore runs contrary to nature. Although the birds offer a better life because they live without such restraints, a city designed in accordance with and in honor of eros is an even greater possibility. Cloudcuckooland can be understood as such a city insofar as we think of Peisetairos as the vehicle by which eros comes to rule. In this sense, Peisetairos' quest to rule is at the same time an attempt to establish eros as the rightful ruler of the universe and therewith to have it honored as the god of all gods.

VI. The Ancient Quarrel between Plato and Aristophanes?

In this chapter, I have sought to provide evidence for the view that Plato's characterization and ultimate criticism of the erotic tyrant in *Republic* IX draws from and even has as its target the main character of Aristophanes' *Birds*. If this is correct and Allan Bloom is right to claim that the choice between "the philosophical and tyrannic lives explains the plot of the *Republic*,"[48] then the choice offered in the *Republic* is between the life endorsed by Aristophanic comedy and the life of Plato's philosopher. Whereas Plato's philosopher directs his eros toward the contemplation of the good and seeks to model his life accordingly by ruling his own psychic constitution rather than the lives of others, a tyrant like Peisetairos directs his life toward the satisfaction of his appetitive desires and the associated quest for power and personal immortality. So understood, the ancient quarrel between philosophy and poetry in the *Republic* is not limited to Books II, III, and X, as a superficial reading of the dialogue might suggest. Instead, the quarrel runs through the entirety of the work precisely because the quarrel, like the *Republic* itself, is ultimately about the kind of life we should live (*Republic* 608b). In the end, Plato's claim that the philosopher lives a life 729 times more blessed than the tyrant's can be understood in terms of the philosopher living a life 729 times more blessed than the life celebrated by an Aristophanic comedy like the *Birds* (*Republic* 587e).

That said, even Plato's attempt to quantify the philosopher's relative superiority has something humorous about it. Indeed, insofar as the reader identifies with the newly appointed philosopher-kings, the *Republic* seems to generate the very feeling of superiority that a comedy such as the *Birds* inspires in its audience. Moreover, the contest between lives and the quarrel between philosophy and poetry that animate the *Republic* seem to draw from the agonistic nature of Old Comedy and therefore suggest that there is something comic even about Plato's construction of the ancient quarrel between philosophy and poetry.[49] And similar to Old Comedy, the *Republic* employs a city–soul analogy in which the private hopes and longings of individual characters are intertwined with and expressed by the utopian political fantasies they generate.[50] Here, the contest of lives morphs into a contest of fantastical political regimes that appear to be outrageous and ridiculous from the standpoint of reigning convention. When coupled with Plato's constant appeal to metaphors, allegories, and images to present philosophical ideas in the *Republic*, one could very well argue, as many have, that Plato is himself a poet, and that in a work like the *Republic*, he is more indebted to comedy than to any other literary genre.[51] If this is right, then the argument of the *Republic* and the nature of Plato's quarrel with the poets cannot be properly grasped without a careful study of Aristophanic comedy and an understanding of Aristophanes' political and poetic wisdom.

Notes

1. The following editions are used throughout this chapter: Plato, *Alcibiades*, trans. D. S. Hutchinson, in *Plato: Complete Works*, ed. John M. Cooper

(Indianapolis: Hackett Publishing Company, 1997), 557–95; Aristophanes, *Birds*, in *Birds and Other Plays*, trans. Stephen Halliwell (Oxford: Oxford University Press, 1998), 14–78; Plato, *Phaedo*, trans. G. M. A. Grube, in *Plato: Complete Works*, ed. John M. Cooper (Indianapolis: Hackett Publishing Company, 1997), 49–100; Plato, *Phaedrus*, ed. and trans. C. J. Rowe (Oxford: Aris & Phillips Classical Texts, 1986); Plutarch, *Alcibiades*, in *The Rise and Fall of Athens: Nine Greek Lives*, trans. Ian Scott-Kilvert (London: Penguin Classics, 1960), 245–86; Plato, *Republic*, trans. Allan Bloom (New York: Basic Books, 1968); Plato, *Symposium*, ed. and trans. C. J. Rowe (Oxford: Aris & Phillips Ltd., 1998); and Thucydides, *The Peloponnesian War*, in *The Landmark Thucydides: A Comprehensive Guide to The Peloponnesian War*, ed. Robert B. Strassler (New York: Touchstone, 1998).

2. Glenn Most, "What Ancient Quarrel between Philosophy and Poetry?," in *Plato and the Poets*, eds. Pierre Destrée and Fritz-Gregor Herrmann (Boston: Brill, 2011), 1–20.

3. In the *Phaedo*, we learn that philosophers are the true Bacchants (69b–c). In the *Phaedrus*, Socrates claims to be speaking in dithyrambs (238d) and refers to bacchants (253a) and the madness of Dionysus (265b). David Sider, "Plato's 'Symposium' as Dionysian Festival," *Quaderni Urbinati di Cultura Classica* 4 (1980): 41–56, has detailed the Dionysian elements of the *Symposium*, most notably the role that Dionysus plays as judge (175e) and Alcibiades' presentation of Socrates as a satyr (215b). See also John P. Anton, "Some Dionysian References in the Platonic Dialogues," *The Classical Journal* 58 (1962): 49–55. Finally, in the *Republic*, we learn that the true lovers of wisdom are not those lovers of sights and sounds who attend every chorus at the Dionysia (475d), but rather the philosophers who long to behold things-in-themselves.

4. Andrea Nightingale, *Genres in Dialogue: Plato and the Construct of Philosophy* (Cambridge: Cambridge University Press, 1995), provides an excellent overview of Plato's engagement with literary genres. Stephen Halliwell, "Plato and Aristotle on the Denial of Tragedy," *Proceedings of the Cambridge Philological Society* 30 (1984): 49–71, sketches reasons for reading the *Phaedo* as Plato's tragedy. William Chase Greene, "The Spirit of Comedy in Plato," *Harvard Studies in Classical Philology* 31 (1920): 63–123, reads the *Republic* as Plato's attempt to vanquish comedy with comedy. M. D. Usher, "Satyr Play in Plato's *Symposium*," *The American Journal of Philology* 123 (2002): 205–28, details the role of the satyr play in the *Symposium*, and Marian Demos, "Stesichorus' Palinode in the *Phaedrus*," *The Classical World* 90 (1997): 235–49, discusses Plato's portrayal of Socrates as a lyric poet in the *Phaedrus*.

5. For a critique of any simplistic reading of the quarrel, see Stephen Halliwell, "Antidotes and Incarnations: Is There a Cure for Poetry in Plato's *Republic*?," in *Plato and the Poets*, eds. Pierre Destrée and Fritz-Gregor Herrmann (Boston: Brill, 2011), 241–67.

6. Versions of this claim can be found in Arlene Saxonhouse, "Comedy in Callipolis: Animal Imagery in the *Republic*," *The American Political Science Review* 72 (1978): 888–901; Greene, "The Spirit of Comedy," 63–123; Allan Bloom, "Interpretive Essay," in *The Republic of Plato*, ed. Allan Bloom (New York: Basic Books,

1968), 305–436; and John Sallis, *Being and Logos: Reading the Platonic Dialogues* (Bloomington: Indiana University Press, 1996). However, most of these readings are based on Plato's apparent borrowing in *Republic* V from Aristophanes' *Ecclesiazusae*. Only Saxonhouse points to the *Birds* as a possible model for the *Republic*. Although I follow her in reading the *Republic* in relation to Aristophanes' *Birds*, I resist some of her assumptions about Aristophanic comedy and some of the conclusions she draws as to how one should interpret the *Republic* in light of its relationship to the genre.

7. Paul Ludwig, *Eros and Polis: Desire and Community in Greek Political Theory* (Cambridge: Cambridge University Press, 2002).

8. One clear exception here is Annie Larivée, "Eros *Tyrannos*: Alcibiades as the Model of the Tyrant in Book IX of the *Republic*," *The International Journal of the Platonic Tradition* 6 (2012): 1–26, who argues that Alcibiades provides Plato with a model for his depiction of the tyrant in *Republic* IX. I find this view entirely plausible. However, it by no means nullifies the thesis I am defending here. In fact, the two positions seem to be mutually supporting. This is because scholars such as Wayne Ambler, "Tyranny in Aristophanes's *Birds*," *Review of Politics* 74 (2012): 200; William Arrowsmith, "Aristophanes' *Birds*: The Fantasy Politics of Eros," *Arion* 1 (1973): 114; Jeffrey Henderson, "Mass versus Elite and the Comic Heroism of Peisetairos," in *The City as Comedy: Society and Representation in Athenian Drama* (Chapel Hill: University of North Carolina Press, 1998), 139; and Michael Vickers, "Alcibiades on Stage: Aristophanes' *Birds*," *Historia: Zeitschrfit für Alte Geschichte* 38 (1989): 267–99, have all noted substantive links between Alcibiades and Aristophanes' Peisetairos. I thank Larivée for sharing her work prior to its publication.

9. Julia Annas, *An Introduction to Plato's Republic* (Oxford: Oxford University Press, 1981), 303ff.

10. See Richard D. Parry, "The Unhappy Tyrant and the Craft of Inner Rule," in *The Cambridge Companion to Plato's Republic*, ed. G. R. F. Ferrari (Cambridge: Cambridge University Press, 2007), 394.

11. See David Halperin, "Platonic *Erôs* and What Men Call Love," *Ancient Philosophy* 5 (1985): 165, for the link between acquisitive eros and wild beasts.

12. See Parry, "The Unhappy Tyrant," 396n9.

13. Annas, *An Introduction to Plato's Republic*, 304.

14. For more on madness, see Dominic Scott, "Erôs, Philosophy, and Tyranny," in *Maieusis: Essays on Ancient Philosophy in Honour of Myles Burnyeat*, ed. Dominic Scott (Oxford: Oxford University Press, 2007), 136–53.

15. As Suzanne Obdrzalek, "Moral Transformation and the Love of Beauty in Plato's *Symposium*," *Journal of the History of Philosophy* 48 (2010): 428n32, remarks, a passage from the *Laws* (731d–732b) indicates that self-love is, for Plato, the cornerstone of all vice.

16. This view seems to conflict with that of Ludwig. Specifically, Ludwig, "Eros in the *Republic*," in *The Cambridge Companion to Plato's Republic*, ed. G. R. F. Ferrari (Cambridge: Cambridge University Press, 2007), 223, contends that what makes the eros of *Republic* IX both possessive and tyrannical is that it is mixed

with spirit or *thumos*. Although *thumos* is certainly at work in the psychic economy of the tyrant, I disagree with Ludwig's view that *thumos* either "asserts the self" or can mean "the whole self" and therefore is essentially associated with the love of one's own (208). On my reading, *thumos* can be and often is closely linked to a sense of self and one's own, but this is not necessarily the case. Specifically, *thumos* is chiefly a sense of indignation at what *appears* to be wrong, shameful, or unjust and the willingness to do battle to protect what *seems* to be right, honorable, and just (*Republic* 440c–d). Although *thumos* and the self are wholly aligned in the case of the tyrant—and perhaps in a figure like Achilles—precisely because the tyrant equates his self and his own with what is good and just, this is not always the case. In what Plato would call nobler souls, the self and one's own, on the one hand, and notions of right, honor, and goodness, on the other, are distinct, and so when there is a conflict between the two, *thumos* is aroused at the violation of the latter rather than at an offense to the former. This is obvious in the case of Leontius. He is angry at and hostile to what is his own, namely, himself and his desire to look at corpses, precisely because he has been led by his desires to act in a way that violates his sense of moral rectitude (*Republic* 439e–440a). Similarly, Plato has Socrates explain that noble souls will not take offense at sufferings done to them when they believe such sufferings are just (*Republic* 440c). If *thumos* were simply about defending oneself, one would always take offense at any harm done to oneself by another. Finally, although, as Angela Hobbs, *Plato and the Hero: Courage, Manliness and the Impersonal Good* (Cambridge: Cambridge University Press, 2007), 19, notes, there is no mention of an agent becoming indignant at the sight of someone else being wronged, one could certainly imagine how *thumos*, when aligned with an objective understanding of justice, could generate a sense of indignation in such cases. Here again, the idea is that in a well-formed soul, *thumos* does not rush to defend one's own, but what is just and good.

17. Parry, "The Unhappy Tyrant," 398, also suggests a turn to literature, but points to contemporary descriptions of drug addicts.

18. See Babette Pütz, *The Symposium and Komos in Aristophanes* (Oxford: Aris & Phillips, 2007), for more on the presence of the *komos* and the symposium in Aristophanic comedy.

19. Waller Newell, *Ruling Passion: The Erotics of Statecraft in Platonic Political Philosophy* (Lanham, MD: Rowman & Littlefield Publishers, 2000), 12ff., identifies two versions of eros in Socrates' encounter with Callicles in the *Gorgias*.

20. Some recent book-length studies devoted exclusively to the *Symposium* include Daniel E. Anderson, *The Masks of Dionysos: A Commentary on Plato's Symposium* (Albany: State University of New York Press, 1993); Thomas L. Cooksey, *Plato's Symposium: A Reader's Guide* (London: Continuum, 2010); Kevin Corrigan and Elena Glazov-Corrigan, *Plato's Dialectic at Play: Argument, Structure, and Myth in the Symposium* (University Park: Pennsylvania State University Press, 2004); Stanley Rosen, *Plato's Symposium* (South Bend, IN: Saint Augustine's Press, 1999); Frisbee C. C. Sheffield, *Plato's Symposium: The Ethics of Desire* (Oxford: Oxford University

Press, 2006); Leo Strauss, *Leo Strauss on Plato's Symposium* (Chicago: University of Chicago Press, 2001). Corrigan and Glazov-Corrigan, Rosen, and Strauss should be credited for giving relatively equal attention to all of the speeches in the *Symposium*, rather than moving quickly to a detailed analysis of Diotima's speech.

21. Richard Kraut, "Plato on Love," in *The Oxford Handbook to Plato*, ed. Gail Fine (Oxford: Oxford University Press, 2008), 286–310.

22. Kraut, "Plato on Love," 305.

23. Kraut, "Plato on Love," 304.

24. See Larivée, "Eros *Tyrannos*," 11. As she notes, Alcibiades' longing for fame is described in erotic terms at *Alcibiades* 124b.

25. I am indebted to Obdrzalek, "Moral Transformation," 427, for this formulation.

26. Obdrzalek, "Moral Transformation," 417.

27. Obdrzalek's position does conflict with a very common reading, which holds that personal immortality is also a concern for the philosopher. The evidence for such a reading comes from *Symposium* 212a, where we are told that those who breed true virtue can also be said to be immortal. There are two reasons for resisting such a reading. First, as Obdrzalek, "Moral Transformation," 442, emphasizes, Diotima's language is guarded. She says that the philosophical lover *would* become immortal, *if* any human could. This, however, is not a promise of immortality. The second and more powerful objection is that it is hard to reconcile understanding immortality as an achievement with the view defended in the *Phaedo* that the soul is, by nature, immortal. In my view, Michael O'Brien, "'Becoming Immortal' in Plato's *Symposium*," in *Greek Poetry and Philosophy: Studies in Honour of Leonard Woodbury*, ed. Douglas E. Gerber (Chico, CA: Scholars Press, 1984), 200f., has correctly resolved this issue by arguing that Diotima's promise of the lover becoming *athanatos* should be understood not in terms of the imperishability of the philosopher's person, but rather in terms of becoming god-loved or blessed like a god.

28. Obdrzalek, "Moral Transformation," 427.

29. See Ludwig, *Eros and Polis*, 54ff., for a similar account.

30. See Ludwig, *Eros and Polis*, 97ff.

31. Larivée, "Eros *Tyrannos*." See note 8 for more on this point.

32. See Ambler, "Tyranny," 205, and Arrowsmith, "The Fantasy Politics," 129.

33. Ambler, "Tyranny," 194.

34. See Stephen Halliwell, "Aristophanic Sex," in *The Sleep of Reason: Erotic Experience and Sexual Ethics in Ancient Greece and Rome*, eds. Martha C. Nussbaum and Juha Sihvola (Chicago: University of Chicago Press, 2002), 124, on comedy as "institutionalized shamelessness."

35. The relativism of Aristophanic comedy might also be the key to resolving the apparent tension between the *Clouds* and a comedy like the *Birds*. Quite simply, Aristophanes criticizes in the *Clouds* the very behavior that seems to be endorsed in the *Birds*. As Ambler, "Tyranny," 202, asks, "by what strange principles would it make more sense for Socrates to be punished than Peisetairos?" The answer is that there are no such principles that govern all agents uniformly in the world of

Aristophanes, and therefore Aristophanes is free to slander a figure like Socrates for holding the very beliefs that his own poetry seems to presuppose and even endorse.

36. See Ludwig, *Eros and Polis*, 84, for a discussion of the link between Peisetairos' self-description as Porphyrion and the description of the circle-people's gigantism in the *Symposium*.

37. Here, I disagree with Saxonhouse, "Comedy in Callipolis," 889, that comedy reveals the ugly side of human existence because it shows our ties to the animal world. Although one can certainly understand comedy in this way, such an evaluation is, I think, deeply embedded in a philosophical tradition that understands reason to be the essential and distinguishing feature of humanity, but this understanding of the human being is ultimately foreign to comedy itself. On my reading, the comic world is one in which human rationality is reduced to the basic drives that we share with animals, but, at the same time, the human animal is then elevated through the artistry of the comic poet to divine status. This is achieved, at least in the *Birds*, by eliminating any cultural or transcendent standard that may make us feel a sense of *shame*. Once we feel ourselves to be the measure of all things, we can experience even the animal part of our existence to be perfect and beautiful in every way.

38. Arrowsmith, "Aristophanes' *Birds*," and Ludwig, *Eros and Polis*, 84.
39. Arrowsmith, "Aristophanes' *Birds*," 156.
40. Ludwig, *Eros and Polis*, 84.
41. Ludwig, *Eros and Polis*, 83.
42. Ludwig, *Eros and Polis*, 86.
43. Ludwig, *Eros and Polis*, 85.
44. Henderson, "Mass versus Elite," 142.
45. Henderson, "Mass versus Elite," 145.
46. My reading largely follows the one proposed by Douglas M. MacDowell, *Aristophanes and Athens: An Introduction to the Plays* (Oxford: Oxford University Press, 1995), 228: "The play shows this ordinary Athenian accomplishing what the ordinary Athenians in the audience can only dream of doing: getting control over everyone else, and using it for his own personal pleasure. It enables the spectator to imagine himself doing the same."

47. Here, I resist a reading that says we are meant to laugh *at* Peisetairos, as if he were a buffoon like Strepsiades.

48. Bloom, "Interpretive Essay," 425.

49. See Most, "What Ancient Quarrel," 6–12, for the view that all four poetic fragments that Plato has Socrates cite as evidence for poets attacking philosophy derive from one genre, Old Comedy. At *Republic* 608b, Plato speaks of an *agon* that concerns becoming good or bad. Not only was an *agon* a formal structure of Old Comedy, but the genre was imbued with a general spirit of contest and competition. For a detailed analysis of the competitive nature of Aristophanic comedy, see Zachary Biles, *Aristophanes and the Poetics of Competition* (Cambridge: Cambridge University Press, 2011). Also, at *Republic* 361d, Plato uses the language of a judgment or *krisis* that will be rendered concerning these two lives. Yun Lee Too, *The Idea of Ancient*

Literary Criticism (Oxford: Clarendon Press, 1998), chap. 1, traces the history of *krisis* and *agon* in ancient Greek literature and highlights the significant role they play in Aristophanic comedy.

50. See Halliwell's comments on the fantasy politics of Old Comedy in "Introduction," in *Aristophanes: Birds; Lysistrata; Assembly-Women; Wealth*, trans. Stephen Halliwell (Oxford: Oxford University Press, 2008), xxi–xxx.

51. I am simply modifying a claim that Nightingale, *Genres in Dialogue*, 172, makes about Plato's entire corpus.

14

Aristophanes' Feminine Comedies and Socratic Political Science

Amy L. Bonnette

Introduction

Amid the playfulness and humor of his plays about women, Aristophanes offers a surprisingly comprehensive treatment of Socratic political philosophy. He alludes not only to the excellence of Socrates' new approach but also to a threat it poses for traditional politics. His provocative imagery suggests that Socrates' new philosophy calls for a new rhetoric to address these practical concerns. Comparing the rude comic impossibilities of these plays with the gentlemanly and moderate Socratic portraits in Plato and Xenophon places one in a better position to see the crux, ultimately, of Socrates' political science.

What is that science? Let us begin from the stunning peak of Plato's *Republic*, rather than from Socrates' numerous denials of knowledge and perplexing cross-examinations. Book V is a reflection on the ultimate unity of human virtue or excellence, linked to a paradoxical conflation of political rule with household rule. Aristophanes pays homage to this insight, at the same time that he ridicules it, in his two most famous plays about women: *Lysistrata* and the *Assembly of Women*. His comic device is to put Socrates' oddly domestic understanding of political science into the mouths of housewives, who save Athens by means of radical political reform: Lysistrata through her notorious women's strike and Praxagora through her even more outrageous communism under the rule of women.

In the *Memorabilia*, Xenophon has Socrates state simply and clearly the strange but pivotal Socratic thesis that the art or science of politics is the same as that of economics in its original sense of household management. Socrates advises a recently defeated aspirant to Athens' highest political office who is bitter, in part, because his rival is a businessman without military credentials:

> Nichomachides, do not hold in contempt men who are skilled at household management [*oikonomike*]. For attending to private affairs differs only in terms of multitude from attending to public ones. Among other very great similarities the greatest one is this: neither comes about without human beings, nor are private affairs accomplished through some human beings, while public affairs are accomplished through other human beings. For those who attend to public affairs don't deal with any other human beings than those whom they deal with in private affairs when managing their households. And those who understand how to deal with these human beings do well [beautifully] both in private and in public affairs, and those who don't strike false notes in both. (*Memorabilia* III.4.12)[1]

Now, Nichomachides presumably has contempt for mere household management because he thinks rule over free men is more important than private household rule (over women, children, and slaves). His conclusion follows from the view that free men (*andres*) and their noble pursuits are simply superior. Socrates, on the other hand, seems to say that human beings are human beings, regardless of their sex or status as citizens. This does not sound particularly controversial to our ears, partly because of our egalitarian politics and partly because we are not attuned to its full implications. Many in our time, for example, accept with nonchalance the Socratic proposal for women soldiers in the *Republic*, a notion that would have appalled a sober political man like Nichomachides, especially with its concomitant family reform.

In Socrates' view, if rulers do not understand the governance of private households, then the nature of their task escapes them. Statesmen tend to be unaware of this need, and private householders, in turn, tend to be unaware of the large role of public law in their household rule. Addressing this dual obliviousness is no simple matter. Socrates alludes to the difficulty in the *Republic* when he, in effect, blames the downfall of the best regime on the rulers' misunderstanding of the nuptial number or, thereafter, in the discussion of regime character formation, on the private grumblings of women and servants.[2]

Although he agrees with Xenophon about Socrates' equation of political and economic science, Plato is reluctant to have his Socrates state it explicitly, in the *Republic* or elsewhere. Socrates does go so far as to mention it toward the end of Plato's *Lovers*, where the nobility of philosophy is coincidentally under question (*Lovers* 138c–39e). But the visitor from Elea is the philosopher in Plato who most clearly enunciates this paradoxical thought, and he does so, perhaps also coincidentally, on the eve of Socrates' famous trial and condemnation in Athens (*Statesman* 258e–59c; cf. Aristotle, *Politics* 1252a). Socrates, who is present in the *Statesman*, does not endorse the Stranger's thesis there. The most we can say is that Socrates observes and does not contradict the Eleatic, remaining silent at the end of the dialogue.[3] On the other hand, in the *Republic*, Plato illustrates, perhaps even more vividly than Xenophon, Socrates' *implicit* adoption of the economic thesis. At the outset of his city's imaginary construction, Socrates discovers the origins of political life in the division of labor for the supply of bodily needs, a topic usually considered under the purview of economics (*Republic* 369b). He then caps off his political theory by turning his virtual city into a single household, much along the lines of Praxagora in the *Assembly of Women*.

A revealing reflection on the implications of this tenet of Socratic political science, stated in the *Memorabilia* and *Lovers* and illustrated in the *Republic*, can be found in the *Meno*, where Plato draws a contrast between Socrates and Gorgias on the subject of virtue and its unity or diversity. When Socrates professes his ignorance about what virtue is—never mind whether it is teachable—Gorgias' student, Meno, takes a stab at a definition:

> But it isn't difficult to say, Socrates. In the first place, if you want the virtue of a man, that's easy. This is the virtue of a man: to be capable of carrying out the affairs of the city and, in doing so, to benefit friends, to harm enemies, and take care that he himself not suffer any such thing. And if you want the virtue of a woman, it isn't difficult to define: she must manage the household well by both preserving its contents and being obedient to the man. And there is one virtue of a child, both female and male, and another of an older man, whether free, or, if you like, slave. There are also very many other virtues, so there is no perplexity in speaking about what virtue is. For the virtue belonging to each of us is related to each task appropriate to each action and time of life. (*Meno* 71e–72a)[4]

Now this seems an eminently sensible initial understanding of virtue. It is associated with our duties as citizens and family members, which differ between males and females as well as between social classes, and which change over our lifetimes as we grow from children to become adults, free or slave, husbands, wives, parents, and grandparents. Aristotle himself endorses this view in the *Politics*, explicitly siding with Gorgias and rejecting Socrates' odd, unified understanding of virtue (1259a–60b).[5]

Against Meno's definition, Socrates wonders whether there isn't one definition of human virtue or excellence, offering the example of bees. Bees do not differ from one another insofar as they are bees. Is not human excellence the same quality in all, he asks, whether it belongs to a man or a woman, just as health and strength are the same in both (73a)?[6] It is difficult to see whether this is Socrates' final position, and if it is, how he might arrive at it. Surely, its mere consideration is morally and politically problematic, given the traditionally different social requirements of men and women, children and parents, slave and free.

Socrates proceeds to restate Meno's earlier assertion, so that the virtue of a man is defined as accomplishing the affairs of the city not in the specifically manly sense—as helping friends and harming enemies—but rather more broadly, as "managing" the city well. In the same way, he defines the virtue of a woman as "managing" a household well, now dropping the important qualification that she must do so in obedience to her husband (73a–b; cf. 71e; *Protagoras* 317b). Thus, Socrates arrives at "management" (*oikein*) as *the* task of human beings. This crucial identification of the fundamental work of human beings provides a reasonable basis for Socrates' identification of economics and politics.[7] Does Socrates teach this art of "management"? He certainly does not profess that he does. While Socrates forces the sophist Protagoras to admit to teaching something similar to this "management" (which Protagoras names "good counsel," *euboulia*), for his own part, in a parallel situation, Socrates denies that he knows the art of politics, except regarding the small subject of eros (*Protagoras* 318e–19a; *Theages* 128b–c).

To return to the *Meno*, Socrates hastens to add next that all individuals must perform their duties well—and so, moderately and justly—whether men or women, children or old men (73b). What, then, he asks, is the universal virtue that belongs to these varied human beings? Prior to this question, we might have been inclined to think that the universal virtue or excellence of human beings is precisely their competency at their work rather than the disposition with which they perform their work. In fact, probably influenced by Socrates' prior suggestions, Meno responds that the universal virtue or excellence they seek is the ability to rule human beings (rather than justice or moderation, as he might have responded on the basis of Socrates' new qualification). But, under Socrates' subsequent pressing, Meno cannot accept the consequence that the virtue of a slave or a child would be to rule the master (73d). We should note that, although there are no sons of Meno present, there are several of Meno's slaves in their company (82b, the same word can be used for "son" or "boy" and "slave," *pais*). Thus, we begin to sense the politically unacceptable implications of Socrates' line of questioning. Socrates, later in the dialogue, has a conversation in front of Meno with one of Meno's slaves. He teaches him geometry, all the while claiming that he does not himself teach the slave anything by his leading questions but that he merely helps him to recollect what he somehow already knew (82b–86c). It does not take an enormous leap of imagination, at least for those who have read the *Clouds*, to infer that this overall Socratic approach to virtue might suggest that educated sons should rule over their uneducated fathers and even beat them if they resist correction (cf. *Clouds* 1410–45). And thus it comes as no surprise that Plato has one of Socrates' accusers, Anytus, appear in this dialogue (89e–90b; cf. Xenophon, *Apology* 30–31). It is this line of thought about human virtue as it relates to the political division of labor that Aristophanes pointedly ridicules in his female plays.

One can see a possible motivation for Socrates' pursuit of this question of the political division of labor in *Alcibiades I*. That dialogue connects happiness via the art of conversation with Socrates' interest in citizens "doing their own business" (and hence with the question of the unity or diversity of virtue). Together with an aspiring ruler, Socrates explores the desire to know oneself (*Alcibiades I* 127b–29e). He looks upon a conversation as an attempt to gaze into the soul of another, which, in turn, forms part of the quest to know oneself (132e–33e). If there is no overlap in the work or function of the various parts of the city, or of the various types of human beings, then one might wonder whether there can be friendship or understanding (*homonoia*) between them, or ultimately even within the individual (for the parts of one's soul are somehow reflected in the diverse parts of the city) (*Alcibiades I* 126d; cf. *Republic* 443a–d, 453b, 620c).

In other words, the city necessarily divides us insofar as it is concerned with the body (and hence with a division of labor), and it must divide us in the first place into male and female, young and old. Is it possible, despite this necessary division, to find a common ground of understanding, such that a human being can be called a human being, as opposed to a man or woman, elder or child? If the specific virtue belonging to the best individual can be understood as ability to rule, and if, in the primary case, rule is self-rule, or the internal harmony of the parts of one's soul, then we might ultimately understand human work as a single activity (*Republic* 443d). Or, on the contrary, must even self-rule necessarily be of two (or more) types because there are two (or more) fundamentally different types of thinking beings, as suggested primarily by our naturally different functions in the community (to say nothing of the divine beings involved in governing that community) (cf. *Oeconomicus* VII.18)?[8]

Aristophanes' ridicule of Socratic thought through his female comic heroines reveals aspects of the division of labor and its relation to virtue in the *Republic*, particularly in Book V, which may remain opaque to us on the basis of Plato alone. This may be partly because, in his shameless appeal to the tastes of the demos, Aristophanes is willing to stoop to forms of slander and indecency that cultivated individuals do not easily abide. In order to consider Aristophanes' feminine plays thoroughly, we must review not just his *Ecclesiazusae* (*Assembly of Women*) and *Lysistrata*, with their female heroines, but also the *Thesmophoriazusae* (*Women at the Thesmophoria*), because its chorus and theme are obviously feminine in spite of the fact that its protagonist is the manly Euripides.

Then, in turn, if we use the presence of a female chorus and theme as our criteria, the *Clouds* itself may be counted as the fourth of Aristophanes' feminine plays. Its chorus is composed of female deities who appear as mortal women to the protagonist Strepsiades (*Clouds* 315, 329, 344). And this association of the *Clouds* with the other female plays is not merely a matter of form: Euripides is an associate of Socrates (*Frogs* 1491–95), and both Euripides and Socrates suffer by the action of Aristophanic females. The females of the *Thesmophoriazusae* quite harshly persecute Socrates' purported student, Euripides, while the females of the *Clouds* are at least indirectly responsible for the burning down of Socrates' school. It is perhaps fair to say that the *Clouds* and the *Thesmophoriazusae* illustrate the potential fallout, for Socrates and for his friends, from his new form of political science—a science, to repeat, that is embodied somehow in Aristophanes' heroines in the *Lysistrata* and the *Ecclesiazusae*. So the four feminine plays can be divided into two subsets: those with female protagonists who present the new Socratic political science, and those with male protagonists who suffer from the fallout of that science.

Now, this coolness or even hostility of females to Socrates and Euripides comes as a surprise to us and calls for an explanation. If we associate

Socratic thought with the *Lysistrata* and *Ecclesiazusae*, then we see that the plays show a radical political change in the public role of women, if only in speech. Moreover, to associate Plato's Socrates and the poet Euripides with what we might call a groundbreaking approach to women accords with their giving prominence to female characters in their own rhetoric, whether it be Socrates' use of Diotima and Aspasia as his purported teachers and mouthpieces or Euripides' use of Medea, Helen, Phaedra, or Andromeda, to name a few of his female roles. Yet while actual women may very well be intrigued by this novelty, it is also understandable if they see a downside to it. The obvious impossibility of Lysistrata's and Praxagora's reforms may provide sufficient explanation, for what conceivable good could come from exposing women to ridicule in this gross manner for no practicable benefit? The manifest ugliness of Praxagora's reform, in particular, could furnish grounds for distrust of Socrates.[9] The Aristophanic characters, Lysistrata and Praxagora, are ostensibly driven to extreme measures because they wish to save Athens from its manifestly self-destructive behavior. Therefore, this ridicule of Athenian politics might serve a practical purpose. But Socrates' strange political thesis is not restricted to the dire straits of Athenian politics. The female choruses of the *Clouds* and the *Thesmophoriazusae* would reasonably consider stable political life as simply necessary. One who puts himself at odds with stable politics, if only by raising uncomfortable questions, would not simply and obviously be a friend to women in general. Perhaps the actual Socrates, like Aristophanes' Euripides, had to work to gain the friendship of women, or at least their respect, if he wanted his own project to have further success. It would not be surprising if the new Socratic rhetoric took this difficulty into consideration. The desire to understand the underlying tension between these two sets of female plays, or to understand Socrates' political science and its political fallout, is the impetus for the following argument.

Lysistrata and the *Assembly of Women*: Socratic Political Science

One cannot prove that Aristophanes had Socrates in mind when he drew the characters of Lysistrata and Praxagora. In fact, at first or second glance, it may seem ludicrous. To begin with the obvious, Socrates is not a woman. Secondly, Socrates famously did not write for himself. So there is no written evidence that the particulars of Socratic political science were widely enough known for popular lampooning.[10] Aristophanes was decades older than Plato or Xenophon. Although there may have been some overlap in their activity at the end of Aristophanes' career, he certainly wrote the vast majority of his plays before their work was written and available.

One is on safer ground in conjecturing that Plato, in turn, referred to these two plays when he wrote his dialogues. Scholars often suggest that Plato had in mind the *Ecclesiazusae* when he wrote the *Republic*, for the parallels between the works are too numerous to ignore.[11] Both Socrates' and Praxagora's political reform make the city look like one household without the walls that divide families, with communal use of property and women, regulated by the city's sole ruler, and with citizens eating at common meals. Less extensively discussed than the parallels between the *Ecclesiazusae* and the *Republic* (but still noticed in the scholarship) is the analogy between political science and weaving connecting Plato's *Statesman* with the *Lysistrata* (*Lysistrata* 568–86; *Statesman* 279ff.).[12] Lysistrata argues that because the women already know the art of weaving, they are competent to resolve the particular difficulties that happen to face Athens. Plato's Eleatic Stranger takes that analogy further, comparing the whole art of politics (statesmanship) to the art of weaving, although he does so without emphasizing that weaving is the art belonging emblematically to women.

Others may argue that, rather than consciously responding to Aristophanic parodies of Socratic thought, Plato was making literary allusions to entirely independent political satires of Aristophanes, which in themselves have nothing to do with Socrates, or even that Plato merely stumbled upon the same widely used images.[13] In any case, we may find that we better understand Socrates as well as Aristophanes by thinking about these feminine plays *as if* they are parodies of Socrates. Surely no harm comes from testing a working hypothesis that Aristophanes intended to address Socrates' thought in some manner in all of his feminine plays and that Plato and Xenophon wrote partly in response to Aristophanes' analysis.[14]

Lysistrata

Lysistrata is the only of Aristophanes' extant comedies named after the protagonist. This outstanding female arranges a clandestine early-morning meeting of Athenian wives with representative wives from the enemy cities, most importantly, Lampito from Sparta. She persuades them all to swear an oath not to enjoy their husbands until the men of Greece reconcile, so as to end the Peloponnesian War and thereby save Greece from self-destruction. Lampito will not agree to this foreign conspiracy until Lysistrata assures her that the Athenian women will take the additional step of seizing Athens' treasury, a step without which she doubts that the scheme can succeed.

In other words, she does not think Lysistrata's approach is sound unless a coup will change the regime in Athens. The "rabble," in her view, cannot be persuaded by the wives' strike. The link between Ares and Aphrodite, as explored in this play, is operationally significant among a limited class of human beings.

Lampito and Lysistrata thus implicitly endorse the view of Socrates, who, in the *Republic*, associates the private influence of women with the transformation of the best regime into the next-best form of government, a "timarchy," or the rule of upper class gentlemen (548a–49e).[15] Socrates presents this form of government as more open to women's influence than democracy, in spite of what is suggested by democracy's devotion to the principles of liberty and equality. Aristophanes exploits this aspect of Socratic political science for laughs in the *Lysistrata* and the *Thesmophoriazusae*, both of which were staged within months around the oligarchic revolution in Athens in 411 BC.[16] Aristophanes can thus, in relative poetic safety, entertain and delight his democratic audience by indirectly lampooning the oligarchs through his farcical women's coups. At the same time, he can speak to the sophisticates in his audience who may be aware of reasons for the link to be found between aristocrats-oligarchs and women in Socrates' political analysis. In the world outside comedy, or mere speech, the natural inequality between the sexes cannot be eradicated or ignored; its consequences can only be ameliorated by different forms of inequality.

Happily for the success of Lysistrata's scheme, she occupies the imaginary world of Aristophanic comedy, in which the virile men of military age are somehow present in their private homes and, at the same time, absent from the city. Therefore, the women may clandestinely occupy the acropolis and then forcibly defend it from the paltry old men who remain to guard the citadel. The military coup (i.e., not the wives' strike) is believable if the young men are away from home on campaign, for the physical differences between old men and women are no longer politically decisive.

Lysistrata and her band of women easily seize and occupy the acropolis, and therefore the Athenian magistrate is forced to reason with her. He asks her to justify the women's claim to rule. It is at this point that we see the full measure of Lysistrata's agreement with Socrates. Like Socrates, she claims that the difference between male and female physical attributes is irrelevant to their just claim to rule. Socrates in the *Republic* compares the difference between men and women to that between bald and hairy men in its relevance to their natural capacity or inclination to be artisans of any type, including warriors and rulers (*Republic* 454c). Lysistrata, more modestly, claims that the women already run the men's household treasuries (which must be all the more true during the war), so of course they are able to run the city's treasury. The magistrate insists that it is not the same thing, citing Hector's judgment in the *Iliad* that "war is the concern of men" (520; *Iliad* VI.483–92), while Lysistrata's assertions (insisting that household and political management skills are essentially the same) echo Socrates' above statement to Nichomachides.

We thus see even in the first few scenes of the play that the author of the *Lysistrata*, like the Socrates of the *Meno* and the *Republic*, is aware of the political significance of differences of age and sex as they relate to the capacity for excellence or virtue and the consequent variety among political regimes. To state only two obvious points from this outrageous comedy: old men are not as courageous as young men, and young men are not as dignified as old men. Even the extremely undignified old men in this play are more dignified than the young men. In relation to this question of dignity, one can speculate more generally about differing capacities for moderation. In the *Republic*, Cephalus acts as Plato's witness to the diminished power of Aphrodite in old age (329a). Diminution of desire may look like moderation from the outside, yet it lacks the element of continence or self-control (which serves as the natural foundation for the virtue of moderation). This difference between young and old, then, cannot quite be comparable to the difference between male and female.

By demonstrating the women's military success on the acropolis, Lysistrata magically overcomes the obvious obstacle to the credibility of Socrates' insistence in the *Republic* on the notion of women rulers, following upon his insistence that they be included in the warrior class. Lysistrata must offer such a demonstration, because there is more at stake for her interlocutor than for the youngster Glaucon, who is reassured by Socrates' assertion that women are always inferior at every art, as they surely must be in the politically significant warrior's art (*Republic* 540c). Socrates claims that women, although equally suited in their natures, are weaker or inferior in ability across the board (*Republic* 455e; cf. 369d). He even uses weaving (and cooking) to support his assertion of women's inferiority, for there are obviously professional male chefs and weavers who surpass the expertise of wives who practice daily the domestic arts of cooking and weaving (455c–d). He therefore allows himself to conclude that the women can never surpass the male practitioners of any art, just as they obviously cannot excel in the physical aspects of the warrior art.

Lysistrata, to the contrary, appeals precisely to the special training or excellence of women in weaving to justify her claim that the women deserve to rule rather than the men. Perhaps she would find Socrates' arguments unpersuasive, if only because of the women's absence from the public realm of professional chefs and weavers. Or she may think of weaving as a stand-in for home economics, or domestic science, more broadly understood. It is not so much the perfection of the technique of weaving, but understanding the underlying need for weaving, which most connects this art to women and perhaps also to that goddess of wisdom, Athena (cf. *Protagoras* 321c–e, and context). At any rate, Lysistrata resembles more the Eleatic Stranger than Socrates on this score. If statesmanship truly is more analogous to weaving than to soldiering, then Lysistrata at least has a more plausible claim for meriting control of Athenian public policy.

We now see more clearly the significance of Socrates' choosing bees as a point of comparison in the *Meno*.[17] The understanding of human virtue as a capacity for "management," when combined with the bee example, points in the direction of Lysistrata's and the Eleatic's analogy of politics to weaving rather than in the direction of Socrates' selection of rulers from the warrior class (cf. *Republic* 374b). The queen bee has by her nature a presiding rather than a protective function. The hive alludes to the rule of women on the basis of their own peculiar abilities rather than on their fanciful participation in masculine abilities. The bee example calls to mind Queen Penelope's skillful and prudent weaving as part of her household management during Odysseus' prolonged absence in Homer. It may also call to mind Xenophon's *Oeconomicus*, where the perfect gentleman Ischomachus recounts to Socrates how he encouraged his young wife to envision herself as a queen bee in order to instruct and inspire her to embrace her duties as household manager (*Oeconomicus* VII.32–40). Of course, Ischomachus, like Nichomachides, does not for a moment think that household management has anything to do with politics, and the whole premise of his education of his wife is that she will perform her household duties in obedience to her husband (*Oeconomicus* IX.1, X.1).

Now, the Eleatic Stranger, for his part, avoids any suggestion of weaving being a woman's art. Therefore, he can also avoid Lysistrata's strange conclusion that the women deserve to rule. Socrates, in the *Republic*, does not even try to avoid that conclusion. He explicitly insists upon their potential for rule while immunizing himself against its abrasive effect by speaking to a youngster, to begin with, and by assuring him that the women are universally inferior in every art, including weaving. He also avoids mentioning in this context the arts of rhetoric, midwifery, and matchmaking.[18] That is, he does not say in the *Republic* that he himself learned certain important subjects from female instructors. Moreover, while making plausible use of animal analogies such as guard dogs, he suppresses his own probable awareness of that gregarious species, the bee, which builds its own community and in which the female is superior in something that looks like rule. On the other hand, the fact that bees are not mammals but insects suggests that such analogies in general are of limited use. They only serve as an impetus to further thought (cf. *Clouds* 1321, 1427; *Birds* 1345–50). Human beings are similar in different aspects to different animals. For example, although they are not winged and do not lay eggs, they live in nests, so to speak, and pair off like birds. Also like birds, cattle, or dogs, they appear naturally to form flocks, herds, or packs, even while they build walls around their communities like bees. Yet, what is most important to notice, what sets human beings apart from all other animals is that the others, with their limited capacity to reason, recognize neither gods nor law and do not use any art, much less such advanced arts as weaving or politics (*Protagoras* 320c–22d).

In spite of her extreme claim, Lysistrata desires only a temporary involvement in statesmanship to pull Athens back from the brink of its political insanity. Following her military and intellectual victory over the Athenian magistrate (and perhaps to distract from it), the action of the play turns to the young wives' marital strike, which is (eventually) completely successful. This success is not entirely fanciful, if the suggestion regarding the influence of women in oligarchic Sparta can be believed. Because of their current dismal military situation, the Athenian men, for their part, would be eager for peace regardless of the wives' strike, as long as the Spartans sue for it. Thus, the ugly physical battle between old men and old women, and the disturbing background notion of the oligarchic coup, is replaced by a compelling and beautiful war of wills between a young husband and wife, Kinesias and Myrrhine. This couple is very much in love with one another, and they both desire what is a natural common pleasure, and hence, one would think, a common good (cf. *Theages* 121b–c; *Memorabilia* II.2.5). Unfortunately, the war has required that the simple unity of this small community be temporarily sacrificed to the good of the larger community. That larger community may ultimately serve the smaller community, but in this particular instance it thwarts it. Individual family communities return to their happy condition only after that divine female, Reconciliation, guided by Lysistrata, accomplishes a negotiated end to the war.

Ecclesiazusae

Praxagora, similarly to Lysistrata, gathers the wives for a predawn conspiracy against their husbands, but her political project is a more radical one than

Lysistrata's. In contrast to Lysistrata's temporary change, Praxagora wishes to replace permanently the existing regime with a new one, and indeed to remove the underlying structure of all existing political regimes, namely, the family. She gains permanent control to establish a new form of politics, and she does so using only fraud and persuasion, whereas Lysistrata uses open force in concert with fraud and persuasion.[19]

Praxagora convinces and trains the women to pretend to be men, in dress and in manner, so as to pack the assembly before dawn and vote that the city be turned over to the women to govern. She first persuades the women by argument in secret, and then speaks to the city at large in disguise. Lysistrata spoke openly as a woman to the elderly citizens and the city's magistrate, with mixed results. Praxagora persuades only her fellow conspirators in her own person. She and her cadre need not genuinely persuade the men, because her voter fraud makes available the legal instrument of democracy, majority vote, an instrument which implicitly acknowledges the claim of brachial strength to rule. By this massive fraud, she overturns the democracy and replaces it with the absolute rule of the one best human being: herself.

Once in power, Praxagora institutes the reform that famously resembles the Socratic reform of politics in the *Republic*, destroying individual families and turning the city into one big household governed by a benevolent despot. As supreme general, she orders state collection and ownership of all property. The women rulers will distribute food in common meals and clothing as needed. Most significant, however, is Praxagora's destruction of traditional family morality in favor of a new, ostensibly egalitarian sexual morality. The custom of marriage gives excessive influence to youth and beauty. If the beautiful are allowed to choose freely even their temporary partners, they enjoy an unequal or unfair advantage. Praxagora counteracts this natural advantage by insisting that the beautiful be with the ugly, especially the elderly, before they may enjoy their chosen partners. Now that the women rule publicly by law, the prerogative that accrued to youthful beauty under the old morality is no longer justifiable. It would be unreasonable to pile convention upon convention in favor of one class of human beings. Of course, even beyond adultery, traditional sexual prohibitions that once supported the family need no longer be sustained, as we see also in the *Republic* Book V (461a–e; *Ecclesiazusae* 1040–42).[20]

Aristophanes' Heroines and Socrates

Praxagora agrees with Lysistrata that the rule of women is justified by the essential similarity of "management" over household and city; that is, they both adopt Socrates' political thesis equating economics with politics.[21] All three political reformers also overturn sexual mores to achieve their novel political goals. These similarities alone might indicate that Aristophanes uses these two females to lampoon Socrates' thought. Yet the resemblances do not end there. There is also the related Socratic insistence in Plato and Xenophon on the education of wives (*Republic* 451d; Xenophon, *Symposium* II.9; *Oeconomicus* III.10–15). A connection between women governing (or women being governed) and women being educated is suggested by Socrates' insistence that his female guardians must be equally educated for their equal tasks. Lysistrata and Praxagora have no visible schooling, yet they clearly managed to inform themselves somehow about the nature of political life.[22] This puzzle is related to another puzzle in Plato that is discussed below after considering the two remaining female comedies: in spite of Socrates making it clear that he received an education himself from the women Aspasia and Diotima and in spite of his making equal education a matter of central concern in the *Republic*, and in spite of his repeated advice to young companions in Xenophon to educate their wives, he himself cannot be seen educating any woman in any work of Plato.

At present, we are in a position to observe that Plato divides the underlying thought of Aristophanes' Lysistrata and Praxagora among three political scientists (Socrates, the Eleatic Stranger, and the Athenian Stranger) in such a way as to allow these respectable philosophers to avoid some of the ridiculousness of these heroines (cf. *Laws* 789e–90a; *Republic* 451a–b). Socrates in the *Republic* bases his reforms in the city in speech upon reasoning such as Lysistrata's, Praxagora's, and the Eleatic's—that the political art is analogous to a domestic art (whether that art be weaving or the very art of household management itself)—but he does not make explicit that underlying reasoning, as he once does briefly in the rather different context at the end of Plato's *Lovers*. Along with this restraint, Socrates focuses on the military as the class from which rulers will be drawn (*Republic* 374b). Conversely, the Eleatic Stranger, in keeping with his weaving analogy, downplays the military component of political rule. At the same time, he steers clear of the explicit egalitarianism concerning the sexes to be found in Socrates, Lysistrata, and Praxagora. Finally, both Socrates and the Eleatic largely abstract from erotic passion in their thematic treatments of political science, while Lysistrata and Praxagora focus more than any decent person should on this matter. Lysistrata does so somewhat beautifully, Praxagora quite appallingly.

The Athenian Stranger of the *Laws* is the most comprehensive and, at the same time, the least outrageous of all five of these figures. He uses the analogy of weaving to politics (734e), insists upon equal education (781b), as well as upon statesmen being able to govern households, in full knowledge of the significance of marriage, birth, and even the swaddling of infants for political science (771e–76b, 779e–85b, 788e–95d). He also directly addresses doubts concerning the providence of the gods, as the others do not, and Praxagora and Lysistrata least of all. Yet he incorporates all of these elements in so moderate a way as to be considered even conservative by some readers (at least in comparison to Socrates, with whom Aristotle, for his part, conflates him) (*Politics* 1265a).

If we take a cue from the discussion of "management" (*oikein*) in the *Meno*, we can see that the management of housewives (in both the subjective and objective use of the word "of") is a primary theme in both of these female plays, as well as in the *Republic* and the *Laws*. These two heroines are at the same time rulers and themselves housewives. Praxagora actively governs Athens and Lysistrata at least arbitrates for all of Greece, but both only *after* securing their influence first over their fellow housewives. In the *Thesmophoriazusae* and the *Clouds* we see two further examples of the need for governing housewives. In the *Thesmophoriazusae*, the wives in the city of Athens take punitive action as a group against Euripides. In the *Clouds*, the topic of an individual ungovernable wife is prominent. Although she is not named and does not even appear, she is somehow an impetus for the two most important actions of the play: Strepsiades' decision to attend Socrates' school and his later decision to burn it down.

The *Thesmophoriazusae* and the *Clouds*: The Fallout from Socrates' Political Science

In the *Thesmophoriazusae* and the *Clouds*, we glimpse a potential for coolness, if not enmity, between Socrates and women, at odds with the suggestion from the *Ecclesiazusae* and *Lysistrata* that Socrates is somehow intellectually close to women, not to say chief among them.[23] Perhaps not surprisingly, female deities also play a significant role in these two comedies. The Athenian housewives in the *Thesmophoriazusae* are on a religious retreat away from their individual homes as they celebrate a festival in honor of the goddesses of the underworld, the mother and daughter Demeter and Persephone. These celebrants are determined to punish their worst enemy, that notorious misogynist (and friend of Socrates) Euripides (*Lysistrata* 283; *Frogs* 1491–95). We do not know whether the women here are aware of Socrates' closeness to Euripides, as it is revealed at the end of the *Frogs*, but they are certainly of the opinion that Euripides teaches that the city's gods do not exist, as Socrates does in the *Clouds* (*Thesmophoriazusae* 451; cf. *Clouds* 381). As for the female deities in the *Clouds*, they are introduced to Athens by Socrates and initially admire him, but ultimately give him a cold shoulder, to say the least. They see for themselves Socrates' unorthodox religious views, some of which obviously serve their interest as newly introduced goddesses. Both of these all-female choruses behave in a punishing manner, but there is a progression toward greater friendliness in the *Thesmophoriazusae*, and one toward lesser friendliness in the *Clouds*.

Thesmophoriazusae

The justification for female hostility against the play's major male character is evident in the case of the *Thesmophoriazusae*. Unlike Socrates, Euripides has thrown down a gauntlet to the women. His tragedies habitually speak ill of women. What possible motive could he have for this ungentlemanly behavior? Rather than actual hostility on his part, Euripides' offensive surface could be masking something different, a defensive maneuver. We watch him as a character in this play taking further action against women, even going so far as to violate civic and religious law. Here, his being on offense is clearly for the purpose of self-defense, because the women have already scheduled a clandestine trial at the Thesmophoria festival in order to condemn and destroy him for his crimes against them.

Euripides' criminality, according to the women, consists in writing predominantly about bad women. Hence, he has made the lives of all women more difficult by making their male relatives suspicious of them (385–428). The women complain that he has not written plays about women like Penelope, but only about those like Phaedra (544–48). They do not mention that when he wrote about that notorious woman, Helen, Euripides portrayed her more favorably than Homer did. He suggests in his *Helen* that she did not really run off to Troy with her lover, but that the Homeric Helen was only an image of the real Helen, who was held captive in Egypt (856).

The Athenian women condemn Euripides at their exclusively female religious festival in honor of the same two goddesses celebrated, coincidentally, by the Eleusinian mysteries. Mocking the Eleusinian mysteries was the charge supporting the capital condemnation of another famous student or friend of Socrates, Alcibiades. In the *Symposium*, not long before Alcibiades was charged with that crime, Plato portrays him showing up late and drunk at the house of Agathon, where Socrates and Aristophanes form part of a group discussing the god Eros at a banquet in celebration of Agathon's popular victory as a tragedian.[24] This Agathon happens to appear prominently in the *Thesmophoriazusae* as a young playwright whose aid Euripides seeks. The *Thesmophoriazusae* begins with Euripides taking a character named Inlaw along to Agathon's house to ask for this poet's help (184–86). Agathon is notoriously effeminate, and so he presumably has a better relationship with women because of his kinship with them. Thus, Euripides reasons, he would escape notice as an infiltrator at the women's gathering, where he might speak on Euripides' behalf disguised as a woman. Agathon refuses on the grounds that his very closeness to the women would make them suspect that he is trying to steal their secrets (204–5). Agathon knows a great deal about women already, as is evident both in his poetry and in his personal equipment (130–45).

In spite of his keen sense of self-preservation, Agathon does not leave Euripides completely hanging. He is willing to groom and dress the Inlaw as a woman so that this old buffoon can serve as Euripides' apologist. The Inlaw, as he is dressed, and later as he listens to the women's secret indictment of Euripides, becomes a witness to certain private womanly behaviors. Naturally, Aristophanes reveals them for the whole audience to see. Aristophanes also (jokingly) portrays women in a bad light, as Euripides had. He shows them professing their intention to clandestinely kill Euripides, because they all recognize even before any trial that he is guilty of hostility toward them. One of them further blames Euripides for his impiety, not primarily on the grounds that impiety is wicked but because her livelihood as a wreath maker has been threatened by Euripides' teaching (450–55).[25]

When the disguised Inlaw has his chance to speak, he defends Euripides by pointing out that the tragic poet could easily have said worse things about women. He helpfully offers a list of feminine misbehavior that Euripides had left unmentioned. The women are outraged by this female's audacity and lack of loyalty to be saying such things out loud. Just as they are about to take revenge on "her," however, rumor comes that a man has infiltrated their festival. It does not take long for them to discover the Inlaw. His response is to steal a swaddled infant from a woman and hold it hostage, threatening its life. This tactic fails miserably, for the beloved "infant" is in fact loved and mourned because it is a disguised wineskin (735–55).

The Inlaw is arrested, on the report of the women, for committing the capital crime of impiety by violating the women's festival (764). The gods, and the civic laws regulating their worship, endorse a proper privacy, distinction, and separation between the sexes, for which these women, at least, are grateful (946–1000; *Oeconomicus* VII.7–8, 16–29). The Inlaw can only hope that Euripides will rescue him. Euripides indeed does so by gradually building a bridge to the women through a series of parodies of his own plays, one of them his *Helen* (850–925). He is finally able to free his defender, with female cooperation. The criminal Inlaw is held under what can be described literally here as the city's brute force in the form of a Scythian policeman. After securing the acquiescence of the women, Euripides lures the ignorant brute away from his duty with a combination of music and a "dancing girl," allowing the Inlaw and Euripides to escape. Euripides' ability to compose music and his willingness to compromise make him a potential ally of the women in mollifying and distracting the brute. At the same time, he remains dangerous to the women through his knowledge of their ways, which he must have gleaned, in part, through his desire to produce realistic images of them for his art, as did Agathon (174).

Clouds

The *Thesmophoriazusae* and the *Clouds* are the only two extant comedies by Aristophanes with male protagonists and female choruses. In each case, the protagonist seeks the help of another Athenian citizen to solve a problem caused by women. It is not evident that Euripides' public difficulty with the whole Athenian womanhood is more problematic than Strepsiades' personal difficulty with his wife. Without ever appearing in the play or even knowing about its action, she is partially responsible for the ruin of Strepsiades, as well as indirectly for that of Socrates. Yet Socrates shows little if any indication in the play that he is even aware of this wife (cf. *Oeconomicus* VII.4).

Strepsiades is a rustic farmer burdened with an outrageously spendthrift and politically ambitious son, all because he married a fancy woman from a powerful family. He reports how he first argued with his wife over her extravagant spending, then over the rearing of their son (10–80). He clearly lost these arguments on the important points. Now, he wants to bring his son with him to seek the help of the wise man Socrates, to learn forensic rhetoric, and thus to escape the family debts in court. The son refuses to attend the school, and Strepsiades is left to become the student himself. He fails his course of instruction, but, during it, Socrates introduces him to the Clouds, the female deities who look like mortal women to Strepsiades (344). After his expulsion, and in his despair, these beings recommend that he insist upon his son's attending Socrates' school (795–96). This suggestion at a critical juncture certainly contributes to Socrates' ruin.

The father is initially pleased with the son's successful education or, we should say, corruption, by Socrates. Yet Strepsiades objects when his son admires the tragic poet with whom we are by now quite familiar, Euripides, who makes obnoxious suggestions about family morality (1372). This disagreement over poetry leads the son to beat his father. Yet it is when the son threatens to beat his mother (Strepsiades' wife) that Strepsiades decides to punish Socrates for the ruin of his family, and so he burns down the school. When Strepsiades complains to the Cloud goddesses for steering him the wrong way, they inform him that they allow wicked men to go astray so as to teach them a lesson (1452–61).

So the *Clouds*, in this manner, brings us back to the common ground that Socrates has with Praxagora on the subject of family morality.[26] Socrates and Praxagora are radical thinkers who do not hesitate to go to the foundations of political science. It would seem that, as a result, there is no room for them in politics proper. Yet Praxagora manages to find a place, at least in Aristophanic politics, as Plato's Socrates does in the *Republic*. Their schemes are utopian, but they are not simply apolitical in the manner of Socrates in the *Clouds*. Lysistrata and the Eleatic Stranger may show us one potential path for that transformation of Socratic thought from apolitical to political by arguing that the weaving art is key for a statesman to master. In the *Statesman*, the Eleatic Stranger ties the art of weaving to the art of matchmaking as the basis of the "social fabric" (305e–8b). Matchmaking, perhaps coincidentally, is the topic with which the *Clouds* begins. In his initial misery, Strepsiades does not curse his wife, per se, but the matchmaker who introduced them (41). Knowledge of the correct formation of marriages plays an important role in the *Statesman* as well as in Plato's two other masterworks of political science, the *Republic* and *Laws*.[27]

While we are on the subject of the feminine arts, we should note the famous Socratic comparison of his own quasieducational activity to the other womanly art that he connects to matchmaking: midwifery (*Theaetetus* 149a–51e). One of the striking aspects of Socrates' claim to possess his mother's art is that he explicitly says that he practices it not on women but on men, even repeating the point just before he goes off to the portico of the King (or of Zeus) to answer the charge brought against him by Meletus (*Theaetetus* 150a–b, 210c–d; *Theages* 121a; *Oeconomicus* VII.1). Now, it would be highly improper for a man to be even a metaphorical midwife to women, particularly as it concerns other men's wives. In the terms of a similar Socratic metaphor, physicians of the soul need to strip the souls of their patients in order to make a diagnosis (*Protagoras* 325a–b). This practice would necessarily come up against the female soul's natural inclination to modesty or secrecy (*Laws* 781a). Physicians of female souls, then, would need properly either to be female themselves or to find a less direct method of practicing their art. We are thus left to wonder whether Socrates ever tried, even privately, to have a midwife-like conversation with a woman, contrary to his assertion in the *Theaetetus*. To put it differently, was Socrates incapable of success in helping a woman to "recollect" what she already knew, as he succeeded to do somehow with even Meno's slave and with several gentlemen's sons, if not necessarily his own (cf. *Memorabilia* II.2)? It is safest and simplest to take his denial in the *Theaetetus* at face value, in spite of his exhortation to other men to educate their own wives (or any other stray incident that may have occurred in Xenophon).[28] Certainly, even in Xenophon, Socrates shows no evidence of having been successful at managing his own wife, as one of his companions is quick to point out.[29]

We recall from the *Thesmophoriazusae* that the Athenian women were concerned with protecting what we might call their proprietary knowledge: Agathon feared that the women would think he was trying to steal their secrets if he were to be caught attending their religious festival. In Plato's *Symposium* and even as early as the dramatic date of the *Protagoras*, Socrates shows an interest in this impressive young tragic poet. So obvious is his attraction that Socrates' onetime favorite, Alcibiades, is moved to directly warn Agathon about Socrates' deceptive courting (*Symposium* 222b–d).[30] Aristophanes' Agathon is knowledgeable, respectful, even wary concerning women, while the elder Euripides is just in the process of learning this necessity. One might conclude, then, that there is good reason for the wise Euripides to seek the younger Agathon's help (*Symposium* 223d).

To return to the *Clouds*, if Socrates found a response to his troubles as Aristophanes portrays them there, just as Euripides found one in the *Thesmophoriazusae*, we are left to piece it together on our own. The *Clouds* and the *Thesmophoriazusae* show us potential grounds of female coolness to Socrates and to his friends, that is, to those who long to be wise in his manner. On the other hand, Aristophanes' female heroines in the *Lysistrata* and *Ecclesiazusae* suggest an intellectual overlap between Socrates and women. Aristophanes' feminine plays as a whole offer us a full range of topics to facilitate an inquiry into whether Socrates and Woman are terms that are fundamentally in tension or agreement.[31] If we wished to investigate the matter in Plato, then Diotima and Aspasia, the two examples of Socrates' teachers, might be the next logical step so as to see whether Lysistrata and Praxagora are the product of Socratic-style thinking on the part of Aristophanes himself or whether they are mere instruments for the effective ridicule of Socrates. We can at least say, based on the above reading of the plays, that Aristophanes sees women somewhere near the center of Socrates' difficulties. If they were important to his difficulties, then it stands to reason that they were important for his solutions to his difficulties.

Conclusion

We have four Aristophanic plays with female choruses of two different types. The difference can be understood in the following way. In two plays we have heroines—with supporting choruses of women—who agree with the paradoxical Socratic thesis that economics and politics are the same thing and hence who indicate a close link between Socratic thought and women. If government were essentially the same as estate management, then expert mistresses of estates would be qualified rulers of cities. In the other two plays, we have female choruses who show discernible coolness, even hostility, to Socrates and his friends.

Taking a hint from Agathon, we might compare this strange situation to present-day intellectual property or patent disputes. Two parties may agree on the importance or usefulness of a particular intellectual insight or technique, but this is no guarantee of a coincidence of economic interests. If politics is based on bodily needs, then with different bodies comes a different set of needs, abilities, and, hence, interests. Differing political interests do not necessarily disappear as a consequence of an intellectual agreement, no matter how significant.

On the other hand, intellectual agreement may reveal grounds for coalition. For example, groups who form a political minority of any sort may find themselves in a situation similar to women, given a comparable inferiority in relative brachial strength in the political community (cf. *Republic* 327c). Hence one can imagine a natural affinity, on some points, between aristocrats and women or between intellectuals and women. They might see a common utility in the art of rhetoric, for example, and learn from one another about its best use (cf. *Menexenus* 235e–36d). Still, before any stable political coalition might form between distinct parties, any grounds of understandable distrust would need to be removed. It is difficult to see how this could occur other than through the persuasion or education of individuals.

All four of these plays contribute to that essential task of education by revealing a partial sketch of Socratic political science, to which Xenophon and Plato fully respond in their beautiful defenses of their teacher. Without these four plays, it would be rather more difficult to understand the reasons why Socrates was so persecuted for his science—both the publicly pronounced reasons and the hidden reasons. Xenophon and Plato each makes a point of referring to such hidden reasons, just as they make a point of referring to Aristophanes. If we do not really understand the persecution of that great man, do we adequately understand his political science?

Notes

1. Xenophon, *Memorabilia*, trans. Amy L. Bonnette (Ithaca: Cornell University Press, 1994), 80. I wish to thank several friends for suggesting improvements to this chapter, in particular Laurence Nee, who proposed a substantial rewriting and offered much concrete advice. I owe too great a debt to Leo Strauss, *Socrates and Aristophanes* (New York: Basic Books, 1966) and *Xenophon's Socratic Discourse: An Interpretation of the Oeconomicus* (Ithaca: Cornell University Press, 1970), as well as to those who introduced me to them, to account for it by textual references. Note: translation here slightly modified from original.

2. *Republic* 546a, 549c–e. The Athenian Stranger in the *Laws* also addresses the problem of private household resistance when he speaks of the near impossibility of persuading even the female slaves to change their practice of swaddling infants (*Laws* 789e–90a).

3. See *Theataetus* 210d; *Republic* 463c–e; *Statesman* 259b. In the *Statesman*, Plato refrains from displaying this common ground between Socrates and the Eleatic. An excessive emphasis on Socrates' notions of political reform might make the corruption charges against him seem more justified. As is suggested below, we must put Plato's Socrates together with his Eleatic and Athenian Strangers to grasp Socratic political science in its relation to economics.

4. Plato, *"Protagoras" and "Meno,"* trans. Robert C. Bartlett (Ithaca: Cornell University Press, 2004), 93–94.

5. In the *Republic*, Socrates indicates that this conventional, diverse, or splintered view of virtue is primarily informed by the opinion of the demos. He accuses the demos of being the greatest sophist or corruptor of the young, for in crowds the demos tells us what it is to be young and old, male and female (*Republic* 492a–c). This "corruption" would seem to begin from the moment of language's development, for the demos is responsible for our primary identification of the classes of beings, such as the difference between human beings and horses (*Alcibiades I* 111c–d; cf. *Clouds* 657–93). Categories such as just and unjust are more complicated, as we can see from Homer, who presents conflicts over the possession of Helen and the treatment of the suitors by Odysseus (*Alcibiades I* 112b). Still, Socrates suggests, our understanding of the proper behavior of male and female, young and old, is not learned, as a subject of study might be, so much as absorbed along with the acquisition of our native language, more or less refined by the poets endorsed by the city (cf. *Republic* 377c; *Protagoras* 325c–e). Socrates allows us to reexamine that initial understanding for ourselves.

6. Below we see better how this example of bees is suggestive. If ruling is the definition of human virtue (73c), the rule of the hive looks rather different from conventional rule in Greek cities but somewhat closer to that of Lysistrata and Praxagora (*Oeconomicus* VII.32–38, IX.15). There were, of course, queens from very ancient times. I wonder whether, prior to modern times, women ruled in republics anywhere other than in the imagination of those like Plato and Aristophanes.

7. The bald statement in Xenophon's *Memorabilia* III.4 is illustrated not only in Plato's *Republic* but also in Xenophon's *Oeconomicus*.

8. We must first know what a human being is before we can properly ask, "Is human being (*anthropos*) the measure?" (*Theaetetus* 152a, 170e, 178b, 179b; cf. 171e, 177d). The *Statesman*, as the sequel to the *Theaetetus* and *Sophist*, treats this question most directly, but the *Republic*, particularly Book V, remains essential preparatory reading. Plato, however, like his contemporary Xenophon, exercises a gentlemanly circumspection in Book V and throughout his dialogues.

9. We cannot use Euripides' portrait of Jocasta in the *Phoenissae* as evidence, for it is not referred to by the women in the *Thesmophoriazusae* (and it may have been written later). Yet it is in the spirit of those women's complaints, if only because Euripides' Jocasta evidently did not react to her shameful situation in the manner of Sophocles' Jocasta, who killed herself upon discovering the true identity of her husband.

10. See Debra Nails, *The People of Plato: A Prosopography of Plato and Other Socratics* (Indianapolis: Hackett Publishing, 2002), esp. 54–56, for one recent account of the relevant dates, many of which are matters of conjecture. At least we can say that these two heroines were presented onstage some years after the *Clouds*. And so we know that Aristophanes had long been thinking about Socrates. When Aristophanes stages the *Clouds* in 424–423 BC (at the approximate age of twenty-seven), Socrates was about forty-six years old. In 411 BC, at the time of the *Lysistrata* and the *Thesmophoriazusae*, Socrates was about fifty-eight years old. He was executed in 399 BC, at the age of seventy, about seven years before the staging of the *Assembly of Women*. Aristophanes, Plato, and Xenophon were all native citizens of Athens and personally acquainted with Socrates, but Plato and Xenophon were at most toddlers at the time of the *Clouds* and in their mid-twenties when Socrates died. Others have conjectured that Aristophanes had one of Socrates' students in mind (say, Plato) rather than Socrates himself when he wrote the *Assembly of Women*, much as he lampoons Euripides in the *Thesmophoriazusae*. This is a reasonable suggestion. On the other hand, death was no barrier to lampooning for Aristophanes, as we know from Euripides and the other dead poets who appear in the *Frogs*.

11. See R. G. Ussher, *Ecclesiazusae* (Oxford: Clarendon Press, 1973), xiv–xx, and James Adam, *The Republic of Plato* (Cambridge: Cambridge University Press, 1963), 345ff., as examples. Cf. Aristotle, *Politics*, 1266a.

12. Alan H. Sommerstein, ed., *Lysistrata* (Warminster: Aris and Phillips, 1990), 183. See Strauss, *Socrates and Aristophanes*, 202: "Lysistrate, anticipating the Eleatic stranger in Plato's *Statesman*, tells him that the women's work in handling wool is a perfect model for bringing order into the disordered affairs of the city. . . . The dignitary does not pause to consider Lysistrate's comparison of the

political art with the arts of wool carding and weaving; he dismisses the women's claim on the simple ground that they do not have the smallest share in the war. This immense stupidity leads immediately to his downfall." Sommerstein, *Lysistrata*, 183, also calls attention to the *Statesman*. Jeffrey Henderson, *Aristophanes' Lysistrata* (Oxford: Clarendon Press, 1987), 142, is remarkably silent on the parallel, although he refers to perhaps related passages in the *Republic*.

13. Henderson, *Lysistrata*, 129, 141–42; Ussher, *Ecclesiazusae*, xvii.

14. Cf. Leo Strauss, *City and Man* (Chicago: Rand McNally, 1964), 61n15. Aristophanes was the first of our three great primary sources who wrote publicly about Socrates by name and probably the only one who did so while Socrates was still alive. Plato and Xenophon, in turn, both occasionally, but unmistakably, reveal that they write about Socrates with Aristophanes' treatment of him in mind (Plato, *Apology*, 18b, 19c; *Symposium* 223c; Xenophon, *Symposium*, VI.8; *Oeconomicus* XI.18; *Cyropaedia* III.1.38).

15. While Socrates in the *Republic* reserves the term "aristocracy" or "rule of the best" for the rule of the philosophers, Aristotle in the *Politics* calls upper class rule "aristocracy" when it serves the common interest of the city and "oligarchy" when it does not (1279a–b). In the *Ethics*, Aristotle, too, uses the word "timarchy" but as the good form of democracy, derived from the word for property qualification, and he compares it to the good relationship between brothers in a household (1160b, 1161a).

16. The dates of the plays' staging are uncertain.

17. See note 6 above.

18. Plato, *Menexenus*, 235e; *Theaetetus* 149a–150a, 210d; cf. Xenophon, *Symposium*, III.10; *Memorabilia* II.6.36; *Oeconomicus* III.13–15.

19. Strauss, *Socrates and Aristophanes*, 264.

20. Strauss, *Socrates and Aristophanes*, 272.

21. *Lysistrata* 495; *Ecclesiazusae* 210–12; *Memorabilia* III.4.12; cf. *Protagoras* 318e–19a. All three also take notice of weaving as the reputed women's art (*Ecclesiazusae* 556; *Republic* 455c–d).

22. Praxagora claims to have learned her knowledge of rhetoric, at least, from the time she spent as a refugee during the war, camped where she could hear the speeches of politicians (*Ecclesiazusae* 244). Lysistrata mentions her native intelligence and listening to her father and elders (*Lysistrata* 500–30, 1124–27). Cf. *Oeconomicus* VII.14.

23. Strauss, *Socrates and Aristophanes*, 281.

24. The date of the festival, and hence the purported victory party recounted in the frame dialogue, is 416 BC. The dramatic date of the frame dialogue itself is a matter of conjecture. We see also in the *Ecclesiazusae* that women, in particular, worship the mother-daughter goddesses celebrated by the Eleusinian mysteries (*Ecclesiazusae* 155–56; Ussher, *Ecclesiazusae*, 97). Alcibiades' alleged impiety (and hence also his teacher Socrates' alleged impiety) somehow hangs in the background of Plato's *Symposium* (Thucydides, *History*, VI.27–29, 61). Consider also Plato's

Protagoras (314c–16a), where Socrates appears to enter Callias' house as though entering a metaphorical house of Hades (the home of Demeter and Persephone) (cf. Strauss, *Xenophon's Socratic Discourse*, 157–58). Socrates sees in that home many of the participants in the *Symposium*, including the favorites Alcibiades and Agathon (some twenty years younger), with the notable exception of Aristophanes. The god Eros, treated in Plato's *Symposium*, is closely related to that other special women's deity, Aphrodite (*Symposium* 180d, 203b–c; *Ecclesiazusae* 189; *Theages* 205). It is less surprising then, that Socrates offers not his own rhetoric about Eros there, but that of his alleged teacher, Diotima.

25. Unfortunately, our information about the Eleusinian mysteries and the worship of Demeter and Persephone in general is quite limited. It is not clear how Aristophanes' mocking of the procedures at the Thesmophoria differs from the mockery that merited capital punishment for Alcibiades.

26. Strauss, *Socrates and Aristophanes*, 272.

27. *Republic* 458c–60a, 546a–47c; *Statesman* 308d–9c; *Laws* 771e–76b.

28. Xenophon, *Symposium*, II.9; cf. *Memorabilia* III.11; *Oeconomicus* X.1; Strauss, *Xenophon's Socratic Discourse*, 136.

29. Xenophon, *Symposium*, II.9; cf. *Memorabilia* II.2.7; *Oeconomicus* VII–XI, esp. X.1. Most instructive of all is the extreme circumspection with which Plato, Xenophon, and Aristotle treat this subject.

30. From the beginning of the *Protagoras* (315d–e) to the end of the *Symposium* (223a–d), decades later, Socrates appears to have had an eye on Agathon, at the same time that he was associating on and off with Alcibiades. Somewhere along the line, he either lost interest in Alcibiades or Alcibiades simply left him to pursue his political career. Agathon is the last man awake with Socrates at dawn on the day following the drinking party.

31. See note 23 above.

Part IV

15

Leo Strauss's UnSocratic Aristophanes?

Devin Stauffer

I. Introduction

Socrates and Aristophanes is one of the least studied of Leo Strauss's major works.[1] This is due in part to the reputation of Aristophanes himself, who, while not entirely forgotten, is less well known or at any rate less respected as a serious thinker than many of the authors about whom Strauss wrote. But although Aristophanes' own reputation is one reason for the neglect of *Socrates and Aristophanes*, it is not the only one. Another is the sheer difficulty of a work that is full of endless puzzles, written by an author who seems to have come to share Aristophanes' delight in laughing while he writes, in constant riddling, and in refusing to descend to the level of heavy-handed clarity. I confess to being as daunted as I suspect most readers are by the playful labyrinth of Strauss's work. The aim of this chapter, then, is simply to highlight some of the puzzles and questions that are at the heart of this bewildering book.

The first puzzle is the source and character of Strauss's interest in Aristophanes. The book includes interpretations of all eleven of Aristophanes' extant plays, but the title of the book suggests that Strauss turned to Aristophanes to learn about Socrates as much as about Aristophanes himself. But what did Strauss think could be learned about Socrates from Aristophanes? Was he seeking historical information about the genuine Socrates, who can be hard to discern beneath the rhetorical cloak in which Plato and Xenophon draped him? Is it possible that Aristophanes, an enemy of Socrates, spoke the truth about Socrates more frankly than did Socrates' friends, who may have had reasons for concealing that truth? Or did Strauss think he could find in Aristophanes a window into the young Socrates, the natural philosopher who would later become the mature Socrates by turning to political philosophy? Each of these answers receives some endorsement from Strauss himself in his Introduction (see 3–4; cf. 314, 316n20). But Strauss also indicates that, though there may be an element of truth in each, none of them can be the last word. Strauss reminds us that the meeting between Socrates and Aristophanes presented in Plato's *Symposium* occurred seven years after the first performance of the *Clouds* (5). In that meeting, the poet and the philosopher, while not without their differences, hardly appear as enemies. In fact, it would be truer to say that they appear to be friends, and there is no sign that they needed seven years to patch up a serious rift. Moreover, that the meeting in the *Symposium* (in 416 BC) took place a mere seven years after the first performance of the *Clouds* makes it difficult to conclude that the *Clouds* was directed only against the "young" or "pre-Socratic" Socrates. To draw that conclusion would require the assumption that the Socrates we see in dialogues such as Plato's *Alcibiades I* and *II*, *Charmides*, and *Protagoras*—each of which is set more than a decade before the *Symposium* and yet presents Socrates already deeply engaged with moral and political questions—was the Socrates who had not yet turned his attention to political philosophy. That conclusion is also rendered doubtful by the *Clouds* itself, for the Socrates we see there, especially the teacher who provides Pheidippides with his "indoor instruction" in rights and obligations, does not confine his studies to natural philosophy (see 41–43).

If Strauss's most obvious answers to the question of his interest in Aristophanes are not his final answers, does he offer others? Not directly. But he provides some indications in the Introduction and by the structure of the book as a whole. In the Introduction, Strauss follows his acknowledgment that Aristophanes was not an enemy of Socrates with a statement on "the problem of Socrates" as seen by the man who first spoke of such a thing. Nietzsche's critique of Socrates, according to Strauss, ultimately raises the question of "the worth of what Socrates stood for" (6), which in turn becomes the question of the worth of rationalism as such (7). Nietzsche's Socrates is "the first theoretical man, the incarnation of the spirit of science, radically unartistic or a-music" (7). And it was this Socratic scientific spirit, with its optimistic belief that reason can dispel all mysteries and that life can be guided by science alone, that Nietzsche saw as the deepest source of the naivety, superficiality, and spiritual exhaustion of the contemporary West. He thus regarded Socratic rationalism as something to be transcended by a philosophy of the future that would no longer be merely theoretical (7). Now, although Strauss does not endorse the whole of "Nietzsche's passionate and extreme attack on the Great Tradition," he does suggest that Nietzsche's attack brings to light a hidden tension within that tradition between the truth-seeking spirit of science and the life-enriching or beautifying spirit of art (7). But did Aristophanes, whose "political posture seems to foreshadow Nietzsche's political posture" (8), see that tension as Nietzsche did?

Perhaps it is best for now merely to offer a general suggestion: Aristophanes, like Nietzsche, can help us to see Socrates and the worth of what he stood for *as a problem*, that is, as something whose goodness is not unambiguous or unquestionable. After dwelling in his Introduction on Socrates and then offering a detailed interpretation of the *Clouds* followed by interpretations of Aristophanes' ten other extant plays, Strauss will return in his Conclusion to speak of Aristophanes' critique of Socrates as the most important source for understanding the ancient quarrel between poetry and philosophy, "as this feud appears from the side of poetry" (311). He will speak there, too, of Aristophanes' conviction of his own superiority to Socrates, especially his superiority in self-knowledge and prudence (311–13). Might Strauss have thought that Aristophanes, who knew Socrates more intimately than Nietzsche did and was closer to him in other ways as well, presents a more powerful critique of Socrates, and perhaps a more compelling alternative to the Socratic life, than Nietzsche does? If Nietzsche's attack on Socrates, as Strauss suggests, "must be understood primarily as a political attack" (7), is it in the laughing Aristophanes, not the lamenting Nietzsche, that we can find the deepest critique of Socrates? And if so, must not all admirers of Socrates and would-be Socratics take Aristophanes' hilarious critique with the utmost seriousness?

II. The *Clouds*

Because Strauss's text is so difficult, let us start from what is clear from the surface. Strauss marks out the special place of his discussion of the *Clouds* by giving that play its own section (Section II) while putting all of the other plays in a single section (Section III), which he titles merely "The Other Plays." His discussion of the *Clouds* is also longer than his discussion of any other play. These features of the book, of course, underscore the importance Strauss accords Aristophanes' critique of Socrates. And that critique itself would seem, at least at first blush, to be fairly straightforward. Aristophanes criticizes Socrates for his reckless imprudence. Aristophanes' Socrates, the

Socrates of the *Clouds*, is an ascetic scientist whose all-consuming dedication to the study of nature—the sun, the moon, flea jumps, gnat guts, and other such wonders—leaves him without a care or a clue about the "ephemerals" with whom he must share the earth, if not his "think-tank." When one such "ephemeral" invades his think-tank to seek Socrates' help in escaping his debts by learning how to defraud his creditors through clever speech, Socrates not only shows no compunction in assisting Strepsiades in his dubious plan, but he proves eager to convince his new pupil to share his heretical view of the gods. Socrates tries at once to convert Strepsiades from the worship of the traditional gods, of whom Zeus was of course the highest, to the worship of new gods or goddesses, the Clouds, for, as Socrates tells Strepsiades, "Zeus does not even exist" (19–21). The movement from Zeus and the other traditional gods to the new goddesses, the Clouds, proves to be merely a stage on the way to Socrates' more radical teaching. Strepsiades' much sharper son, Pheidippides, who must take his father's place when Strepsiades proves too dimwitted to absorb Socrates' instruction, receives the full Socratic teaching. Not only does Zeus not even exist, but neither do the Clouds. Socrates debunks all the gods and teaches the supremacy of Ether and Air (see 21, 24–25, 28, 45). In addition, he teaches Pheidippides that, in part because the gods do not exist and in part for other reasons, it is foolish to respect the law, to have reverence for old-fashioned poets such as Aeschylus, and, above all, to bow before the restrictions that structure and protect the traditional family (see, in particular, 40–45, 48). Anyone who has read the *Clouds* and remembers the flames that consume Socrates' think-tank at the end of the play knows the ultimate price that Socrates pays when the concerns on which he tramples strike back at him.

Aristophanes' Socrates is reckless because he is blind to the natures and attachments of the "ephemerals" on whom he depends more than he knows. He shows no sign of any concern for the city or the family, and, what is perhaps worse from a certain point of view, no awareness even of the passions of most men that tie them to the city and the family (see 48–49). This level of Aristophanes' critique is clear enough. But is it the whole of Aristophanes' critique, or his last and most important word on Socrates? Strauss suggests that it is not. For, as much as he is at pains to elaborate Aristophanes' critique of Socrates for his imprudence, Strauss also indicates that that critique conceals a tribute to Socrates' power and charm. To be sure, the power and charm of Socrates are hard to see in the *Clouds*. But they are pointed to by Aristophanes' indication of their effect on Pheidippides. Because Pheidippides receives those parts of his Socratic education that make the deepest impact on him inside Socrates' think-tank during the second parabasis, Pheidippides' "indoor instruction" is hidden from our view. But we can get an inkling of it by inferring from the speeches and actions of the transformed Pheidippides at least some of what must have gone on behind closed doors (40–45, 50). And the Pheidippides whom we see after the second parabasis is certainly not the same man who earlier expressed his contempt for Socrates and his great reluctance even to visit him. Pheidippides' education inside Socrates' think-tank has destroyed his love of horsemanship and replaced it with a love of speeches. The difference between the newly educated Pheidippides and his father, whose own Socratic education was abortive, is "the difference between a man who has felt in his bones what the denial of the ancestral Zeus means and a man who has not felt it" (45). In fact, Socrates' effect on Pheidippides is so profound that it must be regarded, Strauss says, as "a very great victory," a victory of such importance that, once it has been noticed, "one must wonder whether the victory or the defeat is greater" (50). After all, that a weak and foolish old man turns against Socrates while his much stronger and smarter son refuses to help burn down the think-tank hardly seems to reflect a complete failure on Socrates' part (50).

At this point in Strauss's interpretation of the *Clouds*, one even begins to wonder whether Aristophanes' critique of Socrates is rightly regarded as a critique. Does not Socrates' success in transforming or converting Pheidippides suggest that the *Clouds* is really a disguised tribute to Socrates? Yet, even if the answer to this question in some important respects is yes, we must not forget the suffering caused by Socrates' imprudence, and, more important, we must consider the implications of the fact that Socrates' conversion of Pheidippides is not complete. Although Pheidippides is "captivated by the possibilities that Socrates has opened up for him" (52), it proves to be going too far to say that he has been converted "by Socrates to Socrates" (50). For Pheidippides' failure to try to save Socrates and his think-tank from the attack of his father reflects, according to Strauss, the limits of his conversion: "He has not learned to replace his end by the Socratic end" (52). Pheidippides, Strauss writes, "is not a follower of Socrates; he has not been converted by Socrates to the Socratic ways of extreme continence and endurance" (50). "He has been converted by Socrates' charms only to the way of life recommended by the Unjust Speech" (52).

Pheidippides' eventual conduct toward Socrates, which indicates the limits of his conversion to the Socratic ways, prompts Strauss to raise an arresting question that reveals why the Pheidippides-Socrates saga is the most important part of the *Clouds*: "Is [Pheidippides] a comic equivalent of Aristophanes who, perhaps also charmed or instructed by Socrates himself, also accepts only a part of the Socratic teaching?" (52). Although this question comes only very near the end of his discussion of the *Clouds*, Strauss has prepared us for it by pointing in earlier passages to Aristophanes' closeness to Socrates while also indicating the distance that remained between the two men, especially regarding extreme continence (see, e.g., 31–33, 39, 46–47). After finally posing the question in such a direct and arresting way, Strauss goes a step further with another striking formulation: "The answer to our question depends decisively on whether Aristophanes can be presumed to have agreed with his Socrates regarding the gods" (52).

As striking as this last statement is, it is not immediately clear what Strauss means to convey by it. Why does the question of whether Pheidippides is a comic equivalent of Aristophanes depend on whether Aristophanes can be presumed to have agreed with Socrates regarding the gods? Why isn't the key question rather, as Strauss has encouraged us to think at this point, whether Aristophanes agreed with Socrates regarding the end in devotion to which Socrates exercised his extreme continence? Or does Strauss mean to suggest that even if that more obvious question can be settled by the indications in the *Clouds* that Aristophanes did not embrace the Socratic way of life, the other question remains, that is, the question of whether Aristophanes accepted the Socratic teaching about the gods?

By pointing us to the question of Aristophanes' view of the gods in the context of the more easily settled question of whether Aristophanes embraced extreme continence in devotion to the Socratic end, Strauss directs us to consider two possibilities. The first is that Aristophanes, like his Pheidippides, agreed with Socrates regarding the gods without embracing his way of life. In other words, perhaps Aristophanes accepted Socrates' assertion that Zeus does not even exist but did not think that one had to live like Socrates to come to that view, nor that holding that view would necessarily lead one to live like Socrates. The other possibility is that Aristophanes did not agree with Socrates, at least not entirely, regarding the gods, and that his embrace of a different end or way of life is somehow connected with that at least partial disagreement. Strauss suggests, however, that the question of whether Aristophanes agreed with Socrates regarding the gods cannot be settled on the basis of the *Clouds* alone: "We must turn to the other comedies in order to see whether they supply severally or jointly the answer to the question that is not clearly answered in the *Clouds*" (53, cf. 311). Now, in turning to the other comedies, Strauss will work from their surfaces, and he will thus explore the more obvious ways in which

Aristophanes differed from Socrates more directly than he explores what he here indicates is the deepest question. He will not offer a straightforward answer to that question. But he will search for one and help his readers search for one.

III. The Other Plays

Just as Strauss's interpretation of the *Clouds* moves from Aristophanes' readily apparent critique of Socrates to a deeper question about his relationship to Socrates, so too Strauss's discussion of the other plays operates on more than one level.

The first level is simply an extension, by way of inversion, of Aristophanes' critique of Socrates for his imprudence. Aristophanes himself, and Strauss following him, points repeatedly to Aristophanes' own superior prudence. Whereas Socrates openly declares to all who will listen that Zeus does not even exist and teaches his pupils to look down on the law and the claims of the family, Aristophanes does no such thing. He respects what Strauss calls on more than one occasion "the fundamental requirements of the city" (see, e.g., 193, 304, 312). There would seem to be three such requirements: the affirmation rather than the denial of divine rule, the prohibition against father-beating, and the prohibition against incest (304; cf. 48–49). But more than merely respecting these requirements by not treading on them as Socrates does, Aristophanes comes to sight as a teacher of "the just things," who rebukes the city for its worst tendencies, such as its thirst for war and punishment, and mocks dangerous boasters who threaten the established order (see, e.g., 46–47, 65, 69, 76–77, 134, 140, 157, 193, 311–12). By making radical innovations appear either impossible or ridiculous—or both—Aristophanes' comedies send the edifying message that the traditional ways are not so bad after all. In thus defending the city at the same time that they work to soften its most brutal tendencies, his comedies are "the true Just Speech" (312).

Yet not all radical innovators in Aristophanes are brought to ruin as Socrates is, and Strauss's Aristophanes can hardly be regarded simply as an edifying conservative convinced of the soundness of the old ways. His defense and education of the city, moreover, have as much to do with his desire to defend himself and to secure a place for poetry as they do with a concern for the betterment of the city. For instance, in softening the anger or indignation, the "waspishness," of the city by moving it to laughter, Aristophanes mitigates a danger that confronts the comic poet as much as the Socratic philosopher (see 120 with 216, 220–23, 311). And Aristophanes' poetic means of self-defense are not limited to his unrivaled ability to make his audience laugh. They extend also to his clever manipulation of divisions lurking within the city itself (see, e.g., 66–67, 233–35) and to his willingness to take on all sorts of disguises, hiding his wisdom even in the lowliest of rags (see 63–65). Indeed, comedy itself, in its apparent lowliness and its embrace of all that is ridiculous and crude, is a kind of disguise that conceals the wisdom of the comic poet. When Aristophanes' Dikaiopolis borrows from Euripides a set of filthy rags in which Euripides had cloaked one of his tragic heroes, Strauss suggests that Aristophanes is able, as it were, to fashion for himself an even filthier and subtler sets of rags. For his comedies persuade the audience not to take him too seriously but instead to regard him as merely a laughable and unthreatening force within the city, even as he is able to critique and transform the city by means of the very conceits that make him appear so harmless (see again 63–65 with 139–40, 192–93, 233–35). Thus comic poetry, unlike Socratic philosophy, provides both a shield and a sword in the battle against its would-be persecutors. And since, according to Aristophanes, comic poetry, or indeed poetry as such, can transform the city only so much, the prudent poet's need for such weapons will always remain.

Now, the more Strauss calls our attention to Aristophanes' concern with self-protection and even with a kind of power within the city, the more likely we are to come to doubt that the key difference between Aristophanes and Socrates is that Aristophanes is more devoted to the city. Is not Aristophanes' action within the city similar to that of Dikaiopolis, who pursues peace with Sparta not so much to free Athens from the evils of war as to serve his own private aims (69, 71–77)? It is true that Dikaiopolis' action in convincing the Acharnians to accept his truce with Sparta can be made to appear harmless and even public spirited, as Socrates' actions cannot. But that appearance conceals the fact that Dikaiopolis seeks his own good every bit as much as Socrates does. His peace proves ultimately to be a private peace, even "a monopoly of peace," which he happily exploits for his own profit and pleasure (see especially 74, 76–77). If Dikaiopolis, according to Strauss, is a stand-in for Aristophanes himself (69, 75), so too is Trygaios, the hero of the *Peace*, who also achieves a peace by means of "actions unauthorized by the city" (158; see also 139, 152–53). In the case of Trygaios, those actions begin with his ascent to heaven on the back of a dung beetle and escalate into a confrontation with Zeus himself, who has allowed Polemos (War) to bury Eirene (Peace) in a deep pit. To be sure, Trygaios' astonishing mission brings about a public peace that benefits not only Athens but all of the Greeks, whereas Dikaiopolis' maneuvering secured only a private peace (158). But there is reason to wonder whether Aristophanes is not compelled to present Trygaios' motives and mission as more just than Dikaiopolis' to compensate for their greater impiety. If the two heroes are taken together, it is hard to see where the comic poet, as represented by each and thus also by the compilation of the two, differs from Socrates: "While Socrates denies the existence of the gods and turns his back on the city, the comic poet in the *Acharnians* turns his back on the city but does not act against the gods, and the comic poet in the *Peace* acts in harmony with the city but against the gods" (158; cf. 198). That Aristophanes divides "his" actions into two separate plays indicates his awareness that it is unwise to display one's injustice and one's impiety at the same time (cf. 191–94). But while that may be a sign of the superior prudence of the comic poet, it is hardly a powerful expression of his greater devotion to the city.

Is there no difference, then, between Aristophanes and Socrates beyond Aristophanes' superior prudence and his discovery in comic poetry of a set of rhetorical weapons that give strength to his prudence? Here we may begin by returning to Dikaiopolis, the first of the two stand-ins for the comic poet and the one who is more clearly no more devoted to the city than Aristophanes' Socrates. For although Dikaiopolis shares Socrates' detachment from the outlook of committed citizens, he does not share his end. In his interpretation of the *Acharnians*, Strauss carefully traces the steps in "the revelation of Dikaiopolis' end" (73), which is the main task of the second half of the play (see 72). What is Dikaiopolis' end? It is true enough but too general to say that it is his own profit and pleasure. For in what does his pleasure, in particular, consist? Given the luxurious dinner that Dikaiopolis uses his private peace to procure for himself, the first answer would seem to be feasting—or "present feasting," as Strauss puts it, because Dikaiopolis impatiently speeds up the preparation of his meal and eats alone, without waiting to share his meal with anyone else (71–74). But Dikaiopolis desires more than delicious food. He also desires wine and sex, each of which, if not quite in the same way, involves a pleasure that is less solitary than the pleasure of dining alone. And it is in the context of highlighting "the shift that is taking place toward the end of the play from the pleasures of food to those of drink and sex" (75) that Strauss reminds us that Dikaiopolis is Aristophanes in disguise. Does that mean Aristophanes himself relished the pleasures of drink and sex? Yes. But it also means that the pleasure that Aristophanes undoubtedly took in composing his comedies is "akin in different ways to the enjoyment deriving from wine and from sex, rather than to the enjoyment deriving from food, however delicious" (77). "Comedy, whose mother is laughter, gives birth to laughter. The comic poet's enjoyment is essentially social, although it is not simply political" (77).

In thinking about Aristophanes' enjoyment of a pleasure akin to the pleasures deriving from wine and sex, not to mention his enjoyment of those pleasures themselves, we are reminded of Pheidippides and the limits of his conversion by Socrates. For the demand for extreme continence in devotion to the Socratic end was precisely the aspect of Socrates' teaching that Pheidippides did not embrace. And while there was no sign that Pheidippides intended to begin writing comic poetry, Strauss suggested that he was converted to the way of life recommended by the Unjust Speech, central to which are surely the pleasures of drink and sex (52; see also 31–32, 317n7). Our consideration of Dikaiopolis thus brings us back to—and helps to confirm—the suggestion conveyed in Strauss's interpretation of the *Clouds*, namely, that Aristophanes differed from Socrates not only in his superior prudence but also in his end. If "Socrates is continence incarnate" and "Dikaiopolis is the opposite" (77), that difference cannot be understood without taking account of the end in devotion to which Socrates restrained his desires and the end or ends in the enjoyment of which Dikaiopolis-Aristophanes unleashed his. Whereas Socrates tethered his heart for the sake of knowledge of the things aloft, Aristophanes would seem to have been more open to earthier experiences and pleasures.

But what does this have to do with the question of the gods? Insofar as Aristophanes is Trygaios, too, and not just Dikaiopolis, does that suggest that he shared Socrates' impiety while not fully embracing his end? Or does Aristophanes' difference from Socrates regarding the end reflect a disagreement regarding the gods? These are versions of the questions that we were led to raise at the end of our consideration of the *Clouds*, and nothing that we have seen so far has given us an adequate basis for settling them. We must go, then, to a deeper level of Strauss's discussion of the other plays and try to uncover Aristophanes' own teaching about the gods. The Socratic teaching is clear: Zeus does not even exist. But what is the Aristophanean teaching? It proves to be much harder to say.

Let us start from a point that Aristophanes may well have regarded as a mark of his superiority to Socrates on the question of the gods. Whereas Socrates—Aristophanes' Socrates—denies the existence of the gods on the basis of his study of the heavens while failing to see the power of gods in the hearts of men like Strepsiades, Aristophanes carefully examines the human roots and the complex character of piety. Of course, "carefully examining" for Aristophanes does not take the form that it does in most authors. Still,

Aristophanes can convey more by a few outlandish conceits than most authors can convey by volumes full of grave arguments. And he suggests, especially in the *Peace*, the *Birds*, and the *Plutos*, that piety is rooted in human neediness and in the inability of human beings to secure all of the good things they desire through human effort alone. Given the power of nature and chance, the arts can do only so much to provide human beings with the goods they desire. The gods, by contrast, hold out the promise that human beings can be freed of their burdens and have their desires fulfilled without the burdensome labor and frequent disappointment that attend their own efforts (see 148, 168–69, 295–97). Yet, is it not the case that the gods only *promise* human beings such help as they yearn for? The gods—at least the gods as Aristophanes portrays them—do not seem truly to meet the needs they promise to meet. Furthermore, if human beings initially turn to the gods for the help they desire, it would seem that a more serious, but also darker and more problematic, relationship arises between the gods and at least some human beings. For the gods are not willing, as it were, to serve as mere providers of the goods men need, or, perhaps better, human piety is not so simple as it first appears. The gods are important not only for the goods they bring or promise to bring but also for the support they give *as rulers* to the fundamental requirements of the city (see, e.g., 44–48, 120, 181–82, 192–93, 304). But do not the gods, as rulers and as superior beings, threaten human beings with evils even as they entice them with goods? In this connection, we are led to wonder about the meaning of Nikias' proof in the *Knights* that the gods must exist because they hate him (80, 82–83) and about the significance of the fact that the deepest reason in the *Wasps* for Philokleon's obsession with condemning is his fear of the gods' wrath if he is too compassionate and fails to carry out his duty (116–19, 125, 128; cf. 190). These examples would seem to point to a more complex and interesting side of piety, but one for which Aristophanes has little sympathy (see, e.g., 117–21, 234). For this side of piety, rooted in despair or fear-bred moralism, exacerbates those very same forces in the human soul and contributes to the belief in gods who introduce new terrors into human life and "impair man's self-esteem" (83; cf. 156, 163).

Given the threat that Aristophanes thought piety could pose to human happiness, it is not surprising that he reflected on its mutability and tractability. Now, the mutability of piety, if not its complete tractability, is suggested by Aristophanes' presentation of a number of radical and successful theological revolutions. I have already alluded, for instance, to Trygaios' triumph in the *Peace* over Zeus, who had forbidden the disinterring of the goddess Eirene (Peace). To that example may be added the even more striking revolutions of the *Plutos* and the *Birds*. In the *Plutos*, the reign of Zeus is replaced by the reign of Plutos (Wealth), and not only does this revolution prove to be successful, but it also ushers in a new age of justice, in which just men are rewarded with wealth, as they were not under Zeus' reign (299–304). Plutos proves to be a more philanthropic ruler than his predecessor, and with his ascendance the tyrannical Zeus fades into insignificance as even his priests desert him (see 296–97, 303–7). If the *Plutos* suggests that under the right economic conditions—conditions of abundance and just distribution—men might worship only gentler and more generous gods like Plutos, the *Birds* asks us to envision an even more radical scenario (consider 304–5). What if the gods were replaced by the birds? Or, beyond even that, what if a human being were to become the highest of the gods by using the birds as his allies? The human being in question is Peisthetairos, the visionary who launches a crusade against the Olympic gods in the *Birds* out of a desire to establish a city free of the condemning spirit that dominates life in Athens and that is tied to the Athenians' fear of gods like Zeus (consider 163, 190). Unlike Socrates, Peisthetairos does not deny the existence of Zeus or any other god. Rather, he acts on the premise that Zeus' power is not all that it is cracked up to be and that it will break when tested (171, 178–79; cf. 146). To test it, he introduces new gods, the birds, who promise to provide men with a more reliable supply of goods such as health, prosperity, and long life—at a lower cost and with fewer threats and other strings attached—than they could ever get under the reign of Zeus and his fellow Olympians (see 168–69, 172). But, as attractive to men as the rule of the birds proves to be, the birds themselves turn out in the end to be mere foot soldiers in Peisthetairos' revolution. It is Peisthetairos himself who ultimately becomes the highest of the gods. It is he—a human being, not a bird—who marries the beautiful Basileia (Kingship) and so prevails over both his rivals and his friends that he can feast on some of his most delicious allies (187–89).

Peisthetairos' triumph is shocking, and not only because he eats some of his allies who are also supposed to be his new gods. But what does Aristophanes think of his triumph? Does he endorse Peisthetairos' revolution? There does not seem to be a simple, unambiguous answer to this question. Certainly Strauss gives us reason to think that Aristophanes would have been sympathetic with the original motives of Peisthetairos' revolution, especially Peisthetairos' desire to overcome the spirit of condemnation by replacing the gods who reflect and intensify that spirit (see again 162–63, 190). But Strauss also points to the difference between Aristophanes and Peisthetairos. Unlike Dikaiopolis and Trygaios, "Peisthetairos is not the comic poet" (170).

And Peisthetairos' vast ambition to radically transform the government of heaven and earth goes far beyond Aristophanes' own much more moderate desire merely to enlarge the traditional pantheon to include new and improved gods like the Clouds (162–63, 170, 190–94; cf. 47). Yet was it not Aristophanes who decided to present without evident condemnation the shocking triumph of his brainchild Peisthetairos? Still, as shocking as Peisthetairos' triumph is, and thus as outrageous as Aristophanes seems to be in presenting it, his triumph is not *that* shocking. It is not as shocking, Strauss suggests, as it would have been for Aristophanes to present a triumphant Socrates. After all, not only is Peisthetairos' action manifestly impossible—Zeus cannot really be dethroned by an army of birds—but even in the fantastical vision of his triumph, the city still looks up to gods, and father-beating remains forbidden: "radically differing from Socrates, Peisthetairos acts in accordance with the fundamental requirements of the city" (193; cf. 182–86). Thus, Peisthetairos' triumph is as much a lesson in the limits of even the most extreme theological-political transformations as it is a celebration of one particularly fantastical transformation. By indicating those limits, Aristophanes respects and teaches "the impossibility of successfully denying the fundamental requirements of the city," even if he also suggests that those limits, including the city's need to bow to divine rule, are necessary evils (192–93; cf. 182, 234, 257–59, 304, 312).

None of our observations so far about Aristophanes' treatment of piety and the gods requires that Aristophanes was himself pious, and at least some of them would seem to point in the opposite direction. Should we draw the conclusion, then, that Aristophanes was every bit as atheistic as his Socrates, and that he differed from Socrates only in having, as he saw it, a deeper grasp of the character and grip of piety, and thus also of the need to treat the question of the gods with greater rhetorical delicacy than Socrates did? There are passages in Strauss's text that would seem to support this conclusion. The most striking and direct one comes in Strauss's discussion of the *Peace*. There, Strauss develops the suggestion that in Aristophanes' comedies natural explanations of phenomena (e.g., thunder, lightning, and war) "appear to be the comic equivalents of theological explanations" and vice versa, that is, "theological explanations are the comic equivalents of natural explanations" (143). After remarking that "from the point of view of the Aristophanean Socrates" comic equivalents "par excellence or in the strictest sense" occur only in "the region in which *theologia* and *physiologia* diverge," Strauss turns to the theme of boasting, "the preferred theme of comedy" (143). This leads in turn to a very striking statement about Zeus, which would seem to be the key statement to which Strauss will refer back much later in a well-known passage of the Conclusion. In that passage, he follows the suggestion that Aristophanes himself, the comic poet who celebrates successful transgressions of sacred laws, is "the boaster par excellence" with this arresting but enigmatic remark: "How this judgment must be restated in the light of his suggestions regarding the being of the gods has been stated with utmost clarity in the proper place" (313). If the "proper place" is indeed our earlier passage, then the key statement is this:

> Now if Zeus, who claims, or on whose behalf men claim, that he is the father of gods and men, that he is most powerful and wise, and that he deserves the highest veneration, does not even exist, as Aristophanes' Socrates indeed asserts, he is the greatest example of boasting that can be imagined. His case is the most perfect case of contrast between claim and being; he is the absolute subject of comedy; the comedy par excellence is the comedy of the gods. (143)

So does this statement, echoes of which can be found in other passages (see 179, 188, 234), settle the matter of Aristophanes' answer to the most crucial question about the gods, the question of their existence? Perhaps. But there are several considerations that should give us pause. The first is that even in the statement just quoted, which seems at first glance to be the most direct and emphatic affirmation of Aristophanes' atheism in the book, Strauss gives us reasons to hesitate. For the claim that Zeus does not even exist is explicitly ascribed, even here, only to Aristophanes' Socrates, and it is referred to here, as it is elsewhere, as an assertion (compare 143, "Now, if Zeus . . . does not even exist, as Aristophanes' Socrates indeed asserts," with 45, 53, 173). In addition, immediately after delivering this striking statement, which culminates in the memorable formulation that "the comedy par excellence is the comedy of the gods," Strauss concludes what he indicates has been a digression with the remark: "But let us return to Aristophanes himself" (143). Two pages earlier, he made a similar remark. There, after suggesting that Socrates would not have traced the ruin of Greece to Zeus but would have regarded it as a predicable consequence of a fratricidal war, Strauss went out of his way to issue the reminder: "But Aristophanes is not Socrates" (141; cf. 261). Now, it would be going too far to take these remarks to mean that whereas Socrates replaces theological explanations with natural explanations, Aristophanes would simply do the reverse. But they do introduce some doubt as to whether Aristophanes shared Socrates' confidence in the soundness of the natural explanations offered by *physiologia* and whether he would dismiss Zeus as a risible boaster as readily as his Socrates does.

As we try to find our way on this question, there are two other passages that especially call for consideration. The more difficult and opaque of the two is pointed to in the same passage of the Conclusion in which Strauss pointed us back to the statement we have been considering. In that passage of the Conclusion, which is an enigmatic summary of Aristophanes' critique of Socrates that dwells especially on the question of the gods, Strauss directs us back also to his discussion of what he calls "the birds' theocosmogony" (313). That is a reference to the account of the origins given in the first parabasis of the *Birds*, Strauss's discussion of which is perhaps the most mystifying of the many riddle-filled passages in *Socrates and Aristophanes*. But especially given Strauss's indication of its importance, we cannot avoid wading into that thicket. To prepare ourselves, however, let us first take up the other—at least somewhat clearer—passage that bears on our question: Strauss's discussion of the whipping contest in the *Frogs*.

The occasion of the whipping contest in the *Frogs* is as follows. The god Dionysos, having fallen in love with Euripides' poetry, has conceived the idea of bringing the dead poet back from Hades. Fearing that the gods below will see him, discern his plan, and thwart it, he decides to travel to Hades disguised as Herakles. But when his Heraklean guise leads to a harsh reception by Aiakos, the gatekeeper of Hades, he suggests to his slave Xanthias, who has accompanied him, that they switch roles: Xanthias should take on the guise of Herakles, and Dionysos will disguise himself as a luggage-carrying slave. Xanthias, in his courage and his pride, accepts the new plan, and he is delighted when it leads to his invitation to a feast held in his (i.e., Herakles') honor. But that same invitation to Xanthias-Herakles makes Dionysos reconsider the change of roles and insist on returning to the role of Herakles. Having become Herakles again, however, he soon finds that Herakles is not quite so welcome as it had seemed in Hades—there are those who wish to punish the figure they take to be Herakles for past crimes committed in Hades—and so Dionysos-Herakles reconsiders yet again: let Xanthias be Herakles after all! Although the courageous Xanthias initially accepts the reversal of the reversal of the roles, he finally reaches his limits when, once again disguised as Herakles, he is seized by Aiakos' henchmen and prepared for punishment. Xanthias snaps, denies to Aiakos that he has ever even been in Hades, and suggests that Aiakos discover the truth of his story by submitting his slave (the disguised Dionysos) to severe torture. Of course, enduring severe torture was never part of Dionysos' plan, and so, finding himself now squarely at odds with his own disguised slave, he reveals his identity as Dionysos, a god, and tries to blow Xanthias-Herakles' cover by declaring that he is merely his slave. Aiakos is understandably confused by this barrage of claims and counterclaims. Thus, facing two beings each claiming to be a god, he consents to a joint Xanthias-Dionysos proposal that they both be whipped to see which is truly the god he claims to be: the first to cry out will reveal his humanity and belie his divinity.

What is the significance of this elaborately constructed whipping contest? It would seem to lie in what is revealed by the outcome, or rather in what is not revealed by it: the whipping contest proves to be inconclusive. The contest, it turns out, does not enable Aiakos to discern which of the two purported gods is truly a god, and so he must turn the matter over to Pluton and Persephone who, because they are gods themselves, are able to resolve the question he cannot. In turning matters over to Pluton and Persephone, Aiakos, as Strauss puts it, "acts on the assumption that no being known to be a god to the other gods can be a mortal in the guise of a god" (245). Strauss then further remarks: "This could be thought to imply that only gods can know whether a given being is or is not a god, or that human beings as such can not know gods; *deus est quem dei deum esse declarant*" (245). Of course, the principle stated here—"a god is he whom the gods declare to be a god"—does not solve the problem for human beings, since, as Strauss also remarks, "[t]his obviously leads to the further question of the veracity of the presumed or genuine gods" (245). One might be tempted, therefore, to return to the whipping contest and argue that, while a god cannot be confirmed by such means, an imposter can be revealed. It is true that the whipping contest renders Dionysos' divinity "wholly questionable," insofar as Dionysos proves to be vulnerable to pain and hardly distinguished by his prudence (245). But the contest does not disprove his divinity. In fact, a human being judging by its most manifest (or audible) results—Xanthias' and Dionysos' cries of pain—would risk drawing the wrong conclusion from that inconclusive evidence (cf. 248–49, 254–59; see also 150–51, 296–97).

The whipping contest, then, would seem to be a lesson in the limits of human knowledge of the gods. With that in mind, let us turn to the theocosmogony of the birds in the *Birds*. For there, too, we find a lesson or reflection of sorts on the limits of human knowledge. The theocosmogony of the birds is, as the name implies, an account of the origins of the gods and the cosmos given by the birds themselves, Peisthetairos' allies. Although the birds are Peisthetairos' allies, their account of the origins, Strauss suggests, is more poetic than anything Peisthetairos could have come up with: "They are less intelligent than their savior, but better singers than he; their account of the origins reminds us of Hesiod's" (170–71). If their account reminds

Strauss of Hesiod's, it does not remind him of Socrates'. The birds' account "expels that of Prodikos," who "apparently was as much a 'Melian' [i.e., an atheist: see 25, 163, 318n49, 318n54] as the Aristophanean Socrates" (171), and it differs in important ways also from Socrates' account. What is the birds' account? And how is it different from Socrates'?

The birds' account of the origins is dark in more than one sense. Of the four principles at the beginning—Chaos, Night, Erebos, and Tartaros—Night is the one that got things started. Without impregnation, Night laid an egg in the infinite womb of Erebos and thus was born Eros, who (or which?) then mated by night with Chaos and generated the birds themselves. The birds, although conceived by night, are "the first things brought to light"; their generation precedes the emergence of heaven, ocean, earth, and the gods. Heaven, ocean, earth, and the gods emerged when, after generating the birds by mating with Chaos, Eros mated with the other first principles (Chaos, Night, Erebos, and Tartaros). Now, while the birds speak of Eros' role in the genesis of heaven, ocean, earth, and the gods, they do not speak of air, even though, as birds, they would be expected to appreciate air. Their silence about the origin and status of air, "the principle par excellence of Socrates' account" (171), is one of the two crucial dark points to which Strauss calls our attention. The other is the status of Eros: "Is Eros, who antedates the birds and still more all the other gods, himself a god?" (171). The unanswered question of Eros' divinity, given the role ascribed to Eros, helps to shroud the birds' entire account of the origins of the world and the gods in mystery. This "darkness regarding Eros," however, should not be taken as a denigration of Eros. Far from it. For as striking as is the darkness of the birds' account as a whole, equally striking is its elevation of Eros. If air is "the Socratic principle," the birds "replace air (or ether) by Eros" (171–72).

The theoretical differences between Socrates and the birds are not without their practical consequences or correlates. And Strauss seems very concerned to consider, if not to explain clearly, the connection here between the theoretical and the practical. Now, the birds' doctrine, as much as Socrates', leads to a critique of law in the name of a life that is according to nature (172). The practical opposition, then, is not a moral or political opposition: "Both doctrines transcend the sphere of *nomos*, of the city or of justice; both doctrines permit father-beating" (173). Still, there is a practical opposition: "The birds' doctrine of the origins leads to the recommendations set forth by the Unjust Speech, just as the rejected Socratic doctrine leads to the demands for extreme continence and endurance" (172–73). How should we understand this? Let us start from the Socratic side of things. Why would the Socratic doctrine, which "asserts the primacy of air or ether" (173), lead to the demands for extreme continence and endurance? Perhaps the connection is this: to hold that the first principle, the "principle par excellence," is air or ether is to hold that nature in its most important aspects may be intelligible, but that there is nothing truly shining, beautiful, or responsive about it. It would seem to follow from such a view that all that we can reasonably ask of nature is to know it, insofar as it is knowable, and that extreme continence and endurance are warranted and necessary to keep one's vision clear and to see nature as it really is. More than that, it would seem that, in order to attain and preserve clarity about the primacy of air or ether, one must not only tether one's heart, but also ruthlessly debunk all exalted claims about nature that obscure the truth about that primacy. As Strauss puts it, "Socrates is led to debunking the things aloft; if we disregard, as we must, his provisional or outdoor teaching regarding the Clouds, we see that he does not leave room for any things by nature beautiful or noble" (173). That is Socrates. It is not the birds: "The birds however, by asserting the primacy of Eros, assign an unassailable place to the naturally festive and golden" (173; cf. 302, 307, 313). In speaking here of the *unassailable* place that the birds assign to the *naturally* festive and golden, Strauss points to the birds' own view of nature and its practical implications. If confronted by the debunking Socrates, the birds would argue, in their musical way, that Socrates fails to appreciate a joyous dimension of nature that inspires those who embrace it not just to think but also to sing.

But what about Aristophanes himself? Are we to think that the birds' doctrine expresses his own view? Strauss's next line, immediately after his remark about the unassailable place the birds assign to the naturally festive and golden, would seem to suggest that Aristophanes agrees with the birds: "As a consequence of this," Strauss writes, "Aristophanes is more tolerant of Zeus and the other gods than is his Socrates" (173). But what does this enigmatic line mean? Does it mean that Aristophanes' appreciation of the power and beauty of Eros makes him more sympathetic to the gods who are, among other things, beautiful expressions of natural human yearnings and passions? It may mean that (consider 154–55, 164, 296, 306, 313). But even if it does, I think that it also means something else. Strauss also intends, I think, to indicate that because Aristophanes himself embraced the naturally festive and golden and did not impose on himself the demands of extreme continence in devotion to knowledge, it was not as crucial to him as it was to Socrates to demonstrate the nonexistence of Zeus. For Socrates, everything, so to speak, leads to and depends on the truth of his assertion that Zeus does not even exist. If that assertion is false, his life is an enormous mistake. And even if it merely cannot be known to be true, he is a tremendous boaster who gives up so much for an unattainable end. But Aristophanes, for his part, may have thought that the origins are too dark for any human being to be sure of the truth of the Socratic assertion and, further, that that state of things is not such a tragedy because there is a life more worth living than the Socratic life. A less restrained life, more open to an array of naturally attractive experiences, he may have thought, is in fact in greater harmony with the full range of our erotic human nature (see 29–33, 75–78, 139–40, 252–53, 299, 302, 307, 317n9). That is not to say that Aristophanes simply accepted as true the birds' doctrine of the origins. Indeed, that doctrine is so dark that it is unclear what it would even mean to accept it as true. But Aristophanes' view may have been that the very darkness of the origins is further reason to take one's bearings by the naturally festive and golden and not by the deeply hidden and obscure. Strauss puts it this way: "If Aristophanes had been compelled to choose between Socrates' doctrine and the birds' doctrine, he would have chosen the birds' doctrine, a doctrine that, with the help of Parmenides and Empedocles, could easily have been stated in philosophic terms. This entitles us perhaps to say that Aristophanes is not opposed to philosophy simply, but only to a philosophy that, disregarding Eros, has no link with poetry" (173).[2]

IV. Conclusion

If these last reflections are on the right track, then we have at least the beginnings of an answer to our earlier question about the possible connection between Aristophanes' thought regarding the gods and his difference from Socrates regarding their ends (see pages 336 and 340 above; cf. Strauss 311). For if Aristophanes thought that Socrates' way of life rested on an excessive confidence in his fundamental assertion about the gods and a narrow, unerotic view of nature, we can begin to grasp why Aristophanes was willing to travel only so far with Socrates and why he was unwilling to abandon the pleasures of Dionysus, Aphrodite, and the Muses, especially the comic Muse. Furthermore, Aristophanes may well have regarded his embrace of a less continent life, not only as a more robust and reasonable response to our human condition in its joys and its limits, but also as an essential aid in coming to a more complete appreciation and understanding of human life as a whole (see 48–49, 139–40, 313; cf. 82 on "Demosthenes' decision to drink wine and thus to bring his thought or life to its highest pitch").

For this reason, Aristophanes would surely resist a simple formulation of the difference between Socrates and himself that would hold that Socrates placed wisdom before pleasure whereas he did the reverse (cf. 311). That is not to deny that Aristophanes would readily admit, and even stress, that he poured far less energy than Socrates did into "worrying" about the things aloft (on "worrying," see 220, 235, 313).

How would Socrates respond to Aristophanes? That is a question one cannot help wondering about throughout Strauss's book, and it is a question Strauss himself raises on his last page (see 314). But, as with many of the most important questions he raises, Strauss is not very forthcoming in laying out a full answer. The question, he warns us, is difficult. We cannot simply turn to Plato and Xenophon for the answer, because "[i]t is certainly impossible to say whether the Platonic-Xenophontic Socrates owes his being as much to poetry as does the Aristophanean Socrates" (314). And while it is of course true that the Socrates we see in Plato and Xenophon is hardly the same man we see in Aristophanes, "[i]t is almost equally difficult to say whether the profound differences between the Aristophanean Socrates and the Platonic-Xenophontic Socrates must not be traced to a profound change in Socrates himself" (314). Although Strauss points us here to the Socratic turn, he says little about what was involved in that turn or about whether Aristophanes grasped its full significance. Those are not questions that Strauss tries to settle in *Socrates and Aristophanes*. Still, he does provide some direction by emphasizing the deep concern that the Platonic-Xenophontic Socrates shows, not with contemplating air or ether, but with understanding human life, especially in its moral, political, and erotic dimensions. Indeed, he goes so far as to say that, for the Platonic Socrates, "the true knowledge of souls, and hence of the soul, is the core of cosmology (of the knowledge of the things aloft)" (314). To understand that remark, one would need to follow Strauss's direction, given in the most important passage of his book, and turn to the friendly but far-reaching dispute between Socrates and Aristophanes in Plato's *Symposium* (see 173). Among other things a consideration of that dispute would reveal is that Socrates would not grant to Aristophanes that their differences, both practical and theoretical, are due to his disregard of Eros, as opposed to his different and deeper understanding of it.

Notes

1. Although very little has been written on *Socrates and Aristophanes*, there are a few notable exceptions to its neglect. Amy Bonnette's essay "Family and

Politics in Aristophanes" is not a direct analysis of Strauss's work, but it is, by her own description, "based on an attempt to understand *Socrates and Aristophanes*" (see *Poets, Princes, and Private Citizens*, eds. Joseph Knippenberg and Peter Augustine Lawler [Lanham, MD: Rowman & Littlefield Publishers, 1996], 121–41, especially 140n1). Heinrich Meier makes a number of illuminating remarks about *Socrates and Aristophanes* in his *Leo Strauss and the Theologico-Political Problem* (New York: Cambridge University Press, 2006); see, in particular, 26–27 and 91–94. See also the review of Strauss's book by Arnaldo Momigliano, "Philosophy & Poetry," *Commentary* 44 (no. 4, 1967): 102–4.

The general neglect of *Socrates and Aristophanes* is despite the importance Strauss himself accorded the work. Consider the following remark he made in a 1962 letter to Alexandre Kojève: "I am preparing for publication three lectures on the city and man, dealing with the *Politics*, the *Republic* and Thucydides. Only after these things have been finished will I be able to begin with my real work, an interpretation of Aristophanes" (*On Tyranny: Revised and Expanded Edition, Including the Strauss-Kojève Correspondence*, eds. Victor Gourevitch and Michael S. Roth [Chicago: University of Chicago Press, 2000], 309).

All unspecified references in my text are to *Socrates and Aristophanes* (Chicago: University of Chicago Press, 1966).

2. Regarding the reference to Parmenides and Empedocles in this statement, see Aristotle, *Metaphysics*, A4.

About the Authors

Wayne Ambler is co-director and associate professor in the Herbst Program of Humanities at the University of Colorado, Boulder. He has written on Aristotle and Xenophon and has translated Xenophon's *Education of Cyrus* (2001) and *Anabasis of Cyrus* (2008) for Cornell University Press. He also served as Dean of the University of Dallas' Rome Campus and Program.

Christopher Baldwin is an assistant professor of political science at Rhodes College. He has also taught at the Honors College at the University of Houston and at the University of California, Davis. Interested in the history of political philosophy (especially classical political philosophy and late modern political thought), he has authored articles on Camus, Nietzsche, and Leo Strauss, as well as presented numerous papers on Plato, Aristophanes, Thucydides, Nietzsche, and Heidegger. He is currently writing a book-length study of Nietzsche.

Amy L. Bonnette is a visiting scholar in the political science department at Boston College. In addition to essays on Aristophanes and Jane Austen, she has published a translation of Xenophon's *Memorabilia* (Cornell, 1994) and is currently translating his *On Horsemanship*.

Timothy W. Burns is professor of political science at Baylor University. He is the author of *Shakespeare's Political Wisdom* (Palgrave MacMillan, 2013) and co-author (with Thomas L. Pangle) of *Political Philosophy: An Introduction* (Cambridge, 2014). He is editor of *After History? Francis Fukuyama and his Critics* (Rowman and Littlefield, 1994), *Recovering Reason: Essays in Honor of Thomas L. Pangle* (Lexington, 2010), and the forthcoming *Companion to Leo Strauss' Writings on Classical Political Thought* (Brill, 2015). He is co-editor (with Bryan-Paul Frost) of the forthcoming *Philosophy, History, and Tyranny: Re-examining the Debate Between Leo Strauss and Alexandre Kojève* (SUNY, 2014). He has translated Marcellinus's *Life of Thucydides* and is the author of articles on Homer, Thucydides, Aristophanes, Dionysius of Halicarnassus, Shakespeare, Hobbes, Strauss, Fukuyama, Putnam, Chesterton, John Courtney Murray, and modern liberal republican theory.

Bryan-Paul Frost received his BA from St. John's College, Santa Fe, and his MA and PhD from the University of Toronto. He is currently the James A. and Kaye L. Crocker Endowed Professor of Political Science at the University of Louisiana at Lafayette. He is editor and co-translator (with Robert Howse) of Alexandre Kojève's *Outline of a Phenomenology of Right* (Rowman and Littlefield, 2000); contributor and co-editor (with Jeffrey Sikkenga) of *History of American Political Thought* (Lexington, 2003); and contributor and co-editor (with Daniel J. Mahoney) of *Political Reason in the Age of Ideology: Essays in Honor of Raymond Aron* (Transaction, 2007). In addition to the above, he has published articles on Aristotle, Cato the Younger, Cicero and Roman civic education, and Emerson and Tocqueville.

Khalil M. Habib, MA (political science, University of Toronto), PhD (philosophy, Boston University) is associate professor of philosophy and director of the Pell Honors Program at Salve Regina University, Newport, Rhode Island. His publications include articles or chapters on Ibn Khaldun, Machiavelli, and Tocqueville. He also contributed a chapter on Aristophanes' *Birds*, written for a volume on Western classics edited by Harold Bloom (*The Grotesque: Bloom's Literary Themes*, Chelsea House, 2009). Professor Habib is also co-editor of a volume of essays titled *Citizens without States: Cosmopolitanism in an Age of Globalization* published by the University Press of Kentucky (2011), in which his essay on Ibn Tufayl's *Hayy Ibn Yaqzan* appears.

John Lombardini received his BA from Rutgers University and his PhD from the Department of Politics at Princeton University. Currently, he is assistant professor of government at the College of William & Mary. His work has been published in *Political Theory, History of Political Thought*, and *Polis*.

Kenneth DeLuca is an adjunct associate professor at Hampden-Sydney College, Hampden-Sydney, Virginia, where he teaches courses in Western culture and political philosophy. He is the author of *Aristophanes' Male and Female Revolutions* (Lexington, 2005) as well as "On the Argument of Casablanca and the Meaning of the Third Rick" in *Political Philosophy Comes to Rick's* (Lexington, 2005) and "Spielberg's Deus ex Machina: *Saving Private Ryan*" (Poroi, 2005).

About the Authors

Paul W. Ludwig was educated at Oxford and the University of Chicago and currently teaches at St. John's College, Annapolis. He has also taught at the University of Chicago and in Harvard's Government Department. He has published articles on Aristophanes in the *American Political Science Review* and the *American Journal of Philology*. He specializes in ancient and modern accounts of love and friendship, on which he has published chapters in the *Cambridge Companion to Plato's Republic* and Blackwell's *Companion to Ancient Political Thought*, among others. His books are *Eros and Polis* (Cambridge, 2002) and, forthcoming from Cambridge, *Civic Friendship*.

Matthew Meyer in an assistant professor in the Philosophy Department at the University of Scranton. He recently received a joint PhD-MA degree from Boston University in Philosophy and Classics, and he is working on a book on Friedrich Nietzsche and ancient philosophy under contract at Walter de Gruyter with the title *Reading Nietzsche Through the Ancients: An Analysis of Becoming, Perspectivism, and the Principle of Non-Contradiction*.

Jeremy J. Mhire is an assistant professor of political science at Louisiana Tech University. He has also held postdoctoral fellowships at the University of Virginia and Harvard University. His research interests include political philosophy (ancient, modern, and contemporary); classical and modern republicanism; and politics, philosophy, and literature. He has published on the intersections of classical and modern political philosophy and on constitutionalism broadly construed.

Stephanie Nelson is associate professor and chair of the Department of Classical Studies at Boston University. She holds a BA from St. John's College in Annapolis, Maryland, and an MA and PhD from the Committee on Social Thought at the University of Chicago. Her first book, *God and the Land: The Metaphysics of Farming in Hesiod and Vergil* (Oxford, 1998), deals with Vergil's use of Hesiod's *Works and Days* in the *Georgics*. *Aristophanes' Tragic Muse: Comedy, Tragedy and the Polis in Classical Athens* (in press) argues for a self-conscious symbiosis in the opposite views of fifth-century comedy and tragedy. She is now working on a monograph on the relation of the *Odyssey* and Joyce's *Ulysses*.

Peter Nichols attended Yale University (BA, history 1974), the Georgetown University Law Center (JD, 1977), the University of Toronto (MA, political science, 1985; PhD, 1990). He was admitted to the New York Bar in 1978 and to that of New Jersey in 2009. He is currently an attorney with a private law firm and served as a Manhattan Assistant District Attorney from 1981 to 1984. He also taught as an adjunct professor in a number of universities in New Jersey and New York (philosophy, political science, Western civilization, and expositional writing). He is the author of *Aristophanes' Novel Forms: The Political Role of Drama* (Minerva Press, 1998) and several law review articles.

Arlene W. Saxonhouse is the Caroline Robbins Collegiate Professor of Political Science and Women Studies and an adjunct professor of classics at the University of Michigan. She is the author of *Women in the History of Political Thought: Ancient Greece to Machiavelli* (Praeger, 1985); *Fear of Diversity: The Birth of Political Science in Ancient Greek Thought* (Chicago, 1992); (with Noel Reynolds) *Hobbes's Three Discourses: A Critical Modern Edition of Newly Identified Works by the Young Thomas Hobbes* (Chicago, 1995); *Athenian Democracy: Modern Mythmakers and Ancient Theorists* (Notre Dame, 1996); *Free Speech and Democracy in Ancient Athens* (Cambridge, 2006); and individual articles on the political thought of Thucydides, Plato, Aristotle, the ancient playwrights, Hobbes, and Machiavelli.

Devin Stauffer is an associate professor of government at the University of Texas at Austin. He is the author of *Plato's Introduction to the Question of Justice* (SUNY, 2001); co-author and co-translator of *Empire and the Ends of Politics: Plato's Menexenus and Pericles' Funeral Oration* (Focus Philosophical Library, 1999); and author of *The Unity of Plato's Gorgias: Rhetoric, Justice, and the Philosophic Life* (Cambridge, 2006). He has also published articles on classical and early modern political philosophy in journals such as the *Review of Politics* and the *American Political Science Review*.

John Zumbrunnen is professor of political science and director of the American Democracy Forum at the University of Wisconsin, Madison. Zumbrunnen's scholarly work has largely focused on the intersection of ancient Greek political thought and contemporary democratic theory. He has published two books. *Silence and Democracy: Athenian Politics in Thucydides' History* was published by Penn State University Press in 2008. *Aristophanic Comedy and the Challenge of Democratic Citizenship* was published by the University of Rochester Press in 2012. Zumbrunnen has also published articles on Thucydides, Aristophanes, Nietzsche, constitutionalism in Wisconsin, and the complexity of American conservatism.

Index

Acharnians, 65n5, 70, 73–77, 82–83, 92–97, 117–22, 246–49
Adam, James, 325n11
Adkins, A. W. H., 24n1
Aeschylus, 188–99
Akestor (Sacas), 166–67
Alcibiades, 285–89
Allen, Danielle, 16, 26n11–12
Allen, Woody, 124
Ambler, Wayne, 157n25–26, 298n8, 300n32–33, 300n35
Anderson, Daniel E., 299n20
Annas, Julia, 277, 298n9, 298n13
Anton, John P., 297n3
Aquinas, St. Thomas, 257n18
Aristophanes: critique of rhetoric, 73–76; importance of rhetoric, 69–73; and the meaning of citizenship, 91–107; and politics and despotism, 58–64; quarrel between philosophy and poetry, 47–64; and recent scholarship, 47–48; relation to polis paradoxical, 109–25; and rhetorical resources, 76–81; Socrates as a threat to politics, 56–64; *See also* individual plays, individual characters
Aristotle, 71, 85n4, 91, 99, 104, 106, 123, 136n54, 162, 179n2, 183, 199n1, 223n4–5, 224n13, 256n9, 256n15, 257n18, 306, 351n2
Arnott, Peter D., 128n14, 130n25
Arrowsmith, William, 132n35, 133n39, 293–94, 298n8, 300n32, 301n38–39

Assemblywomen (Ecclesiazusae), 76–83, 103–6, 215, 259–72, 303, 314–15
Athens (Athenians), 53–64, 161–79: character of democratic deliberation, 13–18; freedom and imperialism in, 161–79; in decline, 184

Bacon, Francis, 44n18, 223n2
Bailey, Cyril, 131n31
Bakhtin, Mikhail, 125n3, 130n25
Bakola, Emmanuela, 127n7, 128n9, 129n18
Barret, David, 272n1
Bdelycleon, 75–76, 252–55
Benardete, Seth, 175, 180n8, 180n18, 181n20
Berg, Stephen, 25n1
Berns, Walter, 256n11
Bible, 201, 205, 208, 219–21, 223n1, 226n30
Biles, Z. P., 127n7, 127n9, 128n10, 132n32, 134n46, 301n49
Birds, 117–22, 161–79, 288–96; and Athenian imperialism, 161–65; different kinds of birds in, 167–71; and the Olympian gods, 165–66; and the Persian Empire, 163–64; and Thrace, 172–79
Blaiklock, E. M., 132n35
Blepsidemus, 202, 205–6
Blepyrus, 263–64, 266–67
Bloom, Allan, 45n26, 273n1–3, 274n13, 274n15–16, 274n18, 295, 297n6, 301n48

357

358

Index

Bolotin, David, 256n13
Bonnette, Amy, 350n1
Bowie, A. M., 86n15, 127n6, 128n14, 129n21, 131n29, 132n33, 133n39
Bowie, E. L., 130n28, 131n31–32
Brasidas, 139, 143, 145, 150, 229, 233
Bremer, J. M., 126n3, 126n6
Brock, R. W., 128n14
Bruell, Christopher, 256n13
Burns, Daniel, 258n29
Burns, Timothy W., 255n1, 225n4
Burnyeat, Myles, 25n1

Carey, Christopher, 127n6, 130n28, 132n32
Carion, 204, 206–9, 215–16
Carter, D. M., 125n1, 134n42
Cartledge, Paul, 26n6, 126n6
Ceccarelli, Paola, 133n37
Chremes, 262–63, 266–67
Chremylus, 79–81, 202–23
Christianity, 201–2, 205, 218, 222–23
Churchill, Winston, 111, 126n5
Citizen, 265–67
Cleon, 16–17, 111–12, 139, 143, 145, 150, 229–55
Clouds 13–24, 29–43, 47–64, 82–84, 260, 271–72, 308–9, 320–23; as a defense of political life, 50–64; Just and Unjust Speech, 39–40, 65n11, 245–46
Connor, W. R., 16, 25n5, 130n23
Cooksey, Thomas L., 299n20
Corrigan, Kevin, 299n20

Dante, 226n37
David, E., 224n11
Dearden, C. W., 132n35
Demos (of Pnyx), 74, 250
Demos, Marian, 297n4
Demosthenes, 232–33, 249
Diceapolis (Dikaeopolis, Dikaiopolis), 73–77, 92–97, 118–20, 246–49

Dillon, Matthew, 223n11
Diodorus Siculus, 257n19
Diodotos, 234–44
Dionysus, 183–99
Dissident, 78–79
Dobrov, Gregory, 133n35, 133n39, 134n43, 134n45
Dorion, Louis-André, 27n27
Dover, Kenneth, 24n1, 26n17, 26n19, 27n23, 83, 87n16, 129n21, 130n28, 134n46, 135n48–49, 136n53–54
Dunbar, Nan, 130n25, 130n27, 132n33, 132n35, 133n37–38

Edmunds, Lowell, 25n1, 126n6, 129n17, 131n29, 131n31
Edwards, Anthony T., 85n3, 125n3
Ehrenberg, Victor, 127n6, 133n36, 224n15
Empussa, 186
Euben, J. Peter, 25n1, 85n3
Euelpides, 164–79, 289–92
Euripides, 144, 156n17, 158n31, 184–99, 247, 265, 308–9, 325n9–10

Fisher, N. R. E., 27n20, 131n29, 131n31–32
Foley, Helene, 101, 108n14, 108n16, 108n18, 108n21, 129n19, 130n28, 131n31–32, 134n45, 273n2
Forrest, W. G., 126n6, 132n32
Friedrich, Rainer, 126n4
Frogs, 123, 183–99; and the contest between Aeschylus and Euripides, 188–99; and divine justice, 185–88; the skill of Aristophanes as a poet, 196–99

Gillespie, Michael Allen, 223n1
Glazov-Corrigan, Elena, 299n20
Goldhill, Simon, 125n1, 125n3, 126n6, 134n43
Gomme, A. W., 85n3, 126n6, 132n32
Greene, William Chase, 297n4, 297n6

Index

Griffin, J., 125n1
Griffith, M., 133n42
Griffiths, E., 129n17

Habash, Martha, 131n29
Hades (Pluto), 185–89, 195
Halliwell, Stephen, 85n3, 125n3, 127n6, 127n8, 225n19, 225n23, 297n4–5, 300n34, 302n50
Halperin, David, 298n11
Hamermesh, Daniel C., 274n8
Hansen, M. H., 15, 25n3–4
Harriot, Rosemary, 135n48
Harvey, David, 128n9
Havelock, Eric, 24n1
Heath, Malcolm, 70, 85n3, 125n1, 127n6, 128n9
Heiden, B. A., 134n45
Henderson, Jeffrey, 44n22, 85n2, 86n12, 121, 125n3, 126n6, 129n21–22, 132n33–34, 133n41, 134n43, 298n8, 301n44–45, 326n12–13
Heracles, 185–88
Hermes, 140–41, 144–46, 149–52, 215–17
Herodotus, 15, 89–90, 110, 163–64, 172–76, 180n6, 180n8, 180n18–19, 181n23, 181n27
Hesiod, 33, 158n27
Hesk, Jon, 85n8
Hierocles, 147–48
Hobbes, Thomas, 256n10
Hobbs, Angela, 299n16
Hoffman, R. J., 131n29
Holtermann, Martin, 274n19
Homer, 33, 65n13, 148, 157n19, 157n24, 158n27–28
Hooker, J. T., 135n48
Hubbard, Thomas, 86n8, 132n34–35, 134n45
Humphreys, Sally, 104, 108n19
Hunt, Peter, 134n44
Hutchinson, G. O., 135n46

Informer, 209–11, 214
Isocrates, 27n22

Jesus, 202, 219, 221
Johnson, Laurie M., 256n14
Just Man, 208–10

Kant, Immanuel, 225n21
Kelly, Walt, 136n52
Kleinknecht, H., 128n14
Kleve, Knut, 25n1
Knights, 16, 74–76, 82–83, 114–17, 249–52
Kojève, Alexandre, 351n1
Konstan, David, 25n1, 85n3, 126n6, 132n35, 134n43, 223n11
Kossatz-Deissmann, A., 129n17
Kraut, Richard, 285, 300n21–23
Kremer, Mark, 30, 33, 43n3–6, 44n15–16, 45n24

Larivée, Annie, 289, 298n8, 300n24, 300n31
Leibowitz, David, 43n2
Levin, Mark, 274n14
Lévy, Edmond, 224n11
Lowe, J. C. B., 157n23
Lowe, N. J., 131n31
De Luca, Kenneth, 65n2, 273n5
Ludwig, Paul, 65n2, 66n20, 107n11–12, 226n33, 293–94, 298n7, 298n16, 300n29–30, 301n36, 301n38, 301n40–43
Luther, Martin, 201
Lysistrata (Lysistrata), 97–103, 303, 309–15

MacDowell, Douglas M., 26n10, 86n15, 126n6, 128n14, 129n17, 129n21, 130n28, 131n31, 132n34–35, 301n46
Machiavelli, Niccolò, 223n2
Mansfield, Harvey C., 223n2
Manville, Philip Brook, 90–91, 99, 107n3–5

McGlew, James F., 86n14, 131n31
McLeish, Kenneth, 127n8, 128n12
Meier, Christian, 126n4
Meier, Heinrich, 351n1
Meigs, R., 133n40
von Möllendorf, P., 130n25
Momigliano, Arnaldo, 351n1
Most, Glenn, 297n2, 301n49
Moynihan, Daniel Patrick, 209, 224n14

Nails, Debra, 325n10
Newell, Waller, 299n19
Newinger, H.-J., 130n28, 132n32, 134n46
Newman, Rafael, 126n3
Nichols, Mary, 25n1, 43n2, 44n11–13, 44n17, 44n20–21
Nichols, Peter, 131n31, 135n49, 274n9
Nicias, 230–32, 249
Nietzsche, Friedrich, 146, 197, 199n11, 273n4, 274n17, 332–33
Nightingale, Andrea, 297n4, 302n51
Nussbaum, Martha, 23, 24n1, 27n24, 43n2
Nygren, Anders, 223n3

Obdrzalek, Suzanne, 286, 298n15, 300n25–28
Ober, Josiah, 16, 26n7–9, 27n21–22, 86n10, 107n3
O'Brien, Michael, 300n27
Old Oligarch (pseudo-Xenophon), 110–11
Old Woman, 211–15, 217
Olson, S. Douglas, 129n17, 129n22, 130n28, 131n29, 156n13, 156n17, 224n11
Orwin, Clifford, 256n13, 257n17, 257n20
Osborne, Robin, 126n4
Ovid, 129n16

Pangle, Thomas L., 157n25, 256n15
Parke, H. W., 131n29
Parker, L. P. E., 130n28, 131n31
Parker, R., 129n20
Parry, Richard D., 298n10, 298n12, 299n17
Peace (Peace), 70, 137–54; conditions and limitations of, 138–43; critique of the Olympian gods, 143–152
Peace of Nicias, 138–39, 143, 229
Peisetairos (Pisthetairos), 120–21, 161–79, 288–95; character of, 288–95
Pelling, Christopher, 132n32, 133n42
Peloponnesian War, 138–43, 231–44
Pericles, 15–16, 110, 112, 140, 244
Pheidippides (Pheidippedes), 14, 18, 21–22, 39, 41, 245
Philocleon, 75–76, 252–55
Plato, 23–24, 85n5, 110, 199n10, 224n15, 256n15, 258n29, 259–60, 267–72, 275–88; adaptation of Praxagora, 267–72; and Aristophanes compared, 270–72, 295–96; and eros, 281–88; and erotic tyranny, 277–88; works by: *Alcibiades I*, 307; *Apology*, 24, 65n10, 69, 259; *Gorgias*, 24, 71; *Lovers*, 305; *Meno*, 305–6, 312–13; *Phaedo*, 275–76; *Phaedrus*, 275–77, 281–83; *Philebus*, 24; *Protagoras*, 13, 111; *Republic*, 65n6–8, 66n19, 91–92, 116–17, 259–60, 267–72, 275–88, 303–24; *Statesman*, 305, 310; *Symposium*, 119, 259, 275–88
Platter, Charles, 110, 125n3, 129n20, 133n42
Plutarch, 128n13, 255n4
Poe, J. P., 130n25
Pope, Maurice, 107n2
Poverty (Penia), 80–81, 205–11, 214
Praxagora, 76–79, 103–6, 260–72; revolutionary designs of, 260–67
Priest, 217

Index

Pütz, Babette, 299n18

Rahe, Paul A., 43n2, 44n9
Rau, P., 129n20
Reckford, Kenneth J., 129n18, 132n33, 134n45, 136n52
Redfield, James, 136n55
Reinders, P., 128n14
Rhodes, P. J., 125n1
Rogers, Benjamin B., 85n2
Romer, F. E., 132n35
De Romilly, Jacqueline, 256n12
Rorty, Richard, 274n14
Rosen, R. M., 128n10
Rosen, Stanley, 43n7, 44n19, 299n20
Rosenbloom, D., 126n6
Rösler, W., 125n3
Rothwell, Kenneth S., 86n12–13, 132n33, 273n2
Ruffell, I., 127n7, 128n9, 129n18
Russo, Carlo Ferdinando, 131n31, 135n48
Rusten, J., 129n17

Sallis, John, 298n6
Sausage-seller, 114–17, 250–52
Saxonhouse, Arlene W., 86n11, 86n13, 108n17, 108n20, 297n6, 301n37
Schareika, Helmut, 126n3
Schmitt, Carl, 107, 107n10, 108n22
Schwinge, E.-R., 126n3
Scott, Dominic, 298n14
Scullion, John Scott, 130n25
Seaford, Richard, 125n1
Segal, Charles Paul, 43n2, 135n48, 199n5
Segal, Erich, 129n17
Shakespeare, William, 157n20, 274n20
Sheffield, Frisbee C. C., 299n20
Sider, David, 297n3
Sidwell, K., 127n7, 131n31
Silk, Michael S., 110, 125n3, 127n6, 129n20

Slater, Niall, 85n8, 109, 113, 116, 128n11, 131n29, 133n39, 134n46, 135n50, 274n12
Socrates, 13–24, 29–43, 48–64, 163, 179n3, 267–72, 303–24, 331–50; and asceticism, 30–43; teaching on justice, 36–38
Sommerstein, Alan, 86n12–14, 127n8–9, 128n14, 129n16, 129n18, 129n21, 130n23, 131n29–30, 132n34, 133n38–40, 135n50, 136n53, 212–14, 218, 223n9, 224n11, 225n16, 225n18–19, 226n29, 325n12
Sophocles, 184, 190
Spinoza, Benedict, 221, 223n6
Stanford, W. B., 135n48
de Ste. Croix, G. E. M., 126n6
Stone, L. M., 129n17
Storey, Ian C., 126n6, 128n9, 133n37
Stout, Jeffrey, 26n14–15
Strauss, Leo, 41, 43n2, 44n10, 45n27–28, 65n2, 65n9, 65n17, 66n22–23, 86n15, 94, 107n9, 137, 152, 154n1, 155n7, 158n38, 199n5–8, 224n13, 226n31, 226n38, 255n2, 258n29, 258n31, 274n7, 274n9, 274n11–12, 274n21, 300n20, 325n12, 326n14, 326n19–20, 331–50, 326n23–24, 327n26; and the *Clouds*, 332–37; and the Other Plays, 337–50
Strepsiades, 14–24, 29–43, 50–52, 63; challenge to democratic authority, 18–21; effect of Socratic education on, 40–42; entry into the Thinkery, 31–36; and the language of mockery, 21–23

Taaffe, Lauren K., 273n6
Taplin, Oliver, 129n19, 135n48
Tarcov, Nathan, 223n2
Tarrant, Harold, 25n1, 26n16

Tereus, 161–62, 164, 167–79; and Philomela and Procne, 171–75, 178–79
Thesleff, Holger, 273n2
Thesmophoriazusae, 311, 317–20
Thucydides, 69, 84n1, 90, 99–101, 107n6, 111, 136n52, 138–39, 155n5, 155n8, 199n2, 199n9, 218, 224n15, 226n32, 229–44, 326n24; boastfulness of Cleon, 230–33; and the Mytilenians, 233–44
Tomin, Julius, 25n1
Too, Yun Lee, 301n49
Trygaeus, 137–54

Usher, M. D., 297n4
Ussher, R. G., 273n2, 325n11, 326n13

Vaio, J., 130n25
Vander Waerdt, P. A., 25n1
Vickers, Michael, 298n8
Villa, Dana, 27n25

Wallach, John, 27n26
War, 138–39, 141, 144–45, 149–50, 154
Wasps, 71–72, 75–76, 82–83, 252–55

Wealth (Wealth) 72, 76, 79–82, 201–23; and charity, 203–6; and modern liberalism, 201–2
Weber, Max, 26n13
Welsh, D., 127n9
West, Thomas G., 45n23, 45n25
Whirl, 19
Whitman, Cedric H., 127n6, 128n14, 130n28, 131n31, 133n39, 135n48, 199n5
Wiles, David, 130n25
Wills, G., 135n47

Xanthias, 185–89
Xenophon, 199n3, 199n9, 256n15, 303–24; works by: *Memorabilia*, 24, 304–5; *Oeconomicus*, 24, 313; *Symposium*, 24

Youth, 211–15, 218

Zeus, 14, 19–21, 36–37, 56–59, 79–80, 137–39, 142–46, 148–54, 203–5, 207, 213, 215, 217–18, 221, 245, 251–55
Zuckert, Michael, 43n2, 83, 86n17
Zumbrunnen, John, 65n2, 85n1, 85n6–7, 86n17